D0872415

G 8241 E   78 00

Reconsidering Gallipoli

Published in our
centenary year
~ **2004** ~
MANCHESTER
UNIVERSITY
PRESS

To the memory of
Mollie Vera Macleod
1915–2002

Jenny Macleod

Reconsidering Gallipoli

Manchester University Press

Manchester and New York

distributed exclusively in the USA by Palgrave

Copyright © Jenny Macleod 2004

The right of Jenny Macleod to be identified as the author of this work has been
asserted by her in accordance with the Copyright, Designs and Patents Act 1988.

Published by Manchester University Press
Oxford Road, Manchester M13 9NR, UK
and Room 400, 175 Fifth Avenue, New York, NY 10010, USA
www.manchesteruniversitypress.co.uk

Distributed exclusively in the USA by
Palgrave, 175 Fifth Avenue, New York,
NY 10010, USA

Distributed exclusively in Canada by
UBC Press, University of British Columbia, 2029 West Mall,
Vancouver, BC, Canada V6T 1Z2

British Library Cataloguing-in-Publication Data
A catalogue record for this book is available from the British Library

Library of Congress Cataloging-in-Publication Data applied for

ISBN 0 7190 6742 1 *hardback*

0 7190 6743 X *paperback*

First published 2004

12 11 10 09 08 07 06 05 04   10 9 8 7 6 5 4 3 2 1

Typeset in Minion
by SNP Best-set Typesetter Ltd., Hong Kong
Printed in Great Britain
by Bell & Bain, Glasgow

Contents

List of figures		*page* vi
Acknowledgements		vii
Map of the Gallipoli peninsula		ix
Map of the theatre of operations		x
Introduction		1
1	The official response: the Dardanelles Commission	25
2	The official response: the official histories	57
3	The journalists' response: Ellis Ashmead-Bartlett and C. E. W. Bean	103
4	The soldiers' tale: participants' personal narratives	147
5	The commander's response: General Sir Ian Hamilton's *Gallipoli Diary*	176
6	Post-participant historiography of Gallipoli	209
Conclusion		238
Select bibliography		245
Index		260

List of figures

1 Commodore Roger Keyes, Vice-Admiral J. De Robeck,
General Sir Ian Hamilton and Major-General Walter
Braithwaite on board HMS *Triad* in 1915   *page* 30

2 Portrait of Charles E. W. Bean (1924) by George Lambert   66

3 Mustapha Kemal at Gallipoli in 1915   86

4 The beach at Anzac Cove, showing piled-up stores and
boats landing   119

5 Dug-outs of the 2nd and 3rd Australian Field
Ambulances at Anzac Cove   152

6 *Gallipoli Soldiers* (1960) by Sidney Nolan   217

Acknowledgements

This book was made possible by funding from: the Prince Consort and Thirlwall Fund; the Holland Rose Fund; the Cambridge Historical Society; the Smuts Memorial Fund; the British Federation of Women Graduates Charitable Foundation; the Wilson Fund; the Thornton History Fund; the Scholarship Fund of Pembroke College, Cambridge; the Rydon Fellowship at the Menzies Centre for Australian Studies, King's College London; and the Army History Research Grant Scheme of the Australian Army. The final stages of the process were completed while I was lecturer in defence studies, King's College London, at the Joint Services Command and Staff College. The analysis, opinions and conclusions expressed or implied in this book are mine and do not necessarily represent the views of the JSCSC, the United Kingdom's Ministry of Defence or any other governmental agency.

I gratefully acknowledge permission to quote from private papers granted by: the Trustees of the Liddell Hart Centre for Military Archives, King's College London; the Australian War Memorial; Mrs Rowan Low, the Bodleian Library and the Bonham Carter Trustees; Mrs Margaret Oglander and the Isle of Wight Record Office; the Institute of Commonwealth Studies; the Mitchell Library; and the Harry Ransom Research Centre. Extracts from the Hankey diaries are reproduced by kind permission of the Master and Fellows of Churchill College, Cambridge, and extracts from the Monash, Moorehead and Murdoch Papers are reproduced by permission of the National Library of Australia. Extracts from Ashmead-Bartlett's newspaper articles are made by permission of the Telegraph Group, Ltd. Arnold Publishers have kindly allowed some material previously published in their journal *War in History* to be reproduced in chapter 1. The University of New South Wales have similarly allowed some material from their journal *War &*

Society to be reproduced in chapter 6. Every effort has been made to trace the copyright owners of material used in this book; but, in case of any oversights, those claiming copyright should contact the author.

I must thank the Master, the Fellows, the staff and students of Pembroke College, Cambridge, and the staff of the various libraries and archives where I have worked, particularly those of the Liddell Hart Centre for Military Archives, King's College London. The staff at MUP have been friendly and professional in all my dealings with them. Thank you also to Steve Waites of the JSCSC's graphics department for making the maps.

Many academics have been generous enough to share their expertise with me and to encourage me on my way: Paul Addison, Stephen Badsey, Carl Bridge, John Brown, Jeremy Crang, Ashley Ekins, Bill Gammage, Adrian Gregory, Keith Grieves, Jeff Grey, Ken Inglis, John Lee, Roy and Kimberley MacLeod, Robert O'Neill, Robin Prior, Robert Rhodes James, Dennis Showalter, Nigel Steel, Stuart Ward and, in particular, Gary Sheffield. My greatest debt is to my excellent Ph.D supervisor Jay Winter. Any mistakes in or limitations to the book are my own responsibility.

I would like to apologise to all the friends who I have bored on the subject of Gallipoli; I thank them for being such good company in return. My Cambridge friends bore the brunt: James Cannon, Helen McCartney, Lee Russell, John Phillips, Elliot Vernon, Andy Webster and especially Jeremie Fant. Special thanks also to Mary and Oliver Howie for their hospitality in Canberra, and to my sister in London who kindly put me up during my numerous visits to the archives. My family are the most important people to me and none of this would have been possible without them. Thanks Mum, Dad, Katy, Helen, Chris, Emily and Sam.

Map of the Gallipoli peninsula

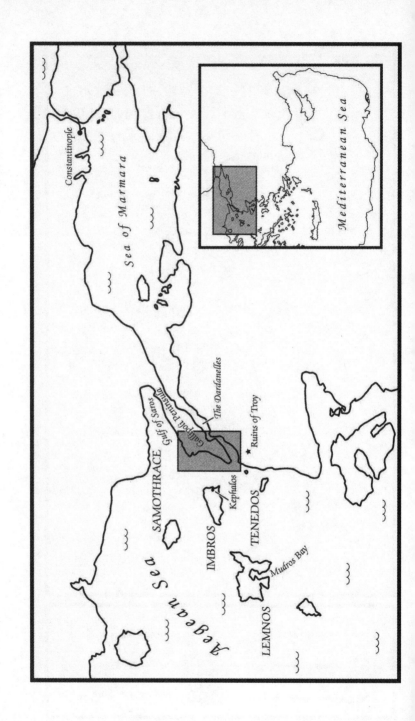

Introduction

> And all our trouble wasted!
> all of it gone for nix
> Still . . . we kept our end up –
> and some of the story sticks.
>
> Fifty years on in Sydney
> they'll talk of our first big fight,
> And even in little old, blind old England
> possibly someone might. (*Anzac*, 1916, by Argent[1])

On 24 May 2002, Australia honoured the passing of Alec Campbell, the last survivor of the Gallipoli campaign of 1915, with a state funeral. The congregation at St David's Cathedral in Hobart, Tasmania, included Campbell's large extended family, Prime Minister John Howard and Chief of Army Lieutenant-General Peter Cosgrove. Campbell was 103 when he died. As a 16-year-old, during the final weeks of the campaign, he had worked as a water-carrier. His death prompted extensive consideration in Australian newspapers – including special supplements – of the significance of the loss of the last living link to the campaign. John Howard announced that the story of the Australian men who had fought there was one of 'great valour under fire, unity of purpose and a willingness to fight against the odds that has helped to define what it means to be an Australian'.[2]

Although the death of Alec Campbell was respectfully noted in the British press, no such national introspection accompanied either this occasion or that of the death, a year earlier, of the last-surviving British veteran Percy Goring, who had lived in Bunbury, Western Australia.[3] Why is such meaning and importance attributed to Gallipoli in Australia, but not in Britain? The campaign was a humiliation for the British empire; so how is such esteem for a disastrous defeat to be explained?

Much of the answer is to be found in the way in which the Gallipoli campaign's history has been written and, in particular, the way that the participants presented the defeat to the world.

The early interpretations of a campaign are of interest because they establish the generally held understanding of the nature of that campaign. That 'understanding' might be better described as its 'myth'. Myth in this sense does not mean falsehood; rather, as Samuel Hynes argues, 'it is a term to identify the simplified, dramatized story that has evolved in our society to contain the meanings of the war that we can tolerate, and so make sense of its incoherence and contradictions'.[4] All subsequent accounts must work in the light of this myth. This book focuses primarily on the early development of *two* myths of Gallipoli in the historiography of the campaign up to 1939, the period during which most of the participant–authors put pen to paper.

Outline of the campaign

The essential purpose of the Dardanelles expedition was to capture Constantinople and thereby defeat Turkey, an ally of Germany. It was also hoped that this strategy would protect Egypt from Turkish attack, and that it would aid Russia and bring the Balkan nations into the war on the side of the allies. The strategy was initiated by First Lord of the Admiralty Winston Churchill. That it was accepted by the War Council had much to do with, on the one side, Churchill's vigorous enthusiasm and, on the other, Secretary of State for War Kitchener's and Prime Minister Asquith's passivity. Initially an attempt was made to force a way by sea alone through the narrow Dardanelles Straits that lead to the sea of Marmora, the Bosphorous and Constantinople. The naval bombardment of the Narrows' defences was unsuccessful and ceased on 18 March 1915. Meanwhile plans developed to support the navy with a landing force, so that what began as a purely naval operation became predominantly a military one with the Royal Navy playing only a supporting role. Given the reduced – and indecisive – role of the navy, this book concentrates on narratives concerning that of the army.

On 25 April 1915 men of the Mediterranean Expeditionary Force (MEF) under the command of General Sir Ian Hamilton landed on the Gallipoli peninsula. The main thrust of the attack focused on five points – beaches named S, V, W, X and Y – along the tip of the peninsula, Cape Helles. The British professional soldiers of the 29th Division carried out these landings. They were supported by a diversionary dawn attack, farther along the Aegean coast of the peninsula at Z Beach, by men of the Australia and New Zealand Army Corps under the command of General Birdwood. This beach was swiftly renamed Anzac Cove, after the corps' acronym. French forces landed temporarily on the Asiatic coast of the Dardanelles, and feint attacks were made at Bulair at the neck of the peninsula. These landings, the first opposed landing by a force armed with modern weapons, were an unprecedented feat of amphibious warfare. Unfortunately they did not lead to decisive gains or the passage of the fleet through the Dardanelles, and several months of intensive trench warfare ensued.

Such were the conditions on the peninsula that almost no location was safe from enemy bombardment or snipers. The food supply was plentiful, if monotonous, but water was at times in very limited supply. In the hot climate, the men, particularly the Anzacs, cut down their uniforms to the bare minimum and sea-bathing was the only respite from the heat and the tension. Care of casualties remained a problem throughout: the burial of the dead lying in no man's land was especially difficult and the campaign's only armistice was held at Anzac on 19 May for that purpose. As a result of these conditions sickness, principally a form of dysentery or enteric fever fuelled by a plague of flies, was rife.

On 6 August an attempt to break the deadlock was made by landing fresh forces at Suvla Bay while forces tried simultaneously to break out from Anzac. This was not successful. The fighting in August was notable for a vicious battle at Lone Pine involving the Anzacs, a futile diversionary attack nearby at the Nek, the brief occupation of the potentially decisive heights of Chunuk Bair by the New Zealanders, and the lethargy of the British efforts under General Stopford at Suvla Bay itself. Hamilton was removed from his command on 15 October. His replacement, Lieutenant-General Sir Charles Monro, swiftly recommended the evacuation of the peninsula. After several weeks of hesitation in London, and a visit to Gallipoli by Kitchener, the decision was made. The evacuation took place in two stages: Anzac and Suvla on 18–19 December, and Helles on 8–9 January 1916.

This book does not discuss in detail the political and military factors behind the defeat at Gallipoli. Suffice it to say that the campaign was severely hampered by two factors. Firstly, it was launched in haste and without sufficient prior planning. This meant that, through no fault of his own, Hamilton lost the asset of surprise and formulated his plans on the basis of scant information. Secondly, the campaign was treated in London as a side-show and was therefore kept short of men and armaments: instead the Western Front continued to receive the lion's share of the limited supplies available. Hamilton's deferential and optimistic nature was partly responsible for this deficiency in materiel in that he did not press hard enough for what was needed for the successful prosecution of the campaign.

Gallipoli's recent historiography

Gallipoli has been a beguiling and fruitful subject for historians.[5] Indeed, the reasons for this are the subject of this book, and, as the next six chapters concern Gallipoli's historiography, the survey which follows is brief.

Since the close of the Second World War, the campaign has spawned five substantial general histories, of which Robert Rhodes James's 1965 volume remains the classic work.[6] Beside these, Gallipoli's historiography may be crudely divided between military and cultural history.

It is the tactical and strategic conundrums of the campaign that explain much about Gallipoli's continuing fascination for historians. As Churchill self-servingly noted, 'the terrible ifs accumulate', and military historians have relentlessly pursued their possibilities. What potential did the strategy have? What went wrong at the landings in April and August 1915? What difference did the commanders make? Complementing such speculation has been academic and professional interest in the achievement inherent in the first modern opposed amphibious landings and the two evacuations staged under the very nose of the enemy and without loss.[7] Moreover, Gallipoli seems to have spawned more than its share of tragic episodes and heroes to be studied.[8] Indeed, a further important theme in Gallipoli's historiography is the role of the individual and his experience.[9] The most recent development in Anglophone military histories of the campaign sees attention directed to the Turkish perspective.[10]

The greater part of Gallipoli's historiography, however, is taken up by explorations of the Anzac legend which grew out of the campaign. Such is the importance of the Anzac legend that it is celebrated and commemorated each year in Australia on Anzac Day, the anniversary of the first landings. It is an event that overshadows November's Armistice Day commemoration and January's Australia Day. The Anzac legend elevates the experience of Gallipoli, and of war, and places it at the centre of Australia's sense of identity.[11] It has therefore been of great interest to Australian historians. Ken Inglis has led the way in this work;[12] he was the first to point to the role of C. E. W. Bean, official correspondent and historian of Gallipoli, in shaping the legend,[13] and his articles have indicated several other rich veins of inquiry: the nature of the Anzacs; the development of the Anzac legend;[14] and its memorialisation.[15]

These investigations into the cultural history of Gallipoli in Australia have few equivalents in British history. The British viewed the defeat at Gallipoli in the context of the entire war; they commemorated the First World War as a whole, and the historiography has reflected this.[16] There are two notable exceptions: Keith Grieves's recent work on Sussex;[17] and Geoffrey Moorhouse's *Hell's Foundations*.[18] Moorhouse explores the impact of Gallipoli and its myths on the town of Bury, home of the Lancashire Fusiliers which lost heavily in the landings at W Beach. Moorhouse's Preface notes the tragic nature of the Gallipoli campaign, and the Australian dominance of its mythology. One of the aims of this book is to counterbalance the historiographical emphasis on the Anzac legend by exploring the British portrayal of the campaign. The romantic tenor of the British portrayal, like that of the Anzac legend, has often been noted by historians; but unlike its Australian counterpart it has never been satisfactorily examined.[19] This book traces and examines what I have termed the heroic–romantic myth through the historiography of the Gallipoli campaign. In doing so, I take 'legend' and 'myth' to be synonymous, but for clarity I use *legend* to refer to the Australian understanding of Gallipoli and *myth* to its British counterpart.

The Anzac legend

What is meant by the romance of war? I take it to mean the fascination, excitement and glamour of battle. In its idiosyncratic way, the Anzac legend is a romantic war myth, and it is probably the most widely known understanding of Gallipoli. It concerns the prowess of the Australasians, but concentrates on the Australian men of Gallipoli.[20] The basic outline of the legend is as follows. In landing at Anzac Cove and pushing recklessly up the steep gullies and ridges of the peninsula, these 'Anzacs' demonstrated tremendous courage and initiative. This was Australia's first major appearance as a nation on the world stage. It was the Australians' 'baptism of fire', the 'birth of a nation'. The sense of national identity uncovered combined courage and self-reliance, athleticism, fierce loyalty to mates, relaxed discipline, egalitarianism, dry humour and a wild streak – ingredients which made them formidable soldiers. George Johnston has powerfully described the Anzac legend. He wrote of the Anzacs:

They seemed to belong, not to the standard conceptions of military prowess and discipline, but to some other, younger, more exuberant world of the spirit. Physical, masculine, their big sunburnt bodies remarkable to an older world, romping naked under shell-fire on the beaches and even fighting naked in their clifftop trenches, activated by simple codes of loyalty, adventure, and comradeship, unmoved by and even sceptical of any thoughts of jingoism or patriotism, admiring and respecting 'Johnny Turk', the enemy, far more than they ever admired or respected their own leaders, these Anzacs were to all outside observers a remarkable new breed of men.[21]

An early popular articulation of the Anzac legend was provided by C. J. Dennis's tales of Ginger Mick in *The Songs of a Sentimental Bloke* (1915) and *The Moods of Ginger Mick* (1916), both of which rapidly sold 40,000 copies on publication.[22] Another early example is *The Anzac Book*.[23] This was a commemorative collection of work by the men of Anzac, edited by Charles Bean. D. A. Kent has argued that this was the first coherent presentation of the legend. By late 1916 it had sold more than 100,000 copies.[24] In its pages a picture is developed of the Anzac as a tough man who endured discomforts with few grumbles and sardonic humour. Despite the fact that most of them were town-dwellers, the Anzac was cast as a bushman,[25] a reluctant warrior who stood by his mates to the end, and whose sense of duty helped him withstand the sacrifices necessitated by the campaign.

Kent argues that Bean's editing made the landing seem 'a glorious dangerous game' and that it inserted a chivalrous regard for the enemy wholly absent from the men's submissions.[26] Furthermore, Kent notes that Bean excluded pieces on experiences of trench-fighting on Gallipoli, together with references to boredom, futility, cowardice, malingering, the anguish of personal loss and even a longing for beer.[27] Bean's purpose was to create a particular image of the Anzac, which was to become the basis of the Anzac legend. Throughout the book I focus on the efforts of Charles Bean in developing the Anzac legend through his dispatches and the official history.

The heroic–romantic myth of Gallipoli

Bean's evangelising work in *The Anzac Book* had its British counterpart in John Masefield's *Gallipoli*, a work of propaganda of the same year.[28] Its key features epitomise the British romanticised response to the campaign, the heroic–romantic myth of Gallipoli. This might be summarised as a retelling of the campaign which emphasises the heroism of the men involved, the campaign's strategic potential and near success, and the lack of support from London, all of which is couched in the most romantic terms. Masefield's concluding paragraph demonstrates this:

> Until then, let our enemies say this: 'They did not win, but they came across three thousand miles of sea, a little army without reserves and short of munitions, a band of brothers, not half of them half-trained, and nearly all of them new to war. They came to what we said was an impregnable fort, on which our veterans of war and massacre had laboured for two months, and by sheer naked manhood they beat us and drove us out of it. Then rallying, but without reserves, they beat us again, and drove us farther. Then rallying once more, but still without reserves, they beat us again, this time to our knees. Then, had they had reserves, they would have conquered, but by God's pity they had none. Then, after a lapse of time, when we were men again, they had reserves, and they hit us a staggering blow, which needed but a push to end us, but God again had pity. After that our God was indeed pitiful, for England made no further thrust, and they went away.'[29]

Masefield had suggested to the Foreign Office that he should write the book following his lecture tour of America, during which he had found that he was frequently challenged about the failure at Gallipoli.[30] In attempting to influence American public opinion, he employed repeated references to *The Song of Roland*, the poem describing Charlemagne's men fighting the Saracens. His atavistic descriptions reinforced the impression of the campaign's grandeur. He referred to Gallipoli as Thracian Chersonese and the Dardanelles as the Hellespont; and, famously, he described the men thus: 'For physical beauty and nobility of bearing they surpassed any men I have ever seen; they walked and looked like the kings in old poems.'[31]

His book was warmly received. Lord Esher privately wrote approvingly of *Gallipoli*: 'It is on a level with Tennyson's "Charge of the Light Brigade", only it is in prose.'[32] Within a year of its publication seven impressions were printed.[33]

The British myth of Gallipoli contains three strands. The first is a romantic view of this campaign, in particular, and of warfare in general. The second is an emphasis on the heroism of the campaign's participants that is used to defend them against criticisms of failure. The third strand is a distinctively British emphasis on the strategy of the campaign. The myth is melancholy in tone. This is understandable given the ultimate failure of the campaign, the terrible living conditions on the peninsula and the constant presence of death – not just the perpetual threat of death but actual wounded and decaying bodies all around. Importantly, however, there is not the anger, futility or irony that Paul Fussell's and Modris Eksteins's claim is notable in memories of the Western Front.[34]

In developing the first two strands of the myth, authors not only convey a favourable view of warfare but make allusions to earlier legendary battles and warriors. The region abounded with classical associations. Given Gallipoli's location, adjacent to Troy, classical references were often made. The Dardanelles was the ancient Hellespont across which Leander swam to reach Hero, and which Xerxes crossed on a bridge of boats. Moreover, the campaign lent itself to comparison with Greek tragedy – explicitly, with a cycle of three distinct parts (landing, trench warfare, evacuation) and perhaps, implicitly, with a proud hero humbled (the British empire). Contemporaries also often described battles and descriptions of battles as 'Homeric'. Another obvious comparison to make in telling of battles against the Turks was with the crusaders who in medieval times sought to liberate Jerusalem and the Holy Land from 'the infidels'.[35]

Paul Fussell has criticised the effect of similar references in David Jones's *In Parenthesis*, which relates to his experience of the Western Front:

> *In Parenthesis* at the same time can't keep its allusions from suggesting that the war, if ghastly, is firmly 'in the tradition' . . . The tradition to which the poem points holds suffering to be close to sacrifice and individual effort to end in heroism; it contains, unfortunately, no precedent for an understanding of war as a shambles and its participants as victims [. . .]
>
> The poem is a deeply conservative work which uses the past not, as it often pretends to do, to shame the present, but really to ennoble it. The effect of the poem, for all its horrors, is to rationalise and even to validate the war by implying that it somehow recovers many of the motifs and values of medieval chivalric romance.[36]

Fussell is making an interesting point about the effect of historical references in war narratives, one that is useful in considering the nature of Gallipoli's heroic–romantic myth. That such references are made relatively frequently in works on Gallipoli points to the weakness in the view that the First World War forced a profound break in the historical condtinuum. Indeed the response of Fussell, a literature professor, to the First World War has provoked strong criticism from military historians.[37]

It should be noted that the Anzac legend also makes comparisons with ancient warriors – how often do books and articles on the Anzacs make use of Compton Mackenzie's ringing phrases of how their beauty should be 'celebrated in hexameters not headlines'?[38] Indeed, Robin Gerster has argued: 'From 1915 on, every mode of Australian war prose, whether "factual", "fictional", "historical" or "imaginative", typically functions either overtly or covertly as publicity for the Australian soldier as a twentieth-century embodiment of classical heroic virtue.'[39] Classical allusions are indeed to be found in Australian writing on Gallipoli,[40] and they are particularly notable in physical – monumental – commemorations of the campaign.[41] Yet there is a difference between the Australian and British purposes in employing them. While the Australian allusions are made to ennoble the men of Anzac, the British purpose seems more often to be to ennoble the campaign *itself.*

This difference in purpose can be seen in discussions of strategy. The Anzac legend scarcely discusses strategy: it is not important to its portrayal of a nation of heroic men.[42] As the junior partners in an enterprise in which they proved themselves to be a formidable and resourceful fighting force, the Australians disclaim responsibility for failure and instead blame another: the British. But the British, both the instigators of the campaign and their defenders, must justify the undertaking: hence the preoccupation with strategy.

The strategy is defended in two ways: in terms of its potential; and in terms of its effect. The idea of attacking in the East is portrayed as an imaginative shortcut to victory. Winston Churchill[43] and official historian Aspinall-Oglander,[44] as well as Basil Liddell Hart,[45] promulgated this idea. Such a peripheral attack utilising the nation's naval power has traditionally been held up as the British way in warfare. Those supporting this maritime strategy, in preference to a more substantial continental commitment, praised it as a relatively inexpensive route towards victory. By contrast, however, Trevor Wilson, in *The Myriad Faces of War*, has provided a succinct unsentimental assessment of the Gallipoli strategy's chances. He writes that 'at no phase was the Gallipoli operation, even if blessed with reasonable military competence and a good measure of luck, assured of success. Rather, the odds against victory were, in whatever circumstances, ominously high.'[46] Yet the prospect of victory in the East retains its potency as an alternative to the grim slaughter of the Western Front. The strategy is defended also as having had decisive results, despite not having secured its most obvious goals. Thus it is frequently claimed that Gallipoli facilitated the later victories in the East by destroying 'the flower of the Turkish army'. Those responsible for the strategy's implementation defended themselves by one further means. Like the

Australians, they blame others – this time, the politicians in London. They argue – albeit in veiled terms – that decisions in London made their task impossible.

The defence of Gallipoli's strategy appeals superficially to the intellect. The first two strands of the myth work more subtly: they form an emotional defence, a sugar-coating for the bitter pill of defeat. The inclination of the British to couch the campaign in heroic–romantic terms had several sources. One is the cult of chivalry that developed in the nineteenth century. This idealised the supposed attributes of the knight of the Middle Ages. The knight, and therefore the gentleman, was thought to be brave, loyal, honourable and courageous, a defender of the Church and of helpless women. Central to these notions was the idea that fighting was not only necessary but glorious.[47] The generation of public-school educated men who fought at Gallipoli had been brought up on martial stories which they were ready to liken to their own experiences. These were stories such as Hector and Achilles, the knights of King Arthur, Richard the Lionheart crusading against the Saracens, Sir John Moore at Corunna and Ivanhoe.[48] Crucially, such stories idealised heroic failures as often as victories. Philip Guedella, in reviewing General Hamilton's *Gallipoli Diary* in 1920, was prompted to consider this British taste for failure:

> There is a certain state of mind, unless perhaps it is a state of health, which prefers its hopes forlorn. It can only breathe in the tense air of disaster, and failure has quite a success with it. Any student of opinion will tell you that with a British posterity one sound, romantic defeat will go twice as far as three vulgar victories ... Contemporaries may be incommoded by the loss of a war; but posterity, if the historians know their business, is a glutton for failure.[49]

Several other popular ideas fed into this cult of chivalry and the romanticising of war. One was the late nineteenth-century glorification of death. An excellent example of this is Tennyson's *The Charge of the Light Brigade*. David Cannadine has explored attitudes to war, death, grief and mourning during Tennyson's time. The combination of social Darwinism, the athleticism sought by the public schools and growing international tensions, with the increasing likelihood that death would be caused by old age, he argues, 'produced an atmosphere in which soldiering and games were equated, in which death was seen as unlikely, but where, if it happened, it could not fail to be glorious'.[50] Such attitudes may be traced through to the poetry of Rupert Brooke, or to the response in Britain to the death of Scott of the Antarctic. Scott had written: 'We are showing that Englishmen can still die with a bold spirit, fighting it out to the end . . . I think this makes an example for Englishmen of the future.'[51] Scott's death, on the eve of the First World War, was futile, but his heroism for heroism's sake was perceived to be glorious. From this, one begins to see the British terms of reference within which the participants in the Gallipoli campaign perceived their experience.

The preoccupation with death emanated in part from the influence of the Romanticism of the late eighteenth and the nineteenth century. This helps to explain the fascination of the British with the ruins of Troy. Other elements of Romanticism, despite its diffuse nature, can be discerned in the portrayal of Gallipoli. One might point to the interest shown in the beauty of the peninsula (wild flowers and brilliant sunsets were a distinctive feature of the battlefield) and in other exotica which enhanced Gallipoli's mystique. The Romantic poet Byron had also made his personal contribution in 1810 by swimming the Hellespont, as Leander had done.

Hellenism, or an interest in ancient Greece, was central to an English public-school education of this period, and thus also an influence on the way in which Gallipoli was perceived. It ensured that Homer's *Iliad* was a familiar text and Schliemann's relatively recent excavation of the site of its battles was well known.[52] Public schools also stressed chivalrous notions and the allied values of sportsmanship and athleticism. This ethos, with its 'romantic' attitude to war, was perpetuated by such popular novels as *Tom Brown's Schooldays* and Henty's adventure stories for boys, and by movements such as Baden Powell's Boy Scouts.[53] With such a background, it is not surprising that many, particularly those socially elite members of the Royal Naval Division, were quick to make the link between modern battle on Gallipoli and its ancient precursors. The circumstances of the death, just prior to the landings on St George's Day, of Rupert Brooke, the most romantic and famous of expublic-schoolboys, only reinforced such thoughts.

Brooke was buried, by torchlight, on Scyros beneath an epitaph proclaiming – in Greek – that he 'died for the deliverance of Constantinople from the Turks'.[54] His friend Charles Lister wrote: 'The Island of Achilles is a suitable resting-place for those bound for the plains of Troy.'[55] Such comparisons were perhaps inevitable following the death of a character like Brooke, but these habits of mind were so deeply ingrained that they applied more widely. As Richard Jenkyns has noted:

> Perfect in physical beauty, perfect in the setting of his death, Brooke was
> fated to be likened to the heroes of epic or romance; but even when men
> died in less cruelly apt circumstances, their friends often found the temp-
> tation to dignify them with the aura of heroic poetry irresistible.[56]

Thus the British heroic–romantic myth drew on long established
patterns of attitudes and beliefs in a way similar to that suggested by
Australian historians who have traced the ready acceptance of the Anzac
legend to its continuation and development of themes and characteristics familiar from convicts, gold-diggers, bushrangers, and so on.[57]

Yet, the questions remain, why was it possible to romanticise Gallipoli
in this way and why did its participants choose to do so? Simply to point
to the romantic frame of mind with which these men began their campaign is not a sufficient explanation of the continuing desire to romanticise Gallipoli. Consider it for a moment in terms of Fussell's flawed but
influential argument. Stripped of its romance, Gallipoli could have been
transformed into the ultimate disillusioning experience. The potential
for an ironic portrayal is certainly there: the possibility that Gallipoli
could have ended the war surely provides the 'dynamics of hope
abridged'[58] which Fussell pinpoints as the fount of the Western Front's
irony. But Fussell's paradigm of disappointed hope leading to ironic portrayal does not apply to Gallipoli, just as it does not apply to the great
mass of literature regarding the Western Front.[59] How then, was it possible for Gallipoli, a campaign which Peter Stanley has described as 'rich
in irony',[60] to be portrayed in its distinctively romantic fashion?

There are several factors that enable recollection of the Gallipoli campaign to be in a manner quite separate from that of the Western Front.
One might be the fact that Gallipoli was a defeat. Failure seems to have
added to the romance of the expedition. This seemingly illogical point
is illustrated by a comment in *The Times* from 1927:

> It began with the achievement of the apparently impossible and it ended
> in failure, a failure which itself gave further glory to the troops engaged. It
> was a proof of the military prowess of the race and a lesson in the relations
> between politicians and soldiers in time of war. It will inspire the youth of
> the future, and it will ever be a warning to statesmen with ideas on war.[61]

To elevate failure in this manner produces an inclusive myth that all can
celebrate – from ardent militarists to pacifists. Indeed this element of
failure may have contributed to the desire to remember Gallipoli amid
the disillusionment of the inter-war period. Hamilton wrote in 1932:

I do not wish them to celebrate anniversaries of resounding victories, because flag-waving over an enemy's defeat must carry with it a sting to the self-esteem of that enemy which may engender a longing for revenge. No, rather would I suggest that we celebrate sheer feats of arms, like those achieved on the beaches of the Dardanelles, as conquests by our soldiers and sailors over every man's enemy – 'The Impossible!'[62]

There are other potent factors that set Gallipoli apart. Its physical separation from France and Flanders is obvious enough, as are its decisively different topography and climate.[63] There is also the way in which it was fought: the extraordinary achievement of the initial amphibious attack, and then the subsequent contrast of individual heroics with the anonymous industrial killing of the Western Front[64] made Gallipoli seem to some extent to be war as it *should* be: noble, daring, imaginative, chivalrous and tragic. Major General A. H. Russell wrote to Hamilton in September 1916:

You may like a line from one of your old divisions on Gallipoli, to whom its campaign on the peninsula will always be the one to which it will look back with the greatest interest. As the French proverb puts it 'On revient toujours à ses premiers amours'. And in truth this fighting on the Western Front, is but a dull affair in comparison: a sordid history punctuated with 5.9s and Minnenwerfers. Certainly lacking the romance attached to our life last year.[65]

But perhaps its cost and timing are the crucial factors. The casualty statistics for almost nine months of fighting at Gallipoli are terrible: official statistics give the total number of casualties from the British empire at nearly 120,000,[66] or two casualties for every nine men sent out to the Dardanelles theatre.[67] Yet the more terrible fact is that these statistics are dwarfed by those for the Western Front, where five in every nine men became casualties. In particular, Gallipoli is overshadowed by the experience of the Battle of the Somme. During the first month of that battle – July 1916, the worst month of the war – losses in France approached 200,000.[68] The Somme was a watershed: it tainted all that came after it. Conversely, the battles that came before – particularly Gallipoli – retain something of the sense of romance and excitement that characterised the earliest days of the First World War.[69]

Therefore, despite Fussell's contention that the First World War constitutes a rupture in cultural history, Gallipoli proves otherwise. Fussell suggests that the profoundly shocking experience of the Western Front made a nonsense of traditional values and required a new, 'modern', mode of thought. Yet the heroic–romantic myth of Gallipoli is resolutely anti-modern. Reactions to Gallipoli support the argument that traditional modes of thought persisted and held resonance for many, that the traditional and the modern co-existed. As Hynes explains: 'Edwardian past and wartime past seemed contradictory realities, one refuting and cancelling the other. But both existed in the minds and imaginations of post-war survivors, and both together defined the troubled post-war world.'[70]

The second of my questions remains: why did the participants of Gallipoli choose to romanticise it? That is to say, what was the purpose of the myth? Selfish motives were certainly at work in some cases. For many of the most prominent figures of the campaign, their portrayals of Gallipoli can be viewed as a personal exercise in saving face. If Gallipoli was almost successful in foreshortening the war and the failure to do so was someone else's fault, that failure is made the more palatable. This thought must be borne in mind in considering the writings of the men involved in its planning, such as Churchill, Hamilton and Aspinall-Oglander. Furthermore, for Australians and others caught up in the failure, such as the serial bankrupt, journalist and lecturer Ashmead-Bartlett, perhaps it was also useful that it was an *important* failure. There was, therefore, a substantial coincidence of interests in making Gallipoli what it became.

In considering the purpose of the myth, it might also be instructive to compare it to two other myths of the First World War that have been identified: Samuel Hynes's myth of the war and George Mosse's myth of the war experience refer to the Western Front. The first is angry and accusatory, expressed in the terms of high culture, its essence being that 'the old betray the young; the past is remote and useless'.[71] The second is a consolatory myth[72] expressed in the terms of popular culture, its main features being the spirit of 1914, war as a test of manliness, the ideal of camaraderie, and the cult of the fallen soldier.[73] The heroic–romantic myth of Gallipoli contains elements of both of these – the accusatory idea of betrayal by the politicians; and the consolatory idealisation of the war experience. Hynes is again useful in suggesting an overarching purpose for such myths:

> We must believe that war narratives also confirm the memories of men who fought but did not write about their wars. Confirm, but also perhaps construct; for the order and meaning that written versions give to the incoherence of war must operate on other memories, making sense of the muddle of images that most men bring back from their wars.[74]

Such assumptions about the thoughts of the silent majority of participants cannot be substantiated, but these thoughts on the purpose of myths for those who propagated and perpetuated them are still helpful. The myths of Gallipoli – both British and Australian – helped to make its failure tolerable. They are about what made it special and different, and what made it worthwhile. They are about elevating the experience above the ignominy of defeat.

Outline of the book

How pervasive, then, was the heroic–romantic myth of Gallipoli? This book traces its development and influence through the assessments of participants in the campaign. That it became the dominant public form of understanding and remembrance of Gallipoli is illustrated by countless newspaper anniversary articles and book reviews of the period. In 1939, for example, the BBC broadcast a documentary about the campaign. It based its text on the writings of Winston Churchill, John Masefield, General Sir Ian Hamilton, Henry Nevinson, Compton Mackenzie and John North – and on Aspinall-Oglander's official history of the war.[75] That it did so illustrates that the works by these authors, all of which are discussed in the book, were considered by the nation's broadcasting voice to be the essential texts of Gallipoli. The result was an absorbing and moving documentary that was heavily influenced by the heroic–romantic myth. Of particular note was the decision to quote several long passages from the romantic work of the poet John Masefield.

Did the heroic–romantic myth pervade all the primary texts of Gallipoli in the same way? I consider participants' assessments in terms of three genres: official, journalistic and individual. They are considered not as historical evidence from which to discern the facts of the campaign, but as narratives that portrayed the campaign in a particular manner for a particular reason. The factual veracity of these various portrayals is therefore not the primary concern here; rather, the nature of their story-telling, their style, tone, emphases and omissions form the focus.

This approach sets the book apart from other work on Gallipoli. For example, as Steel and Hart do,[76] consideration is given here to the testimony of individual participants. However, I uses those testimonies not to piece together the progress and experience of the campaign – not as historical evidence as such – but as a *genre*. This approach mirrors the priorities of these narratives – that is, not to document the progress of the campaign but to record the nature of individuals' war experiences and, in particular, how they felt. In doing so, I apply the ideas of Samuel Hynes's *The Soldiers' Tale* (1997). He imagines that the recollections of all soldiers can be gathered together as one story – a soldiers' tale – which then can be discussed. He suggests that, unlike other war genres, the personal narratives of soldiers

> subvert the expectations of romance. They work at a level below the big words and the brave sentiments, down on the surface of the earth where men fight. They don't glorify war, or aestheticize it, or make it literary or heroic; they speak in their own voices, in their own plain language. They are not antiwar – that is, they are not polemics against war; they simply tell us what it is like. They make war actual, without making it familiar. They bear witness.[77]

However, Hynes generalises too much: not all the participants' published responses to Gallipoli fit his thesis of the soldiers' tale. Many of them are deeply imbued with the heroic–romantic myth. Nor do these personal narratives alone account for the picture of Gallipoli that was presented to the public.

This book places alongside an examination of soldiers' personal narratives and the idea of the soldiers' tale two other genres: official responses and journalists' responses. The official responses are antithetical to Hynes's idea of the soldiers' tale – and to personal narratives in general. The journalists' responses straddle these two genres.

What, then, are the shared characteristics of the British official responses? They give a top–down view in which the experiences and emotions of individuals are largely irrelevant. They work at the levels of high politics and the military details of strategy and tactics. Their purpose is to record the bare facts so far as that is consonant with subduing criticism and controversy so that the memory of the campaign could be laid to rest. The contrast with personal narratives is clear: their task was to secure the memory of their participation and to find some meaning within that. Given this contrast, the journalists can be seen as a transitional group. The response that they developed detailed the facts and progress of the campaign within strict parameters of censorship as laid down by officials, but also interpreted those facts, gave them meaning and considered their impact at the level of the individual.

Almost all of the narratives of Gallipoli contained elements of the heroic–romantic myth of Gallipoli. This book considers their development and their style, and how they related to each other.

The structure of the book is as follows. The first two chapters consider the official responses. The first official interpretation of the campaign was the Dardanelles Commission. Despite the vigorous efforts of General Sir Ian Hamilton, the commission's report was a document which refused either to wholly blame or to exculpate those involved in the campaign. The second British official interpretation was the history of the campaign, the author of which, Brigadier-General Cecil Aspinall Oglander, refused to make the account as bland as his superiors wished, though some elements of the campaign were nonetheless whitewashed. It thus had much in common with other official responses, but was also in important respects different from the model for British official history, Brigadier-General Sir James Edmonds's volumes on the Western Front. Chapter 2 also considers the Australian official history, by C. E. W. Bean. He had entirely different priorities from the British official responses, and this meant that his work shared some characteristics with personal narratives and with his work as a war correspondent. Chapter 3 considers the development of the journalists' responses during the campaign, with particular reference to the writings of the British war correspondent Ellis Ashmead Bartlett and his relations with the officials who attempted to control him. I compare his work with that of Bean. Given the transitional nature of the journalists' responses, they are not considered in strict chronological order within the book. Chapter 4 considers the soldiers' personal narratives and compares Hynes's thesis of the soldiers' tale with the nature of Gallipoli's personal narratives. Chapter 5 looks at a special case among these personal narratives: the commander's response, Hamilton's *Gallipoli Diary*. It will be seen that Hamilton was a major exponent of the heroic–romantic myth of Gallipoli. His work is briefly compared with those of General Sir John Monash and Winston Churchill. Chapter 6 seeks to trace the influence of Hamilton's, Bean's and others' mythologising over the historical assessments of Gallipoli by subsequent generations.

Hamilton's aim was to defend his reputation, which had been severely tarnished by the failure of the Gallipoli expedition. His activities in attempting to influence the public portrayal of the campaign are given particular emphasis throughout the book. I therefore dispute Michael Hickey's assertion that Hamilton 'spent his long retirement, until his death in 1945, caring as best he could for his former officers and men, never repining or *seeking to exculpate himself*, despite the frequent and often shrill judgments passed on his conduct of operations at Gallipoli'.[78]

Because of this emphasis on Hamilton, and because of the historiographical domination of the Anzac legend, the British portrayal of Gallipoli is the main focus of the book. It is placed alongside developments in Australia in order to consider the portrayal of Gallipoli as a whole. For the narration of Gallipoli as the foundation myth of the nation contrasts strikingly with the way the story was told in Britain. Both forms of the reconstruction of one campaign in the Great War reinforce the view that Gallipoli did not destroy the heroic romance of war stories. On the contrary, language and documentation coalesce into what has become the 'history' we share.

Notes

1 Argent, *Anzac*, reprinted in Philip J. Haythornthwaite, *Gallipoli 1915: Frontal Assault on Turkey* (Oxford, 1991), p. 90. Thanks to Major Steve Crouden RM for this reference.

2 Andrew Darby, 'Australia loses its last living link to Gallipoli: Alec Campbell, 103, dies', *The Age* (Melbourne), 17 May 2002, p. 1.

3 'Last hero dies', *Daily Mail* (London), 17 May 2002; 'Obituary of Alec Campbell', *Daily Telegraph* (London), 18 May 2002; Kathy Marks, 'Australia salutes last of the Gallipoli survivors', *Independent* (London), 25 May 2002; Barbie Dutter, 'Last British veteran of Gallipoli dies, aged 106', *Daily Telegraph* (London), 30 July 2001; Max Arthur, 'Obituary: Percy Goring', *Independent* (London), 4 August 2001.

4 Samuel Hynes, 'Personal narratives and commemoration' in J. M. Winter and E. Sivan (eds) *War and Remembrance in the Twentieth Century* (Cambridge, 1999), p. 207.

5 Useful surveys of Gallipoli's historiography are to be found in John Robertson, *The Tragedy and Glory of Gallipoli: Anzac and Empire* (London, 1990), pp. 268–76, and Edward Spiers, 'Gallipoli' in Brian Bond (ed.) *The First World War and British Military History* (London, 1991), pp. 165–88; see also, Fred R. Van Hartesveldt, *The Dardanelles Campaign, 1915: Historiography and Annotated Bibliography* (Connecticut, 1997).

6 Alan Moorehead, *Gallipoli* (London, 1956); Robert Rhodes James, *Gallipoli* (London, 1965); Michael Hickey, *Gallipoli* (London, 1995); Tim Travers, *Gallipoli 1915* (Stroud, 2001); Les Carlyon, *Gallipoli* (Sydney, 2001).

7 Robert Rhodes James, 'General Sir Ian Hamilton' in Field Marshal Sir Michael Carver (ed.) *Military Commanders of the Twentieth Century* (London, 1976), pp. 84–92; Robin Prior, 'The Suvla Bay tea-party: a reassessment', *Journal of the Australian War Memorial*, 7 (October 1985), pp. 25–34; P. A. Pedersen, *Monash as Military Commander* (Melbourne, 1985); Eliot A. Cohen and John Gooch, *Military Misfortunes: The Anatomy of Failure in War* (New York, 1990), pp. 133–63; John Lee, 'Sir Ian Hamilton and the Dardanelles, 1915' in Brian Bond (ed.) *Fallen Stars* (London, 1991), pp. 32–51; Denis Winter, *25 April 1915: The Inevitable Tragedy* (St Lucia, Queensland, 1994); T. H. E.

Travers, 'Command and leadership styles in the British Army: the 1915 Gallipoli model', *Journal of Contemporary History*, 29 (1994), pp. 403–42; John Lee, *A Soldier's Life: General Sir Ian Hamilton 1853–1947* (London, 2000); Geoffrey Till and Gary Sheffield (eds) *Challenges of High Command in the Twentieth Century* (Camberley, 2000); Robert O'Neill, 'Alliances and intervention: from Gallipoli to the 21st century', *RUSI Journal*, 146:5 (October 2001), pp. 56–61.

8 Peter Cochrane, *Simpson and the Donkey: The Making of the Legend* (Carlton, Victoria, 1992) and Peter Burness, *The Nek* (Kenthurst, NSW, 1996).

9 Bill Gammage, *The Broken Years: Australian Soldiers in the Great War* (Canberra, 1974); Nigel Steel and Peter Hart, *Defeat at Gallipoli* (London, 1994).

10 Edward J. Erickson, *Ordered to Die: A History of the Ottoman Army in the First World War* (Westport, CT, 2000); Edward J. Erickson, 'Strength against weakness: Ottoman military effectiveness at Gallipoli, 1915', *War and Society*, 65 (October 2001), pp. 981–1012; Travers, *Gallipoli 1915*; Tim Travers, 'The Ottoman crisis of May 1915 at Gallipoli', *War in History*, 8:1 (2001), pp. 72–86; Tim Travers, 'Liman von Sanders, the capture of Lieutenant Palmer, and Ottoman anticipation of the Allied landings at Gallipoli on 25 April 1915', *Journal of Military History*, 65 (October 2001), pp. 965–79. See also Kevin Fewster, Vecihi Başarin and Hatice Hürmüz Başarin, *Gallipoli: The Turkish Story* (Crows Nest, NSW, 2003 [1985]).

11 Wendy M. Mansfield, 'The importance of Gallipoli: the growth of an Australian folklore', *Queensland Historical Review*, 6:2 (1977), pp. 41–53; W. F. Mandle, *Going it Alone: Australia's National Identity in the Twentieth Century* (Ringwood, Victoria, 1977); Richard White, *Inventing Australia: Images and Identity 1688–1980* (Sydney, 1981); Suzanne Welborn, *Lords of Death: A People, a Place, a Legend* (Fremantle, 1982), reprinted in 2002 as *Bush Heroes*; Jane Ross, *The Myth of the Digger: The Australian Soldier in Two World Wars* (Sydney, 1985).

12 Many of Inglis's articles have been collected in two volumes: *Anzac Remembered: Selected Writings of K. S. Inglis*, ed. John Lack (Melbourne, 1998) and *Observing Australia 1959 to 1999. K. S. Inglis*, ed. Craig Wilcox (Melbourne, 1999); see also, K. S. Inglis, 'The Australians at Gallipoli – I', *Historical Studies*, 14:54 (April 1970), pp. 219–30; 'The Australians at Gallipoli – II', *Historical Studies*, 14:55 (October 1970), pp. 361–75; and K. S. Inglis, *Sacred Places: War Memorials in the Australian Landscape* (Melbourne, 1998).

13 Peter Stanley, 'Reflections on Bean's last paragraph', *Sabretache*, 24:3 (July–September 1983), pp. 4–11; Kevin Fewster (ed.) *Gallipoli Correspondent: The Frontline Diary of C. E. W. Bean* (Sydney, 1983); D. A. Kent, '*The Anzac Book* and the Anzac legend: C. E. W. Bean as editor and image-maker', *Historical Studies*, 21:84 (April 1985), pp. 376–90; John Barrett, 'No straw man: C. E. W. Bean and some critics', *Australian Historical Studies*, 23:89 (April 1988), pp. 102–14; Alistair Thomson, ' "Steadfast until death"? C. E.

W. Bean and the representation of Australian military manhood', *Australian Historical Studies*, 23:93 (October 1989), pp. 462–77.

14 L. L. Robson, 'The origin and character of the First AIF, 1914–1918: some statistical evidence', *Historical Studies*, 15 (1973), pp. 737–49; Kevin Fewster, 'Ellis Ashmead-Bartlett and the making of the Anzac legend', *Journal of Australian Studies*, 10 (June 1982), pp. 17–30; L. L. Robson, 'C. E. W. Bean: a review article', *Journal of the Australian War Memorial*, 4 (1984), pp. 54–7; E. M. Andrews, *The Anzac Illusion: Anglo-Australian Relations during World War One* (Cambridge, 1993); Alistair Thomson, *Anzac Memories: Living with the Legend* (Melbourne, 1994).

15 Philip Kitley, 'Anzac Day ritual', *Journal of Australian Studies*, 4 (June 1979), pp. 58–69; Peter Stanley, 'Gallipoli and Pozières: a legend and a memorial', *Australian Foreign Affairs Record*, 56:4 (April 1985), pp. 281–9; Richard Ely, 'The first Anzac Day: invented or discovered?' *Journal of Australian Studies*, 17 (November 1985), pp. 41–58; Eric Andrews, '25 April 1916: First Anzac Day in Australia and Britain', *Journal of the Australian War Memorial*, 23 (October 1993), pp. 13–20; D. W. Lloyd, *Battlefield Tourism, Pilgrimage and the Commemoration of the Great War in Great Britain, Australia and Canada, 1919–1939* (Oxford, 1993); Jenny Macleod, 'The fall and rise of Anzac Day: 1965 and 1990 compared', *War and Society*, 20:1 (May 2002), 149–68; John A. Moses, 'The struggle for Anzac Day 1916–1930 and the role of the Brisbane Anzac Day Commemoration Committee', *Journal of the Royal Australian Historical Society* 88:1 (June 2002), pp. 54–74.

16 Bob Bushaway, 'Name upon name: the Great War and remembrance' in Roy Porter (ed.) *Myths of the English* (Cambridge, 1992), pp. 137–67; Catherine Moriarty, 'Christian iconography and First World War memorials', *Imperial War Museum Review*, 6 (1992), pp. 63–74; Adrian Gregory, *The Silence of Memory: Armistice Day 1919–1946* (Oxford, 1994).

17 Keith Grieves, 'Remembering an ill-fated venture: personal and collective histories of Gallipoli in a southern English community, 1919–1939' in Jenny Macleod (ed.) *Gallipoli: Making History* (forthcoming).

18 Geoffrey Moorhouse, *Hell's Foundations: A Town, its Myths and Gallipoli* (London, 1992).

19 P. H. Liddle, 'The distinctive nature of the Gallipoli expedition', *RUSI: Journal of the Royal United Services Institute for Defence Studies*, 122:2 (June 1977), pp. 51–6, lists the campaign's unique features but does not discuss them in detail.

20 The New Zealand component of Anzac has been largely overlooked; this book reflects that pattern since it is a consideration of Gallipoli's historiography. Notable work on the New Zealanders at Gallipoli includes: Christopher Pugsley, *Gallipoli: The New Zealand Story* (Auckland, 1984); Jock Phillips, Nicholas Boyack and E. P. Malone (eds) *The Great Adventure: New Zealand Soldiers Describe the First World War* (Wellington, 1988); and Maurice Shadbolt, *Voices of Gallipoli* (Auckland, 1989); see also, Major Fred Waite, *The*

New Zealanders at Gallipoli, New Zealand Popular History Series (Auckland, 1919), vol. 1.

21 George Johnston, 'Anzac . . . a myth for all mankind', *Walkabout* (April 1965), p. 15.

22 Joan Beaumont, 'The Anzac legend' in Joan Beaumont (ed.) *Australia's War, 1914–18* (St Leonards, NSW, 1995), p. 156.

23 C. E. W. Bean (ed.) *The Anzac Book* (London, 1916).

24 Kent, '*The Anzac Book*', p. 390; this article prompted Denis Winter to write '*The Anzac Book*: a re-appraisal', *Journal of the Australian War Memorial*, 16 (April 1990), pp. 58–61. Kent responded in '*The Anzac Book*: a reply to Denis Winter', *Journal of the Australian War Memorial*, 17 (October 1990), pp. 54–5.

25 This misrepresentation is discussed in Robson, 'The origin and character of the First AIF'.

26 Kent, '*The Anzac Book*', p. 386.

27 *Ibid.*, pp. 382–3.

28 John Masefield, *Gallipoli* (London, 1916). Masefield is discussed further in Jenny Macleod, 'The British heroic–romantic myth of Gallipoli' in Jenny Macleod (ed.) *Gallipoli: Making History* (forthcoming).

29 Masefield, *Gallipoli*, p. 183.

30 Constance Babington Smith, *John Masefield: A Life* (Oxford, 1978), p. 158.

31 Masefield, *Gallipoli*, p. 19.

32 Esher to John Charteris, 16 October 1916, quoted in A. D. Harvey, *A Muse of Fire: Literature, Art and War* (London, 1998), p. 79.

33 Kent, '*The Anzac Book*', p. 377.

34 Paul Fussell, *The Great War and Modern Memory* (London, 1975), p. 35; Modris Eksteins, *Rites of Spring: The Great War and the Birth of the Modern Age* (London, 1989), p. 219.

35 The likening of war in the East to a religious crusade was implicit in army thinking before the First World War: see David French, 'The Dardanelles, Mecca and Kut: prestige as a factor in British Eastern strategy, 1914–1916', *War and Society*, 5:1 (May 1987), pp. 45–61.

36 Fussell, *Great War and Modern Memory*, pp. 146–7. See also, Evelyn Cobley, *Representing War: Form and Ideology in First World War Narratives* (Toronto, 1993), p. 192.

37 John Terraine, *The Smoke and the Fire: Myths and Anti-Myths of War 1861–1945* (London 1980), pp. 130–41; Robin Prior and Trevor Wilson, 'Paul Fussell at war', *War in History*, 1:1 (March 1994), pp. 63–71; G. D. Sheffield, ' "Oh! what a futile war": representations of the Western Front in modern British media and popular culture' in Ian Stewart and Susan L. Carruthers (eds) *War, Culture and the Media: Representations of the Military in 20th Century Britain* (Trowbridge, 1996), pp. 63–6.

38 Compton Mackenzie, *Gallipoli Memories* (London, 1929), p. 80.

39 *Ibid.*, p. 5.

40 Bernard Curran, 'The Australian warrior–hero and the classical component', unpublished paper presented at the Australian War Memorial History Conference, 12–15 November 1991; Martin Ball, 'Rereading Bean's last paragraph', and Chris Mackie, 'Troy and Gallipoli: patterns in comparative myth making', unpublished papers presented at the conference 'Australia in War and Peace', 1–4 October 2002, Çanakkale, Turkey.

41 Peter Londey, 'A Greek inscription at the Australian War Memorial', *Journal of the Australian War Memorial*, 23 (October 1993), pp. 50–1; Chris Flaherty and Michael Roberts, 'The reproduction of Anzac symbolism', *Journal of Australian Studies*, 24 (May 1989), pp. 52–69.

42 Bean did make grand claims for the strategy, suggesting that it might have curtailed the war by two years, but this dubious assertion is overshadowed by his emphasis on the nature of the Anzacs: C. E. W. Bean, *The Story of Anzac from the Outbreak of the War to the End of the First Phase of the Gallipoli Campaign, May 4, 1915*, vol. 1 of the Official History of Australia in the War of 1914–1918 (St Lucia, Queensland, 1981 [1921]), p. 174.

43 Winston Churchill, *The World Crisis 1915* (London, 1923).

44 C. F. Aspinall-Oglander, *Military Operations, Gallipoli*, vol. 2: *May 1915 to the Evacuation*, History of the Great War Based on Official Documents (London, 1992 [1932]), p. 380.

45 B. H. Liddell Hart, *The Real War 1914–1918* (London, 1930); and *The British Way in Warfare* (London, 1932)

46 Trevor Wilson, *The Myriad Faces of War* (Cambridge, 1986), p. 130.

47 Mark Girouard, *The Return to Camelot: Chivalry and the English Gentleman* (New Haven, CT, 1981), p. 16.

48 *Ibid.*, p. 281.

49 Philip Guedella, 'Miscellany – defeatism', *New Statesman*, 26 June 1920; Liddell Hart Centre for Military Archives, King's College, London, Hamilton Papers, 17/43, p. 80.

50 David Cannadine, 'War and death, grief and mourning in modern Britain' in Joachim Whaley (ed.) *Mirrors of Mortality: Studies in the Social History of Death* (London, 1981), p. 195.

51 Geoff Dyer, *The Missing of the Somme* (London, 1994), pp. 8–9; see also Max Jones, ' "Our king upon his knees": the public commemoration of Captain Scott's last Antarctic expedition' in G. Cubitt and A. Warren (eds) *Heroic Reputations & Exemplary Lives* (Manchester, 2000).

52 James Bowen, 'Education, ideology and the ruling class: Hellenism and English public schools in the nineteenth century' in G. W. Clarke (ed.) *Rediscovering Hellenism: The Hellenic and the English Imagination* (Cambridge, 1989), p. 179.

53 Peter Parker, *The Old Lie: The Great War and the Public School Ethos* (London, 1987). See also, Michael Paris, *Warrior Nation: Images of War in British Popular Culture, 1850–2000* (London, 2000).

54 Parker, *Old Lie*, p. 234.

55 Richard Jenkyns, *The Victorians and Ancient Greece* (Oxford, 1980), p. 339.
56 *Ibid.*
57 Beaumont, 'Anzac legend', p. 162.
58 Fussell, *Great War*, p. 35.
59 Rosa Maria Bracco, *Merchants of Hope: British Middlebrow Writers and the First World War 1919–1939* (Providence, RI, and Oxford, 1993); Jay Winter, *Sites of Memory, Sites of Mourning: The Great War in European Cultural History* (Cambridge, 1995); Hugh Cecil, 'British war novelists' in Hugh Cecil and Peter Liddle (eds) *Facing Armageddon: The First World War Experienced* (London, 1996), pp. 801–16; Brian Bond, 'British "anti-war" writers and their critics' in Cecil and Liddle (eds) *Facing Armageddon*, pp. 817–30; see also Jay Winter, *Sites of Memory, Sites of Mourning: The Great War in European Cultural History* (Cambridge, 1995).
60 Stanley, 'Gallipoli and Pozières', p. 281.
61 'Gallipoli to-day', *The Times*, 17 July 1927; Hamilton Papers, 17/47.
62 General Sir Ian Hamilton, 'One more drop of blood!', *John Bull*, 30 January 1932; Hamilton Papers, 17/52.
63 The relationship between landscape and the Anzac legend is explored by Peter Hoffenberg in 'Landscape, memory and the Australian war experience, 1915–18', *Journal of Contemporary History*, 36:1 (2001), pp. 111–31. He does not make a distinction between the two theatres in this way.
64 Omer Bartov, *Murder in Our Midst: The Holocaust, Industrial Killing and Representation* (Oxford, 1996), pp. 5, 15–32. This suggestion about individuals, technology and romance must be qualified. It overlooks, for example, the importance of small units in the successes of 1918 or the experience of a man such as Ernst Jünger, author of *The Storm of Steel* (New York, 1975 [1921]; first published in English in 1929).
65 A. H. Russell to Hamilton, 24 September 1916, Hamilton Papers, 8/1/55.
66 'Approximate casualties by months for the Dardanelles campaign (25th April 1915 to 8th January 1916)', *Statistics of the Military Effort of the British Empire During the Great War 1914–1920* (London, 1922), pp. 284–7.
67 'Total per cent of battle casualties and deaths', *ibid.*, p. 248.
68 'Approximate casualties by months in the Expeditionary Force, France', *ibid.*, p. 258. The actual figure is 196,081. Comparative statistics for Australian casualties reflect a similar story. Australian casualties at Gallipoli were approximately 27,500; their casualties at Pozières, during the Somme offensive, numbered 24,000 in less than one-fifth of the time: see Stanley, 'Gallipoli and Pozières', pp. 283, 287).
69 Harvey, *A Muse of Fire*, p. 63.
70 Samuel Hynes, *A War Imagined: The First World War and English Culture* (London, 1990), p. 354.
71 Hynes, *War Imagined*, p. x.
72 J. M. Winter, 'Catastrophe and culture: recent trends in the historiography of the First World War', *Journal of Modern History*, 64 (September 1992), p. 530.

73 G. Mosse, 'The two world wars and the myth of the war experience', *Journal of Contemporary History*, 21:4 (October 1986), p. 492.

74 S. Hynes, 'Personal narratives and commemoration', p. 207. This seems to complement both Bracco's argument regarding middlebrow fiction, in *Merchants of Hope*, and Thomson's ideas about how we compose memories using public languages in order to feel comfortable with them: see *Anzac Memories*, p. 8.

75 Transcript of *Gallipoli*, broadcast Sunday 23 April 1939, 9.10–10.30pm; Hamilton papers, 7/9/19, p. 1. This documentary was produced by Val Gielgud who later told Alan Moorehead: 'I have always been fascinated by the campaign, ever since I was lucky enough to spend an Easter on Jethou with Compton Mackenzie while he was writing *Gallipoli Memories*, and spent very ambrosial nights in reading aloud what he had written': Val Gielgud to Moorehead, 1 May 1956, National Library of Australia, Canberra, Alan Moorehead Papers, MS 5654, box 13, folder 107.

76 Steel and Hart, *Defeat at Gallipoli*.

77 Samuel Hynes, *The Soldiers' Tale: Bearing Witness to Modern War* (New York, 1997), p. 30.

78 Hickey, *Gallipoli*, p. 338 (my emphasis). Hamilton died in 1947, not 1945.

1

The official response: the Dardanelles Commission

The first official assessment of the Gallipoli campaign was undertaken reluctantly. The Dardanelles Commission was conceded by a Government beset by crises. It was marked, unsurprisingly, by strenuous attempts by participants in the campaign to present their actions in a positive light. The Dardanelles Commission sat in late 1916 and 1917 as Britain went through battles at the Somme and Passchendaele on the Western Front. In this chapter I explore the reasons why this distraction from the war's prosecution was allowed; and I discuss some of the concerns of witnesses called before the commission and their manoeuvring behind the scenes in a bid to explain the nature of the reports produced. The chapter, therefore, sheds light on an important historical source, one that is often dealt with too briefly.[1]

A reluctant concession

In mid-1916 Britain contemplated two military defeats. Following an autumn of agonising over the decision, the Gallipoli peninsula was evacuated in January. During the same period fears developed that another expeditionary force was faltering in Mesopotamia. In April 1916 Kut el Amara fell. With this event, the combined impact of these two defeats forced the Government to answer the critics who clamured for an explanation.

As its position weakened, the Government edged towards conceding a commission of inquiry. It had denied a request to lay the relevant papers about the Dardanelles before the House of Commons on 15 November 1915.[2] However, by 1 June 1916, the fact that Prime Minister Herbert Asquith had voluntarily offered to produce papers on Mesopotamia was used by MPs, including Winston Churchill, to force

Andrew Bonar Law, the secretary of state for the colonies, to accept the principle of publishing the papers on the Dardanelles.[3] (The Mesopotamia campaign was the more controversial failure: as *The Times* noted, in discussing the two commissions that were established, 'this business on the Tigris is for the moment paramount'.[4])

Then on 18 July, the Government appeared to have changed its mind. Asquith made a statement to the House that day explaining that the papers could not be published at the present time 'without omissions so numerous and so important that the Papers actually presented would be incomplete and misleading'.[5] He therefore proposed to postpone the publication of the Dardanelles papers, but suggested a debate on Mesopotamia without the publication of its papers instead. The reason for this change of heart was the fierce opposition emanating from within Whitehall. Chief of the Imperial General Staff General Sir William Robertson argued strongly against the publication of all or even part of the relevant documents;[6] and Maurice Hankey, the influential secretary to the Committee of Imperial Defence, wrote two memoranda outlining the case against Bonar Law's promise.[7] Hankey's objections included the difficulty of securing allies' permission for the publication of diplomatic documents, and the risk of assisting the enemy by publishing naval and military documents. It was suggested that any scrutiny of the Dardanelles campaign would signal that efforts in that arena were definitely finished. This would assist the enemy in locating the campaign's defences. Further difficulties arose over the publication of the proceedings of the War Committee – evidence crucial to making sense of events.[8] That evidence was not recorded verbatim; nor had it been circulated among participants for checking in the interests of security. It was therefore considered unfair to publish it. It would also be difficult to go back and ask committee members to check the notes because a chief protagonist, Lord Kitchener, the secretary of state for war, had died in the interim. Moreover, were the precedent of publication to be set, discussions in future meetings might be stifled. In short, serious difficulties surrounded the publication of all relevant papers, and a partial publication would not facilitate a thorough and just investigation. Hankey concluded: 'Unquestionably, without these papers it is impossible to tell the "whole story".'[9]

Hankey's cogent and persuasive arguments were considered and accepted by the War Committee.[10] The committee's decision not to publish the Dardanelles and Mesopotamia papers was greeted with relief in Whitehall. Hankey noted in his diary: 'All the afternoon I was being rung up from different departments by people thanking me for managing this.'[11] Yet Asquith's statement reporting this decision was followed, two days later, by a further reversal of his position and the announcement to the House of commissions of inquiry, 'deliberating under the veil of confidence and secrecy'.[12]

Hankey declared in his diary that the decision was 'sheer cowardice',[13] but the Government's weak political position was more to blame. Asquith's coalition fell in December 1916, its position in Parliament in the preceding months having slowly weakened. In particular, between April and July 1916, two major issues of principle – conscription and Ireland – divided the Government's supporters and weakened its position. The chain of events during this period must also have induced a sense of crisis. Between 24 April 1916 and the promise of the commissions, Asquith's Government faced the Easter Rising in Dublin, the fall of Kut, the battle of Jutland (which at first appeared to be a defeat), the death of Kitchener, and the first day of the battle of the Somme, the bloodiest day in the history of the British Army. Bowing to the demand for commissions of inquiry was the only way that the Government avoided defeat in the House.[14]

The commission was established by the 'Special Commissions (Dardanelles and Mesopotamia) Act, 1916'. It heard evidence on eighty-nine days between late August 1916 and early September 1917, completing reports in February and December 1917. It had been intended to keep the commission small and manageable, but discussions in Parliament swelled its membership to ten (another sign of Asquith's weak position[15]). Lord Cromer was appointed as chairman; after his death on 29 January 1917, another commissioner, Sir William Pickford, a law lord, took his place. Other nationalities which fought at Gallipoli were represented by the New Zealand High Commissioner Sir Thomas Mackenzie and his Australian counterpart Andrew Fisher; the Welsh MP Walter Roch and the Irish Nationalist MP Captain Stephen Gwynn. Two other MPs, Sir Frederick Cawley and James Clyde, left the commission at its mid-point in December 1916 to take up appointments in David Lloyd George's Government. It was agreed in Parliament that the admirals and generals 'shall be tried by men who understand something about modern military matters';[16] and so Field Marshal Lord Nicholson and Admiral William May were added to the commission. Edward Grimwood Mears, a barrister who had worked on the Bryce Committee on the German atrocities in Belgium – the reply to the German 'White Book' – and the commission on the rebellion in Ireland,[17] agreed to act as secretary to the Dardanelles Commission in return for a knighthood.[18]

The establishing Act defined the commission's purpose to be that of

> inquiring into the origin, inception, and conduct of operations of war in
> the Dardanelles and Gallipoli, including the supply of drafts, reinforce-
> ments, ammunition and equipment to the troops and Fleet, the provision
> for the sick and wounded, and the responsibility of those departments of
> Government whose duty it has been to minister to the wants of the forces
> employed in that theatre of war.[19]

Thus it produced two reports, one an interim report concerning the campaign's origin and inception and the final report on the execution of the
campaign.[20] These were concerned, as instructed by the Bill, with the
administrative problems of the campaign and a few crucial episodes.
General Sir Ian Hamilton's dispatches were attached as an appendix to
describe the fighting.

But what was the commission's wider purpose? It was, surely, to
assuage the controversy that had forced its establishment. It therefore
needed to settle the question marks against the reputation both of the
campaign and of some of its leading figures.

Preparing for the commission

The establishing of the commission prompted a flurry of activity. The
inception of the campaign was the first topic of consideration, and the
politicians called before the commission relied heavily on Hankey to
organise their evidence. The extent of the burden thus placed on him
may be gleaned from his diary. This evidence also indicates the manner
in which the politicians cooperated in order to present a united front.
The prospect of presenting the Government's case gave Hankey at least
one sleepless night and 174 hours of extra work in the space of two
months. He described the preparing of the evidence as 'one of the most
dreary tasks that has ever fallen to my lot'.[21] It received close attention
from his colleagues.[22] Hankey sent a transcript of his proposed evidence
to Asquith, Balfour, Grey, Lloyd George and Lord Crewe on 11 August,
and it was further discussed, on 14 and 15 August, at informal meetings
as well as in various other brief conversations. In addition, Hankey coor-
dinated the evidence that his colleagues would present. He heard Fisher
rehearse the whole of his evidence;[23] he 'lunched with Lord Grey to coach
him on his Dardanelles evidence';[24] and he 'coached' Haldane
and Asquith.[25] Hankey himself appeared twice before the commission in
September 1916.

Of all of Hankey's present and former colleagues, it was perhaps Churchill who was most concerned to influence the Dardanelles Commission. He had lost his position as first lord of the Admiralty because of events on Gallipoli, and he was subjected to repeated virulent criticism of his role in the campaign, not least from the *Daily Mail*, which described him as 'a megalomaniac politician [who] risked the fate of our Army in France and sacrificed thousands of lives to no purpose'.[26] Following his departure from the Government that autumn, Churchill spent a brief interlude on the Western Front, and then kicked his heels in London, pushing his case before the commission, making speeches in Parliament and writing newspaper articles, until his return to Government under Lloyd George as minister of munitions in July 1917.[27]

Churchill laboured over his own contribution to the commission between July and November 1916. As his attempts to have the relevant documents published were thwarted by Asquith, he determined to include in his own evidence as many documents as possible.[28] Churchill received help from Lloyd George and the Admiralty in gathering the documentation he needed, but Asquith continued to stand in the way of full publication by refusing to allow Hankey to provide for Churchill a complete set of War Council minutes. Asquith thereby covered up evidence that would reveal his own support for the campaign.[29] Churchill corresponded with Admiral Oliver, outlining the points which he should stress,[30] and renewed his friendship with Jackie Fisher, the volatile first sea lord whose resignation in May 1915 had prompted the formation of the coalition Government and with it Churchill's removal from the Admiralty. The two men corresponded regarding their evidence.[31] Fisher's case was essentially that 'I clung to you! Clung against my convictions!'[32] Accordingly, Churchill tried to tailor his evidence to fit with Fisher's, possibly thereby weakening it, since he denied himself the opportunity to refer to Fisher's erratic thought processes and his mental collapse in May 1915. At no point was Fisher's capricious behaviour referred to before the commission.[33]

One important collaborator for Churchill was his old friend General Sir Ian Hamilton (see figure 1).[34] They began working together as early as June 1916, when it seemed that papers would be laid before Parliament. But their plan to demonstrate the culpability of Kitchener was partially scuppered by the latter's death at sea. (Hamilton describes in his memoirs the tragi-comic scene in which they hear of Kitchener's death from a news-vendor's cry as he and Churchill were about to put the fin-

1 Commodore Roger Keyes, Vice-Admiral J. De Robeck, General Sir Ian
Hamilton and Major-General Walter Braithwaite on board HMS
Triad in 1915

ishing touches to their evidence.[35]) Thereafter, Kitchener remained
the target of Hamilton and Churchill, but it became impossible to
attack him directly. Hamilton wrote to Churchill of a conversation with
F. E. Smith:

> He was strong and clear of your way of thinking throughout. But, he said,
> that as my vindication must be, so far as he could see, at Kitchener's
> expense, it would be necessary if I had counsel that he came down to
> defend [. . .]

> I thought hard all the way and I came to the conclusion I should be
> utterly done for during my lifetime if any act of mine were to draw out a
> Government defence of Kitchener. Once my defence becomes looked upon
> as an attack on a dead hero it would be better for my reputation to lose
> than to win. Further, although our lines are not quite parallel, I am also
> quite certain the popular fury thus raised would react against your own
> case too. It simply is not good enough. As a matter of fact, I don't mean to

attack Kitchener at all although the figures will prove that, witingly or unwitingly [*sic*], he did me very badly.[36]

Following the death of Kitchener, Hamilton and Churchill's cooperation continued in a more limited fashion. For example, Churchill gave Hamilton a copy of the paper he presented to the commission. This was a highly secret document, and Hamilton invited Major-General Sir Walter Braithwaite, his chief of staff at Gallipoli, to come round to read it – 'I cannot, of course, send this paper out of my house.' He told Braithwaite: 'Then when we talk we would do so with a mutual knowledge of the lines of Churchill's case which, up to a point, is our case.'[37] Braithwaite disagreed. He argued vehemently against binding themselves too closely to Churchill: 'But, to follow your simile of the boat; if F. E. Smith is going to pull the stroke oar and Mr. Churchill is going to hold the rudder lines – instead of you – then I am going to be in another boat altogether, even if it is only a canoe which I have to paddle myself.'[38] Hamilton continued to correspond regularly with Braithwaite, but wrote to Churchill less frequently. This may have been due to Braithwaite's ultimatum, but could also be explained in part by Churchill being mainly concerned with the initiation of the campaign and Hamilton with its execution.

Building on his preparation, Churchill took a robust attitude to the proceedings of the commission. The former first lord of the Admiralty demanded the right to present and cross-examine his own witnesses as if it were a court of law. He wrote to Lord Cromer:

> With regard to the procedure of the Commission, I presume that I shall be at liberty to be present during the course of the enquiry. I have a number of witnesses to bring before the Commission. I propose to conduct the case so far as I am concerned myself and not to ask leave to employ counsel.[39]

Although he was not allowed to attend at will,[40] he was, extraordinarily, allowed to question witnesses[41] and to read out a long statement before his own cross-examination began on day five. This was in addition to more than 100 pages of statements and documents that he presented to the commission.[42]

Hamilton, in contrast, having considered and rejected the overtly aggressive stance of employing a barrister,[43] preferred a more covert manipulation of the commission. It is difficult to assess which man's tactics were the more successful, if indeed their effectiveness can be separately gauged. The reports criticised Churchill more strongly than Hamilton, but it was the younger man's career that ultimately revived. Nonetheless, Hamilton's machinations deserve further attention. He skilfully combined a stance of seeming transparency with extensive secret orchestration of 'his witnesses' to present their evidence to the best advantage and to rebut specific allegations made during the proceedings. This endeavour was part of a pattern of activity.

Reputation at stake

From the very first landings on Gallipoli, General Sir Ian Hamilton sought to vindicate himself and the campaign as a whole. The reputation of the two were, and continue to be, inextricably entwined. As it is traced through his dispatches, telegrams and memoranda, then through his dealings with the Dardanelles Commission and subsequently through his writings and speeches, a shift in the emphasis of his vindicative efforts may be seen. During the campaign, Hamilton worked to establish its merits and successes; but, particularly after his removal as commander, he aimed to disperse the clouds of blame and suspicion as well. He described his task to Birdwood thus:

> I have been fated to have to fight for an idea – for a might-have-been. I have been forced in fact to fight before this Commission in vindication of what you and I achieved with our brave troops and also in proving how much more we might have achieved had we been properly supported.[44]

Hamilton fought 'tooth and nail' for 'our good name and reputation'.[45] That was the central contribution he made to the work of the Dardanelles Commission.

Hamilton continued throughout the war to hope for a senior appointment, but that became dependent on a favourable report by the commission.[46] In his evidence to the commission, Hamilton even mentioned that political reasons accounted for his unemployment.[47] In November 1917, it seemed that Hamilton would be appointed to the Eastern Command,[48] but he never received another senior appointment, only the honorific sinecure of lieutenant of the Tower of London in 1918. However, as Hamilton explained to Churchill, being given any particular job was of secondary importance: 'So long as public feeling in the matter is such that the Government could do so if they wished, – that is the main thing, and certainly more vital to me than the bestowal of any non-fighting billet.'[49]

It should be stressed that Hamilton was not motivated by personal ambition alone. He was also concerned on imperial grounds for the reputation of the Gallipoli campaign. In May 1917 he wrote to Hankey:

If my conduct of the operations is to be impugned by the Commissioner's Report, the result would be, to say the least of it, detrimental to future military federation of our forces on Imperial lines [. . .]

I have not suggested this idea, so far, to anyone in the world. But you of all men in our Empire are capable of grasping its import and you will understand at the same time why it was impossible to use such an argument before the Commission and why I now take you into my confidence.[50]

Hankey gave the desired reply: 'I intend to avail myself of any opportunities that may arise to mention the argument as my own in any circles where it is likely to be useful.'[51] This is a clear example of Hamilton's attempts to manipulate the commission, yet it should not be seen as a purely cynical and self-serving exercise. He wrote to Churchill that the first report had done a great deal of harm, but that it was a critical final report that held the greater potential to damage imperial unity. It is worth quoting at length from this letter, since it explains Hamilton's regard for the imperial dimension of the commission and the extent of his moderating activities:

Now what will smash – or go far to smash – you as well as me and, I veritably believe, in the long run our Empire, will be if this second Report does anything to shatter the belief still confidently clung to in the Antipodes, that the expedition was *worth while*, and that 'the Boys' did die to a great end and were so handled as to be able to sell their lives very dearly.

The mischief that a sensational second Dardanelles Report of the Mesopotamia type would produce would be out of all reckoning greater than that produced by the first Dardanelles Report. Our colonies are case-hardened to all sorts of political scandals, treacheries and fiascos. But if the actual conduct of operations is held up to obliquy [*sic*] and most of all if the people of Australia and New Zealand feel their sacrifices went for nothing, then never expect them again to have any sort of truck with our superior direction in preparation for future wars.

What is the moral of all this? I say that whilst the Report is still not quite stereotyped a warning as to the imperial issues at stake might, if put to Pickford, say, by the PM, even at the 11th hour save the situation by determining him to put all his weight on the side of toning down any reflections which may have been made.

Please do not think I would try to stop this Report whatever it may be. I feel it must come out now or people would think the worst. I would only wish the powers that be to realise what the consequences will be if they *emphasise* shortcomings in the conduct of operations. As for myself, if I am unjustly blamed, I shall ask for a Court Martial or at least a military inquiry,

where, by statute, I can be present or be represented if my military conduct
and character is impugned. But I am thinking of wider and bigger things
than that. Amongst them, justice and truth and the maintenance of our
imperial unity.[52]

Hamilton's paramount concern here was not to defend the politicians,
but to defend the conduct of the operations, for adverse comment might
be felt to invalidate the sacrifices of the Anzacs. Indeed, this consideration prompted Hamilton to assert in much of his writing the heroism of
those he commanded. This concern for imperial unity was one of the
reasons why the Murdoch affair – where an Australian journalist sent
an unauthorised and highly critical letter about Gallipoli to his prime
minister – was so dangerous.

Asquith wrote to Andrew Fisher, the Australian prime minister, to try
to minimise the initial damage of this letter:

> This report is now being carefully examined here, and as many of the state-
> ments in it appear to be exaggerated and over-coloured, and some to be
> without foundation, I hope that you and your colleagues will suspend
> judgement and prevent publicity until you have received the report of
> Colonel Hankey and other relevant documents which are being sent to you
> without delay. We all here agree that no praise can be too high for the mag-
> nificent soldiership of the Australian and New Zealand troops.[53]

John Robertson writes that the British Government need not have
worried. Pearce, the minister for defence, was disinclined to rock the
imperial boat. More importantly, W. M. Hughes took over as prime minister on 27 October 1916; his Government thought it had been wrong to
allow Murdoch to visit Gallipoli at all and requested that no Australian
press representative be allowed to visit the front in future without the
prior approval of the Australian Government.[54] A letter by Lieutenant-
General Sir William Birdwood, the British commander of the Australian
and New Zealand Army Corps, also confirms that the Australians were
anxious that the Gallipoli campaign did not damage imperial unity.
Referring to the appointment of High Commissioner Fisher to the
Dardanelles Commission, Birdwood wrote that

> the Commonwealth Government quite disliked his [Fisher's] appointment
> to the Commission from the first, which was I believe hustled through by
> Asquith before Fisher had time to communicate with Australia. The Gov-
> ernment there seemed to think that his appointment might be taken to
> mean that Australia had grievances which they wished investigated, while
> such was by no means their attitude. They were sure to let Fisher know this,
> which may account for his want of keenness![55]

Hamilton's approach to the commission

Hamilton's strategy in approaching the commission combined two seemingly contradictory impulses: openness and secret orchestration. Since he felt that he, personally, had made no major errors, he believed that a full disclosure of the facts was in his best interests. A complete appreciation of the events of 1915 would reveal that he and his force had done the best that was possible in the circumstances. It would also reveal the factors that had let him down, in particular the failure to keep him fully supplied with reinforcements and the murky events that had led to his dismissal and the evacuation of the peninsula. He therefore wrote to Hankey when a commission of inquiry was first mooted:

> I want to tell you that I welcome the completest publicity. From my personal standpoint there exists no letter, cable or paper connected with the Dardanelles campaign I should wish to see withheld from publication. If I possess any documents not accessible to you, I shall be glad to place them at your disposal.[56]

Despite this inclination to openness and to appearing as a man who, as Braithwaite, his former chief of the general staff (CGS), put it, 'had nothing to attack about, and nothing to defend',[57] Hamilton continued to be concerned with the 'devilish difficult thing' of stating his own case 'with full vigour'.[58] His solution was to do all he could to manipulate and orchestrate the proceedings of the commission by assiduous work behind the scenes.

After each witness appeared before the commission, the transcript of his evidence was forwarded to the individual concerned for correction. It seems, however, that Hamilton gained access to all the other evidence too. This was not a privilege unique to Hamilton. Cromer, the first chairman of the commission, had told Churchill in September 1916 that

> the evidence of all the witnesses will be printed, and that, should it appear desirable, for whatsoever reason, that any witness who has been already examined should be placed in possession of the evidence of other witnesses, a copy will be confidentially sent to him. Thus, on the one hand, the Commissioners will have an opportunity of recalling a witness should they think it desirable to do so, and, on the other hand, a witness who has been examined will have an opportunity of requesting that he may be recalled in order to furnish any further explanation which he may wish to make, resulting from the evidence of subsequent witnesses.[59]

Hamilton saw the evidence of at least thirty-one witnesses (from a total of forty-three, including Hamilton, interviewed in the second phase of the commission), probably more than any other interested party;[60] he certainly made the most of the opportunities for reply and re-examination.

Hamilton saw these papers on the strict understanding that he was not to show them to others, but he did nonetheless. He wrote to Braithwaite: 'although I am forbidden and have promised not to show these evidences I regard you as absolutely my *alter ego* in this matter. Only you must either burn or return.'[61] This cloak-and-dagger collaboration was repeated with each of those individuals Hamilton considered an ally. For example, Ellison similarly was also considered his *alter ego* on water matters;[62] Birdwood and Freyberg were warned not to disclose their knowledge of others' evidence.[63] Hamilton shared this information in order to strengthen his defence of the campaign. When he identified a weak point, a false statement or an attack, he garnered information to promote his view and encouraged allies to support it. Indeed, Hamilton had referred to 'my witnesses' in a letter to Braithwaite (a phrase which his former CGS deprecated), and although the phrase was not used again, it is clear that a number of Hamilton's allies were happy to be directed by him in their evidence.[64] He was, therefore, not above attempting to shape others' evidence; for example, he wrote three letters to Birdwood suggesting the points he should bring out.[65] In the third letter Hamilton insisted: 'what I am going to put forward in this letter is not tinctured by selfishness'.[66] Although Birdwood had agreed 'on the necessity of us all standing firmly together',[67] he did not slavishly follow Hamilton's advice. Hamilton had suggested the line he should take on the manner in which Hamilton's replacement as commander, General Sir Charles Monro, decided the peninsula should be evacuated, but Birdwood's evidence did not touch on this.[68] In turn, however, Birdwood did give guidance to Major-General Sir Alexander Godley, general officer commanding (GOC) NZ and A Division, on his evidence.[69] Similarly, Hamilton manipulated General Winter, deputy quartermaster-general of the Mediterranean Expeditionary Force (MEF), and his assistant Lieutenant Colonel Beadon to head off the contentious issue of whether the 'Q' staffs of GHQ and IX Corps worked together efficiently.[70]

To a certain extent, in his correspondence Hamilton was legitimately following up lines of enquiry at the request of the commission,[71] and his actions were openly referred to on occasion,[72] but other comments suggest that much of his activity was highly secret and improper. Hamilton wrote to Braithwaite on 21 September 1916: 'I have heard something about the Commission and Hankey's evidence, but remember we are both (really and truly) liable to be cast into prison if it is known that we know.'[73] To Birdwood, he wrote:

> Be careful, though, about showing my evidence to anyone, or about showing any knowledge of what my evidence was. Strictly speaking I have only been warned to treat as secret such evidences of *other witnesses* as may be shown me by the Commission. Still, I doubt if I am not skating on rather thin ice in having kept a record as I suddenly resolved to do that afternoon when I found you had not time to read the proofs through.[74]

Hamilton's strategy then, was one of seeming transparency combined with secret orchestration of 'his witnesses' on how best to present their evidence and rebut specific allegations made during the proceedings. However, this 'contradiction' might be seen as the difference between means and end: Hamilton's goal was consistent throughout. He wanted to shape the historical record in favour of himself and his men.

Hamilton and the commissioners

Hamilton's manipulation of the witnesses was intended to influence the opinions of the commissioners, and he was anxious to find out how their attitudes were developing. He therefore, for example, used Birdwood's high standing with the Anzacs to explore the attitudes of the commissioners from Australia and New Zealand. Birdwood had a particularly interesting conversation with Sir Thomas Mackenzie, New Zealand's representative on the commission, in June. This conversation took place in private and its content was secret, a fact that did not prevent Birdwood from summarising it for Hamilton. He was able to ascertain that Andrew Fisher, the Australian representative, had lost interest in the commission, having decided that he probably carried little influence with the other commissioners. Birdwood took the opportunity, both verbally and later in writing, to urge the alteration of an unspecified criticism of Hamilton that was to have been contained in the report.[75]

Despite Hamilton's apprehensiveness about Fisher's attitude, prompted, as will be seen, by his involvement in the Murdoch affair; it was the attitude of Field Marshal Lord Nicholson which gave him the gravest concern from the outset. As early as August 1916 Hamilton wrote to Braithwaite:

> Nick's appointment caused me to shiver. On the surface he has always been a friend; under the surface he has been, I know, a persistent crabber of your

humble servant. In any case his delight in mischief-making will certainly find scope in the Commission. But there is one side to his mind which may save us. He hates K. a great deal worse than he hates me. Not that I think he hates me at all, but he has been jealous of me and has always had a mischievous delight in trying to put a spoke in my wheel.[76]

Nicholson had been a long-standing foe of Hamilton's. Their enmity dated back at least to 1905,[77] and possibly to the Boer War when Hamilton, in 1901–2, had acted as Kitchener's chief of staff. Hamilton told Birdwood: 'his clear, unmistakable animus against me dates exactly from the time when I said absolutely and clearly I retained my admiration and gratitude for that great soldier, Lord Kitchener. From that very moment he has done everything he possibly could to do me in.'[78] Another letter to Birdwood suggests that Nicholson's target was not Hamilton directly, but Kitchener via Hamilton: 'Of course Nick himself would always play for safety and he hates Lord K and would like to convict him – through our mouths – of having been a reckless, haphazard creature.'[79] However, an encounter between Braithwaite and Nicholson in December 1916 – before the second phase of the proceedings began – seemed to indicate that Nicholson's mind was 'still in a state of flux about the matter'. Braithwaite took his opportunity to assert that the landing was 'the most splendid military feat ever performed' and to defend some criticisms of Hamilton's command.[80] However, the hope that Nicholson was still open to persuasion seems to have been in vain: with his access to so much evidence, Hamilton was able to chart the manner in which Nicholson was asking leading questions.[81] Birdwood was able to confirm these suspicions as to Nicholson's activities in his private conversation with Mackenzie. Birdwood told Hamilton: 'What he very guardedly mentioned was that Nick was apparently out to do all he could to whitewash Stopford, and on for adopting a different attitude towards you.'[82]

Given the 'malign' influence of Nicholson, it was comforting that Pickford asserted a moderating authority as chairman. His presence enabled Hamilton and Braithwaite to retain their confidence in the integrity and fairness of the commission. Braithwaite wrote: 'I have a good deal of faith in Mr Justice Pickford's acumen, and think that his experience as a Judge will enable him to size up not only what people say, but how they say it, and I am inclined to think that he is the dominant mind on the Commission.'[83] Hamilton shared his faith, writing: 'Lord Justice Pickford is a fair minded man; so I still have hopes that right may prevail and that the feasibility of the Dardanelles Expedition may be made clear.'[84] It does seem possible, however, that 'nasty old

Nick'[85] had a considerable effect on the final report. In part, this was due to the influence he gained from being the only military man on the commission – although Hamilton thought that the only area of judgement where this would come into play would be over the question of his intervention at Suvla on 8 August.[86] An extraordinary document among Hamilton's papers suggests the degree of influence Nicholson wielded, despite others' efforts to see fair play:

> XXX repeated that there is not a shadow of doubt that if Lord Nicholson had not been on the Commission Sir Ian would have been completely exonerated. As it is, he casts imputations and makes suggestions till they are not sure whether they are right after all. The first Report which was on the point of coming out a month ago was a complete vindication of Sir Ian.[87]

It is unwise to rely solely on this document, given its lack of attribution, but it is corroborated by Hamilton's earlier suspicions. He wrote to Commodore Roger Keyes: 'Had it not been for Lord Nicholson's presence on this Commission I would have been absolutely vindicated'.[88]

Murdoch and the commission

Nicholson's was not the only bias that Hamilton feared. He believed that the actions of the Australian journalist Keith Murdoch had turned the authorities in London against the campaign in the autumn of 1915 and had prompted General Monro to make up his mind for evacuation before even reaching the peninsula to make his report.[89] He also feared that it had affected the view of Andrew Fisher. Murdoch's experience provides an opportunity to show how one witness was treated by the commission and how Hamilton tried to counter his potential influence.

Murdoch's role in the Gallipoli campaign deserves comment. He had come second to Charles Bean in the journalists' ballot to elect Australia's official war correspondent; but had nonetheless managed to visit Gallipoli for four days on his way to take up an appointment as the managing editor of a cable service housed in *The Times*' office in London. It appears to have been his own idea to make use of his journey to look in to the postal service and banking arrangements for the Australian Imperial Force in Egypt.[90] He then wrote a 'wheedling'[91] letter to Hamilton in order to secure a trip to Gallipoli. He was strongly influenced by the charismatic though pessimistic journalist Ellis Ashmead-Bartlett, who persuaded him that the campaign was disastrous and that he should carry home a letter explaining – free from the rigours of censorship – to

Asquith the situation in Gallipoli as he perceived it. This letter was seized by British intelligence officers when he reached Marseilles; but when Murdoch reached London he wrote his own version. This he sent to his friend Andrew Fisher, the prime minister of Australia. He showed it also to British cabinet ministers and Asquith had it printed and circulated as a Committee of Imperial Defence document.[92]

Murdoch's letter was powerfully written, full of emotive phrasing and generalisations proclaiming patriotically the virtues of the Australians, the pitiful nature of new British recruits, and the deplorable incapacity of British officers and particularly the staff.[93] Murdoch also mentioned the slow and bloody progress of the campaign, the failing morale, the scandalously poor water supply, and he alleged that sometimes laggards were shot by their officers. Most of this was given without specific examples, although Hamilton, Braithwaite and Birdwood were singled out for criticism.

Murdoch forwarded this letter to Asquith on 25 September, but only on October 13 did Hamilton receive a copy. He sent a cable in reply the next day; it was a restrained piece that questioned Murdoch's ability to make his judgements and pointed out Murdoch's pro-Australian bias, his inaccuracy and tendency to exaggerate.[94] On 15 October, Hamilton was relieved of his command. He always believed that Murdoch's letter had played a crucial role in this, and Hamilton hated him for it. He later described Murdoch as 'my bête noir' and told Churchill that 'the imputations cast on all British Officers and men under my command are too black to be forgiven'.[95] Hamilton vented his fury in a full response to Murdoch's letter, which was printed as a Committee of Imperial Defence document on 26 November 1915. In it Hamilton expanded on his criticisms of Murdoch. Note, for example, the sarcasm in his description of Murdoch's fleeting visit to the peninsula and his bias:

> His visit was of the briefest. He resisted the temptation to visit Helles, twelve miles distant, despite his original 'intense anxiety' to visit the sacred shores of Gallipoli, and despite the facts that transport was always available and that he had my full permission to go anywhere and see anything. In short, Mr. Murdoch had hardly a bowing acquaintance with the peninsula, and he knows it. But this does not deter him from dealing out unrelieved condemnation to every section of the force: men, officers, staff, generals, lines of communication, base and home administration – always excepting the Australians.[96]

Hamilton alluded to the malign influence of Ashmead-Bartlett; highlighted Murdoch's civilian ignorance of the work of the staff and its usual interaction with journalists and the men; refuted the 'vile' allegation that laggards were shot and denied that men died from thirst alone. He asserted that Murdoch's account was ungenerous and unjust, his behaviour ungentlemanly. But the most scandalous feature was the importance given at home to these ill-founded and overblown allegations:

> Since I have returned I find everywhere my own soldierly reputation has been undermined, and I catch everywhere echoes of phrases printed in the Committee of Imperial Defence memorandum.
>
> In my absence, I, a British General and a member of the Committee of Imperial Defence, have had circulated amongst my brother members aspersions against my honour, and libels against my troops. No chance was vouchsafed me of proving the malignancy of these attacks, or of showing how far they might be inspired by personal animus. A fortnight before I had ever heard of their existence they had already been elevated to the rank of State papers, and passed round from hand to hand, and mouth to ear through the most influential circles in the land.[97]

The role of Murdoch in Hamilton's and the campaign's downfall was still uppermost in the general's mind a year later when preparations were underway for the Dardanelles Commission hearings. Hamilton believed that Murdoch had influenced some commissioners' attitudes towards himself, and he wrote to Braithwaite: 'There are several points on which I have been attacked and on which I have reasons to think I shall be attacked in the Commission by persons whom Murdoch has influenced.'[98] Hamilton therefore seized his first opportunity to influence their view of Murdoch. He replied to a request from the commission's secretary, Mr Grimwood Mears, for suggestions as to witnesses to be summoned. In Hamilton's list, only Murdoch is mentioned as someone whose views needed refutation. For this purpose he suggested Major-General Sir E. A. Altham, inspector general of communications, and Surgeon-General Sir W. Babtie, who could counter particularly unfair criticisms that had been made. Hamilton also suggested that Phillip Schuler should be called. He, like Murdoch, was a civilian pressman invited to the Peninsula by Hamilton, but his views were more substantially based on personal experience: 'The only difference between his qualifications and those of Mr. Murdoch are that he stayed longer on the Peninsula; that he saw fighting, and that he has since joined up and is serving in the ranks.'[99] He went on to suggest that Ashmead-Bartlett's dispatch be laid before the commission; for this, in combination with Murdoch's letter, 'were the final causes of a momentous, and I believe, ruinous decision'.[100]

This letter from Hamilton was not placed before the commissioners, and so he faced the decision whether to press his attack in person when he appeared as a witness. He had corresponded with Mears during the winter, occasionally referring to Murdoch; Mears advised him to 'get up and rub it in',[101] but Andrew Fisher's presence on the commission gave Hamilton reason to hesitate. He told Braithwaite about his day at the commission on 8 January:

> Fisher asked me no questions at all and made himself exceedingly agreeable. On leaving the room he shook me warmly by the hand; said I had had a long and tiresome day but – and here he nodded his head and smiled in a sort of way to make me understand I had come out of it splendidly.
>
> I have a sort of impression that this is his way of saying, 'You leave Murdoch alone and I will be nice about you'. Well, if this is so, would I not be wise to play up to his hint? He may sell me, of course, in the secrecy of the conference and go against me all the same.[102]

Braithwaite's reply shows an equal degree of suspicion about the whole process: 'Very glad things went so well . . . Should not lightly dispense with evidence against Murdoch otherwise you are likely to be had behind your back.'[103]

In his evidence on the following day, however, Hamilton did not mention Murdoch or Ashmead-Bartlett. Braithwaite himself was asked about the war correspondents and took the opportunity to tell the story of Ashmead-Bartlett and Murdoch in remarkably calm terms.[104] By far the greatest damage to Murdoch's credibility, however, was done by his own testimony. His poor performance has been described by John Avieson: 'Murdoch was an unwilling, evasive, defiant, and rebuked witness. The climax was an admission, under close and decidedly hostile cross-examination, that part of what he had written was a deliberate fabrication.'[105] Murdoch explained that his main impression had been that the expedition had 'reached a desperate crisis and that a full consideration of the position was essential'.[106] The questions to be asked, therefore, should have been: was that impression correct and was he right to take drastic steps to communicate this crisis?

Murdoch robustly defended the morality of his actions, arguing that the War Office allowed correspondents to address a minister of the crown, and that the correspondent's declaration which he had signed did not prevent him from carrying a letter from another to the British prime minister. On the subject of Murdoch's own correspondence with the Australian prime minister, the recipient of that letter, Andrew Fisher, now a commissioner, took care to help out his friend's testimony, arguing that Murdoch was in a special position. Fisher had asked him to communicate his impressions, and wrote to him:

> You therefore considered yourself in a privileged position as carrying a mandate from one self-governing dominion which was directly concerned with the operation of their forces in Gallipoli and elsewhere, to give your best impressions of what you saw? – I considered that I was charged with the duty of reporting to my Government in Australia to the best of my ability.[107]

That was Murdoch's trump card. Given the sacrifice of Australian men, it would have created difficulties in imperial relations to deny Australia's right to know, by whatever means, how its men were being employed. Murdoch argued that he patriotically risked his career in order to ensure that the expedition be considered afresh. He went on to stress that he was never censured by the politicians he spoke to in Britain, and indeed was so well regarded that he had recently been granted an interview with the British prime minister.

Though he would not be bullied, Murdoch had difficulty in justifying his assumed role as an expert on the campaign. His sources were weak – he was reluctant to name specific officers who, he said, had criticised their superiors and he was forced to admit that he never met the British generals he so violently criticised. His ignorance, as a civilian, of the working of the army was made clear. Field Marshal Lord Nicholson questioned him particularly aggressively on the technicalities and distinctions of the staff, to which Murdoch could only weakly reply: 'Well they wear red.'[108] He blamed Ashmead-Bartlett for the initial suggestion to break the censorship, and he admitted that he made his own letter purposefully highly-coloured to maximise its effect and that in doing so he was unjust to Birdwood. At the end of his testimony Murdoch requested a copy of Hamilton's memorandum about him. Murdoch feared that it would influence the commission. Pickford's reply was extremely sharp: 'I assure you we shall not, any more than we shall be influenced, if I may say so, by a good many hearsay statements which are in your statement, and as to which you have not given us any evidence.'[109]

And yet Murdoch did influence the commission – not by his evidence, but through the original letter. For all the vagueness of its sources and its exaggerations and overstatements, it helped set the 'agenda' of the commission. Many of the letter's concerns were the same as the commission's: poor staff work, the suffering of the wounded and the failure at Suvla.

Despite this poor performance, Hamilton remained concerned about Murdoch. He wrote to Mears suggesting another witness, Henry Nevinson, a senior war correspondent who would be able to refute Murdoch's and Ashmead-Bartlett's evidence. This 'little personal note' to Mears reflects the frank and co-operative correspondence which had developed between the secretary and the general:

> Nevinson is, as I have said in my original letter about Press correspondents, a high class man – a crank perhaps in some things but one whose word would carry great weight with his own profession. If you think there is even a lingering belief in the minds of any of the Commission that Mr. Murdoch had anything whatever to go upon except Ashmead-Bartlett and his own imagination when he spread this untruth, then I certainly think Nevinson should be called* [. . .]
>
> *In any case he is a head & shoulders in intellect and everything above Captain W. Maxwell & such like conceited little shrimps.[110]

The final report did not mention the controversial actions of Murdoch and Ashmead-Bartlett – perhaps they did not impress as witnesses, or perhaps Hamilton's campaign against them worked. A more plausible explanation might be a desire to avoid controversy, either for its own sake or for reasons of imperial unity.

An intentionally bland report

The reports of the Dardanelles Commission treated Hamilton kindly. The following is its harshest comment on him:

> Though from time to time Sir Ian Hamilton represented the need of drafts, reinforcements, guns and munitions, which the Government found it impossible to supply, he was nevertheless always ready to renew the struggle with the resources at his disposal, and to the last was confident of success. For this it would be hard to blame him; but viewing the Expedition in the light of events it would, in our opinion, have been well had he examined the situation as disclosed by the first landings in a more critical spirit, impartially weighed the probabilities of success and failure, having regard to the resources in men and material which could be placed at his disposal, and submitted to the Secretary of State for War a comprehensive statement of the arguments for and against a continuance of the operations.[111]

But its view that the operation should have been sufficiently considered beforehand by Kitchener, that the requirements of other operations should have been taken into account and that political considerations in London forced delay at an important time[112] were all most helpful to Hamilton's belief that the failure was not the fault of those who were actually at Gallipoli.

Hamilton's reactions to the report suggest that he felt at least partially exonerated by the commission. He chose not to push for a court martial – an idea floated by Hankey in 1917[113] – and he sought the publication of the final report, and even of the minutes of evidence.[114] This demonstrated a continued belief that he could only benefit from openness. Similarly, Churchill continued to press for the publication of the evidence,[115] and he welcomed the fact that the burden of blame no longer rested solely upon his shoulders but was 'now shared with the most eminent men which this country has produced'.[116]

The report's treatment of Hamilton was extended to most of the soldiers involved in the campaign. The commission's restrained verdict blamed some officials – political, military and medical – rather than soldiers. There was the failed bureaucracy at the War Office where the general staff became moribund;[117] the failure, as bureaucrat and politician, of First Sea Lord Fisher in his attempts to oppose the initiation of the campaign;[118] the unhappy position of Churchill, the overpowering chief;[119] the failure of Hamilton to communicate effectively with his superiors or to work his general staff efficiently;[120] of Surgeon-General Birrell to properly organise medical evacuations;[121] of Major-General Poett to properly organise the water supply at Suvla;[122] and Stopford's failure to ensure that the staff work was done well.[123] Only Generals Sitwell, Hammersley and Stopford were criticised on their fighting abilities.[124]

There were calls in Parliament prior to the commission to 'get to the bottom of the matter, and see that the people who are incapable are severely dealt with',[125] but this was not possible. In wartime the competence of the political and military commanders who continued to hold positions of power could not be seriously impugned. The result was a intentionally bland report, publication of the military part of which was delayed until the peace of 1919.

The manner of the first report's criticisms was commented on during the parliamentary debate that followed its publication. Colonel Sir Mark Sykes said:

It seems to me also that the Report as it stands is unsatisfactory from the point of view of the people of this country as a whole. If people are supposed to have done wrong, I suppose you accuse them and take evidence against them, and some day you say they have done it or not. This Report does not seem to run on those lines at all, but gives scraps of evidence here and there. It does not give one a fair picture of the whole thing. It seems to damn with faint blame all along, with a little faint praise here and there. There is no real opportunity for those who are accused or blamed of really speaking fully on these points.[126]

After the publication of the final report, *The Times*' 'correspondent on war' made a similar point about the difficulty in discerning what criticisms had actually been made. He wrote: 'their conclusions, which are for the most part wise and balanced, have almost literally to be crushed out of the quartz'.[127] An editorial in the previous day's paper commented on the report's reticence. In particular, the failure to tackle the question of whether Hamilton had been the right man to command the expedition was noted and Mackenzie's supplementary report was commended for showing 'much more vigour in pronouncing a decided verdict'.[128]

The publication of the first report was followed by a debate in Parliament on 20 March 1917.[129] It began with extended speeches by Asquith and Churchill that reiterated their own position, but was dominated by discussion, not of the reports' findings, but of the rectitude in respect of publishing and discussing the report in wartime and of putting out a bowdlerised version of the report. This was as nothing compared with the three-day debate, starting on 12 July 1917, which greeted the publication of the Mesopotamia Commission's report. Balfour described the Mesopotamia commissioners as 'criminals', and Sir Austen Chamberlain resigned from the Government.[130] Such controversy is scarcely surprising in relation to a report on which Lord Curzon confidentially commented: 'a more shocking exposure of official blundering and incompetence has not in my opinion been made, at any rate since the Crimean War'.[131]

The final report of the Dardanelles Commission, when it was eventually published on 17 November 1919, provoked even less controversy than had the first instalment. Curiously, its publication does not appear to have provoked a debate in Parliament. An article in *The Scotsman* commented upon the contrast: 'The Commission's first report raised almost as much controversy as the matter with which it was concerned. Their final judgements are of a character that will command general assent even if criticism may still fix upon details.'[132]

The newspapers' verdicts on the report appear to have attached greated blame to the politicians while almost universally commending the men's heroism. Several touched upon the poor staff work at Gallipoli, but the verdict on Hamilton was mixed: his friend Nevinson's comment in the *Manchester Guardian* all but cleared him of blame, while the *Daily Express* took a scathing view of his culpable failure.[133]

This muted response to a bland report had been connived at by some of the soldiers who testified to the commission. Babtie and Aspinall wrote to Hamilton of their decision to avoid controversy in their evidence.[134] Aspinall felt that criticism would be subversive of all military discipline and he declined to make such comments without an order from the War Office.[135] Major-General De Lisle, commander of the 29th Division, suspected that the politicians were trying to pin the blame on the soldiers, and accordingly took extra care with his evidence.[136] Birdwood perhaps spoke for many soldiers when he wrote to Hamilton of his distaste for controversy:

> Personally I cannot help thinking that it is such a mistake asking us for opinions at all, as I cannot think what they possibly hope to get in the way of valuable information. It is of course all right if we agree with and confirm what you say, but it would be a nice kettle of fish if we went in for criticising what you have done![137]

Sir Thomas Mackenzie noted this tendency in his supplementary report:

> With reference to the evidence tendered, whilst undoubtedly it was, in many aspects, full and complete, yet one felt that some of the officers called as witnesses could have disclosed a great deal more than they did. Probably their reticence arose from a sense of loyalty to the Service and a disinclination to say anything against their comrades. As a consequence of this and the natural desire of the Commission to give those chiefly concerned the benefit of any doubt, some of the conclusions arrived at may be somewhat different from what they otherwise might have been.[138]

In not tackling the nature of the campaign's fighting, nor condemning it as an outright failure, the commissioners left space for other narratives to interpret the campaign. This may be its ultimate significance. The commissioners had relied on Hamilton's dispatches, attached as an appendix, to describe the action of the campaign. It was not until the official histories of Britain and Australia were published that a serious attempt to piece together an account of the campaign was made.[139] Nor did the commissioners prescribe improvements for the future; that was left to a joint services report after the war. The first report of the commission had touched on the idea that it might be useful in the future, but explicitly rejected the means to render it so:

> [I]f our enquiry is to be of any real practical use for future guidance, we should not confine ourselves to a bald statement of facts, or even to the mere assignment of a proper share of responsibility to individuals or departments in connection with past events, but that we should go some-what further and indicate briefly and in general terms the conclusions at which we have arrived in respect to the merits and demerits of the original, as also of the revised organisations which have been instrumental in conducting the war. It would, however, be exceeding the scope of our functions if we were to discuss in detail the measures which should be taken to remedy any administrative defects which the light of recent experience has revealed.[140]

Therefore, in 1919, the Admiralty ordered the Mitchell Committee to report secretly on the attacks on the Dardanelles. Its terms of reference looked to the developing of guidance for the future:

> It is not intended that the Committee should in any way criticise the actual conduct of the operations, but it should confine itself to drawing lessons from what actually took place, and thereon make proposals for the preparing for, and carrying out of combined operations in the future.[141]

As was the case with the Dardanelles Commission, in Hamilton's eyes the limiting effect of these terms was compounded by cautiousness in writing the report. He commented in a letter to Churchill:

> As to the value of the Report, I am disappointed. Interesting and useful evidence, it is true, has been collected but the Committee as a body have not shown boldness and, to preserve unanimity, they have sacrificed effective comment: also, I think, they have been victims of Admiralty manipulation.[142]

Moreover, the report was so secret that even a member of the committee and the man collecting records for the Australian official history were refused access to it.[143]

The Dardanelles Commission succeeded in taking the heat out of the debate in the short term, but it failed to assuage the controversy in the long term. Its blandness and its limited release did not satisfactorily and decisively clear anyone's reputation. As Hankey commented later:

> Personally, though I was almost the only person who received some sort of faint commendation in the report of the earlier Commissions I never discovered any advantage of any sort or description which was obtained from

these two inquiries. No controversy was finally settled – for controversy on these matters has continued ever since and will continue to the end of time. On the other hand, an immense amount of suffering and injustice was inflicted on men who had done their best to serve their country in conditions of terrible responsibility and with inadequate means at their disposal, in the confident belief that the country would see them through. At least one brilliant officer was consigned to the 'scrap heap' so that the country lost the benefit of his services and experience for the remainder of the war.[144]

The Dardanelles Commission was limited in the questions it asked and in the verdict it gave. It was the first part of the official response. It asked 'what happened?' and 'who was to blame?' and it gave limited answers to those questions. It searched for administrative and political reasons for failure. It did not piece together the military details of the campaign; nor did it consider the nature of the experience. This meant that the full story of Gallipoli was left to be told elsewhere.

Notes

1 There are some exceptions. My article discussing further evidence on this subject – 'General Sir Ian Hamilton and the Dardanelles Commission', *War in History*, 8:4 (2001) – was published almost simultaneously with Tim Travers's *Gallipoli 1915* (Stroud, 2001) which includes the chapter 'Ian Hamilton and the Dardanelles Commission: collusion and vindication'. John Robertson, *The Tragedy and Glory of Gallipoli: Anzac and Empire* (London, 1990), pp. 224–44 discusses the commission from the Australian perspective. Personal views of the commission are to be found in Martin Gilbert, *Winston S. Churchill*, vol. 3: *1914–16* (London, 1971), vol. 4: *1916–22* (London, 1975); Lord Hankey, *The Supreme Command 1914–1918*, vol. 2 (London, 1961); and Stephen Roskill, *Hankey: Man of Secrets*, vol. 1: *1877–1918* (London, 1970). John Lee, *A Soldier's Life: General Sir Ian Hamilton 1853–1947* (London, 2000) devotes a chapter to assessing the fairness of the commission's criticisms of Hamilton's leadership.

2 M. P. A. Hankey, 'The presentation to Parliament of papers in regard to the military operations in Mesopotamia and the Dardanelles', 8 July 1916, Public Record Office, London (hereafter PRO), CAB 17/132.

3 The Secretary of State for the Colonies (Mr Bonar Law), *House of Commons Parliamentary Debates*, vol. 82 (1 June 1916), cols 2976–7.

4 'A study in surrender', *The Times*, 21 July 1916, p. 9; see also 'The Mesopotamia Commission', *The Times*, 25 July 1916, p. 7; and Paul K. Davis, *Ends and Means: The British Mesopotamia Campaign and Commission* (Cranbury, NJ, 1994).

5 The Prime Minister (H. H. Asquith), *House of Commons Parliamentary Debates*, vol. 84 (18 July 1916), col. 851.

6 W. R. Robertson, 'The publication of papers on the Dardanelles operations', 9 July 1916, PRO, CAB 17/184.

7 Hankey, Memorandum to Prime Minister, CID 529, 5 June 1916; and memorandum of 8 July 1916, PRO, CAB 17/132.

8 The release of the secretary's notes of the War Council proceedings continued to be a problem after the commission was set up. The issue provoked an hour-long row at the committee on 20 September 1916. The compromise appears to have been reached that the commission would rely on a compilation of the pertinent extracts made by Hankey. Two commissioners were allowed to consult his original notes in order to check that nothing had been kept back. Hankey to Asquith, 20 September 1916, Modern Papers Reading Room, Bodleian Library, Oxford, Asquith Papers, II/30, fol. 202a–d.

9 His comments refer specifically to the exclusion of the diplomatic correspondence, but they may be taken as indicative of the problem of releasing any relevant papers.

10 Hankey to Robertson, 15 July 1916, PRO, CAB 17/132. For further details see Davis, *Ends and Means*, pp. 178–9, and PRO, CAB/42/16/4–5.

11 Hankey, *Supreme Command*, 1, p. 520.

12 The Prime Minister (H. H. Asquith), *House of Commons Parliamentary Debates*, vol. 84 (20 July 1916), cols 1236–40.

13 Hankey's diary, 20 July 1916, Churchill Archives Centre, Churchill College, Cambridge, Hankey Papers, HNKY 1/1.

14 Trevor Wilson, *The Downfall of the Liberal Party 1914–1935* (London, 1966), p. 87; see also John Turner, *British Politics and the Great War: Coalition and Conflict 1915–1918* (London, 1992), pp. 112–52.

15 Robertson, *Anzac and Empire*, pp. 229–30.

16 Admiral of the Fleet (Sir H. Meux), *House of Commons Parliamentary Debates*, vol. 84 (27 July 1916), col. 1911.

17 Grimwood Mears to Lord Hardinge, 1 August 1916, Asquith Papers, II/30, fols 186–9. Mears is referring to his work as secretary of the Bryce Committee which investigated the allegations of German atrocities during the invasion of Belgium and France in 1914 and disclosed its findings in the *Report of the Committee on Alleged German Outrages Appointed by His Britannic Majesty's Government and Presided over by the Right Hon. Viscount Bryce, OM*, Cd 7894 (London 1915). It was published in the same month as the German White Book, the German Government's response to the accusations. It was not therefore a direct reply to the White Book, but acted as such retrospectively. I am grateful to John Horne for this information.

18 Hardinge to Lord Cromer, Private, 1 August 1916, Asquith Papers, II/30, fols 184–5.

19 *First Report of the Dardanelles Commission*, Cd 8490 (Parliamentary Papers 1917–18, vol. 10), para. 1.

20 *Final Report of the Dardanelles Commission*, Cd 371 (Parliamentary Papers 1919, vol. 13). There was also a brief *Supplement to First Report* (Cd 8502, Parliamentary Papers 1917–18, vol. 10) issued which paraphrased the excisions that had been made. The reports have recently been published as *The Dardanelles Commission Part 1: Lord Kitchener and Winston Churchill, 1914–15*, ed. Tim Coates (London, 2000) and *Defeat at Gallipoli – The Dardanelles Commission Part 2: 1915–16*, ed. Tim Coates (London, 2000).

21 Hankey, *Supreme Command*, 2, p. 523.

22 Hankey's diary, 4, 11, 14, 15 August and 4 September 1916, Hankey Papers, HNKY 1/1.

23 *Ibid.*, 9 August 1916.

24 *Ibid.*, 25 September 1916.

25 *Ibid.*, 17 and 30 October 1916.

26 Gilbert, *Churchill*, 3, p. 811. Churchill was deeply concerned by this comment on matters he considered *sub judice* at the time; Churchill to Cromer, 17 October 1916, Churchill College, Cambridge, Churchill Papers, CHAR 2/74/93–4.

27 Gilbert, *Churchill*, 4, ch. 41.

28 Gilbert, *Churchill*, 3, p. 790.

29 *Ibid.*, p. 805.

30 *Ibid.*, p. 813.

31 *Ibid.*, pp. 803–8

32 Fisher to Churchill, 15 August 1916, quoted in *ibid.*, p. 803.

33 Gilbert, *Churchill*, 3, p. 804.

34 Churchill's Boer War chronicle, *Ian Hamilton's March*, was published in 1900.

35 Hamilton, *Listening for the Drums* (London, 1944), p. 254 and repeated in Gilbert, *Churchill*, 3, p. 780.

36 Hamilton to Churchill, 11 November 1916, Hamilton Papers, 8/1/16. Similarly, Churchill was advised by Graham Greene, permanent secretary to the Admiralty, that he should employ 'a little more reserve' in referring to Kitchener in his narrative of events: W. Graham Greene to Churchill, 9 September 1916, Churchill Papers, CHAR 2/7/64–72.

37 Hamilton to Braithwaite, 5 October 1916, Hamilton Papers, 8/1/13.

38 Braithwaite to Hamilton, 18 November 1916, Hamilton Papers, 8/1/13.

39 Churchill to Cromer, 12 August 1916, Churchill Papers, CHAR 2/74/37–8.

40 Cromer to Churchill, 20 September 1916, Churchill Papers, CHAR 2/74/75–8.

41 On day 14 of the Dardanelles Commission he questioned Admiral Wilson, Captain Hall, Vice-Admiral Bacon and Sir William Graham Greene. At the next session he questioned Admiral Oliver and Commodore Bartolomé.

42 PRO, CAB 19/28.

43 Braithwaite to Hamilton, 11 November 1916; Hamilton to Braithwaite, 14

November 1916; Braithwaite to Hamilton, 18 November 1916, Hamilton Papers, 8/1/13.

44 Hamilton to Birdwood, 3 February 1917, Hamilton Papers, 8/1/11.

45 Hamilton to Braithwaite, 8 February 1917, Hamilton Papers, 8/1/13.

46 Hamilton was offered the governor-generalship of Ireland, which he rejected in March 1916. Controversy in the Commons in May 1916 over the Dardanelles dissuaded Asquith from appointing Hamilton to the Eastern Command; see I. B. M. Hamilton, *The Happy Warrior*, p. 417.

47 Evidence of General Sir Ian Hamilton, Thursday 29 March 1917 (day 69), Dardanelles Commission, q. 25508, PRO, CAB 19/33.

48 Hankey's diary, 23 November, 1917, Hankey Papers, HNKY 1/3; Hamilton to Churchill, 23 November 1917, Hamilton Papers, 8/1/16.

49 Hamilton to Churchill, secret, 7 October 1917, Hamilton Papers, 8/1/16.

50 Hamilton to Hankey, personal, 11 May 1917, Hamilton Papers, 8/1/31.

51 Hankey to Hamilton, private and personal, 10 May 1917, Hamilton Papers, 8/1/31.

52 Hamilton to Churchill, 30 June 1917, Hamilton Papers, 8/1/16.

53 Asquith to Andrew Fisher, Prime Minister of Australia, draft telegram, October 1915, Asquith Papers, II/29, fols 239–40.

54 Robertson, *Anzac and Empire*, p. 158.

55 Birdwood to Hamilton, quite private, 21 June 1917, Hamilton Papers, 8/1/11. Andrew Fisher was not considered to be officially representing Australia on the commission and attended only 37 of the commission's 89 sittings.

56 Hamilton to Hankey, 28 June 1916, PRO, CAB 17/132.

57 Braithwaite to Hamilton, 18 November, 1916, Hamilton Papers, 8/1/13.

58 Hamilton to Braithwaite, 14 November 1916, Hamilton Papers, 8/1/13.

59 Lord Cromer to Churchill, 20 September 1916; reprinted in Gilbert, *Churchill*, 3: *Companion part 2, May 1915–December 1916* (London, 1972), p. 1560.

60 Testimony from these 31 men can be found in the Hamilton Papers, 8/2.

61 Hamilton to Braithwaite, 10 February 1917, Hamilton Papers, 8/1/13.

62 Hamilton to Ellison, 16 February 1917, Hamilton Papers, 8/1/21. Major-General G. F. Ellison was briefly deputy inspector general of communications at Mudros.

63 Hamilton to Birdwood, 26 February 1917, Hamilton Papers, 8/1/11; Hamilton to Freyberg, 21 December 1916, Hamilton Papers, 8/1/26. Lieutenant-Commander Bernard Freyberg VC of the Royal Naval Division did not give evidence before the commission. One Ernest Townley was made to sign the following declaration dated 12 March 1917: 'I hereby undertake that I will in no wise indicate the source of any information regarding General Maude which may be given me this evening by Sir Ian Hamilton': Hamilton Papers, 8/1/43.

64 Hamilton to Braithwaite, 14 November 1916, Hamilton Papers, 8/1/13.

65 Hamilton to Birdwood, 8 December 1916, Hamilton Papers, 8/1/11; Hamilton to Birdwood, 26 January 1917, Australian War Memorial, Canberra, Birdwood Papers, 3DRL 3376/11/5; Hamilton to Birdwood, 27 January 1917, Hamilton Papers, 8/1/11.

66 Hamilton to Birdwood, 27 January 1917, Hamilton Papers, 8/1/11.

67 Birdwood to Hamilton, 7 August 1916, Birdwood Papers, 3DRL 3376/11/5.

68 Evidence of Lieutenant-General Sir William Birdwood, Tuesday 6 March 1917 (day 56), Dardanelles Commission, PRO, CAB 19/33.

69 Birdwood to Hamilton, 4 December 1916, Hamilton Papers, 8/1/11.

70 See Macleod, 'Dardanelles Commission', pp. 430–5.

71 For example, Pickford asked him to investigate whether the administrative staffs of GHQ and the IX Corps had any conferences prior to the Suvla landing; Hamilton to Braithwaite, secret, 4 August 1917, Hamilton Papers, 8/1/13.

72 For example, Lord Granard states that Hamilton alerted him to a statement made about him by Ashmead-Bartlett: evidence of Lieutenant-Colonel The Earl of Granard, KP, GCVO, Tuesday 10 July 1917 (day 79), Dardanelles Commission, PRO, CAB 19/33.

73 Hamilton to Braithwaite, 21 September 1916, Hamilton Papers, 8/1/13.

74 Hamilton to Birdwood, 26 January 1917, Birdwood Papers, 3DRL 3376/11/5.

75 Birdwood to Hamilton, 28 June 1917, Hamilton Papers, 8/1/11.

76 Hamilton to Braithwaite, 17 August 1916, Hamilton Papers, 8/1/13.

77 Hamilton wrote to Birdwood of 'the intense jealousy Nick has always borne to me and to my works. It came out so clearly in his comments on my Manchurian Reports'. (Hamilton had served as Military Representative of India with the Japanese Field Army in Manchuria, 1904–5): Hamilton to Birdwood, 25 June 1917, Hamilton Papers, 8/1/11.

78 Hamilton to Birdwood, 3 July 1917, Hamilton Papers, 8/1/11. The context of this quoted statement does not make it clear quite when Hamilton had expressed his view of Kitchener, but my assumption seems plausible.

79 Hamilton to Birdwood, 13 January 1917, Birdwood Papers, 3DRL 3376/11/5. Hamilton may well have been trying to play on Birdwood's loyalty to Kitchener. Birdwood was close enough to Kitchener to have received a bequest in his will.

80 Hamilton to Churchill, 29 December 1916, Hamilton Papers, 8/1/16.

81 Hamilton to Braithwaite, 8 February 1917, Hamilton Papers, 8/1/13. Hamilton's Papers contain a memorandum noting Nicholson's leading questions often referring to the general's leadership: Hamilton Papers, 8/2/28.

82 Birdwood to Hamilton, quite private, 21 June 1917, Hamilton Papers, 8/1/11.

83 Braithwaite to Hamilton, 11 February 1917, Hamilton Papers, 8/1/13.

84 Hamilton to Keyes, 5 May 1917, Hamilton Papers, 8/1/38; Jean Graham Hall and Douglas Martin, _A Perfect Judge: Cases and Reports of Lord Sterndale, Master of the Rolls_ (Chichester, 1999) warmly praises Pickford but provides no further illumination on the Dardanelles Commission.

85 Hamilton to Shaw, 14 February 1917, Hamilton Papers, 8/1/57.

86 Hamilton to Birdwood, 25 June 1917, Hamilton Papers, 8/1/11.

87 'Summary of conversation held between XXX and XXX, Thursday, 12th July 1917', Hamilton Papers, 8/2/29.

88 Hamilton to Keyes, 5 May 1917, Hamilton Papers, 8/1/38.

89 Hamilton to Mears, 22 November 1916, Hamilton Papers, 8/1/46.

90 An official replied to Murdoch that 'the Minister will be glad to avail himself of your offer to inquire into and report to him upon certain matters in Egypt on the occasion of your projected journey to London': acting secretary, Department of Defence, Commonwealth of Australia, to Murdoch, 2 July 1915, No. 35598, National Library of Australia, Canberra, Murdoch Papers, MS 2823/2/1.

91 This is Hamilton's description; 'Memorandum by General Sir Ian Hamilton on a letter from Mr K. A. Murdoch to the Prime Minister of the Australian Government (CID paper G-25)', CID paper G-42, 26 November 1915, Murdoch Papers, MS 2823/2/1.

92 John Avieson, 'The correspondent who stopped the war', _Australian Journalism Review_, 8 (1986), pp. 64–71; Desmond Zwar, _In Search of Keith Murdoch_ (Melbourne, 1980); see also his unpublished biography, _K. M. . . . A Life of Keith Murdoch, Newspaper Reporter_, Murdoch Papers, MS 2823/11/9.

93 Murdoch to Fisher, personal, 23 September 1915, Murdoch Papers, MS 2823/2/1; an edited version of this letter is given in Zwar, _Murdoch_, pp. 31–9.

94 Zwar, _Murdoch_, p. 42.

95 Hamilton to Churchill, 26 January 1917, Hamilton Papers, 8/1/16.

96 'Memorandum by General Sir Ian Hamilton on a letter from Mr K. A. Murdoch to the Prime Minister of the Australian Government (CID paper G-25)', CID paper G-42, 26 November 1915, Murdoch Papers, MS 2823/2/1.

97 _Ibid._

98 Hamilton to Braithwaite, 14 November 1916, Hamilton Papers, 8/1/13.

99 Hamilton to Mr Grimwood Mears, 22 November 1916, Hamilton Papers, 8/1/46.

100 _Ibid._

101 This is Hamilton's description; Hamilton to Braithwaite, 8 January 1917, Hamilton Papers, 8/1/13.

102 _Ibid._

103 Braithwaite to Hamilton, 9 January 1917, Hamilton Papers, 8/1/13.

104 Evidence of Braithwaite, qq. 13750–6.

105 John Avieson, 'Sir Keith Murdoch: the unwilling witness', _Australian Journalism Review_, 11 (1989), p. 43.

106 Evidence of Keith Murdoch, q. 16361.

107 *Ibid.*, q. 16420.

108 *Ibid.*, qq. 16521–2; this onslaught against Hamilton's enemy indicates that Nicholson was perhaps more even-handed than Hamilton credited.

109 Evidence of Keith Murdoch (no question number).

110 Hamilton to Mears, 6 March 1917, Hamilton Papers, 8/1/46.

111 *Final Report*, General conclusions, para. 9.

112 *Final Report*, General conclusions, paras 1–5.

113 Hankey to Hamilton, private and personal, 10 May 1917, Hamilton Papers, 8/1/31.

114 Hamilton twice made this suggestion in speeches; see *Daily Telegraph*, 26 April 1929, Hamilton Papers, 17/47; and *Evening News*, 5 December 1929, Hamilton Papers, 17/52.

115 Churchill to Lord Justice Pickford, no date given, reprinted for the Committee of Imperial Defence, PRO, CAB 17/184. The Proceedings of the commission became available to the public only on 1 January 1968.

116 Mr Churchill, *House of Commons Parliamentary Debates*, vol. 90 (20 March 1917), col. 1786.

117 *First Report*, para. 40.

118 *Ibid.*, para. 91.

119 *Ibid.*, para. 121(e).

120 *Final Report*, para. 33.

121 *Ibid.*, General conclusions, para. 34.

122 *Ibid.*, General conclusions, para. 19.

123 *Ibid.*, General conclusions, para. 19.

124 *Ibid.*, General conclusions, paras 7, 8.

125 Mr Holt, *House of Commons Parliamentary Debates*, vol. 84 (26 July 1916), col. 1715.

126 Colonel Sir Mark Sykes, *House of Commons Parliamentary Debates*, vol. 90 (20 March 1917), col. 1772.

127 Correspondent on war, 'The Dardanelles Report. The operations at Suvla Bay', *The Times*, 19 November 1919, p. 14.

128 'The Dardanelles verdict', *The Times*, 18 November 1919, p. 13.

129 *House of Commons Parliamentary Debates*, vol. 90 (20 March 1917), cols 1753–827.

130 Davis, *Ends and Means*, pp. 210–14.

131 Lord Curzon, 'Memorandum on the report of the Mesopotamia commission', printed for the War Cabinet 1917, PRO, CAB 17/191.

132 *Scotsman*, 18 November 1919, Hamilton Papers, 17/38, p. 37.

133 H. W. Nevinson, 'The new Dardanelles Report', *Manchester Guardian* (no date); 'Why we failed in Gallipoli. Scathing Report of the Dardanelles Commission', *Daily Express*, 18 November 1919, Hamilton Papers, 17/38, pp. 40–1.

134 Babtie to Hamilton, 11 December 1916, Hamilton Papers, 8/1/7; Aspinall to Hamilton, 15 January 1917, Hamilton Papers, 8/1/4.

135 Aspinall to Mears (copy), 10 December 1916, Hamilton Papers, 8/1/4.

136 De Lisle to Hamilton, 14 December 1916, Hamilton Papers, 8/1/40.

137 Birdwood to Hamilton, 4 December 1916, Hamilton Papers, 8/1/11, or Birdwood Collection, 3DRL 3376/11/5.

138 Sir Thomas Mackenzie, Supplementary report in *Final Report* (unnumbered paragraph).

139 Brigadier-General C. F. Aspinall-Oglander, *Military Operations, Gallipoli*, vols 1 (1929) and 2 (1932), History of the Great War Based on Official Documents; C. E. W. Bean, *The Story of Anzac*, vols 1 (1921) and 2 (1924) of the Official History of Australia in the War of 1914–1918. Prior to these Charles Callwell had produced a history that gave a fairly detailed account of certain phases of the campaign, but was not intended as a complete history and was above all concerned with the strategic implications of the campaign: Major-General Sir C. E. Callwell, KCB, *Campaigns and Their Lessons: The Dardanelles* (London, 1919).

140 *First Report*, para. 10.

141 *Report of the Committee Appointed to Investigate the Attacks Delivered on and the Enemy Defences of the Dardanelles Straits*, PRO, AIR 1/2323, p. xiv. The Mitchell Committee's report is discussed in Ian Speller, 'In the shadow of Gallipoli? Amphibious warfare in the inter-war period' in Jenny Macleod (ed.) *Gallipoli: Making History* (forthcoming).

142 Hamilton to Churchill, 24 August 1920, Hamilton Papers, 13/24.

143 Brigadier-General C. J. Perceval to Historical Section, 14 April 1929, PRO, CAB 45/244; Edmonds to Heyes, 13/C/40–49, c.1925–6; Bean Papers, AWM38 3DRL 8042, item 47.

144 Hankey, *Supreme Command*, 1, p. 524.

2

The official response: the official histories

The first two volumes of Charles Bean's official history of Australia in the First World War, which relate the story of the Australian Imperial Force (AIF) at Gallipoli, were published in 1921 and 1924.[1] The two volumes of Cecil Aspinall-Oglander's British official history of the Gallipoli campaign were published in 1929 and 1932.[2] With unmatched access to information on the campaign, they provided definitive factual accounts that remain important sources of reference. Bean's history has been massively influential, both on the Anzac legend and on the historiography of the campaign. What has been less widely acknowledged is the influence of Aspinall's history on the British view of the campaign.

In Britain, the first part of the official response, the Dardanelles Commission, had relied on General Sir Ian Hamilton's dispatches to provide a narrative of the campaign. It was for the official histories, therefore, to establish what happened at Gallipoli. Australia, however, had played almost no part in the Dardanelles Commission;[3] and the priorities of officialdom there were very different. This chapter considers the contrasting purposes and priorities of the official histories produced by these two nations. I show that from these priorities flowed profound differences in construction, style, focus and argument. But first the notion of *official history* and its implications must be investigated.

The purpose of official history

The early British official military histories, which date from the Crimean War, aped the model established by Prussia that aimed to improve the performance of the national army.[4] The official history of the First World War was produced under the auspices of the Historical Section of the Committee of Imperial Defence, which was run by its secretary Colonel

E. Y. Daniel, an officer of the Royal Marines. He referred difficult matters to Maurice Hankey, the secretary of the Committee of Imperial Defence and a fellow Royal Marine.[5] The decision to undertake such a project was considered by a committee under Vice-Admiral Sir Edmond Slade and was announced in Parliament by Asquith on 28 June 1916.[6]

That decision reflected more than a precedent. It was prompted by several factors that were discussed in a series of memoranda prepared by Hankey and Daniel. The first consideration was that the strict levels of censorship and secrecy had resulted in a great deal of ignorance of the war among the general public and the armed forces.[7] Hankey therefore proposed that a 'popular' work should be produced, with a more detailed technical staff history coming later. The aim should be 'an authoritative history for the general reader' rather than something that would 'sell like smoke on railway bookstalls'.[8] Such volumes, Daniel explained, would 'provide an antidote to the usual unofficial history which, besides being generally inaccurate, habitually attributes all naval and military failures to the ineptitude of the Government'.[9]

The first report on the work of the Historical Section in 1919 expanded on this theme, confirming both the perceived failure of existing popular works and of generals' dispatches:

> The necessity for an account founded on official documents, elaborated by statements and private records of officers and German information, has become more and more apparent. Many complaints have been heard and received with regard to the garbled and misleading accounts given in their books by Sir A. Conan Doyle, and J. Buchan and others. The writers were of course glad to get anything to fill their pages, and accepted statements from officers who had been sent home as failures, and from those who wished to advertise their units, while others who were doing the fighting in the various theatres of war refused them information when applied to. The first thought that naturally occurred was that it would be sufficient to elaborate the dispatches; but the publishers who have been consulted with regard to this, and other authorities, are most emphatic that *the public do not trust dispatches*, and that a book of such a class would not have a large number of readers.[10]

In 1922, Daniel wrote:

> The general effects of post-war literature are becoming clear; if widely read it owes its popularity to the amount of secret information which the author has divulged, or to the extent to which he has entered into personal controversies. It would be morally wrong to leave either the public or the services to such guidance; it is a matter of honour and common sense that the

country's unprecedented effort between 1914 and 1918 should be analysed and its effects made clear.[11]

Daniel argued that the official history should address both the general public and the services to counter criticisms of the war. However, it would be wrong to imply that the British official history's purpose was to justify the war or guard its memory; rather it was to educate the public, or perhaps, more specifically, the ruling classes, in order to provide a proper basis for future decision-making.[12] Above all, the official history addressed the services, not as disillusioned participants but as professional soldiers to be trained. From 1927 the official histories were set for army promotion examinations.[13] The primary purpose of the official histories therefore remained, as it had almost always been, the education of military professionals. As Hankey had written in 1915, 'history is the "memory" of the Services, and without it the lessons will be forgotten alike by statesmen, sailors and soldiers'.[14]

The case was thus made for an authoritative history of the war for the purpose of educating both the military and the public; but why did that history have to be *official?* There were several benefits in having the historian of the war under the control of government and recognised as the official historian instead of using the services of an independent professional historian. Such benefits accrued from practical matters of access and support. Much of the evidence to be used for the history was highly secret and access to it had to be controlled. Rather than becoming entangled in the attempt to choose from among the various historians who might apply for access, were it to be generally available, it was preferable to grant this privilege to one specially licensed historian.[15] (This explanation, incidentally, gives a further reason why there was a need to supplement the Dardanelles Commission. Such was the secrecy of the statements and evidence presented to the commission that permission to release those documents to the Australian Government was refused as late as 1927.)[16] This arrangement would have the further benefit of improving the historian's access to the participants of each action. Trust would be put in an officially designated historian with whom governmental officers would feel able to co-operate in a manner that would have been impossible with a private individual.[17]

The second issue was financial support from government. The private individual would never be able alone to fund the work and that of the necessary clerical assistants; moreover, it was argued, government had a moral responsibility to fund such an undertaking:

Private historians as a rule have access to archives on the collection and arrangement of which thousands of pounds and years of highly skilled labour have been spent, and even with the path thus smoothed for them the work will never yield a living wage. It must always be a labour of love or subsidized. In this case quite apart from the obvious need of a complete record of the war for official information, a subsidy appears fully justified in the interest of national education alone. If, as is now generally admitted, national education in its broadest sense is an elementary duty of government then the study of the war is one which specially calls for reasonable state assistance; and when we consider the vast cost at which our experience was bought, the amount that is being spent on making that experience available for educative purposes comes clearly within the limits of sound economy. In actual money values the cost of the war for six minutes exceeded the annual cost of making its lesson available by means of the Historical Section.[18]

Therefore, despite some Treasury pressure and questions in Parliament regarding expense in 1922,[19] it was argued that the value of the histories could not be judged merely by their receipts: 'It is by the standard of their value for professional educational purposes that official histories must be judged', it was asserted. 'It is doubtful if they will ever pay.'[20] Official histories, argued Hankey, were comparable to Hansard and the proceedings of royal commissions.[21]

The powerful arguments in favour of an official history overcame not just the financial objections to the preparation of the histories, but objections to writing contemporary history and engaging government in a subject so fraught with controversy as well. In 1919 Hankey wrote:

Is it feasible to write Official Histories of events that have only just occurred? The author, however discreet he may be, is in a very awkward dilemma. However sparing he may be of personal comment, the manner in which he marshals his facts, more especially when unsuccessful operations have to be recorded, is liable to reflect on one leader or another, on this department or on that. The very absence of personal comment must weaken the interest in the book. Is it fair to publish the narrative when events are so recent that all the principal actors are still on the stage of public life?[22]

Such histories, published piecemeal over a number of years, he continued, would be liable to serial attacks and therefore be 'very troublesome in the aggregate'.

Ultimately, the outcome was an insistence that strict attention would be paid to its style and contents. In both Britain and Australia, contemporary history under the official imprimatur was felt to require particular attention to the accuracy of the narrative. In the British official history, however, this Rankean empiricism was extended, and led to the avoidance not only of inaccuracies but of criticism and controversy, and overt assessments in terms of failure. The solution in the case of the British naval official history was to attach disclaimers to both the official histories of the First and Second World Wars and, in the latter case, to drop the description 'official' altogether.[23]

James Edmonds and the writing of the British official histories

The decision to go ahead having been taken, how were the British official histories written? The process was laborious and time consuming. There were three stages in writing a single volume. A first narrative, compiled from primary documents, was circulated among participants and then revised to take in some of their criticisms. From the revision the historian would produce a first draft, which, again, would be circulated among participants, this time the higher commanders. A final draft would be follow which was subject to some further alterations in preparation for publication. A memo outlining the process commented on the benefits of such painstaking attention to detail:

> The student in years to come will, no doubt, check portions of the narrative, and, when he finds it full and accurate, will feel that he can trust the remainder. His thanks, although he may be only able to express them as prayers for the faithful departed, will be the narrator's ultimate reward.[24]

A consideration of the sources available to the official historian further illuminates the magnitude of the task. There were three kinds of British documents that had to be consulted:
- those regarding policy, that is documents pertaining to the inception of a project, such as minutes of war committees;
- those regarding intelligence, such as telegrams, which reveal information that was available to the commander of a project; and
- those regarding the execution of the operation, such as dispatches and ships' logs,[25] or unit war diaries.

Brigadier-General Sir James Edmonds, the director of the Historical Section, also encouraged the utilisation of allies' and enemy's records.[26] This material was augmented by the testimony of surviving officers, who were the source of a voluminous correspondence. The opportunity to access such invaluable and irreplaceable information was used as a further justification for embarking at once on so potentially controversial a project.[27] In addition to producing its own histories, the Historical Section assisted in the production of regimental histories and Dominions' official histories. It also provided information to the Ministry of Pensions and the Imperial War Graves Commission.[28]

Who were selected to undertake this task? In August 1915, Sir Julian Corbett, a lecturer in history at the Royal Naval College, Greenwich, naval theorist and author of many works, including *Confidential Naval History of the Russo-Japanese War*,[29] began work on the naval history and Sir John Fortescue, the royal librarian and author of *The History of the British Army*[30] began the military history of the Western Front. Both were to be popular rather than technical works.[31] In the spring of 1919, Captain G. S. Gordon began work on the history of the Dardanelles campaign. It was mooted in 1922 that 'men of outstanding literary reputation', such as G. M. Trevelyan, Rudyard Kipling, Sir Arthur Quiller Couch, Sir Henry Newbolt or John Buchan, should be associated with the histories, so that their sales might be maximised.[32] Newbolt did indeed take over the naval history on the death of Sir Julian Corbett, but T. E. Lawrence, Maurice Baring and John Masefield declined preferred appointments as official historians, 'mainly because they were unable to face the enormous and exacting research work entailed'.[33]

The most important appointment was that of Brigadier-General Sir James Edmonds (1861–1956), who in 1919 became the director of the Historical Section, Military Branch. Edmonds had been at Staff College with Haig and Allenby, had written a history of the American Civil War and had worked at GHQ for most of the war.[34] His job at the Historical Section entailed organising the records and superintending the compilation of the histories. He took on the additional work of historian of the Western Front on the resignation of Fortescue in December of 1919.[35] He oversaw the production of the fourteen volumes of official history on the Western Front that were completed in 1948; the official history series was completed in 1949.

Edmonds's personality had a huge impact on the nature of these official histories. He was responsible for the shift from a popular account of the Western Front towards a more technical staff history that favoured detailed and accurate information and eschewed overt expressions of opinion. He had found Fortescue's work to be 'very readable but very inaccurate';[36] he forced Fortescue's resignation following the latter's intemperate comments about Field Marshal Lord French[37] – an official historian could not be controversial or partisan.[38] Edmonds thereafter chose to produce a work more akin to a staff history, modelled on the official German history of the Franco-Prussian war.[39] This shift in purpose is also evident from Edmonds's prefatory comments. In volume 1, published in 1922, he contends that the official history has in mind a dual purpose: to inform both the general reader and the student at 'military school'.[40] By 1928's volume 4 he was bluntly stating: 'The purpose of military history is to discover what actually happened, in order that there may be material for study, and that lessons for future guidance may be deduced.'[41]

Edmonds also influenced the structure of the official histories as a whole. It had originally been conceived that the naval history would be the linchpin of the series of official histories.[42] Edmonds, in his waspish unpublished memoirs, written at the age of 90, was scornful. Of Sir Julian Corbett, who he unfairly described as 'a barrister and amateur writer of naval history', he wrote:

> He actually proposed that the general story of the war should be told in the naval, not the military volumes. I took the opportunity to remind him
> 'Now far from St. Helena are the capes of Trafalgar,
> A longish way, a longish way, with ten years more to run',
> and told him that the Navy in 1914–18 was no more than guard of the lines of communication. It was not this, however, which caused his sudden death in his bedroom in 1922.[43]

However, Edmonds's and Corbett's volumes covering the period of the Dardanelles campaign show that it was the naval history that considered the question of grand strategy. Edmonds's volume on 1915, which covers the battle of Aubers Ridge and others, scarcely mentions the Dardanelles, despite the controversial nature of the decision to attack both there and at Gallipoli in May.[44] Moreover, Aspinall had to be allowed to mention Aubers Ridge in his volume on Gallipoli.

Most importantly, Edmonds's involvement reinforced the existing tendency to avoid criticism and controversy. This derived from Edmonds's close identification with his former comrades and was compounded by the circulation of drafts to participants. This contrived to give the British official history what Ken Inglis describes as 'the character of a committee's report'.[45] Edmonds considered the purpose of official history to be the education of the military, but he chose not to make the lessons of a campaign too explicit. He gave the facts and left staff to draw their own conclusions.[46] Edmonds explained himself in 1928:

GENERAL EDMONDS said that two persons could not write in the same style. He had been inclined to hint a thing rather than to state it baldly. Taking the Battle of Loos, when Lord French and General Joffre were clamouring to have as many Divisions as possible, he put in the History what Divisions were sent to France, and at the same time said that four Divisions were sent to the Dardanelles, but he did not rub it in. We did not, he considered, want *everybody to see the troubles we had had and the mistakes we made.*[47]

Churchill, who attended this meeting, replied immediately that the contrary was the case, that all our mistakes should be made clear to avoid their repetition by our children. Churchill, of course, had an axe to grind on this specific point. It is the crux of his argument that a choice should have been made between reinforcing the Western Front and reinforcing the Dardanelles.

Edmonds's refusal to engage in controversy and to comment freely on episodes, and his habit of hiding difficult episodes in footnotes or leaving them out altogether, have been widely discussed.[48] Edmonds's confidant, Liddell Hart, wrote of this self-defeating tendency:

In the early years of his task, he often said that he could not state the damaging truth in an official history, because of loyalty to the Service yet wanted to make it known privately to other historians – which he did. That practice became a fatal hindrance to the chance of getting the lessons of World War I clear in time for the next generation to profit by them in World War II.[49]

The pressure to avoid controversy in an official publication was just one of the various distorting influences to which the official history was subject. Others flowed from the purpose of these volumes and the authors' personal approach and bias. The emphasis on its educative role for the army instead of aiming to enhance public understanding of the experience of the war, for example, led to the suggestion that the Battle of the Somme and the other battles of attrition and stalemate required comparatively little attention. In 1922, Major-General Romer, director of staff duties in the War Office, wrote:

From the point of view of the education of the Army it was important that very good accounts should be written of the following periods: – 1914 to the end of the first Battle of Ypres, March 1918 to the Armistice, Allenby's Campaign in Palestine, and the operations in the Dardanelles. He was of opinion that a less detailed account might be prepared of the war in France from 1915 to 1918.[50]

Each of the first two volumes on the Western Front did indeed cover just over two months; 1918 was covered in four volumes, compared to 1916's two; and Passchendaele got one – inadequate – volume. This weighting has not been replicated in the subsequent historiography of the Western Front. Although 1914 has received substantial attention, it is the attritional battles of 1916 and 1917 that have loomed largest. This is not so much due to those battles' military value but because of the unprecedented and terrible losses they inflicted and the ensuing psychological impact on their participants and on the nation.

A further distortion resulted in part from the histories' purpose of staff education and in part from Edmonds's personal experience and bias. Edmonds wrote from the point of view of a staff officer. He admitted in old age that he had largely decided what he would write from his memories of GHQ. This coloured his entire approach:

> The secret of rapid work is to make up one's mind what one is going to write, and not revising too much. A good memory is indispensable, and fortunately I had in Mr Tarsey an assistant who knew as much about the war as I did myself and could read my handwriting at its worst. I had of course the advantages of having been at GHQ France for most of the war, and thus of understanding its course from the inside;[51]

Edmonds did note that information became more distorted nearer to the top of the chain of command, i.e. nearer to GHQ. However, he did not recognise how this potentially devalued his chosen method of work:

> Regimental accounts on both sides were extraordinarily accurate; as one ascended in the hierarchy from brigade to division, division to corps, the story became more and more distorted and, on the German side, the casualties reduced. This distortion was not intentional; the higher staffs could not follow the fluctuations of a battle.[52]

This statement amounts to an unwitting endorsement of the methods employed by Charles Bean, the official historian of the Australian Imperial Force. Like Edmonds, he dominated his country's official history, but his work provides a stark contrast.

Charles Bean and the Australian official history

Charles Edwin Woodrow Bean (1879–1968) was born in Bathurst, New South Wales. In photographs he peers out from behind wire-framed glasses, a tall, thin man with a shock of red hair (see figure 2). He was educated at Clifton College, Bristol and at Hertford College, Oxford,

2   Portrait of Charles E. W. Bean (1924) by George Lambert

where he studied classics and then law. He returned to his native
Australia in 1904 and, after a brief period as a barrister and a teacher, he
worked as a journalist for the *Sydney Morning Herald*. In 1914 he was
nominated by the Australian Journalists' Association to work as the official correspondent with the AIF. One of his most notable assignments as
a journalist had produced a series of articles on the wool industry. In
those articles Bean had taken a potentially dry subject and transformed
it by describing the lives of the men involved. He thereby systematically

presented some outstanding national types.[53] Bean had discovered his
main interest, what his biographer McCarthy summarises as 'human
subjects and their doings';[54] an innocuous interest to hold, perhaps, but,
when applied in the field of military history, as it was then practised, a
radical one.

When he was selected as official correspondent it was agreed with the
Defence Department that on his return he would write a history of the
war. This was to be 'an account of the Australian part in it for a permanent record for Australian libraries, schools, and the Australian people
generally'.[55] It was not going to be another staff history, but a commemorative work. Indeed, he wrote: 'I shall not write the military history of
it, I shall write the national history – if I come through it – the history
that will be read by my nation as long as it exists.'[56] Bean sought to ensure
that this would be possible, recommending that the 'sales shall be so
organised that all Australians shall have an opportunity, if they care to
take it, of purchasing the work'.[57] The commemorative point was emphasised at the time of the renewal of his contract in 1924:

> It has to be borne in mind, too, that the Government, when it decided in
> 1919 to undertake the production of the National Histories had in con-
> templation not an ephemeral work but one that would endure. Books of
> the former class could doubtless have been hurriedly compiled and abun-
> dantly disposed of, but the work of *constructing the permanent memorial in
> writing* of Australia's effort in the war must needs be deliberate and if, on
> that account, the opportunities of the immediate post-war market are lost,
> the national value of the Histories can justifiably be counted against the
> expenditure.[58]

This conception of the official history was integral to establishing a creation myth that pinpointed the Anzac experience as the 'birth of a
nation'. It will be seen that the construction of 'a permanent memorial
in writing' brought with it peculiar responsibilities and emphases.

Bean's 1919 scheme for the official histories, drawn up at the same
time as his proposal for what became the Australian War Memorial,
makes clear the unusual emphases of his work. He suggested that three
different types of history should be written: national histories; professional histories; and unit histories. The national histories would com-
prise twelve volumes: six to cover Gallipoli and France, then one volume
on each of Palestine, Rabaul, the Royal Australian Navy, the Australian
Flying Corps and the effort of Australia, plus 600 annotated photographs. Bean would be the editor and official historian for these. A

second group of histories were to be closer to the British vision of a military history:

> The PROFESSIONAL HISTORIES (medical, engineering, legal, veterinary, administrative, military schools, etc., artillery and desert warfare) are needed for the traditions of those branches of the Army; and the four first-named will probably be welcomed by their civil professionals in Australia as the basis of a great tradition in their professions also.[59]

Thus the volume to be used for military education was of only secondary importance and was comparable with traditions in other professional occupations. Bean suggested that the professional military volumes were 'most urgently necessary if the experience of the war . . . is not to be forgotten and wasted', and he therefore advised that 'the General Staff should be asked if it requires these or any such series. If so, that it be asked to appoint the writers, and that the Department make such arrangements as it desires to meet the immediate expense.'[60] The official medical history was eventually brought under Bean's general editorship, but the other technical histories were not.[61] After the first intensive period of work, Bean also supervised the writing of regimental histories.[62]

A second distinctive feature of the Australian official histories was that Bean secured a promise from the Government: 'The Commonwealth shall not censor or alter the National Histories as written, annotated or edited by the Official Historian.'[63] Bean had explained to the Military Board that

> the volumes written by himself would necessarily include his own opinions on many subjects, in addition to the historical facts described, and he also admitted that his work could be taken as apportioning praise and blame to units and individuals. At the same time Mr Bean frankly stated that he raised no objection to the inclusion of an official notice that he alone was responsible for such opinions.[64]

The Military Board accepted Bean's request, but in consequence objected to the use of the terms 'Official History' or 'National History', suggesting that the series be entitled 'Australia and the Great War', the sub-title to be ' "The Story (or Narrative) of the AIF" by C. E. W. Bean, Official War Correspondent'.[65] Bean's response was fierce:

> Restriction on the term 'national' and the ruling of the term 'history' out of the title I cannot agree to, nor to the style of myself as simply 'Australian War Correspondent'. It was not in that capacity that I compiled three

hundred volumes of notes, the most complete record ever kept by an historian. I was requested by the Government at the beginning of the war to obtain material with a view to writing the National History of the War, and if I am now appointed to do this I do not see why the book should not say so.[66]

A glance at the front page of his first volume confirms that Bean won the argument. His Preface gratefully acknowledged his freedom from censorship but does not suggest that he alone was responsible for the opinions of the history.[67]

Bean began work on the official history with a small staff of clerks and draftsmen in late 1919 at Tuggeranong, twelve miles outside of Canberra. His staff numbers reached their peak during the first few months of work when he was assisted by four clerks and four draftsmen. From 1925 onwards there were only two clerks and one draftsman.[68] He expected the task to take five years – in fact each volume took, on average, three years to complete. Bean drew on a vast array of sources – forty different classes of records, the official documents from Australia alone comprising 21,500,000 foolscap sheets – and used them with meticulous care.[69] He was nonetheless closely involved in all stages of the preparation of the official history of this relatively small Australian force. He disapproved of the British authors' reliance on others to prepare a précis of events.[70] In constructing his history, Bean acted very much as a pathfinder: 'Few people', he wrote, 'realise to what an extent no guide even now exists to much of the history of the Great War.'[71] Bean wrote of this unique opportunity and responsibility: 'I regard our work as something like that of the photographer who must fix certain pictures on his plate or film, else they will be lost forever . . . What we have to do is "fix" that history for posterity.'[72] It was the chance to write the definitive, authoritative discourse on the campaign.

Prior to 1917, when the Australian War Records Section under Captain J. L. Treloar was set up, the official records were deficient.[73] Bean wrote in respect of the Gallipoli campaign that 'the official records were so bare and, as I know by my own observation and researches during the campaign, so inaccurate, that any history based chiefly upon them could only be a travesty of the truth.'[74] He therefore found, particularly when considering the human side of the story, that his own papers formed his most important source: these diaries, regimental records and historical notes had the advantage of having been 'collected by a trained investigator, mainly at the time of events, and in most cases from the actors themselves.'[75] Since he knew from the beginning that he would eventually write a history, he took notes in far greater detail than a war correspondent ordinarily would.[76]

Denis Winter has sounded a fierce note of caution concerning the use of one of Bean's personal sources: his diaries. In a review of D. A. Kent's article on *The Anzac Book*, Winter describes Bean's diaries as a 'ragbag of notes and jottings' which were written up in 1916 and substantially reworked in 1924.[77] It is clear from Bean's diaries that he went back over them adding notes, but not to the extent that Winter has suggested. The scope of these allegations and the mendacity implied seem implausible in the light of Bean's character.[78] Moreover Bean himself was well aware of the possible pitfalls of relying on a diary. He ensured that the following warning, written on 16 September 1946, was attached to all his diaries:

> These writings represent only what at the moment of making them I believed to be true. The diaries were jotted down almost daily with the object of recording what was then in the writer's mind. Often he wrote them when very tired and half asleep; also, not infrequently, what he believed to be true was not so – but it does not follow that he always discovered this, or remembered to correct the mistakes when discovered. Indeed, he could not always remember that he had written them.
>
> These records should, therefore, be used with great caution, as relating only what their author, at the time of writing, believed. Further, he cannot, of course, vouch for the accuracy of statements made to him by others and here recorded. But he did try to ensure such accuracy by consulting, as far as possible, those who had seen or otherwise taken part in the events. The constant falsity of second-hand evidence (on which a large proportion of war stories are founded) was impressed upon him by the second or third day of the Gallipoli campaign, notwithstanding that those who passed on such stories usually themselves believed them to be true. All second-hand evidence herein should be read with this in mind.[79]

Perhaps the greatest difficulty regarding Bean's use of sources – for the Gallipoli volumes in particular – is that it resulted in the official history relying on the perceptions of one man to an inordinate degree. Bean's official history is therefore influenced to an unusual degree by the diarist's preoccupations and attitudes. The freedom of expression given to him can only have reinforced this. E. M. Andrews concurs:

> He based too much of his writing on the diary of his experiences (the sights he had seen and the conversations he had held) as a war reporter. His preju-

dices and misconceptions at the time, despite his care, therefore slanted some of his later views. Again, his class background, education (public school and Oxford), rank and position created an unbridgeable gulf between him and the ordinary soldiers . . . being in headquarters so much put Bean apart from the ranks, so that he did not understand what occurred at the cutting edge . . . His history, therefore, is slanted history, despite his great strength – his unrelenting search for the *factual* story.[80]

It is perhaps unfair to say that there was an *unbridgeable* gulf – at least Bean attempted to break it down. He may have been taken into the HQ's staff's confidence more than other reporters, but he also spent more time near the frontline than the others. Yet his democratic credentials are impaired by suggestions that he tended to gather evidence only from officers.[81]

However, as Andrews notes, Bean's remarkable diligence in gathering evidence counterbalanced some of these problems. Bean explained his methods thus: 'The writer himself, either on the day of battle or soon afterwards, visited as far as it lay in him to do so, every important trench or position mentioned in this and the following five volumes and of most of them he kept detailed notes.'[82] Like Edmonds, Bean recognised the strength of eyewitness testimony for the particularities of battles – and the corollary of that, the weakness of evidence from further up the chain of command. Unlike Edmonds, however, who was working on a far greater scale, Bean was able to base his work on this highly detailed evidence.[83] In 1933 he wrote:

The story that emerges from this first-hand evidence is often widely different from the story in the leaders' despatches . . . This imputes no blame to the leaders – they had to go on conducting the war and trying to snatch victory, not to devote themselves to sifting out evidence of past events. But it does mean that the historian – if he has the means – must ascertain for himself who were responsible for successes or failures, since the official reports are no certain guide.[84]

Bean suggested that this healthy mistrust was the product of nationality: 'Probably the colonial writer regards more sceptically than those of older countries the despatches both of statesmen and of generals.'[85] This assertion was not backed by any evidence, and it should be noted, as in the above quoted passage, that Edmonds himself recognised that 'the public do not trust dispatches'.[86] Furthermore, Andrews has suggested that later in the war, at Bullecourt for instance, Bean's scepticism concerning British activities was coupled with a disposition to believe Australian soldiers' statements.[87]

Nonetheless, in relying on eye-witness accounts, Bean found that it was 'a perpetual marvel to me how exactly their narratives dovetail'.[88] He further became convinced that evidence given by the wounded, like second-hand reports, were unreliable.[89] This diligent gathering of evidence and scrupulous archival work were central to Bean's quest for the truth, and he relished the opportunity he had to find and present 'the truth':

> [T]o all of us there was the excitement of constantly discovering unsus-pected facts, or the truth as to events of whose causes we had previously known only one side; and of exhibiting to our own people and others many facts that would have undoubtedly been disputed unless accompanied by their discovered proofs; and, above all, of being able to right many wrongs, and to bring to thousands of actions recognition that they would never otherwise have obtained.
>
> Few people have the power that falls to a war historian in this way.[90]

Bean's wealth of first-hand evidence facilitated the principal charac-teristic of his history: its frontline perspective. His narrative is full of individual incidents, each supplemented by footnotes giving the personal details of its participants – a unique feature of his histories. This detail was crucial to its commemorative aim. For the history to be a dignified and worthy memorial it had to be authoritative, and that required detailed proof substantiating his account. A microscopic focus, further-more, gave him the opportunity to detail many instances of heroism, and to record endurance and self-sacrifice that if not recorded would be lost to posterity.[91] A further benefit, presumably, was that the large number of individuals mentioned was likely to boost sales of the volumes among those men. Such a close focus was made possible by the relatively small size of the AIF.

There were, however, drawbacks to Bean's frontline view. E. M. Andrews argues – with some justification – that Bean's highly detailed narrative tended to swamp the overall picture of the battle's progress.[92] He further suggests that Bean had a 'weakness in analytical ability'[93] and that he 'deliberately covered up Australian weaknesses'.[94]

Bean's tendency to place too much faith in Australian accounts and to downplay Australian failures is concomitant with his patriotic–commemorative aim. In his words, he wished to commemorate 'the reac-tion of a young, free, democratic people to this great test'.[95] In 1938 he described the questions he believed required answering in his history:

> How did the Australian people – and the Australian character, if there is one – come through the universally recognized test of this, their first great

war? Second was the question: What did the Australian people and their forces achieve in the total effort of their side in the struggle? Third: What was the true nature of that struggle and test so far as Australians took part in it? How well or ill did our constitution and our preparations serve us in it? What were their strengths or weaknesses? And what guidance can our people or others obtain from this experience for future emergencies?[96]

Thus the concerns of this journalist creating a history for a new nation, were radically different to those of a staff officer preparing a history for the army of a great imperial power. Their implications for the nature of the Australian official history were profound. The nature of these questions is a further reason why the impact of the author's personality is far more tangible in Bean's histories than in any other work of official history. Therefore, despite his desire to write 'the bare and uncoloured story',[97] Bean's attitudes are revealed throughout his work.

Bean shared many of his generation's beliefs and preoccupations. In his official history can be seen the collision of nineteenth-century values and twentieth-century warfare. Bean's unique response to this provides another example which disproves the argument of Fussell and others that this collision led to crisis, to modernism, or else it resulted in strangely anachronistic responses. Bean's value system withstood this test. His views were heavily influenced by his English public-school education. Robin Gerster details his tendency, *Vitae Lampada*-style, to employ sporting analogies – with rowing, cricket, a football crowd, racehorses – in describing warfare and attributes this to his Newboltian public school.[98] Inglis reproduces Newbolt's poem about his and Bean's old school *Clifton Chapel*. The following extract seems an uncanny precursor of the Anzac legend:

> To set the cause above renown,
>   To love the game beyond the prize,
> To honour, while you strike him down,
>   The foe that comes with fearless eyes;
> To count the life of battle good,
>   And dear the land that gave you birth,
> And dearer yet the brotherhood
>   That binds the brave of all the earth –
>
> My son, the oath is yours: the end
>   Is His, who built the world to strife,
> Who gave His children Pain for friend,
>   And Death for surest hope of life.

> Today and here the fight's begun,
>   Of the great fellowship you're free;
> Henceforth the School and you are one,
>   And what You are, the race shall be.[99]

The most consequential of Bean's beliefs was his social Darwinism. It informed the central thrust of his work. Thomson explains:

> He shared the ideas of contemporary social Darwinism, which assumed that there was an innate relationship between race and moral and cultural traits, and he was convinced that the English were pre-eminent because of their superior characteristics. Bean's racial attitudes would change, but the notion that the character of each individual exemplified distinctive national traits would remain the central explanatory tool of his life's writing. This idea dovetailed with a typically Victorian personal philosophy which assumed that an individual of sound character could determine his (rarely her) own fate, regardless of personal privilege or economic power.[100]

Thus Bean, believing that war afforded the opportunity to observe national traits, could write an article entitled 'Sidelights of the war on Australian character' with only a small scholarly qualm about generalising. Bean's racialist attitudes are apparent in his portrayal of the Turks as stupid[101] and sometimes inhuman (an opinion moderated during the course of the campaign);[102] and in his portrayal of British troops as decent and brave, yet lacking initiative and drive. These attitudes were also informed by eugenicist ideas. After the disappointing failures of the British troops at Suvla, Bean wrote in his diary:

> The truth is that after 100 years of breeding in slums, the British race is not the same, and can't be expected to be the same, as in the days of Waterloo. It is breeding one fine class at the expense of all the rest. The only hope is that these puny narrow-chested little men may, if they come out to Australia, or NZ or Canada, within 2 generations breed men again. England herself, unless she does something heroic, cannot hope to.[103]

These ideas culminated in his deep admiration for Australian troops:

> The Australian came of a race whose tradition was one of independence and enterprise, and, within that race itself, from a stock more adventurous, and for the most part physically more strong, than the general run of men. By reason of open air life in the new climate, and of greater abundance of food, the people developed more fully the large frames which seem normal to Anglo-Saxons living under generous conditions. An active life, as well as the climate, rendered the body wiry and the face lean, easily lined, and thin-lipped.[104]

Given the priorities of his history and the personal beliefs that fuelled them, Bean's theme throughout is the nature of the men produced by the young nation of Australia. He argues that the experience of working and surviving in the bush had percolated through Australian society, and that in combination with the egalitarian nature of its society, this produced men who were independent, resourceful, adventurous and full of initiative.[105] This classlessness brought with it a disrespect for hidebound tradition and a reputation for indiscipline.[106] These qualities made Australians outstanding and excellent fighters. These ideas are most explicit in the final chapter of his final volume, on 1918. Written during the Second World War, it is a hymn of praise to the qualities of the AIF, particularly their fighting prowess.[107] E. M. Andrews disputes Bean's thesis. He argues that Bean wrongly attributes to the Australians at Gallipoli the efficiency that they developed by the end of the war.[108] Furthermore, he contends that the idea that Australian soldiers were different or better than other soldiers in the British army is illusory.[109] Considering their lack of experience and training, this is a fair judgement on the Australians at Gallipoli.[110]

Another nineteenth-century idea – the romance of warfare – took a battering at the Western Front. With no grand cavalry charges to describe in exalted terms, but a great deal of random death by remote and impersonal technology to record, it became very difficult to apply the old idioms of heroic warfare.[111] Bean, however, managed to redefine and rejuvenate the notion of heroism as a test of endurance.[112] He complained in his diary about those who devalued heroism by overstatement, and he expressed his definition of heroism thus:

> There is plenty of heroism in war – it teems with it. But it has been so over-written that if you write that a man did his job people say: Oh, but there's nothing heroic in that! Isn't there? You come here and see the job and understand it and get out of your head the nonsense that is written about it. There is horror and beastliness and cowardice and treachery, over all of which the writer, is anxious to please the public, has to throw his cloak – but the man who does his job is a hero. And the actual truth is that though not all Australians, by any means, do their job, there is a bigger proportion of men in the Australian Army that try to do it cheerfully and without the least show of fear, than in any force or army that I have seen in Gallipoli. The man who knows war knows that this is magnificent praise. The public can never know it.[113]

The manner in which he described this heroism also was vital. As a result of his emphasis on the frontline of battle and his detailed eyewitness evidence he was able to describe individual deeds. The actions of many individuals were recounted: men with names and home towns and jobs, all carefully referenced in the footnotes. This made abstract deeds real – it brought them home. Anticipating later criticisms, Bean's hope was that this detail would illuminate rather than clogg his work, and would tie 'this national history into the everyday life of our people'.[114] The following extract illustrates how this personalised focus generated a sense of pathos and reinforced the heroism of the sacrifice:

> It was near this spot that some of Swannell's men were under a Turkish fire to which it was difficult to reply. Swannell had felt sure that he would be killed, and had said so on the *Minnewaska* before he landed, for he realised that he would play this game as he had played Rugby football – with his whole heart. Now, while kneeling in order to show his men how to take better aim at a Turk, he was shot dead.[115]

A vital element was Bean's deliberately plain and clear style of writing, combined with frequent small sketch maps in the margin. These maps were well suited for understanding specific incidents, but not for trying to follow the course of a battle – in line with Andrews's criticisms of his overall coverage. Bean's writing style reflected his view that the military jargon of old-fashioned history books made it impossible to follow the action of a battle.[116] To have perpetuated that lazy habit would have been 'fatal' to his aim of communicating the deeds of Australians to the nation:

> In the first place our volumes were written for the general reader – women as well as men. In the second, they were intentionally detailed, and jargon obscures detail – you use a set term to cover all sorts of different actions and experiences, whereas we felt that it was our particular business to describe those experiences and the reactions of the person who underwent them, whether these were scouts creeping along a ditch or generals waiting anxiously for news of the welfare of men whom they have committed to a nasty night attack.[117]

His writing is often interesting, it is lucid and rarely indulges in the hyperbole that is notable in much military writing. It is even exciting at times. Indeed, Bean deliberately chose to recount episodes from the viewpoint of the participants, at first revealing only what they knew before moving on to explain the wider context so as to make the episode dramatic and thereby enable the reader 'to feel suspense, anxiety, relief as they felt it'.[118]

Bean's individual focus, the bareness of his description and the mass of anecdotal detail means that there are strong similarities in his work to the personal narratives of soldiers as they have been identified by Samuel Hynes.[119] Despite the fact that Bean had not been a soldier, he too was bearing witness. There are, of course, many points of difference between Bean's and Hynes's work, not least the level of factual detail and contextual information in the former's work. However, perhaps the most important point is that Bean's purpose went beyond merely bearing witness: he aimed to commemorate the soldiers. This commemorative aim is the essential reason why I argue that Bean's official history is romantic.

The romance of Bean's portrayal of war has not always been accepted. It has been noted that, for example, in contrast to many other writers on Gallipoli, Bean, a classics' scholar, made no reference to the legendary associations of the area. Bean did not need them. John North wrote that 'the only mention of Troy is that of a private soldier of the name, born in the severely unclassical locality of Geraldton, Western Australia'.[120] Robert Rhodes James has called the official history 'almost chilling in its curt factuality'.[121] Even Bean's friend John Gellibrand commented: 'His only failing, an inability to rise to the occasion. His pen was cold.'[122] Robin Gerster disagrees, he describes Bean's writing style approvingly: 'The result of the incorporation of so much material illustrative of individual experience into the narrative is that the *Official History* has the intimacy of a military memoir and the variety and dynamism of a good war novel.'[123] Bean may not have been conventionally romantic, but he re-fashioned notions of heroism for a new nation and found a formula with great resonance.

The strength of Bean's portrayal of the Anzacs as heroic–romantic also derives from his overall argument. Crudely put, this stated that the failure of the campaign was not due to Australian shortcomings. As Inglis notes:

> The disaster evident by 4 May 1915 was of imperial, not colonial, making. Bean implies throughout the narrative and proclaims on its last page that for the soldiers whom he was writing to honour – the two thousand dead as well as the men still alive on 4 May – those ten days of Anzac were a triumph.[124]

Bean noted, with misplaced optimism, that the forcing of a passage through the Dardanelles and the capture of Constantinople could have shortened the war by possibly two years.[125] However, in detailing the manner in which the plan developed he singled out the impetuous Churchill for propelling it to tragic fruition in disadvantageous circumstances.[126] He argued that the campaign had valuable results but they were hardly sufficient to justify the losses involved. He concluded:

> The real stake – the opening of communication with Russia, the crushing of Turkey, and the securing of allies in the Balkans – was worth playing for, provided that it was attainable by the means employed; but nothing could justify the initiation of the enterprise by means which could not attain its goal.[127]

For the Anzacs to have fought so manfully in such circumstances makes their story all the more heroic and poignant. Their failure was not of their making. Similarly, Bean's depiction of the Turks also contributes to the heroic and romantic picture of the campaign. He described the Turks as honourable fighters. He may have castigated their stupidity, but he respected their steadfastness in protecting their homeland. His portrayal of the country bears none of the extreme distaste that was reserved for Germany and her 'utterly abhorrent' *Kultur*.[128] In particular, Bean admired the commander of the 19th Turkish Division, Mustafa Kemal. He argued that Kemal's actions were vital to the Turks' success. Such respect for the enemy dignifies defeat; perhaps to fail against an admirable leader and an admirable race is palatable.

What Bean left out or played down was in some ways just as important as what he argued and emphasised. Both constitute choices that built his romantic image of the campaign, and both are revealing of his attitudes. Following his original vision of separate professional volumes, Bean's discussion of weaponry, technology and tactics were somewhat limited. Yet he did criticise, for example, the overly ambitious tactics of the landing or a decision to advance in daylight. He also went into some detail concerning the difficulty of the artillery at Anzac. This coverage is adequate for the non-military readers at whom he was largely aiming. It should also be noted, as A. J. Hill does, that Bean's focus on the front-line did not prevent him from moving back along the whole chain of command.[129] In considering the balance struck by Bean's narrative, it is worth remembering that warfare perhaps retains more of its romance if success or failure rest on troops' endeavours rather than the accuracy of artillery calculations.

There is an absence of horror and suffering in Bean's writing, and that also assisted the development of a romantic view of the campaign. Certainly, we are told of the annihilation of the Light Horse Brigade at the Nek in the August offensive, or occasionally of a bomb blowing off a man's arm, and an entire chapter is given to describing the prevalence of sickness at Anzac. We are left in no doubt that very many heroic men died. Yet the description of the armistice of 24 May – the prime opportunity for conveying the deeply unpleasant nature of life on Gallipoli – is limited. There are hints that bullet wounds can be so destructive of flesh that bodies appear to have been mutilated;[130] however, as Inglis writes:

> The reader is given no help in these pages to imagine what bullets, shrapnel and bayonets do to flesh and blood and bone; and the only photograph of wounded men shows them as in need of a helping hand, but whole. The historian had emancipated himself from the rhetoric of the illustrated papers, but his pursuit of the truth stopped short of horror.[131]

More important still are Bean's omissions concerning character – his primary interest. He did not mention personality clashes. He did not frankly admit the diversity of the fighting men and their attitudes, including the diversity in their quality. Thomson argues that 'Bean's readiness to make generalisations about the typical Australian ... in effect defined other behaviour as aberrant'.[132] Bean chose to highlight the exceptionally brave or inspiring, and to limit his portrayal of incompetence, cowardice or unwarranted viciousness. Therefore, as Thomson notes, while Bean is frank in comparison to Edmonds's volumes, he did use footnotes to discuss unsavoury behaviour and provide explanations of brutal behaviour, thereby lightening the impact on his glowing portrayal of the men.[133] In doing so, Bean was repeating one of Edmonds's techniques for minimising controversy. In the following example of a rare revelation of weakness and disharmony, Bean's moderate language belittles the significance of the disagreement:

> The 14th (Victorian) Battalion was hampered by a certain feebleness of some of its senior officers, and about this time there occurred some alleged default which caused bad blood between it and the 15th (Queensland). The event left an unfortunate tradition, which, encouraged by foolish partisans, persisted until after the Evacuation.[134]

Bean's propensity to minimise both criticism and the inclusion of personal failings in his volumes stemmed from careful consideration. He explained to Keith Murdoch in 1921 that he hoped he had achieved a fair balance which maintained the authority of his work while conveying his personal view:

> People will turn up our records some day, and they will find here and there some very strong, sometimes untempered, foolish things, said about units by men writing on the spur of the moment; Pompey [Elliot], for example wrote scathingly of men of other brigades in France, and there is a great

deal written by staff officers, here and there, about the straggling at the landing. I try to give just so much of those things as they are worth in their proportion to the whole, so that when letters or diaries are someday published speaking of them the readers will say: 'Oh yes, Bean dealt with that – it was only an unimportant section . . . (or) a passing phase . . . and he gives you the reason for it.' I promise you that the full reason for my feeling in regard to the AIF (and you know what that feeling is) will be plain to every intelligent reader of these six volumes, and I think most of them will acquire something of it.[135]

Bean's approach to official history, unlike Edmonds's straitjacketed method, was romantic and original. Drawing upon themes and notions from the nineteenth century he refashioned familiar concepts and applied them to the army of a new nation. Bean's impact on the development of the Anzac legend has been the subject of a considerable historiography. Between the cold staff emphasis of Edmonds and Bean's commemoration of the individual, the British official historian of Gallipoli, Cecil Aspinall-Oglander, found a middle way. He wrote under the same strictures as applied to the other volumes of the British official history; yet, as in the Australian volumes, his volume bears the imprint of the author's opinions, including his essentially romantic and benevolent view of the campaign.

The British official historians of Gallipoli

Prior to Aspinall-Oglander's involvement, two other historians had attempted to produce this work. Ill-health prevented Captain G. S. Gordon, Professor of English Language and Literature at Leeds University, from completing his work.[136] Major-General Sir G. F. Ellison succeeded him on 1 August 1923. Ellison resigned on 24 January 1925 and was himself succeeded by Aspinall-Oglander.[137] The British official history of Gallipoli was published in two volumes in 1929 and 1932.

Gerald Ellison's tenure as historian was somewhat controversial. Like Aspinall, he had been on the headquarters' staff of the Mediterranean Expeditionary Force in 1915, holding the position of deputy inspector general of communications there from late July. He was unwilling to follow Edmonds's policy of presenting facts without conclusions in his volume since he wished to express his strongly held view that the campaign's failure was due to grand strategic and political mistakes. This was the reason for his resignation. He later published *The Perils of Amateur Strategy as Exemplified by the Attack on the Dardanelles Fortress in 1915* in a bid to publicise the Dardanelles Commission's findings. He also argued therein that important areas of government should be taken over by military professionals, that there was never any hope that the attack on the Dardanelles would succeed and that therefore it should never have been undertaken.[138] Such suggestions would have been unacceptable in an official history.

Cecil Faber Aspinall-Oglander (1878–1959) was educated at Rugby and entered the Royal Munster Fusiliers in 1900. He attended the Staff College in 1908 and went on to work on the general staff in India and at the War Office. He joined the MEF as a general staff officer (GSO2) in the operations branch and during the campaign he was promoted from captain to lieutenant-colonel. He was involved in planning the notably successful final evacuation of Gallipoli, and his professional skills as a staff officer were widely recognised. He was mentioned in dispatches ten times during the First World War, and retired in 1920. His second marriage was in 1927 to Florence Joan Oglander, a member of a prominent Isle of Wight family. He added Oglander to his surname by deed poll but continued to sign his letters Aspinall.[139] He went on to write several books, including a biography of Roger Keyes (1951).[140] In 1929, the *Daily Sketch* described him thus:

> Soldiers, as a rule, though they are always neat, do not usually show taste in civilian clothes. They look as if they were all dressed according to plan by some military outfitter. General Oglander is an exception. His clothes are those of a man of taste and culture, redolent of the intellectual salon rather than the battlefield, and he wears a monocle. His conversation is erudite and interesting – in fact, in this respect he might well be compared with his friend, Sir Ian Hamilton, with whom he was associated in the Gallipoli campaign.[141]

'Holding the official pen': Aspinall-Oglander's official history

Aspinall-Oglander the official historian cannot be separated from Aspinall-Oglander the staff officer. While he adhered to many of the conventions of the British official histories of the Western Front, his own volumes were distinctive. Hamilton described them as 'something entirely out of the line of ordinary official histories and having, by some miracle, escaped from the official mill still trailing a few wisps of battle smoke and glory after it'.[142] They reflect the sensibilities of a British staff officer who participated in the campaign – therefore the influence of the heroic–romantic myth may be discerned. In particular, the volumes reflect the need to respond to misrepresentations of the campaign.

Aspinall's official history describes and explains the military operations of the forces of the British empire at Gallipoli. It was therefore a supplement to the Dardanelles Commission which had not adequately covered this ground. But Aspinall's history was also a response to the commission reports' other inadequacies and the sense of failure which had prompted the commission's establishment. The reports' bland style and limited circulation had failed to dispel the sense of failure attaching to the campaign. Yet many of its participants, Aspinall included, felt that the campaign had not been an unmitigated failure. It remained, therefore, for the official history to justify and explain the value of the campaign, to rationalise its failures and criticise its mistakes. Aspinall's history was also a supplement and a reply to the Australian official history. He aimed to correct the latter's parochial individualism and biased pride. The British official history of Gallipoli was therefore the product of a British staff officer who was deeply engaged with his subject matter, who aimed to capture what he perceived to be the nature of a unique campaign and to place it in its proper perspective, albeit constrained by the requirements of its primary function of military education.

Aspinall's central task in his official history was to refute the idea that Gallipoli was an unmitigated failure. He felt that 'the truth about it [the campaign] has never yet been told. It has been referred to as a "colossal blunder" and "a hopeless task from the first".'[143] How did he set out to correct that view? His most important point was that the overall strategy had been a good idea. This gives the ensuing heroism and suffering value. Second, he argued that the aim of the campaign had been almost achieved: like Hamilton in his *Gallipoli Diary*, he described the campaign's achievement as coming 'within an ace of triumph'.[144] Third, despite its ultimate abandonment, he argues – without Bean's equivocation – that the campaign had useful effects. Fourth, he wanted to prove that though mistakes were made on the peninsula, the crucial mistakes were made in London and owed much to the lack of an authoritative general staff at the War Office. Indecision there ensured that the expeditionary force was kept short of men and arms. This argument is made clear in his Preface where he adds a fifth important point, namely that the campaign's losses simply do not compare with those at the Western Front.[145]

In writing his official history Aspinall faced serious opposition from Edmonds and the Army Council. Edmonds felt that he was unduly outspoken. He warned Aspinall:

> So far the press has treated all the military volumes very kindly. I am much concerned that there should not be a failure and the Branch should not be accused of issuing a biassed narrative brilliantly written but without the cold judgment that an official historian should display. Remember that you are not writing as yourself, but merely holding the official pen.[146]

Edmonds objected particularly to Aspinall's critical observations,[147] and the Army Council also remarked on the differences between the Gallipoli and France volumes. Thus it was noted in an annual report of the Historical Section:

> The Army Council consider that these chapters are written in a lucid and instructive manner and that they bring out clearly the lessons to be learnt. They are, however, compelled to observe that the tone of this particular history differs materially from that adopted in writing the histories of other campaigns in the Great War, in which the facts are stated and the reader left to form his own conclusions.[148]

Aspinall sought to resist the imposition of changes by his superiors. He forced the consideration of the issue at a meeting in March 1928 of the Sub-Committee for the Control of the Official Histories. Almost thirty years later Aspinall recounted the situation to Liddell Hart thus:

> I was also amused to hear what he [Edmonds] told you about his dislike of telling the truth in an official history! That explains why he was so 'down' on my Gallipoli, and tried to persuade me to water it all down. I eventually had to go to Winston, who attended a special meeting of the CI Defence to discuss the whole matter, with Edmonds and me as witnesses, and at which, thanks to Winston's support, I was successful all down the line. But I remember Edmonds telling me that 'In ten years' time your book will carry no more weight than an article in the Sunday Press; it will lower the reputation of the War Histories, and you'll live to be ashamed of having written it!'[149]

The main problem discussed at this meeting was Aspinall's reference to the indecisiveness in government that had allowed both the second battle of Krithia and the attack at Aubers Ridge on the Western Front to go ahead when there was a shortage of ammunition. To Aspinall, this

episode was symptomatic of the failure in London to support the
Gallipoli campaign and give it the backing it required to succeed.
Aspinall defended his ability to make such comments, saying 'he could
not see the value of a history written in blinkers or read in blinkers',[150]
and he stressed that he was not implying that Aubers Ridge was wrong,
but that going ahead with *both* attacks was wrong. This was the meeting,
referred to earlier in this chapter, where the self-interested Churchill
robustly argued that it was 'absolutely indefensible and absurd' to suggest
that a monograph on one campaign should not make reference to the
general context of the war, since to do so would make the story unintel-
ligible.[151] Churchill opposed Hankey's suggestion that a passage should
be inserted detailing the dilemma faced by the politicians in London.
Hankey pushed for the Army Council's views to be taken into account
and thereby restated the official history's purpose and the particular constraints on such volumes:

> [U]nless there is something at stake, we ought to give every possible defer-
> ence to the views of the Chief of the Imperial General Staff. The history
> was written on the basis of information supplied almost exclusively by the
> War Office, and the largest market for the book would be soldiers. He felt
> in that case, subject to any principle, everything possible should be done to
> meet the CIGS.[152]

It was agreed that Aspinall would collaborate with Edmonds on this
and other controversial passages, and the pressure for more subtle
changes continued.[153] However, from Aspinall's 1957 comments to
Liddell Hart and from the published version, it does not appear that he
moderated his comparatively outspoken comments. The comment of
Cyril Falls, another official historian, on Aspinall's first volume also
demonstrates his success: 'In the Gallipoli campaign what happened
in London was really more important than what happened on the
Peninsula, and the political aspects are here clearly depicted.'[154] The
Gallipoli volumes were subjected to strong constraining pressures
(including diplomatic concerns), but not to the kind of massive alterations and changes of opinion that Tim Travers details in his study of
the writing of the later volumes on Passchendaele.[155]

Aspinall's justification of the strategy was the first step in demonstrating that the campaign had not been a blunder, but there was a need
also to rationalise the mistakes made by its participants. He explained
mistakes in terms of leadership failures, but was careful to explain also
the extenuating circumstances. The most important of these were the

decisions taken and the indecisiveness displayed in London which ensured that there were always too few men and too few guns for the task. The rugged ground and the amphibious nature of the campaign, which brought immense tactical and logistical difficulties, were also influential factors. Finally, like Bean, Aspinall highlighted the presence in the enemy camp of an outstanding leader, Mustapha Kemal, the 'Man of Destiny' (see figure 3).[156] However, it is possible that this flattery was exaggerated for diplomatic reasons, since the Foreign Office wished to present specially bound copies of the history to the Turkish leader.[157] Nevertheless, these difficulties both explained leadership failures and served to underline how remarkable the forces' achievements were.

Aspinall's emphasis on leaders rather than battle plans as an explanation of failure can be seen as the product of his staff officer's perspective. Therefore Hunter Weston at the Helles landing and Stopford at Suvla received a good deal of criticism for their faulty implementation of otherwise viable plans. Stopford and the Suvla operations have been the subject of a re-appraisal by Robin Prior,[158] who has usefully pointed out how subsequent accounts have been based on just two sources: a report by a staff officer at the time and the official history. Both were written by Aspinall. Moreover, as one of the planners of the Suvla operation, he was scarcely an independent witness. Prior argues that the Suvla plan could never have delivered a crucial victory and that Stopford has been made a scapegoat. In this criticism of Stopford, Aspinall was assisted by Hamilton, Churchill, Birdwood and Keyes, each of whom had a vested interest in finding 'a military buffoon who by his incapacity had ruined the whole enterprise'.[159]

The most important failed leader on the peninsula was, of course, Hamilton. Aspinall praised his character but made several telling criticisms. The most acute was that Hamilton was 'loyal to a fault':[160] his deference to Kitchener, compounded by his tendency to gloss over the difficulties of the situation, contributed to the mistakes made in London. Hamilton also overemphasised the need for secrecy and thereby hampered the dissemination of intelligible orders at crucial junctures and effectively abdicated power to subordinates during large operations. Nonetheless Aspinall was most sympathetic to the difficulties of Hamilton's task. Quoting Enver Pasha, he wrote that the commander had been set to 'thread a needle with his toes'.[161]

Aspinall himself was subject to some criticism concerning this portrayal, not from Hamilton, but from Stephen Gaselee, the Foreign Office librarian:

3   Mustapha Kemal at Gallipoli in 1915

It is curious to notice how this very definite impression grows on one in reading the History carefully and critically as I have done. The author nowhere shows hostility to the Commander-in-Chief; nowhere is openly censorious of his decisions; and even provides, from time to time, excuses for his failures. All the same, the impression to which I refer grows more and more definite as the author continues his story, as if the facts he marshals are too insistent to be obscured or softened by the explanations offered. I have the feeling that in justice to the Commander in chief somewhat more might be advanced in the ways of explanation than has been done.[162]

Echoing one of Hamilton's concerns prior to the Dardanelles Commission, Gaselee suggested that in the interest of relations with France and the Dominions, whose troops had served under Hamilton, it would be politic for the official history to record and explain the general's difficulties and to present him in a favourable light 'so far as is compatible with historical truth'.[163]

In explaining the value of the campaign and that it was not a 'colossal blunder', Aspinall not only dealt with strategy and tactics, but (unusually for an official historian) he conveyed something of the drama and romance of the campaign. This is particularly notable in his Preface and Epilogue in which he perhaps had more leeway for personal expression. He summarised his sentiments about the campaign at the beginning of the Epilogue:

The drama of the Dardanelles campaign, by reason of the beauty of its setting, the grandeur of its theme and the unhappiness of its ending, will always rank amongst the world's classic tragedies. The story is a record of lost opportunities and eventual failure; yet it is a story which men of British race may ponder if not without pain yet certainly not without pride; for amidst circumstances of unsurpassed difficulty and strain the bravery, fortitude and stoical endurance of the invading troops upheld most worthily the high traditions of the fighting services of the Crown.[164]

Perhaps the most obvious – and the most typically British – way in which Aspinall made the campaign seem romantic was his references to classical antiquity. The first reference was oblique: 'The campaign was enacted upon the most historic of all stages for a noble feat of arms.'[165] At the beginning of the second volume he reproduced a paragraph by Aeschylus which, with its description of a besieging force afflicted by vermin and the heat, seems an uncanny parallel to the campaign.[166] The final part of the quotation is repeated at the very end of the volume and encapsulates Aspinall's argument: 'What need to repine at fortune's frowns? The gain hath the advantage and the loss does not bear down the scale.'[167] This reinforces the idea that the advantages and achievements of the campaign outweighed its cost. Aspinall's fellow staff officer Orlo Williams discerned a sense of such classical romance working at a more subtle level in the official history:

> [F]rom his first volume, I derive the hope that he will be able, without distorting his facts or transgressing his limits, to reproduce the dramatic rhythm which, as surely as on the stage of Æschylus, pulses through the story of Gallipoli. Here, as there, neglect of principle and human overconfidence brought their inevitable Nemesis.[168]

This is not to say that Aspinall rejected all the norms of style of an official history. Aspinall's prose was necessarily moderate and measured, as a comparison with Hamilton's will illuminate. Hamilton, having read draft chapters from the second volume, suggested an alternative opening paragraph. First, here is Aspinall's draft:

> The middle of May 1915 marked a critical juncture in the Gallipoli operations. The British hopes of a short campaign, crowned by a far-reaching victory, had ended in disappointment. Success at the Dardanelles could no longer be purchased without the expenditure of a very large military effort . . .

Hamilton advised instead, 'You must begin your attack from a picturesque angle', his suggestion begins,

> What the Ides of March were to Imperial Caesar the middle of May was to the GHQ at Gallipoli. The British hopes of gaining a big victory with small forces had ended in disappointment. They were up against the hard fact that a vast military Empire like that of Turkey could only be over thrown by an adequate force . . .[169]

The published version remained close to Aspinall's draft. Another illustration of the constraints on Aspinall's writing style comes from a manuscript fragment, in Aspinall's handwriting, of a chapter regarding Suvla. Its colourful but flippant metaphor was obviously deemed unsuitable for inclusion in the official history:

> On the 6/7th August indeed, the 9th Corps can be compared to nothing so well as to a motor car whose hurried assembly had only been completed by the inclusion of spare parts of various different makes. Some of them were new, others old, a few of them were already quite worn out and none of them were made to fit. The car had arrived from Ireland with a high reputation; it had a fresh coat of paint, it bore a reputed maker's guarantee, and

every confidence was reposed in it. Doubtless, before using it for important work, Sir Ian Hamilton ought to have tested it. But he had no space to test it in before it reached the peninsula, and he knew that its first journey was along an easy road, with no gradients to speak of, and no serious obstacles.

No sooner was the car set in motion that its inherent faults became apparent. Violent noises came from under the bonnet. The carburettor choked, the bearing heated, the driving shaft snapped, the differential broke, the steering gear collapsed, and the engine fell to pieces.[170]

Aspinall's volumes were nonetheless well written – Liddell Hart thought them 'so much better, and better written, than his [Edmonds's] own'.[171] His account of the landings exemplifies his achievement. He described events carefully, explaining the disposition of the troops, their actions and progress from the point of view both of the invader and of the enemy. He explained where mistakes were made, but he also built tension. For example: 'During the hour of inky darkness that preceded the dawn the faint night breeze died suddenly, and the surface of the Ægean grew smooth and still as glass. In face of the coming drama, the very elements appeared to hold their breath.'[172] He did not shrink from admitting that severe casualties had been inflicted. His classically inspired description of V beach is vivid and dramatic:

[W]hen the boats were only a few yards from the shore, Hell was suddenly let loose. A tornado of fire swept over the incoming boats, lashing the calm waters of the bay as with a thousand whips. Devastating casualties were suffered in the first few seconds. Some of the boats drifted helplessly away with every man in them killed. Many more of the Dublins were killed as they waded ashore. Others, badly wounded, stumbling in the water, were drowned.[173]

Aspinall was averse to dwelling on the suffering of the wounded. Later, however, he did graphically describe the revolting living conditions and health problems on the peninsula. In the same way that emphasising the strategic and tactical difficulties underlined the forces' achievements, dwelling on these extremely trying circumstances served to throw the heroism of the men into sharp relief.

The romantic image created by Aspinall in his well-written and dramatic account was possible only in the context of a worthwhile campaign, and it contributed, in its turn, to the sense that the campaign was valuable. This romance differentiates the Gallipoli campaign from the Western Front, and its official history from that of Edmonds's volumes. Aspinall and Bean were reflecting the perception of the campaign's participants that it was romantic, and in doing so they reinforced and perpetuated that perception. As has been seen, Bean created a sense of romance and heroism through a focus on the individual moment. The discovery of the nature of those individuals, not the strategic achievement of the campaign, was what made the campaign worthwhile to Bean. Indeed Bean's discussion of strategy is not prominently placed. His emphasis on the individual led, perhaps, to an overstatement of the prowess of the Anzacs; and that was something Aspinall was keen to counteract. Perhaps in getting the role of the Australians into perspective by diminishing their achievement, Aspinall felt he would make the plans look better and the British troops look better still.

In 1927 Aspinall wrote to Edmonds of the distorting dominance of the Australian version of 25 April 1915:

> This chapter was a difficult one to write because the truth about the Australian has never yet been told and in its absence a myth has sprung up that the Anzac troops did magnificently against amazing odds. The anniversary of the landings at Gallipoli is called Anzac Day, and very many people would be surprised to learn that any other troops but Australians took part in the landing operations in Gallipoli.[174]

In particular Aspinall was critical of Bean's emphasis on the frontline soldier: 'An unbiassed history can hold no brief for the troops on the spot.'[175] This comment makes fully explicit the contrasting approaches of the British and Australian official historians. As with other narratives of Gallipoli then, Aspinall was writing to correct the perceived failings of an earlier narrative: Bean's official history, published in 1921 and 1924. This attitude had the potential for great controversy. Aspinall's draft version of the Anzac landing, a sacrosanct episode for the Australians, proved explosive. His description, which included references to large numbers of stragglers (men who had returned to the beach and were possibly shirking their fighting duties), has been discussed in an article by Alistair Thomson, who commented:

> Cecil Aspinall was able to perceive straggling from outside the Australian national viewpoint, though his perception may well have been affected by a different investment in the Anzac story. Bean suspected as much when he wrote of Aspinall's history in a letter to his friend and compatriot Brudenall [sic] White, 'I can't get away from the notion that he is on the defensive, and thinks that too much has been made of the Australians, and that he will even things up somewhat if he shows that they were no great shakes after all.'[176]

Aspinall described the campaign from the imperial perspective. He included all participants of the British empire and, writing from the centre of that empire, he sought also to give the political and strategic context. Bean's aim was far more intimate and unique, yet limited, too: he sought to tell only *The Story of Anzac*. Bean admitted that his Australian history 'must inevitably be but a partial history'.[177] The British were occasionally critical of this tendency. Edmonds' report of 1928 referred thus to the latest draft of Bean's work:

> The Australian official account of the Australians in the battles of the Somme, close on a thousand closely typed pages, were sent to me for remarks and criticism. This absorbed a considerable amount of time, as the historian, Mr. Bean, had taken rather a parochial view, has no great military knowledge, and was inclined to write as if the Australian divisions were in 1916, when they arrived in France, the perfect instrument they were in August 1918, and to attribute their early failures in 1916 to British generals.[178]

This criticism stemmed from Edmonds's staff emphasis, an emphasis replicated by Aspinall. His accounts of battle did not describe the actions of individual men, but took the officers' point of view. It was therefore also a partial history. This approach resulted not only from Aspinall's origins as a staff officer but from his method of gathering evidence. There was for him no equivalent to Bean's diaries and frontline interviews. Aspinall was reliant on War Office records and the voluminous correspondence that resulted from the circulation of draft chapters to *officers*, 260 in the case of the second volume.[179] Indeed the British were disdainful of Bean's methods. Edmonds wrote: 'He founds his narrative far too much on general gossip without reference to documents, and has little idea of how Armies are commanded and Staff work done.'[180]

Bean's letter of congratulation to Aspinall on the completion of his official history was generous in its praise. It was also perceptive in its description of an official history's relationship with the public and its recognition of the former staff officer's comparative strengths and differing priorities:

> It seems to me that the public has accepted your work as the standard authority on the subject, and I feel quite sure that it will never lose that status. I feel sure also that you will never regret having adopted the freedom which you employed in stating your own views. We here have often been criticised for this, but without that frankness your great work would have lost its authority and its interest for the public. As it is, everyone who wants to know the true history of Gallipoli will go to your book. No other can

approach it as *an authority for what was planned*. Our Australian history
will supplement it as an authority, perhaps, upon the human side of it, what
was done and suffered. Not that your book in any way lacks its human side.
It is a fair, balanced, interesting human story, and I am just a little envious,
and I congratulate you with all my heart.[181]

Conclusion: the official response

The contrasting styles of Edmonds, Bean and Aspinall are indicative of
their differing conceptions of the purpose of an official narrative. British
official history took a top–down view that minimised criticism and controversy, and was essentially exculpatory in intent. It therefore sought to
dissipate imputations of blame and failure to the campaign and its participants. This can be seen in regard to Gallipoli in the twin strategies of
denying the outright failure of the campaign and in rationalising the failures of its participating leaders. It was not feasible to deny all failure nor
to avoid all criticisms, but the highlighting of compensatory results and
the inclusion of muted criticism were possible. In the final chapter such
characteristics and purpose are to be seen in the bland conclusions of
the Dardanelles Commission. They are particularly evident also in
Edmonds's approach to official history. He consciously limited his narrative in order to avoid overt criticisms. Therefore, although his volumes
were written specifically for military education, they were insufficient for
that purpose. It was left to the Kirke report to draw useful lessons from
the First World War for internal army consumption.[182]

Aspinall's tussle with Edmonds was not simply about how frankly criticism could be made: it was about who was to be exculpated. Both men
wrote command narratives: they told the story from the leadership's point
of view; but Aspinall's purpose was more narrowly focused in that he
sought to exculpate in particular the British leaders on the ground.
Edmonds wrote for future staff officers; Aspinall wrote to protect his
fellow staff officers, and unlike Bean he held 'no brief'[183] for the men. This
Aspinall achieved by touching on some elements of the heroic–romantic
myth of Gallipoli, particularly its imaginative strategy, by giving the wider
context of political indecisiveness and by diminishing the burgeoning
prestige of the Anzacs. Like the Dardanelles Commission reports, his is
essentially a narrative of the professional military.

By contrast, Bean wrote a narrative for a citizens' army. It is full of
pride in the achievements of its individuals. It bears witness to their
heroism, and in greater detail than any other official narrative it bears

witness to their experiences. In doing so, Bean shares some of the characteristics of Hynes's idea of the soldiers' tale. Bean elevates the aim of bearing witness by seeking to commemorate the Australians in a national epic narrative. In doing so Bean blurs the boundaries between the official mode of response and the soldiers' tale. This will be seen more clearly in chapter 3, which concerns the journalists' responses. Theirs are transitional narratives between the experiential narratives of the individual and the exculpatory narratives of officialdom.

Notes

1 C. E. W. Bean, *The Story of Anzac from the Outbreak of War to the End of the First Phase of the Gallipoli Campaign, May 4, 1915*, vol. 1 of the Official History of Australia in the War of 1914–1918 (St Lucia, Queensland, 1981 [1921]); C. E. W. Bean, *The Story of Anzac from 4 May, 1915 to the Evacuation of the Gallipoli Peninsula*, vol. 2 of the Official History of Australia in the War of 1914–1918 (St Lucia, Queensland, 1981 [1924]).

2 Brigadier-General C. F. Aspinall-Oglander, *Military Operations, Gallipoli*, vol. 1: *Inception of the Campaign to May 1915*, History of the Great War Based on Official Documents (London, 1992 [1929]); *Military Operations, Gallipoli*, vol. 2: *May 1915 to the Evacuation*, History of the Great War Based on Official Documents (London, 1992 [1932]). The New Zealand official history was a modest popular volume: Major Fred Waite, *The New Zealanders at Gallipoli* (Auckland, 1919).

3 See John Robertson, *The Tragedy & Glory of Gallipoli: Anzac and Empire* (London, 1990), pp. 224–44.

4 Jeffrey Grey, *A Commonwealth of Histories: The Official Histories of the Second World War in the United States, Britain and the Commonwealth*, Trevor Reese Memorial Lecture 1998, Sir Robert Menzies Centre for Australian Studies, Institute of Commonwealth Studies, University of London (London, 1998); Hans Umbreit, 'The development of official military historiography in the German Army from the Crimean War to 1945' in Robin Higham (ed.) *Official Histories: Essays and Bibliographies from Around the World* (Kansas, 1970), pp. 160–8; Jay Luvaas, 'The first British official historians' in Higham (ed.) *Official Histories*, pp. 488–91.

5 James Edmonds, unpublished memoirs, ch. 32: 'The Historical Section of the Committee of Imperial Defence, 1919–49', p. 1, Liddell Hart Centre for Military Archives, King's College, London (hereafter LHCMA), Edmonds Papers, III/16.

6 Colonel E. Y. Daniel, 'Memorandum on the work of the Historical Section, Committee of Imperial Defence', 12 July 1922, pp. 1–4, PRO, CAB 103/82 (also filed at CAB 27/182).

7 Hankey, Memorandum for the Prime Minister, 23 December 1915, p. 4, PRO, CAB 103/68 and CAB 103/76.

8 *Ibid.*, p. 6.

9 Daniel, 'Historical Section', 12 July 1922, p. 8, PRO, CAB 103/82.

10 'Historical Section (Military Branch)' p. 10 (no date, no author, but probably by Edmonds soon after March 1920), PRO, CAB 103/1 (my emphasis); see also Keith Grieves, 'Early historical responses to the Great War: Fortescue, Conan Doyle and Buchan' in Brian Bond (ed.) *The First World War and British Military History* (Oxford, 1991), pp. 26–7, 30–3.

11 Daniel, 'Historical Section', 12 July 1922, p. 41, and repeated in similar memo of 1938(?), p. 8, PRO, CAB 103/82.

12 Daniel, 'Report on the work of the Historical Section by the secretary', COH 33, 22 February 1933, p. 6, PRO, CAB 16/52.

13 Daniel, 'Historical Section, Committee of Imperial Defence', 1938(?), p. 8, PRO, CAB 103/82.

14 Hankey, Memorandum to Prime Minister, 23 December 1915, p. 9, PRO, CAB 103/68.

15 Daniel, 'Historical Section', 12 July 1922, pp. 36–7, and 1938(?), pp. 6–7, PRO, CAB 103/82.

16 Proceedings of meeting, i.e. Sub-Committee for the Control of the Official Histories, COH 4, 11 February 1927, p. 4, PRO, CAB 16/53.

17 Daniel, 'Historical Section', 12 July 1922, p. 37, and 1938(?), p. 7, PRO, CAB 103/82.

18 Daniel, 'Historical Section', 12 July 1922, p. 35, PRO, CAB 103/82.

19 *House of Commons Parliamentary Debates*, vol. 155 (13 June 1922), cols 277–86.

20 Daniel, 'Official histories – memorandum by the secretary of the Historical Section of the Committee of Imperial Defence', CID 238–B, October 1919, p. 3, PRO, CAB 103/83.

21 Daniel, 'Historical Section', 12 July 1922, pp. 10–11, PRO, CAB 103/82.

22 Hankey, 'Cabinet. Official histories. Note by the secretary', 28 October 1919, p. 2, PRO, CAB 103/83.

23 Sir Julian S. Corbett, *Naval Operations*, 3, History of the Great War Based on Official Documents (London, 1923); S. S. Wilson, *The Cabinet Office to 1945* (London, 1975), p. 122.

24 Colonel J. S. Yule, 'Provisional note for the guidance of narrators in the compilation of first narratives for histories of military operations', 15 September 1941, p. 4, PRO, CAB 44/428.

25 Daniel, Memorandum, 1938(?), p. 9, PRO, CAB 103/82.

26 Cyril Falls, 'Edmonds, Sir James Edward (1861–1956)' in E. T. Williams and H. M. Palmer (eds) *Dictionary of National Biography 1951–60* (Oxford, 1971), p. 328.

27 Daniel, Memorandum, 1938(?), p. 7, PRO, CAB 103/82.

28 Wilson, *Cabinet Office*, p. 126.

29 This is the title as given by Daniel, 'Historical Section', 12 July 1922, p. 9, PRO, CAB 27/182. He is probably referring to J. S. Corbett, *Maritime Operations in the Russo-Japanese War, 1904–5* (Annapolis, 1994).

30 J. W. Fortescue, *A History of the British Army*, 13 vols (London, 1899–1930); see Keith Grieves, 'Fortescue, Conan Doyle and Buchan', pp. 18–19.

31 Daniel, 'Historical Section', 12 July 1922, p. 8, PRO, CAB 103/82; and Wilson, *Cabinet Office*, p. 124.

32 Hilton Young to H. A. L. Fisher, 'Memorandum on war histories', 4 October 1922; and letter from H. A. L. Fisher to Lt-Commander E. Hilton Young, MP, 11 October 1922, PRO, CAB 103/73. Buchan, besides writing 24 volumes of *Nelson's History of the War* (London, 1915–19), revised as *History of the Great War*, 4 vols (London, 1921–2), went on to write *The History of the South African Forces in France* (London, 1920). Kipling edited and compiled *The Irish Guards in the Great War* (London, 1923).

33 Daniel to Cecil Longhurst, 10 January 1939, PRO, CAB 103/102.

34 David French, ' "Official but not history?" Sir James Edmonds and the official history of the Great War', *RUSI: Journal of the Royal United Services Institute for Defence Studies*, 131:1 (March 1986), p. 58.

35 Edmonds, unpublished memoirs, ch. 32, p. 3, Edmonds Papers, III/16.

36 Commander H. R. Moore, 'Minutes of meeting of the Committee on the Historical Section of the Committee of Imperial Defence of 27 July 1922', OHW 1st conclusions, p. 5, PRO, CAB 27/182.

37 J. W. Fortescue, 'Lord French's "1914" ', *Quarterly Review*, 461 (October 1919). Fortescue commented in his review (p. 363): 'The author has descended to misstatements and misrepresentations of the clumsiest and most ludicrous kind in order to injure the reputation of a subordinate [Smith-Dorrien], who is forbidden to defend himself; and, coming from one in his high position, this brings shame and dishonour not only upon the Field-Marshal himself but upon the Army.'

38 Edmonds, unpublished memoirs, ch. 32, p. 3, Edmonds Papers, III/16. Denis Winter's *Haig's Command: A Reassessment* (London, 1991), pp. 242–3, alleged that Edmonds plotted to get rid of Fortescue. He suggests that Fortescue was trapped into making his unacceptable comments by being invited to review French's book, the contents of which were likely to have been like a red rag to a bull. These assertions are entirely unsubstantiated by the sources referenced. In footnote 8, p. 352, Winter lists several sources: the first, a note by Edmonds dated 12 September 1919, is not properly referenced and I have not been able to locate it; the second, a letter by Edmonds denigrating Fortescue's work, does exist but it was addressed to E. Y. Daniel and not to 'Sandhurst' as Winter states. There is no evidence of Edmonds's plotting in CAB 103/83, and 'Minute 1 in CAB 635' is referred to in a memo in CAB 103/83 as War Cabinet 635, Minute 1. Winter implies he has read it, though I have been unable to locate such a file. Furthermore, the veracity of *Haig's Command* has been effectively demolished by Jeffrey Grey's

review in *Journal of the Society for Army Historical Research*, 71:285 (spring 1993), pp. 60–3. Winter's subsequent comments on the writing of the official histories are therefore not included in this book.

39 Moore, OHW 1st conclusions, 27 July 1922, p. 5, PRO, CAB 27/182.

40 Brigadier-General Sir James E. Edmonds, *Military Operations, France and Belgium, 1914*, 1: *Mons, the Retreat to the Seine, the Marne and the Aisne, August–October 1914*, History of the Great War Based on Official Documents (London, 1925 [1922]), p. v.

41 Brigadier-General Sir James E. Edmonds, *Military Operations, France and Belgium, 1915*, 2: *Battle of Aubers Ridge, Festubert and Loos*, History of the Great War Based on Official Documents (London, 1928), p. viii.

42 Moore, OHW 1st conclusions, 27 July 1922, pp. 4–5, PRO, CAB 27/182.

43 Edmonds, unpublished memoirs, p. 1.

44 Edmonds, *Military Operations, France and Belgium 1915*, 2 (London, 1928); Corbett, *Naval Operations*, 3.

45 K. S. Inglis, *C. E. W. Bean, Australian Historian*, John Murtagh Macrossan Lecture 1969 (St Lucia, Queensland, 1970), p. 22.

46 So reported Hankey to the meeting of the Committee on the Historical Section on 27 July 1922, OHW 1st conclusions, p. 6, PRO, CAB 27/182.

47 Proceedings of meeting, i.e. Sub-Committee for the Control of the Official Histories, COH 5, 9 March 1928, p. 9, PRO, CAB 16/53 (my emphasis).

48 Tim Travers, *The Killing Ground: The British Army, the Western Front and the Emergence of Modern Warfare 1900–1918* (London, 1987), chs 8 and 9; David French, ' "Official but not history"?', pp. 58–63; David French, 'Sir James Edmonds and the official history: France and Belgium' in Bond (ed.) *The First World War and British Military History*, pp. 69–86.

49 B. H. Liddell Hart, 'Responsibility and judgment in historical writing', *Military Affairs* (spring 1959), p. 36.

50 'Conclusions of Committee on the Historical Section', 31 July 1922, p. 1, PRO, CAB 27/182.

51 Edmonds, unpublished memoirs, ch. 32, p. 10, Edmonds papers, III/16.

52 *Ibid.*, p. 12. Edmonds was largely successful in ensuring the factual accuracy of his volumes.

53 Dudley McCarthy, *Gallipoli to the Somme: The Story of C. E. W. Bean* (London, 1983), p. 65; Bean published these articles as *On the Wool Track* (1910).

54 McCarthy, *Gallipoli to the Somme*, p. 72.

55 Bean to GSO 1st Australian Division., 27 June 1915, Australian War Memorial, Canberra, Bean Papers, AWM 38 3DRL 6673, item 270.

56 Bean to Capt. R. Muirhead Collins, RN, Official Secretary for the Commonwealth, 12 May 1916, Bean Papers, AWM 38 3DRL 6673, item 271.

57 Bean, 'Australian records of the war, Official Historian, AIF', 14 August 1919, Bean Papers, AWM 38 3DRL 6673, item 11.

58 E. K. Bowden, 'Australian war histories. Renewal of engagement of Official Historian (Mr. C. E. W. Bean)', 4 June 1924, Bean Papers, AWM 38 3DRL 6673, item 11 (my emphasis).

59 Bean, 'Australian records', 14 August 1919, Bean Papers, AWM 38 3DRL 6673, item 11.

60 Bean, 'Australian war records – full scheme of publication', Memorandum for the secretary, Department of Defence, 26 June 1919, Bean Papers, AWM 38 3DRL 6673, item 180.

61 The medical history was published as A. G. Butler (ed.) *The Australian Army Medical Services in the War of 1914–1918* (Melbourne, 1930).

62 C. E. W. Bean, 'The writing of the Australian official history of the Great War – sources, methods and some conclusions', *Royal Australian Historical Society, Journal and Proceedings*, 24:2 (1938), p. 88.

63 'Agreement between C. E. W. Bean and the Commonwealth of Australia', 1919(?), Bean Papers, AWM 38 3DRL 6673, item 11. The only exception was in case of libel.

64 'Copy of Minute by Military Board' in Bean, 'Australian records', p. 9, Bean Papers, AWM 38 3DRL 6673, item 11.

65 Bean, 'Australian records', 14 August 1919', Bean Papers, AWM 38 3DRL 6673, item 11.

66 *Ibid.*

67 Bean, *The Story of Anzac*, 1, p. lix.

68 Bean, 'The writing of the Australian official history', p. 88.

69 Bean details these sources in 'The writing of the Australian official history', pp. 93–6. He describes his methodology in 'The technique of a contemporary war historian', *Historical Studies Australia and New Zealand*, 2:6 (November 1942).

70 Bean, 'The technique of a contemporary war historian', p. 70.

71 Bean, 'The writing of the Australian official history', p. 89. In the Preface to the first edition, Bean lists the more important books and writings he consulted. Many of these were personal memoirs or inherently unreliable such as Hamilton's dispatches, his *Gallipoli Diary* or John Buchan's *Nelson's History of the War*.

72 Bean writing in the *Sydney Morning Herald* in 1925, quoted in Denis Winter (ed.) *Making the Legend: The War Writings of C. E. W. Bean* (St Lucia, Queensland, 1992), p. 14.

73 Bean, 'The technique of a contemporary war historian', p. 66.

74 Bean, 'The writing of the Australian official history', p. 90.

75 *Ibid.*, p. 100.

76 Bean to Commander Pethebridge, Defence Department, 16 October 1914, Bean Papers, AWM 38 3DRL 6673, item 270.

77 Denis Winter, '*The Anzac Book*: a re-appraisal', *Journal of the Australian War Memorial*, 16 (April 1990), p. 60.

78 David A. Kent's '*The Anzac Book*: a reply to Denis Winter', *Journal of the*

Australian War Memorial, 17 (October 1990), pp. 54–5, effectively refutes Winter's article. I am grateful to Ashley Ekins for supplying me with a copy of this article.

79 This warning can be found on any of the diaries in his papers: Bean Papers, AWM 38 3DRL 606.

80 E. M. Andrews, *The Anzac Illusion: Anglo-Australian Relations during World War One* (Cambridge, 1993), p. 214.

81 Jane Ross, 'Review: *Frontline Gallipoli*, etc.', *Australian Historical Studies*, 24:97 (October 1991), p. 478; also suggested to me by Sir Robert Rhodes James.

82 Bean, *The Story of Anzac*, vol. 1, pp. lxiii–iv.

83 Edmonds was writing about a 60–division army, while Bean covered a 5–division corps.

84 C. E. W. Bean, 'Writing the war history', *Reveille* (1 June 1933), p. 3.

85 Bean, *The Australian Imperial Force in France 1916*, vol. 3 of the Official History of Australia in the War of 1914–1918 (Sydney, 1938), p. vi, quoted in Inglis, *C. E. W. Bean*, p. 23.

86 Edmonds(?) 'Historical Section (Military Branch)', March 1920(?), p. 10, PRO, CAB 103/1 (no date or author given).

87 E. M. Andrews, 'Bean and Bullecourt: weaknesses and strengths of the official history of Australia in the First World War', *Revue Internationale d'histoire militaire* (August 1990), p. 45.

88 Bean, 'The writing of the Australian official history', p. 109.

89 *Ibid.*, p. 110.

90 Bean, 'The technique of a war historian', p. 79.

91 Bean, 'The writing of the Australian official history', p. 93.

92 Andrews, 'Bean and Bullecourt', p. 44.

93 *Ibid.*, p. 43.

94 *Ibid.*, p. 45. Andrews's comments are specific to two difficult battles of 1917, but his general criticisms of Bean should be borne in mind when considering the Gallipoli volumes.

95 Bean, 'The technique of a war historian', p. 79.

96 Bean, 'The writing of the Australian official history', p. 91.

97 Bean, *The Story of Anzac*, 1, p. lxiv.

98 R. Gerster, *Big Noting: The Heroic Theme in Australian War Writing* (Melbourne, 1987), p. 78.

99 Inglis, *C. E. W. Bean*, p. 8. Inglis notes that this poem was published during Bean's final year at Clifton: see *The Island Race*, which also contained *Vitae Lampada*.

100 Alistair Thomson, *Anzac Memories: Living with the Legend* (Melbourne, 1994), p. 49.

101 Bean, *The Story of Anzac*, 1, pp. 152, 470; and 2, p. 507.

102 Bean, *The Story of Anzac*, 1, p. 421; and 2, p. 162.

103 Bean's diary, Sunday 29 August 1915, Bean Papers, AWM 38 3DRL 606, item 10.

104 Bean, *The Story of Anzac*, 1, pp. 4–5.

105 *Ibid.*, p. 5; see L. L. Robson, 'The origin and character of the First AIF, 1914–1918: some statistical evidence', *Historical Studies*, 15 (1973), pp. 737–49; and John Barrett's criticisms in 'No straw man: C. E. W. Bean and some critics', *Australian Historical Studies*, 23:89 (April 1988), p. 109. In his later work – e.g. *The Old AIF and the New* (Sydney, 1940) – Bean attributed the Australians' qualities to the egalitarian and democratic nature of their society.

106 Bean, *The Story of Anzac*, 1, p. 6.

107 C. E. W. Bean, *The Australian Imperial Force in France during the Allied Offensive, 1918*, vol. 6 of the Official History of Australia in the War of 1914–1918 (St Lucia, Queensland, 1983 [1942]), pp. 1074–96.

108 Andrews, *Anzac Illusion*, p. 147.

109 *Ibid.*, p. 4.

110 Christopher Pugsley, 'Stories of Anzac' in Jenny Macleod (ed.) *Gallipoli: Making History* (forthcoming).

111 This type of description did, however, continue to be used in the press and propaganda, e.g. regarding winners of the Victoria Cross.

112 Alistair Thomson, ' "Steadfast until death"? C. E. W. Bean and the representation of Australian military manhood', *Australian Historical Studies*, 23:93 (October 1989), p. 468.

113 Bean's diary, Sunday 26 September 1915, Bean Papers, AWM 38 3DRL 606, item 17.

114 Bean, 'The technique of a war historian', p. 79.

115 Bean, *The Story of Anzac*, 1, p. 297.

116 Bean, 'The writing of the Australian official history', p. 92.

117 Bean, 'The technique of a war historian', p. 76.

118 *Ibid.*, p. 77.

119 Samuel Hynes, *The Soldiers' Tale: Bearing Witness to Modern War* (New York, 1997); I discuss in detail Hynes's ideas and personal narratives in ch. 4.

120 John North, *Gallipoli: The Fading Vision* (London, 1936), p. 19.

121 Robert Rhodes James, *Gallipoli* (London, 1965), p. 351.

122 Quoted in Winter (ed.), *Making the Legend*, p. 15.

123 Gerster, *Big Noting*, p. 66.

124 K. S. Inglis, Introduction to 1980 edition of *The Story of Anzac*, published by University of Queensland Press, 1, p. xxxvii.

125 Bean, *The Story of Anzac*, 1, p. 174.

126 *Ibid.*, ch. 9; and *The Story of Anzac*, 2, p. 764.

127 Bean, *The Story of Anzac*, 2, p. 909.

128 Bean, *The Story of Anzac*, 1, p. lxvi.

129 A. J. Hill, Introduction to 1980 edition of *The Story of Anzac*, published by University of Queensland Press, 2, p. xxvii.

130 For example, the discovery of Sergeant Larkin's apparently savagely slashed body: Bean, *The Story of Anzac*, 1, p. 421.

131 Inglis's Introduction in *ibid.*, p. xxxv.

132 Thomson, ' "Steadfast until death" ', p. 467.

133 *Ibid.*, pp. 465–6.

134 Bean, *The Story of Anzac*, 2, p. 90.

135 Bean to Murdoch, 1 November 1921, Bean Papers, AWM38 3DRL 6673, item 2.

136 Daniel, 'Historical Section', 12 July 1922, p. 20, PRO, CAB 103/82.

137 Daniel to Cecil Longhurst, 10 January 1939, PRO, CAB 103/102.

138 Lieutenant General Sir Gerald Ellison, KCB, KCMG, *The Perils of Amateur Strategy as Exemplified by the Attack on the Dardanelles Fortress in 1915* (London, 1926), p. 34; and Note by Lt-General Sir Gerald Ellison on the history of the campaign, undated, PRO, CAB 45/238.

139 These details are from County Record Office, Newport, Isle of Wight, Aspinall-Oglander Papers, and from his *Times*, 25 May 1959, obituary.

140 C. F. Aspinall-Oglander, *Roger Keyes* (London, 1951).

141 'Our best dressed general', *Daily Sketch*, 26 April 1929, Aspinall-Oglander Papers, Press cuttings.

142 Hamilton to Aspinall, 22 November 1932, Aspinall-Oglander Papers, OG 111.

143 Hand-written note by Aspinall, the text of which indicates that it was written in 1927: Aspinall-Oglander Papers, OG 112.

144 Aspinall-Oglander, *Military Operations*, 1, p. 198.

145 *Ibid.*, pp. viii–ix.

146 Letter fragment from Edmonds to Aspinall (undated), Aspinall-Oglander Papers, OG 111.

147 Edmonds to Aspinall, 2 April 1928, Aspinall-Oglander Papers, OG 114.

148 Extract from War Office letter quoted by Daniel in 'Report on the work of the Historical Section. Report by the secretary', 15 February 1928, p. 9, PRO, CAB 16/52.

149 Aspinall-Oglander to Liddell Hart, 31 December 1957, LHCMA, Liddell Hart Papers, LH 1/23/5.

150 Proceedings of meeting, i.e. Sub-Committee for the Control of the Official Histories, COH 5, 9 March 1928, p. 6, PRO, CAB 16/53.

151 *Ibid.*, p. 1.

152 *Ibid.*, pp. 12–13.

153 H. J. Creedy to the secretary, Historical Section [Daniel], 23 February 1929, Churchill College Archives, Cambridge, Churchill Papers, CHAR 2/164/9 and 10; Aspinall-Oglander to Churchill, 23 November 1931, Churchill Papers, CHAR 2/177/72.

154 Cyril Falls, *War Books* (London, 1989 [1930]), p. 3.

155 Travers, *Killing Ground*, ch. 8.

156 Aspinall-Oglander, *Military Operations*, 1, p. 185.

157 Gaselee to Aspinall, 14 October 1931, Aspinall-Oglander Papers, OG 112.

158 Robin Prior, 'The Suvla Bay tea-party: a reassessment', *Journal of the Australian War Memorial*, 7 (October 1985), pp. 25–34.

159 *Ibid.*, p. 33.

160 Aspinall-Oglander, *Military Operations*, 2, p. 5.

161 Aspinall-Oglander, *Military Operations*, 1, p. 353.

162 Extract from Foreign Office letter, copy, 26 April 1927, probably from Stephen Gaselee, the Foreign Office librarian: Aspinall-Oglander Papers, OG 111.

163 Gaselee to Daniel, private, 28 July 1927, Aspinall-Oglander Papers. OG 111.

164 Aspinall-Oglander, *Military Operations*, 2, p. 479.

165 *Ibid.*, 1, p. v.

166 *Ibid.*, 2, p. v.

167 *Ibid.*, p. 486.

168 Orlo Williams, 'The Gallipoli tragedy: part I', *The Nineteenth Century and After*, 106 (July–December 1929), p. 85.

169 'Official history vol. II, comments by Hamilton on chs i–vi', p. 1, LHCMA, Hamilton Papers, 7/9/15. It is a clever overstatement to start referring to Turkey as a 'vast military Empire'.

170 Hand-written opening of chapter on Suvla in Aspinall's handwriting (undated): Aspinall-Oglander Papers, OG 116.

171 Liddell Hart to Aspinall-Oglander, 1 January 1958, Liddell Hart Papers, LH 1/23/7.

172 Aspinall-Oglander, *Military Operations*, 1, p. 173.

173 *Ibid.*, p. 232; this may be a reference to Herodotus's description of the angry order issued by Xerxes that the Hellespont should be struck with a whip 300 times.

174 Hand-written note by Aspinall, the text of which indicates that it was written in 1927: Aspinall-Oglander Papers, OG 112.

175 *Ibid.*

176 Alistair Thomson, ' "The vilest libel of the war"? Imperial politics and the official histories of Gallipoli', *Australian Historical Studies*, 25:101 (October 1993), p. 635; correspondence regarding this controversy is to be found in Bean's Papers, AWM 38 3DRL 7953, items 27 and 29.

177 Bean, *The Story of Anzac*, 1, p. lxv.

178 'Report on work of Historical Section, 1st December 1927 to 30th November 1928', PRO, CAB 103/6, p. 4.

179 'Report on work of Historical Section (Military Branch) 1st December 1930 to 30th November 1931', PRO, CAB 103/9.

180 'Report on work of Historical Section (Military Branch) 1st December 1931–30th November 1932', PRO, CAB 103/9.

181 Bean to Aspinall-Oglander, 3 October 1932, Aspinall-Oglander Papers, OG 111 (my emphasis).

182 The Kirke Committee and the influence of its reports are briefly discussed by David French, 'Sir James Edmonds and the official history: France and Belgium', pp. 84–5.

183 Hand-written note by Aspinall, the text of which indicates that it was written in 1927: Aspinall-Oglander Papers, OG 112.

3

The journalists' response:
Ellis Ashmead-Bartlett and
C. E. W. Bean

Australia's official historian Charles Bean worked throughout the war as an official war correspondent. His British counterpart at Gallipoli was the highly experienced Ellis Ashmead-Bartlett. Their position as war correspondents was an anomalous one. They were at once part of the official machine and observers of it. Their job was to convey only what the armed forces wished the public to know about the current military situation, while describing the experience of that situation for the public. Their narratives bridge the gap between what could be produced under the official imprint and what was later produced by other individuals recounting their experiences on their own terms. The journalists' response can therefore be seen as a transitional work which lies between the official responses and the soldiers' tale.

Through a focus on Ashmead-Bartlett in comparison to Bean, this chapter considers the nature of the journalists' response. It explores also the tensions generated by the anomalous quasi-independent role of the journalist by tracing Ashmead-Bartlett's resistance to becoming an arm of government.

The journalists at Gallipoli

Journalists were made unusually welcome during the Gallipoli campaign. They owed their good fortune in this to General Sir Ian Hamilton's belief that the public at large should be kept informed about the war. Ellis Ashmead-Bartlett, chosen by the Newspaper Proprietors' Association to represent the London press, was therefore among at least fifteen men who filed journalistic dispatches from Gallipoli. He was one of three correspondents accompanying the MEF in April 1915. Ashmead-Bartlett travelled from London with the myopic Lester Lawrence,[1] the Reuters representative, who was the only correspondent to witness both evacuations at Gallipoli; unfortunately, however, he was inexperienced as a war correspondent.[2] Bean, an Australian educated in England who had been working for the *Sydney Morning Herald*, won the nomination of the Australian Journalists' Association to be the country's official representative. He was the only correspondent to be present for the duration of the campaign, staying with the AIF throughout the war. Malcolm Ross, New Zealand's official representative, arrived at Anzac in June and remained there until December, when he left during the evacuation suffering from typhoid fever. He, like Bean, was held in high regard.[3] Compton Mackenzie, the novelist turned staff officer, filed several articles in June during Ashmead-Bartlett's brief return to London.

From 14 July these men were joined by Henry Nevinson, an experienced and highly respected journalist representing the Provincial Press, Herbert Russell, acting for Reuters, and Sydney Moseley, for the Central News.[4] These last two remained on the peninsula little more than a month, leaving by 19 August.[5] Sydney Moseley seems to have been an unpopular character at Gallipoli. Ashmead-Bartlett referred to him on his arrival as 'a terrible Jew boy'.[6] Hamilton's report described him as 'unfitted to associate on terms of social equality with officers or his fellow correspondents. The latter very strongly resented his presence in their camp . . . He has no knowledge of military matters, and the few dispatches he did write while here were partly direct falsehoods.'[7] Moseley went on to write a strongly pro-Hamilton book, *The Truth About the Dardanelles*.[8] Hamilton, recognising an ally, later wrote to apologise and confide that he had been misinformed about Moseley and had therefore written to the War Office to correct matters. This is revealed in a subsequent book, *The Truth About a Journalist*, which also strongly defended Hamilton and criticised Ashmead-Bartlett's 'private vendetta' against the commander.[9] Keith Murdoch, who had come second in the ballot to elect the Australian representative, made his brief but ultimately significant visit to the peninsula in September.

In addition to these, Major Oliver Hogue, writing as 'Trooper Bluegum', submitted articles to the censor in Australia, describing his experiences with the light horse in Gallipoli and Palestine.[10] Similarly, Private Arthur Godsman of the 2nd Highland Field Ambulance, formerly a reporter for the *Aberdeen Daily Journal* and the *Evening Express*, sent home via the censor at least one account of his experiences;[11] H. E. Yarra also sent several accounts of fighting to the Brisbane *Patriot* before the censors stopped this.[12] A. B. 'Banjo' Paterson, a veteran reporter of the Boer War, filed reports for the *Sydney Morning Herald* from Egypt. Phillip Schuler of the Melbourne *Age* and C. P. Smith of the Melbourne *Argus* were also based in Egypt but managed to visit the peninsula.[13] G. Ward Price, Ashmead-Bartlett's ultimate replacement as the representative of the Newspaper Proprietors' Association,[14] filed at least one dispatch from the Dardanelles in the latter stages of the campaign.[15] No Frenchman was authorised to act as correspondent.[16]

Ashmead-Bartlett's character and career

The British war correspondent Ellis Ashmead-Bartlett (1881–1931) was the first journalist to describe the landing of the Australians and New Zealanders at Gallipoli. He has been credited with thereby establishing the foundations of the Anzac legend,[17] but he was also the most trenchant critic of the campaign. Before the land campaign was one month old his independent-minded and pessimistic attitude had brought him into conflict with Hamilton and his staff. Charles Bean provides a contrast in personality, attitude and work: he was a diligent and conservative man, where Bartlett was conceited and rebellious. Bean is well respected as a reliable witness of the Gallipoli campaign, but his journalistic work has been overshadowed by his achievements as Australia's official historian of the First World War. Even while he was on the peninsula Bean had one eye on the long-term portrayal of the campaign, and this may have had an effect on his dispatches. This chapter focuses on the now less well known Ashmead-Bartlett, exploring his reliability as a witness, his relations with the censors, and the style and emphases of his work.

Ashmead-Bartlett was a charismatic man, brilliant in conversation, but also cantankerous and egotistical. Bean described Bartlett and his recollections of his early life thus:

> He is a chap with an exceedingly nice nature but vilely brought up in the sort of wild selfish third rate society that surrounded his father. He frankly tells you that his mother and father were unsuited – that his mother, though always very kind to him, would have irritated anybody she lived with. He hated his school days at Marlborough – and the compulsory cricket and football, and his schoolmasters – almost every one of them, and their families. The only part he looks back on with pleasure is his active rebellion – as when he and a friend exploded 10 lbs. of mine powder on a neighbouring hilltop during the solemn procession of the masters and their wives and families to chapel.[18]

His conceit is apparent in his diary comment on his departure from the campaign: 'All were genuinely upset at my departure. Poor devils. They will have a poor time now that I have gone. At least I have fought for their rights and but for me they would have been completely crushed beneath the iron heel.'[19] As this comment shows, he saw his role at Gallipoli as a battle against the staff, a struggle to resist being drawn entirely into the official purview. By contrast, Bean wrote to the Australian Secretary of Defence: 'Our Staff has stood by me splendidly in this and I do not think that I have written a word that has caused them a moment's anxiety – which is really the achievement I am proudest of.'[20]

Ashmead-Bartlett was 34 in 1915. He was tall (5 ft 10 in) and slim with grey eyes and fair hair.[21] He had first witnessed war at the age of 16 when he accompanied his father Sir Ellis Ashmead-Bartlett, former civil lord of the Admiralty, as a guest of the Sultan during the Graeco-Turkish War. Ashmead-Bartlett junior fought in the South African War and first worked as a war correspondent during the Russo-Japanese War. He was attached to the French Army during the Moroccan campaign of 1907 and returned to Morocco in 1909 for Reuters, accompanying the Spanish Army. He achieved major scoops in his next three assignments: with the Italian Army in Tripoli in 1910; and for the *Daily Telegraph* during the First Balkan War, in 1912, and the Second Balkan War in 1913. At the outbreak of the First World War he was on an assignment for the *Telegraph* with the Austrians fighting the Serbs. Prior to the Dardanelles expedition he had accompanied the armies of Britain, France and Belgium at the Western Front.[22]

In 1910 he had twice contested parliamentary seats, and was eventually elected Conservative MP for North Hammersmith in 1924. He resigned his seat when he was declared bankrupt in 1926. He had previously faced insolvency in December 1914,[23] no doubt as a consequence of his extravagant lifestyle – even while in the eastern Mediterranean he ensured that he had a supply of champagne.[24] Nevinson described his style thus:

> About him hung an atmosphere of magnificence that often astonished me, as when, among the rocks of that savage island, among the pigs and sheep that infested our camp searching for the last leaves and grapes of summer in a vineyard hard by, he would issue from his elaborately furnished tent dressed in a flowing robe of yellow silk shot with crimson, and call for breakfast as though the Carlton were still his corporeal home.[25]

His cash-flow problems, exacerbated by ill-health after his return from the campaign, explain some of his behaviour, and are one reason why his activities and opinions should be treated with caution.

During the campaign Bartlett had made the suggestion that the Turks should be offered ten shillings and a free pardon to encourage them to desert. In response Hamilton wondered to himself 'what would Ashmead-Bartlett himself do if he were offered ten shillings and a good supper by a Mahommedan when he was feeling a bit hungry and hard-up among the Christians.'[26] Ashmead-Bartlett was certainly keen to maximise his financial gain from his involvement in the campaign. In addition to his primary task of writing dispatches, for which he was paid £2,000 per annum,[27] Ashmead-Bartlett took photographs that were widely published, particularly in May 1915, and for which he was presumably paid.[28] An admitted inability on his part to 'draw a line . . . either straight or crooked' did not prevent him responding positively to a request from an editor for sketches of interesting scenes at Gallipoli.[29] During his brief return to London, in June 1915, he asked for a salary rise from the Newspaper Proprietors' Association,[30] he signed a deal for a book on the expedition with an advance of £500 and the promise of a large royalty,[31] and he agreed to a 45 per cent share of the profit from the film he planned.[32] Once he had returned for good from the campaign he signed a lecturing deal with Jack White, manager of Thomas Beecham, and the Berry brothers, proprietors of *The Sunday Times*, entailing twenty-five lectures for a fee of £100 per lecture, with an option on a further seventy-five lectures;[33] one of his letters suggests that this deal was worth £10,000.[34] After an abortive lecture tour of America, he went on to lecture in Australia, agreeing with J. and N. Tait to give twenty-five two-hour lectures at £100 each.[35] While he was in Australia, he agreed to sell his papers on Gallipoli to the Mitchell Library in Sydney for £200–£300.[36]

Ashmead-Bartlett published three books featuring the Gallipoli campaign. *Ashmead-Bartlett's Despatches from the Dardanelles: An Epic of Heroism*, brought out swiftly, reprinted his articles covering the period prior to the Suvla landings.[37] *Some of My Experiences in the Great War* also reproduced some of his journalistic work. This volume, written during the war, contained one chapter on Gallipoli describing general scenes on the beaches and in the trenches.[38] His most important book came out ten years later. *The Uncensored Dardanelles* (1928)[39] was a highly critical work which had been planned even while Bartlett was at Gallipoli. One of his letters discussed a deal with the publisher Sir George

Hutchinson; he was being pressed to bring something out swiftly, but Bartlett argued:

> Now if I am given time I am convinced I can produce a work which will have a far greater sale than one which would merely be more or less of a rehash of what has already appeared in the Press. The subject is too vast and too great to spoil by over haste. I will stake my opinion against the most astute publisher that the interest in this expedition will last for years and years and that its conduct will arouse more bitter controversies than any other event in English History for several centuries. It will be the really authoritative book which will have the big and permanent sale and not one produced red hot like the generality of war books. This is outside their pail [*sic*] altogether. In the first place I have been allowed to see everything and I know every detail of what has taken place and until one is allowed to make the book really interesting by the publication of all those thousand details which no censor would allow at the present time it would hardly be worth while publishing it at all.[40]

The book enabled Ashmead-Bartlett to express his opinions on the strategy and tactics of the Dardanelles campaign – something that had not been permitted in his wartime dispatches. In *The Uncensored Dardanelles*, Bartlett argued that the idea of capturing Constantinople was a brilliant one, but that Hamilton's faulty strategy and tactics had brought on failure, despite the most heroic efforts of his force. Many of his criticisms are well founded – save perhaps for his oft-repeated assertion that Hamilton should have attacked at Bulair at the neck of the peninsula.[41] Cyril Falls, a veteran of the Western Front and a well-regarded historian, commented that the book was

> chiefly interesting as an explanation of the prejudice and distrust which soldiers cannot avoid when they have to do with war correspondents of a certain type. It also illustrates to what follies vanity and cocksureness may lead a man in the position wherein Mr Ashmead-Bartlett found himself, even when that man is strikingly able, a clear writer, and an experienced war correspondent.[42]

Moreover, it should be considered that were an author to attempt to construct an argument most likely to please readers and maximise his sales, he would do well to avoid an attack on the overall plan of the campaign while emphasising the heroism of those involved, providing a recognisable scapegoat and presenting an alternative route to victory. Fewster, similarly, has suggested that Bartlett changed his lecture rhetoric, becoming more optimistic and praiseful of the Anzacs and of the campaign in Australia, in order to attract a larger audience.[43] Furthermore, the possibility must be considered that it suited Bartlett throughout to make the Dardanelles campaign important, for that made its most able witness important and valuable too. Contemporaries certainly suggested as much: Moseley repeated a statement from the publication *Truth* commenting on the 'great personal profit and kudos' gained from the campaign by Bartlett.[44]

There is a further difficulty in relying on Ashmead-Bartlett as a witness, in particular in using his private papers as supplementary evidence to his published work. Bartlett lost all his papers when the *Majestic* sank on the night of 26–27 May 1915. Therefore his accounts of the early stages of the campaign, including what purports to be a daily diary, were actually written at a later date. At the Dardanelles Commission, he claimed that he wrote up the diary entries immediately using his initial notes from a little notebook, presumably on his journey back to London; he accepted only that his recollection of conversations might not be verbatim.[45] However, some of Ashmead-Bartlett's diary comments show a remarkable and dubious prescience. It is possible that he doubted the campaign's chances from the beginning, but not that he could have foreseen, as he alleges, the nature of the campaign's difficulties to such an exact extent that he could warn Hamilton on 22 April, three days before the first landings: 'General, the task ahead is one of the most difficult that has ever been undertaken, and the Expedition can only succeed if you have sufficient troops to push right inland at the start, and if the Government keep you well supplied with reinforcements.'[46] Hamilton claimed that this warning was never made and that Bartlett had written it weeks later.[47] Similarly, did Bartlett actually wonder as early as 2 May 'whether Sir Ian Hamilton would really face the true facts and let the Government know the real state of affairs'?[48] Perhaps most telling is the lack of mistaken predictions among his forecasts. However, this is not to say that Ashmead-Bartlett made no forecasts at all during the campaign. In fact, his pessimistic pronouncements were so widely known that he was likened to Jeremiah, Jonah and Cassandra; he was rebuked by Braithwaite; and, according to Mackenzie, staff officers at Helles on one occasion hid behind rocks so as to avoid lunching in his disagreeable company.[49] Nonetheless, in retrospect, Bartlett's contemporaneous criticisms and predictions seem well placed. His 'diary' and other papers are here used in conjunction with articles published under his by-line in the *Daily Telegraph* and reproduced elsewhere.[50]

Ashmead-Bartlett's articles are valuable sources. Their authenticity is not affected by the sinking of HMS *Majestic*, nor do his financial problems impinge here. He perhaps sought to make his articles as interesting and graphic as possible, but this is a normal journalistic pursuit. His reports of the campaign are by far the best of those featured in the *Telegraph*. Their descriptions are powerful, their narratives engaging; they do not make wild claims of progress as do those by some 'special correspondents', nor are they vague and bland as the official dispatches are. The greatest difficulty in relying on them as evidence is that they were seriously affected by censorship. Yet it seems that although Bartlett was prevented from fully expressing his pessimism, he was taken as being one of the most reliable sources of information. His writings contained truth, but not the whole truth. For example, in August, *The Globe* condemned the effects of censorship and relied on Ashmead-Bartlett to confirm the accuracy of other reports:

> There is nothing in . . . [Ashmead-Bartlett's] dispatch which gives the least confirmation to the optimistic narrative whose publication was authorised by the Press Bureau at the beginning of the week. If the Turks in the Gallipoli peninsula have been cut off the official Eye-Witness knows nothing of the fact. When the rosy narrative appeared we expressed a strong opinion that nothing of the kind ought to be authorised unless there were good grounds for believing it to be true. We regret to be compelled to repeat that observation with added emphasis. The public has been buoyed up by exaggeration, and the disappointment and reaction are to-day proportionately great. Why should the Press Bureau pass falsehoods when they are agreeable, and suppress the truth when it is not?[51]

Bean, however, struck a note of caution in his diary: 'He's perhaps not quite so accurate in detail as the English papers think him, but he is most honest in giving the real outline and trend of events.'[52]

The influence of Ashmead-Bartlett's dispatches

The attention given to war correspondents by politicians, generals and censors is indicative of the formers' potential power. Information flowing from the peninsula – for example, Hamilton's public and private dispatches – affected both policy and public perceptions of the expedition. Before considering the official limitations placed on the flow of information from the journalists, I look at the nature of the journalists' work that did reach the public. These dispatches were important in shaping public perceptions of the expedition. Elements of the Anzac legend and the heroic–romantic myth can be seen in them. A comparison of Bean's and Bartlett's response to the Anzac landings provides an ideal opportunity for contrasting the work of these two men and for tracing its impact on subsequent accounts of the event.

The first news of the landing came on 27 April with the publication of the previous evening's War Office announcement that a 'completely successful' landing had occurred.[53] Over the following ten days further reports and official dispatches were published, the details of which tended to be scant, some of them wildly inaccurate; for example, a special correspondent's report of 29 April from Athens said that Allied troops had advanced twenty miles from their landing-point at Enos.[54] The first detailed, descriptive account was Ashmead-Bartlett's. His article appeared in the *Daily Telegraph* on 7 May.[55] He had submitted his cables to be censored on 27 April, and was happy to learn two days later that Lawrence had yet to submit any cables of his own. Frustratingly, however, Bartlett's cables were held up by General Hamilton's official dispatches, which took precedence.[56] The British authorities in Alexandria held up Bean's account until 13 May. It was published in the *Commonwealth of Australia Gazette* on 17 May.[57] The potential influence of Bartlett's and Bean's accounts of the landing was recognised and reinforced by the swift decision of the New South Wales Department of Public Instruction to publish them, in edited form, as a pamphlet on 18 May 1915.[58]

The two accounts demonstrate the strengths that were to mark out each writer's work. Bartlett's is dramatic and vivid; Bean's the more detailed and careful. Bartlett is particularly effective in building tension as the expedition gets under way and the 'twelve snakes of boats' slowly steam past:

> Every eye was fixed on that grim-looking line of hills in our front, so shape-less, yet so menacing in the gloom, the mysteries of which those in the boats, which looked so tiny and helpless, were about to solve. Yet for some time, not a sound and not a light was heard or seen; it appeared as if the enemy had been completely surprised, and that we would get ashore without opposition.[59]

He makes the beginning of the fighting sound more spontaneous and adventurous than does Bean:

> It was a trying moment, but the Australian volunteers rose as a man to the occasion. They waited neither for orders or for the boats to reach the beach, but springing out into the sea, they waded ashore, and, forming some sort of rough line, rushed straight on the flashes of the enemy's rifles.
>
> Their magazines were not even charged, so they just went in with cold

steel, and I believe I am right in saying that the first Ottoman Turk since the last crusade received an Anglo-Saxon bayonet in him at five minutes after five a.m. on April 25.

Typically, Bean explains the reason why they began to fight in this way:

So far not a shot had been fired by the enemy. Colonel McLagan's orders to his brigade were that shots, if possible were not to be fired till daybreak, but the business was to be carried through with the bayonet. The men leapt into the water, and the first of them had just reached the beach when fire was opened on them from the trenches on the foothills which rise immediately from the beach.

Bean interrupts the flow of his narrative to detail the topography of the area, likening it to the Hawkesbury River country in New South Wales; Bartlett relies on a more vivid description, accessible to all readers, to convey the challenging landscape. He describes how this landscape is ideal for snipers and how adept the Australians and New Zealanders are at this kind of warfare, which requires great endurance and individuality. Such praise is typical of Bartlett's report. He is able to create memorable and insightful phrases – for example, 'a race of athletes' hits on a theme to be found throughout writings on the Anzacs: their magnificent physiques. In writing 'they were happy because they knew they had been tried for the first time in the war and had not been found wanting' he encapsulates an important reason for Gallipoli's power and impact. There had been a secret fear that Australians wouldn't be good enough,[60] but that had now been categorically disproved. Bartlett went on to award the ultimate accolade at this stage in the war: 'These raw colonial troops in those desperate hours proved worthy to fight side by side with the heroes of Mons and the Aisne, Ypres, and Neuve Chapelle.' By contrast, Bean's comparison is weaker. As an inexperienced war correspondent he could only draw upon his knowledge of military history to link the operation to the battle of the Heights of Abraham in 1759.

Some of the hallmarks of Bean's writing are apparent in this early article. One such is his tendency to identify particular men and incidents. Early in his account he describes the origins of a brigade to have been largely those of miners from the Broken Hill and Westralian gold-fields, but perhaps in this case Bartlett's similar point that these were 'men who six months ago were living peaceful civilian lives' is the more powerful: he makes them Everyman. However, Bean's specificity comes into its own later in his account. When he describes the brave and inspiring actions of one officer, he focuses on the individual moment and makes the expe-

rience real and comprehensible. From this example he is able to extrap-
olate to the general moral point that his life has not been wasted. Huge
losses are justified, therefore, through a personal example: 'It would be
absurd to pretend that the life of an officer like that one was wasted. No
one knows how long his example will live on amongst men.' Bean's
descriptions of the fighting, in this article as also later, are particularly
effective and evocative. However, as Fewster points out,[61] the most
important facet of Bean's work, a stress upon the nature of the Australian
character, had not yet developed.

Those details which were left out of the articles are also important.
Evacuation had been seriously considered during the course of the night,
and Bartlett knew this but did not mention how close to disaster the
landing came. Similarly, both Bean and Bartlett refer only briefly to
the wounded; their numbers are not detailed and the hard work of the
stretcher-bearers is instead emphasised. In particular, Bartlett points to
the high spirits of the wounded. Yet what seems to have been a draft of
Bartlett's dispatch contained scathing criticism:

> As usual the medical arrangements were awful, and terribly mismanaged,
> and the accommodation on the two Hospital Ships speedily gave out. There
> seemed to be no-one in supreme authority to direct the boats full of
> wounded, for whom no accommodation could be found in the two
> Hospital Ships, to any of the now empty transports lying off the coast. It
> was a pathetic sight watching these lighters packed with the dead and
> dying and the maimed, being towed or rowed aimlessly round from ship
> to ship only to meet with the same reply 'we are full up'.[62]

It would not be accurate, however, to imply that Bartlett left out all the
difficult aspects of the operation. It may be impossible to ascertain from
his article the scale of casualties incurred, and the failure to achieve all
of the operation's aims is not mentioned – indeed the precise aims of the
operation are never explained, whether in terms of operational tactics or
of grand strategy. Yet Bartlett did not exaggerate the landing's achievement, and he concluded with the sobering note that siege warfare would
probably develop.

The strength of Ashmead-Bartlett's landing dispatch and the role of
the war correspondent in describing the nature and experience of a military event might be further illuminated through a comparison with the
commander's official dispatch. Sir Ian Hamilton's official account of
the landing was published on 7 July 1915.[63] This is a more detailed
account of the preparation and execution of the landing. It gives specific

information, detailing geographic features on the peninsula and naming units involved, and it gives some explanation of the tactics of the landing. It does include various explanations of the failures to push onwards and the following tacit admission of the failure of these early operations to achieve their goal: 'Hopes of getting a footing on Achi Baba had now perforce to be abandoned – at least for this occasion.' But, as is suggested by this statement, Hamilton's dispatch was rooted in optimistic expectation of progress, and it ends not with a warning, as Bartlett's does, but with salutes to the navy and to his commanders. It also contains some literary touches, including this attempt to emulate Ashmead-Bartlett's successful portrayal of the tension prior to the landing: 'The morning was absolutely still; there was no sign of life on the shore; a thin veil of mist hung motionless over the promontory; the surface of the sea was as smooth as glass.' That this and other such comments are unusual in an official dispatch are perhaps revealed through comparison with Admiral De Robeck's official dispatch, which contains only the usual details of the operation and commonplace tributes to its participants. The landing, for example, is described merely thus: 'At 4.20 a.m. the boats reached the beach and a landing was effected. The remainder of the infantry of the covering force were embarked at ten p.m., 24th.'[64]

Ashmead-Bartlett's account of the landing of 25 April 1915 was the most important dispatch from Gallipoli. Bean later wrote of it:

> [T]he despatch describing the Anzac landing electrified the world . . . it displayed the first terrible struggle on Gallipoli, and the qualities of the Australian and New Zealand soldiers, in one brilliant flash before the eyes of every nation and the world has never forgotten. Even today the tradition of the Anzac landing is probably more influenced by that story than by all the other accounts that have since been written . . . He was the first to impress on the world the main facts of the landing and the impression is still there.[65]

Bartlett won the race to tell this story and continued to outshine Bean throughout the campaign. Bean's reaction to the news that his work on the Anzac and Suvla evacuation could not be sent suggests that he felt this disappointment keenly:

> This was like an unexpected shrapnel shell in the pit of the stomach. The despatch on which I had poured out more care than anything of which I have written here – the only chance one has had of even attempting to rival Bartlett's work (which no man ever censored in this degree). However, the authorities are quite right.[66]

Kevin Fewster has pointed to Ashmead-Bartlett's dispatch in combination with his brief film of the campaign and his lecture tour as being instrumental in 'first shaping then institutionalizing a legend'.[67] It has been difficult for subsequent accounts of the landing to deviate from its heroic tone – witness the furore over Aspinall-Oglander's allegations of stragglers at the landing. Ashmead-Bartlett's dispatch was history's first rough draft.[68]

Accuracy, exaggeration and romance

Bean's dispatches were the rough draft of his history in a more literal sense. For example, his description of the bravery of two nonchalant stretcher-bearers in one of his despatches[69] is very close to his description of the same scene in the first volume of his official history.[70] His writing style was similar in both works and, like Bartlett's, was clearly the product of his working habits. Bean worked assiduously and meticulously, talking to as many frontline participants as he could. Ashmead-Bartlett was less likely to risk his life in this manner, preferring to stand back from the action and attain an overview of developments. Fewster, quoting a comment attributed to Bartlett, 'Oh – Bean – I think he almost counts the bullets!', compared the two men's approaches:

> The Englishman preferred to stand back and absorb the full scene – listen as the commanders expounded their strategy, watch it unfold and subsequently interview the wounded when they were returned to the ships. This approach gave his work a majestic broad sweep which Bean's stories sometimes lacked. Bartlett, at the same time, was more susceptible to error, often relying on hearsay where Bean usually could depend on his personal observations.[71]

That Bean's dispatches were based on personal observation gives a distinctive quality to his work, full of small details of the individuals who were 'our men'. Much of his description is written from the point of view of the frontline and includes even snippets of speech.[72] He was perhaps less likely than others to use the passive voice, an authorial technique which has the effect, according to Paul Fussell, of throwing a scene into 'merciful soft focus'.[73] Bean's work is more intimate and articulates the reality that otherwise can be concealed in grand phrasing and platitudes.

Although Bean had written in a cable that Bartlett's writing was 'thoroughly reliable', particularly in comparison to cables originating in the Greek islands,[74] privately, he was highly critical of Bartlett's tendency to exaggerate. While the latter did not make unfounded claims as to the achievements of the campaign overall, he did add some extra colour to his articles. Bartlett's description of the attack, on Sunday 8 August, by Maori soldiers at Anzac is a good example of this. He had received details of the attack from Malcolm Ross, the New Zealand correspondent. Bartlett's dispatch included this: 'Although few in numbers they closed on the Turks with fury using their rifles as clubs, swinging them round their heads and laying out several with each sweep.'[75] Bean wrote in his diary after Bartlett had left the peninsula:

> When Ross supplied him with an account of what the Maoris and N. Zealanders had done on Aug. 6–10 I was most surprised to see something about the Maoris advancing (apparently on Chunuk) using their clubbed rifles, knocking down 3 men at each blow. I knew it was not true of this attack – and I didn't believe it to be true of any – and I wondered at Ross writing in this way. I asked Ross and he told me as a matter of fact he had not written it. Bartlett had said to him afterwards: 'I say, I hope you didn't mind my inserting one or two things in your account – one or two things I heard from officers.' And that was it – Bartlett wouldn't invent a description like that. But he had heard something of the sort from some NZ officer and he inserted it without hesitation in a report which the article said he had received from Mr. Ross, the NZ Official Correspondent. Bartlett has a real regard for truth – and that is the astonishing part about him, that and his industry.[76]

When Bean had heard of a similar story he dealt with it in a much more cautious manner:

> It is said that one huge Queenslander swung his rifle by the muzzle, and, after braining one Turk, caught another and flung him over his shoulder. I do not know if this story is true, but when we landed some hours later, there was said to have been a dead Turk on the beach with his head smashed in.[77]

Bean was also critical of a description of the brief capture of Hill 70 by the dismounted British Yeomanry on 23 August. Bartlett wrote:

> It was now almost dark, and the attack seemed to hang fire when suddenly the Yeomanry leapt to their feet, and, as a single man, charged right up the hill. They were met by a withering fire, which rose to a crescendo as they neared the northern crest, but nothing could stop them.
>
> They charged at amazing speed, without a single halt from the bottom to the top, losing many men and many of their chosen leaders, including gallant Sir John Milbanke.
>
> It was a stirring sight, watched by thousands in the ever-gathering gloom . . . From a thousand lips a shout went up that Hill 70 was won.[78]

Bean commented:

> I can't write about bayonet charges like some of the correspondents do. Ashmead-Bartlett makes it a little difficult for one by his exaggerations, and yet he's a lover of the truth. He gives the spirit of the thing: but if he were asked: 'Did a shout really go up from a thousand throats that the hill was ours?' he'd have to say 'No, it didn't.' Or if they said 'Did the New Zealanders really club their rifles and kill three men at once?' or 'Did the first battle of Anzac really end with the flash of bayonets all along the line, a charge, and the rolling back of the Turkish attack,' he'd have to say 'Well, – no, as a matter of fact that didn't occur.' Well, I can't write that it occurred if I know it did not.[79]

As was the case later with his histories, Bean's achievement in avoiding overtly romantic descriptions attracted some criticism of his clinical style. In June 1915, the Sydney *Bulletin* complained of his dispatches: 'they don't serve the Australian who wanted the story of Australian arms to be written so that he could visualise it. The fact is he's too small for the job. It demanded a man able to make images with the vocabulary of a literary man and the eye of a photographic lens, and it got – a reporter.'[80] Melbourne's *Argus* and *Age* came close to discontinuing their use of Bean's work in September 1915,[81] and in April 1916 the *Argus* was still sniping about his work's lack of appropriate spirit.[82] However, as I said in chapter 2, Bean's original style and concerns, in particular his focus on the individual, had their own romantic effect in developing the Anzac legend.

In contrast to Bean's, Bartlett's writing style was closer to the usual romantic portrayal of war.[83] There are numerous examples of his vivid powers of description. One such refers to the action of 12 July:

> At the same moment, as if animated by a common will, the regiments of the brigade leapt from their trenches and surged forward towards the great redoubt and the network of saps and trenches. The whole scene resembled some picture from the Inferno, for our guns, shelling the works behind, made a great background of earth and smoke; whilst no sooner did our advance become apparent than the enemy's batteries, which had been keeping very quiet, opened upon our infantry with shrapnel and high explosives, smothering his own works which we were about to enter. The ground resembled a gigantic steaming cauldron, into whose thick vapours the gallant brigade poured without once hesitating or looking back. Individuals soon became swallowed up in the mist, and all you could see were black dots rushing about or jumping into the trenches with bayonets flashing in the shrouded sun amidst a continuous roar of musketry, which showed that the Turks were resisting valiantly.[84]

Ashmead-Bartlett had the ability to portray war as a dramatic and exciting event. He was also able to inject great pathos into his accounts, such as his description of 'a Colonial, an Englishman, a Maori, and a Gurkha all lying dead side by side',[85] who had died in the attempt to capture Chunuk Bair on 10 August. With writing such as this, doubtless bolstered by his exaggerations, Ashmead-Bartlett laid some of the groundwork for the heroic–romantic myth of Gallipoli. His tendency to include picturesque and historical features also contributed to the glamorous aura surrounding the campaign. It has already been seen in Bartlett's description of the Anzacs leaping from their boats that he was keen to frame the operation in terms of a modern-day crusade. Prior to the launch of the campaign, for example, he writes of restoring Constantinople's Saint Sofia to Christianity[86] and of avenging 'the chivalry of the Middle Ages'.[87] Such references lend the campaign an air of grandeur, placing the allies' actions in a historical continuum. He also compares operations to other great military feats, such as Wellington's Peninsular Campaign[88] and Wolfe at Quebec,[89] and the Turks (when they are fighting particularly stubbornly) to their predecessors under Osman at Plevna,[90] and thereby measures their achievement. Unlike many other commentators, however, he does not take the opportunity to link the campaign to its classical forerunners.

Another important element in the romantic atmosphere of Gallipoli was its beautiful setting and its rugged grandeur,[91] an exotic theatre different from the familiar dreary plains of North-Western Europe. He wrote of the surrounding islands sparkling 'like great jewels',[92] and of the 'reckless and beautiful profusion' of colourful wild flowers.[93]

Bartlett was careful, however, not to allow these picturesque descriptions to overpower his writing, and since, in most instances, they featured in pre-landing articles, they were probably included, at least in part, for the sake of filling out those pieces. He does, however, continue to praise the men's heroism and make historical comparisons throughout the campaign. A note in his papers explains what he considered to be the most effective style of writing for dispatches:

The great secret of all good discriptive [sic] writing is simplicity in style and in the language employed. At all costs avoid straing [sic] after effect. Try and write as if you were talking to some intimate friend who merely wished to hear what had happened. At except on very rare instances high flown picturesque sentences entirely destroy accounts of great events. They shake the reader's faith in the truth of the story and they fail to give him a correct idea of what happened.[94]

4 The beach at Anzac Cove, showing piled-up stores and boats landing

Such a contrast is evident when we turn to the novelist Compton Mackenzie. Mackenzie was on the staff at Gallipoli, and while Bartlett returned to London in June following the sinking of the *Majestic*, Hamilton asked the novelist to work as an eyewitness. Hamilton probably hoped to get a tamer eyewitness in Mackenzie – and to obviate the need for the difficult Ashmead-Bartlett to return. However, Bartlett did return, and Mackenzie refused to continue in this work.[95] Mackenzie's articles describe the scenes at Gallipoli in poetic language, dwelling for instance on the smoke of shell-bursts, and spending less time and detail in describing fighting actions, so that it is difficult to ascertain from his dispatches what has occurred. Both men recounted the loss of the *Majestic*. Mackenzie wrote:

> Among the transports and trawlers and various craft at anchor, a small green whale, all that is now visible of the Majestic, waited motionless upon the water. She was subsiding rapidly, they said: and already in the watery sunlight she gave the illusion of slowly assuming to herself the nature of the waves that splashed against her still rigid sides. Such a dream of a ship's transmigration to her own element vanished in the billows of dust ashore, vanished in that queer heartlessness of war that is really the desperate occupation of the mind with something to do and therefore no time to dream.[96]

In contrast, Bartlett, who had been personally affected by this sinking, was more matter of fact, stressing how old the ship was before describing its final end. The bracketed words are those the censor deleted, presumably to avoid distress:

> The final plunge was so sad but grand that for a few seconds you forgot about the large numbers of officers and men who were still clinging to her like limpets when she went down. [There was a great deal of cries and shouting as these unfortunates were precipitated into the water mixed up with the foam and steam. Many] Some were dragged down by the fatal nets before they could get clear others were probably killed inside by the explosion. Nevertheless the loss of life was small numbering only fifty.[97]

If Ashmead-Bartlett had allowed the picturesque and the romantic aspects of the campaign to overwhelm his articles, Hamilton might not have found him so objectionable. While Ashmead-Bartlett put a positive spin on events where it was feasible, he attempted to combine these with frank criticisms and observations. Take, for example, the following extract from an article assessing the achievements of the landing and the future prospects of the campaign:

> Those who in their ignorance of the true state of affairs on the Gallipoli peninsula expected a speedy and triumphant success will be disappointed, but those who have studied the lessons of modern warfare in France and Poland will at once realise that the Anglo-French armies have not only accomplished marvels considering their strength, but also that the soldiers of both nations in two weeks of continuous fighting have performed deeds which have never been surpassed in the history of either nation.
>
> It is only just that all false illusions as to the task before us should be cleared away, once and for all. Victories leading to decisive results can no more be gained in a day on the Gallipoli Peninsula than they can be in France or Belgium.[98]

Ashmead-Bartlett and censorship: phase one

The balance struck between making optimistic interpretations of events and criticising where necessary was the result of ongoing negotiations between the censors and the journalist. This quandary is at the heart of the quasi-independent situation of the journalist. The impact of the censors should therefore be explored.

During the campaign, the flow of information from the peninsula to Britain was very tightly controlled. This was contrary to early indications. Since the campaign was initially conceived as a naval attack, the question of press access came under the Admiralty's – and therefore Churchill's – authority. In contrast to Kitchener's obstructive attitude, Churchill allowed Lawrence, Ashmead-Bartlett, Bean and Ross to act as official reporters from the outset of the campaign.[99] Hamilton's attitude matched Churchill's. At their first meeting the commander was most friendly to Ashmead-Bartlett and explained to him that

> he thoroughly disapproved of the manner in which the public had been kept in the dark throughout the campaign, and that he was entirely in favour of having reputable war correspondents with the Army. He said that of course, this passage would have to be censored, but that he would see that nothing was taken out except that which came within the category of military secrets.[100]

Given the nature of the campaign, the censorship arrangements were complex. Since the campaign involved both naval and military operations, dispatches were subject both to the chief naval censor and to the War Office censors at the Press Bureau. In practice, it appears, the navy was broadly in charge of censorship in the early stages, while military involvement steadily grew. Ashmead-Bartlett was therefore initially censored by the navy.[101] Commodore Keyes was a benevolent censor who allowed Ashmead-Bartlett (to his surprise) to point out, for example, the extreme difficulties ahead following the failure of the naval attack of 18 March.[102] Bartlett's difficulties appear to have developed after GHQ took over control of censorship following the landing.[103]

The exact source of opposition to journalists' freedom is difficult to locate within the army at Gallipoli. The commander appears to have retained his benevolent view of the press at this point since it was his personal intervention that had secured Nevinson's employment at Gallipoli amid disagreement among editors and upheaval at the Admiralty.[104] Hamilton continued to make speeches of welcome – he spoke to Moseley upon his arrival, just as he had to Ashmead-Bartlett. Moseley suspected that it was Hamilton's subordinates who were the cause of the problems.[105] Ashmead-Bartlett had himself expected the censor, Maxwell, a former correspondent for the *Daily Mail*, to take a 'fiendish joy in cutting up my despatches', but he found these fears to be groundless.[106] However, N. P. Hiley identifies the commander as the source of Bartlett's difficulties. He suggests that Hamilton's understanding of press freedom was crucial: 'Hamilton carefully separated freedom of information from freedom of opinion, believing that the correspondents had no right to disagree with his optimistic interpretation of events.'[107] Again this points to the tension obtaining between the journalists' role as, on the one hand, official conduits of information and, on the other, interpreters of that information.

These tensions became overt in the aftermath of the second battle of Krithia of 6–8 May. Bartlett's account of the landing was published in the *Daily Telegraph* on 7 May. By that time reinforcements had arrived on the peninsula and the next great engagement was underway. The second battle of Krithia involved every nationality present on the peninsula in three days of frontal attacks from all along the allied lines at Helles. Almost 30 per cent of the total number of allied troops on the peninsula became casualties for a gain of about 600 yards.[108] This failure to take Krithia and Achi Baba signalled the end of the hope that the Gallipoli peninsula might be captured swiftly and cheaply.

It seems that Bartlett was forced to conceal his true opinion in reporting the attempt to capture Krithia, a battle he described grandly in his dispatch as the 'Battle of the Nations'.[109] It is apparent that the battle involved much terrible and furious fighting, but the wounded and the dying are not described, nor are the absolute exhaustion, the mutilating effect of gun-fire, pain, suffering, confusion, fear – all elements of the battle. In describing the attack in the early evening of the third day, for example, Bartlett writes of the infantry dashing forward with the sun glittering on their bayonets. He employs language to obscure some of the horror of the scene: the bullets 'patter' like gentle rain; men don't die in agonising pain but 'melt away'; the fusillade may be 'dreadful', but the fallen are replaced and the attack continues:

> They were met by a tornado of bullets, and were enfiladed by machine-guns from the right, and the artillery in vain endeavoured to keep down this fire.
>
> The manner in which these Dominion troops went forward will never be forgotten by those who witnessed it. The lines of infantry were enveloped in dust from the patter of countless bullets in the sandy soil and from the hail of shrapnel poured on them, for now the enemy's artillery concentrated furiously on the whole line.
>
> The lines advanced steadily as if on parade, sometimes doubling, sometimes walking, and you saw them melt away under this dreadful fusillade only to be renewed again as the reserves and supports moved forward to replace those who had fallen.

He concludes that considerable ground has been gained, though not the main objective, and that the men are determined not to budge; patience will be required to capture Achi Baba, and in the meantime 'our men have done everything mortal man can do'.

Despite such obfuscation Ashmead-Bartlett's dispatches were more informative and closer to reality than the pronouncements of Hamilton or the politicians. Kitchener's statement to the House of Lords, for example, was unduly positive:

> The handling [at Gallipoli] was a masterpiece of organisation, ingenuity and courage which will long be remembered. The progress of our troops is necessarily slow since the country is most difficult. But the Turks are gradually being forced to retire from positions of great strength, and though the enemy is being constantly reinforced, the news from this front is thoroughly satisfactory.[110]

Some newspapers noted the contrasting tone of the pronouncements on the battle: the *Pall Mall Gazette*, for instance, described Hamilton's official dispatch as 'more hopeful' than 'Mr Ashmead-Bartlett's vivid battle-picture'.[111] The discrepancy between Ashmead-Bartlett's account and the others demonstrates the importance of journalistic dispatches as a source of information. *Truth* noted:

> Mr Ashmead-Bartlett's illuminating dispatches from the Dardanelles are admirable supplements to the meagre reports which reach us from Sir Ian Hamilton. We now know, what was anticipated in *truth* from the first, that the process of clearing the Gallipoli Peninsula of Turkish troops will be a slow one.[112]

If the tone of Ashmead-Bartlett's dispatches was comparatively pessimistic, he was more outspoken still in private. He wrote in his diary of the late stages of the battle:

> I again went to the shore to watch the final stages of the attack on Achi Baba, which culminated in a final charge of both armies simultaneously that is the French and English at 5.30 p.m. Of course this ridiculous [*sic*] of conducting warfare except a further slaughter [*sic*], and by 6 o'clock we knew that the first stage of the campaign had definately [*sic*] failed, and that it would be impossible to make another move of any sort until the arrival of large reinforcements from home. This means that we are now settled to a great campaign in France and another of huge dimensions in the near East. We have voluntarily brought this on ourselves by attacking the Turks, when we would have done far better to have let them stew in their own juice until the grand settlement which must follow the termination of the War.[113]

What appears to be a draft for a chapter of a book is even more damning.[114] Bartlett describes the attack as being hopeless and desperate, 'an old-fashioned attack in which flesh and blood were pitted against entrenchments, barbed wire and concealed machine-gun positions, and [which] ended in failure as such attacks generally do'.[115] He quotes from Hamilton's dispatch of 26 August 1915 to demonstrate the commander's absurd logic and to condemn the continuation of the battle on 8 May:

> It is best therefore to quote his own words: 'The troops were now worn out. The new lines needed consolidating, it was certain that fresh reinforcements were reaching the Turks. Balancing the actual state of my own troops against the probable condition of the Turks, I decided to call upon the men to make one more push before the new enemy forces could get into touch with their surroundings.' Probably no more extraordinary statement has ever been written by a Commander in Chief, and his deductions seem to have been based on the inverse ratio to the facts. Note the three first statements. His troops were now worn out. His new lines needed consolidating. It was certain that fresh reinforcements were reaching the Turks. Thus there were three reasons which made the continuation of the attack both undesirable and even dangerous.[116]

He also notes that this battle was an attempt finally to reach the first day's objective, a point ignored by Hamilton in his dispatch. Indeed Hamilton's conclusion on this battle sounds complacent: 'for the first time I felt that we had planted a fairly firm foothold upon the point of the Gallipoli Peninsula'.[117] Bartlett further comments:

> Sir Ian Hamilton's statement is far from complete or satisfactory. He does not mention his real objectives, the village of Krithia and the mountain of Achi Baba, but it must be borne in mind that his despatch was written after the failure of all his efforts against these two positions, and that there is probably a natural desire to limit his objective when writing of a defeat, for by thus limiting his objective, he could make it appear to the authorities at home that he had accomplished all he set out to do.[118]

This is unfair. Hamilton had in fact sent a frank telegram to Kitchener on 8 May about the battle. Like Ashmead-Bartlett's differing accounts, Hamilton's demonstrates the gap between permissible public and private expression:

> The result of the operation has been failure, as my object remains unachieved. The fortifications and their machine-guns were too scientific and too strongly held to be rushed, although I had every available man in today. Our troops have done all that flesh and blood can do against semi-permanent works and they are not able to carry them. More and more munitions will be needed to do so. I fear that this is a very unpalatable conclusion, but I can see no way out of it.[119]

Bartlett later wrote of the impossibility of being able to fully express his opinions and knowledge of this episode:

> It is heartrending work having to write what I know to be untrue, and in the end having to confine myself to giving a descriptive account of the useless slaughter of thousands of my fellow countrymen for the benefit of the public at home, when what I wish to do is to tell the world the blunders that are being daily committed on this blood-stained Peninsula.[120]

The episode demonstrates both that Hamilton's dispatches were misleading and the restrictions placed on the expression of opinion of war correspondents in war. In his 1928 book *The Uncensored Dardanelles*, the embittered Ashmead-Bartlett created an official bulletin which could be applied to any of the attacks on Gallipoli (it is attributed to 15 July, but also seems in keeping with this earlier attack):

> After a concentrated bombardment our infantry advanced against the demoralised enemy and speedily captured four lines of trenches. We were on the verge of taking Achi Baba when unfortunately something (generally the French) gave way on our right, leaving us with an exposed flank. Our centre then had to retire, suffering heavy casualties. On our left something else gave way, and the enemy was unfortunately able to reoccupy his old positions. We are now back on the same line from which we started this morning. The enemy's counter-attacks were most gallantly repulsed with enormous losses. At least ten thousand of his dead are lying in front of our lines and it is reported that thirty thousand wounded have been evacuated to Constantinople. Our troops are much elated by their success, and declare themselves ready to attack again at any time. We have made a distinct advance of at least five yards in some places.[121]

How does Bartlett's experience of censorship compare with Bean's? The Australian certainly did not have the same difficulties; however, in addition to his conservative attitude to authority, his articles had entirely different priorities which did not lead him into conflict with the censor. He wrote in a letter protesting at the plan to move him, with the other correspondents, to Imbros:

> I have not attempted to sum up the general trend of the campaign except in one small reference to events already published in England long before. I do not know, I do not want to know and of course I have not attempted to touch on, even remotely, any possibilities as to future plans.
>
> The only news I could get at Imbros would be of a general character relating to the movements and plans of the whole force which are the interest of most correspondents but which I do not need and cannot obtain at

Anzac. The news which I cannot get at Imbros is the harmless details as to the life, scenes, bearing of men, which is what the nation that I represent wants to hear.[122]

Bean's freedom of movement had not been curtailed; nor was he alone in his attitude to authority. It seems that Ashmead-Bartlett's difficulties regarding censorship stemmed from his particular attitude to official control. Hiley, in studying war correspondents between 1914–16 both at Gallipoli and on Western Front, found Bartlett to be unique:

What Ashmead-Bartlett did which was of great importance, and which was unique among the official war correspondents, sprang from his conviction that he remained free to record his own impressions. Whatever his motives, he attempted to describe exactly what he saw and to report precisely what he felt, holding that this was not inconsistent with his official status, and the significance lies not in the influence that this may have had with politicians at home, but in the reactions of his fellow journalists. Remarkably they all agreed with the military that in performing this simple function he had gone beyond his rightful duties.[123]

Ashmead-Bartlett and censorship: phase two

The impact of Bartlett's unique attitude became particularly apparent from late May onwards. Such was his frustration at not being able to get the truth home that on 19 May he decided to submit an extremely frank letter to the press. He did not expect it to be passed by the censors – and it was not – but he wished to test how far the truth was being allowed to get home. He later wrote of this day in his diary:

I feel certain the Military Authorities out here are concealing the truth from the Authorities at home and that they will not tell them the real facts about the situation because they are afraid they will be withdrawn altogether and then good bye to KCBs KCMG and all the other damned Gs and Peerages they have in mind. But this is only plaing [*sic*] with a great question when the whole safety of your country is at stake. But our leaders in the field are very little men. That is the trouble.[124]

On 26 May he was told that it was impossible to send his letter home, 'Then I knew', wrote Bartlett, 'what was going on and became still further convinced that the truth was not known either in private or public circles at home.'[125] Bartlett's relations with Hamilton and Braithwaite became very strained. They were never to recover: witness the usually chivalrous Hamilton's conversation with Nevinson two months later. Nevinson recorded in his diary that he 'was asked in to Ian Hamilton alone. Very pleasant, but he ages. He burst out agst Bartlett very hot.'[126] Bartlett, in typically conceited fashion, later wrote in his diary, pinpointing the causes of the staff's animosity following his frank letter to the press, that they now realised three unforgivable things:

> Firstly that I had a perfectly clear conception of the extent of our so called success up to date. Secondly that I knew too much and disapproved of the strategy of the campaign and thirdly they saw for the first time that I was *not prepared to be an official eyewitness but was determined to remain an independent critic* who could not be got at in any one's interests.[127]

On the night of 26–27 May, the *Majestic* was torpedoed and sunk. In expectation of this, the crew had apparently been sure to make the best of the champagne and port on board the previous night. Ashmead-Bartlett lost all his possessions, including his papers, and therefore returned to London to re-equip himself. Hamilton's attempts to curtail Bartlett's activities continued when he cabled to the governor of Malta, Lord Methuen, to prevent Bartlett sending off any cables, since he was a 'Jeremiah'. Bartlett wrote: 'This confirmed my previously conceived opinion that the Staff were determined not to let the whole truth be known and that they dreaded above all else my return to England lest I should let the cat out of the bag.'[128] En route, Bartlett met two King's Messengers, Captain Stanley Wilson, MP, and Captain Somers Somerset; both men had apparently found Hamilton's staff similarly obstructive. Bartlett noted: 'It appears that although entrusted with His Majesty's most confidential despatches, the General Staff had evinced a very strong desire not to have them actually up to the front for fear they would return home and tell the truth about the real state of affairs.'[129]

It was possibly these two officers who persuaded Bartlett to write a memorandum to Prime Minister Asquith, explaining the situation in Gallipoli. In it he recounted how close disaster had been on 25 April and the difficulty of the present situation. He wrote that further progress would be impossible without at least another five divisions. He also touched on the problems regarding the flow of information: 'very erroneous reports', he said, had appeared in the press.

> These statements and many others have been allowed by the Censor at home to appear in the papers, thus hopelessly misleading the public and rendering the subsequent disappointment all the more keen. It is surely one of the first duties of a Censor to stop these ridiculous and ludicrous lies, as it is for him to suppress the truth when he considers it might be harmful.

As a matter of sober fact, the Allies are only a few hundred yards further onward than they were three days after the landing.[130]

When he met Asquith, Bartlett was asked to summarise this memorandum so that it might be presented to the Cabinet.[131] Bartlett also engaged in a vigorous round of breakfast, lunch and dinner meetings, at which he explained the situation in Gallipoli as he saw it to Dardanelles committee members, Sir Edward Carson, Andrew Bonar Law and Arthur Balfour; to the permanent secretaries of the War Office and Admiralty, Sir Reginald Brade and Sir William Graham Greene; to General Callwell, the director-general of military operations; to Harry Lawson, proprietor of the *Daily Telegraph* and chairman of the Newspaper Proprietors' Association; and to Winston Churchill. He wrote that he had taken care not to be used in the political intrigues of the day, but his actions would have inevitably involved him in them.[132] Bartlett also met Colonel Repington, the military correspondent of *The Times* who had revealed the shells' scandal in May. He took care not to feed him information that would generate a further scandal.[133] Perhaps he was wrong not to produce something similar to Repington's famous scoop; Compton Mackenzie certainly felt that Ashmead-Bartlett had wasted his opportunity, wrongly stressing his pet strategic plan of Bulair to those in authority when he should have repeated the call for 'guns and shells'.[134]

Hamilton had objected to Ashmead-Bartlett's return to London in the middle of operations, but hoped to turn it to his advantage by requesting that 'some more cheerful correspondent should be sent in his place'.[135] However, since Ashmead-Bartlett represented the entire London press, it would have been necessary for Hamilton to have provided a more 'definite objection' than his vague assertions of pessimism in order to prevent Ashmead-Bartlett's return.[136] Ashmead-Bartlett was therefore allowed to return to Gallipoli. Arriving on 25 June, he received a frosty reception:

> On arriving at GHQ I was seen by the Chief of Staff who at once began to abuse me because he said it had been brought to his notice that I had openly criticised the conduct of the campaign about the camp. He said that as a private individual I might hold what views I liked but that *as a War Correspondent I had no right to any except those which were officially given me.* This is a new aspect of the case. He said it was a grave offensive [*sic*] to criticise the conduct of the campaign as it destroyed the morale of the army. I denied ever having done so in public which is perfectly true although in the course of private conversations I might have said something. Certainly I have never said a word to any officer in the front line having returned a stock answer to all requests for information namely 'That the Government

were absolutely united and were sending out large reinforcements'. What really amuses me is the fact that the people who really criticise the campaign are the members of the Headquarters Staff itself. They are always coming to me with some fresh complaint. The Chief of the Staff said anyone who criticised them would be sent straight home an empty threat which was quite lost on me because it is their not in their interests [*sic*] to let anyone home at present.[137]

Hamilton continued to attack Ashmead-Bartlett's position. He seized the chance to allow more correspondents to report from Gallipoli. The arrival of Nevinson, Russell and Moseley on 14 July signalled the dilution of Bartlett's influence. In late June, as referred to above, the correspondents were herded into a single camp at Imbros as a means of controlling Ashmead-Bartlett, but the reliable Bean and Ross were allowed to roam freely as before.[138] In August, with the arrival of Major Delmé Radcliffe, another press officer, it seemed that the correspondents' freedom of movement might be further curtailed, but a deputation to Hamilton led by Nevinson secured a guarantee of freedom.[139]

Ashmead-Bartlett grew increasingly frustrated with the censorship, and on 18 July he had a further run in with the censors:

I thought there were limits to human stupidity but now I know there are none. The censorship has now passed beyond all reason. They won't let you give expression to the mildest opinions on any subjects. They apply it to taste style poetry and events of which the enemy are by now fully cognisant and which have already appeared in the press. The long article I wrote on Lancashire Landing has been returned without a single word being passed. The reason is that they state it makes the people on W beach look as if they were afraid. I wrote the article to please those on W beach and they were tickled to death with it? There are now at least four censors all of whom cut up your stuff. Maxwell starts it then Ward then General Braithwaite and finally Sir Ian Hamilton. All hold different views and feel it their duty to take out scraps. Thus only a few dry crumbs are left for the wretched public. The articles resemble chicken out of which a thick nutritious broth has been extracted.[140]

The next day he wrote to Harry Lawson to warn him of his difficulties and the effect they were having on his work:

I am afraid you will find a great falling off in the quality of my work but this is entirely due to the censorship on letters which is the severest I have ever known ten times more so than when I was with our Army in France. It is in fact applied to everything and not confined to what might be of value to the enemy, which was the standard laid down and adhered to in

Flanders. I think it only fair to me that the Newspapers Proprietors Association should know of the difficulties under which I now work. On the
other hand the censorship as applied to cabled discriptions [*sic*] of fights
is excellent and we are allowed to mention regiments Brigades and Divisions. It is the censorship of long and purely discriptive [*sic*] letters of which
I speak.[141]

What were the effects in practice of this censorship? In Ashmead-
Bartlett's papers there are some telegrams which bear the censor's marks.
Among the passages that were cut are a frank appraisal in August of the
lack of progress on the peninsula: 'but of course the real work of driving
the enemy back and getting astride of the peninsula thus completely
cutting off his armies south of the Narrows at this hour remains yet to
be accomplished'.[142] In September, a passage concerning the huge losses
and the failure of the 'New Armies' was also cut,[143] just as a warning about
the support and supplies required from home had been excised in July:

> [A]nd to achieve these ends unlimited men unlimited ammunition and
> unlimited grenades are required stop our men cannot be surpassed in
> bravery and determination and cheerfulness under all conditions but our
> supplies of ammunition and our grenades are unfortunately limited and
> the stock is apt to run low before an engagement has been fought out to a
> finish whilst the Turk seems to have an inexhaustible supply of grenades of
> which he makes most effective use in his counter attacks stop[144]

However a frank description of the fighting was allowed to remain in this
article:

> [T]he cost of this particular kind of warfare can be worked out with almost
> mathematical exactness for so many men must be sacrificed so many shells
> fired and so many grenades are required for every fresh houndred [*sic*]
> yards of ground occupied stop it is bludgeon work brutal and unattractive
> and giving little or no scope for skill in tactics or strategy[145]

In September, Hamilton wrote to Harry Lawson to state his opinion
that Bartlett was unsuitable to act as a war correspondent. Bartlett's later
comment was: 'This is quite true, because I have always refused to write
to dictation what I do not believe to be true, at anyone's request.'[146]
Ashmead-Bartlett's frustration culminated in a sensational attempt to
step outside the constraints of censorship. He wrote another letter to
Asquith about the campaign and persuaded the visiting Australian journalist Keith Murdoch to smuggle it to London. When this letter was
seized from Murdoch by the military police, he wrote his own version
and forwarded it to the British Cabinet and to his friend Andrew Fisher,

prime minister of Australia. Ashmead-Bartlett's actions resulted in his dismissal: Braithwaite confronted Bartlett with the evidence of his actions on 28 September and he left Imbros on 2 October 1915.[147]

Other breaches of official control

The journalists' dispatches formed only one of many sources conveying information home about the campaign. Hamilton and his staff tried to control each one. Hamilton's influence over his communications with Kitchener and his published dispatches are obvious; and the misleading and partial nature of the latter have already been touched on, as have his alleged interference with King's Messengers. As was usual in times of war, the troops' letters would have been censored. There were other interesting attempts to convey information home. The first involved a privy councillor, the Earl of Granard, who wished to inform the king as to the situation. Granard told Bartlett that he had written to Hamilton saying:

> 'I feel it my duty as privy Councillor to write the truth of all that has occurred out here to the King. Perhaps under these circumstances you would prefer that I should not serve under your command.' Hamilton replied that in wartime Privy Councillors did not count and that all became soldiers and left the matter at this. On the same day he telegraphed over to de Lisle stating that Granard's letters were to be censored like everyone else's. This was passed on from Corps Headquarters for Granard to see. He inatiled [*sic*] it and then sent it back. Hamilton hates Granard like poison because he knows that nothing can stop his corresponding directly with the King and in telling him the truth. Granard sent in his next letter and received a note back from Ellison the Quartermaster General saying that he himself had sent it off. This shows how GHQ love one another. Never in fact was an army in a more deplorable state of moral disintegration.[148]

Granard went before the Dardanelles Commission to correct Ashmead-Bartlett's lurid account of his actions. He denied that he had hated GHQ or had denounced Sir Ian Hamilton, but confirmed that he had written to the commander on August 19 to warn that he was writing to the king. However, he described that letter as 'criticism in a certain sense' only and explained that his criticism was confined to the 'breaking up of the 10th Division and a few minor incidents'.[149]

A further unregulated source of information was another messenger, Major Guy Dawnay, sent to London in September at about the same time as Keith Murdoch. Dawnay had been educated at Eton and Magdalen College, Oxford, and was a close associate of Cecil Aspinall – both men working in the Operations Division at GHQ, Dawnay having begun the campaign as a general staff officer, 3rd grade. Compton Mackenzie described him thus:

> Dawnay stood there, a fragile figure with something of exquisitely fashioned porcelain in the finely chiselled features of his small face [. . .]
>
> [H]e had a dry, sometimes indeed a wry wit, and he did not bother to spare those he disliked or, it might be more accurate to say, those he despised.[150]

In returning to London Dawnay had the blessing of Hamilton, who believed he would press for reinforcements. A cipher officer, Orlo Williams, commented in his diary: 'His instructions are ridiculous "To answer all questions truthfully but in no way pessimistically".'[151] Dawnay's journey resulted from his determination, shared with his fellow staff officers, Aspinall, George Lloyd and Wyndham Deedes, that the truth had to be told at home.[152] That truth was that Hamilton and Braithwaite had to go. Having read through Hamilton's correspondence with the War Office, Dawnay had a series of interviews with important officials, Cabinet ministers and men of influence. He spoke first to Kitchener and then to Churchill. Both of these interviews were in the presence of the chief of the Imperial General Staff and the director of Military Operations. Then Dawnay saw Dardanelles Committee-member Andrew Bonar Law and parliamentary under-secretary for the colonies Arthur Steel Maitland, and thereafter he saw the king. He also talked to another member of the Dardanelles Committee, Sir Edward Carson, Kitchener's private secretary Colonel Fitzgerald and Prime Minister Asquith. Dawnay was shown a copy of Murdoch's letter, which he annotated for Kitchener.[153]

Robert Rhodes James believes that Dawnay's trip was far more significant than the actions of Murdoch:

> Ministers were impressed by the weight of his evidence and his transparent integrity. Murdoch could possibly be laughed off, but not Dawnay. In all the history of the Gallipoli campaign, nothing is more surprising than the spectacle of this exceptionally competent young staff officer advising Ministers to over-rule the authority of his own commander-in-chief.[154]

However, Ashmead-Bartlett was dismissive of Dawnay. He wrote 'a more unfitting choice could hardly have been made. Dawny [*sic*] is both ignorant and stupid.'[155] By contrast, the biographer of Dawnay's friend Wyndham Deedes noted that 'in Dawnay an extreme intellectual clarity was combined with a sensitive and highly-strung temperament'.[156] Moreover, Dawnay had no high regard of Ashmead-Bartlett either. He wrote of him in June:

> His descriptions – though frequently incorrect – are not so bad, but his judgement is puerile, – & naturally so since it is founded on no knowledge of the information & other data on which the operations are based so that he has to rely on guesses & deductions which are invariably wrong. He went home after the sinking of the Majestic & we were truly thankful to be rid of him . . . When we found out the false impression which he was circulating in London we asked for him back here, where he can do less harm.[157]

Dawnay, well informed and disinterested, was the most substantial critic of the campaign at this stage. He was not the only subordinate of Hamilton to go behind the commander's back. General Sir Frederick Stopford, the disgraced commander of the IX Corps, submitted what he called an unofficial report directly to the military secretary, when it should have been passed through Hamilton. Hamilton argued that this breach in the regulations had seriously affected the decision to relieve him of his duties.[158] The final sources of information, General Monro and Kitchener himself, reported through the proper channels after Hamilton had been relieved of his command. They eventually led to the evacuation of the peninsula. In addition, Ashmead-Bartlett continued to publicise his point of view once he had returned to London. He was interviewed in *The Sunday Times* and began lecturing on the campaign.

Conclusion: Ashmead-Bartlett and the journalists' response

What was Ashmead-Bartlett's purpose in attacking the leadership of the campaign in the autumn of 1915? It was the same as Dawnay's: to get Hamilton and Braithwaite removed. In his letter to Asquith, Bartlett recognised that evacuation of the peninsula was probably politically impossible and he argued that adequate preparations for winter should entail the evacuation of the Anzacs and new leadership since 'the confidence of the troops can only be restored by an immediate change in the supreme command'.[159] He excused his breach of the censorship regulations on the basis of his suspicion that the authorities were not properly informed – a suspicion, he says, that was shared by many officers:

> I have taken the liberty of writing very fully because I have no means of knowing how far the real truth of the situation is known in England and how much the Military Authorities disclose. I thought therefore that

perhaps the opinions of an independent observer might be of value to you
at the present juncture [. . .]

I have been requested over and over again by officers of all ranks to go
home and personally disclose the truth but it is difficult for me to leave
until the beginning of October.[160]

Bartlett's diary suggests that he would have continued his campaign
against Hamilton and Braithwaite had it proved necessary. Following a
lunch with Winston Churchill, Bartlett wrote:

He told me that Ian Hamilton and his Chief of Staff had both been recalled.
This is at least a step in the right direction. It saves me agitating any further
on this score. I was determined to go on making exposures of their deceit-
fulness and incompetency until matters had reached a crisis.[161]

Bartlett wrote to Churchill in November that since his return he had
'refrained from any real criticism',[162] although he did write to *The Times*
to highlight the deception of speeches by Asquith and Churchill. He
came to write the 'true history' of the Dardanelles in 1928, in *The Uncensored Dardanelles*, in which he expressed his opinions in a manner he had
been unable to do in his dispatches. Yet even then his views had to be
curtailed, now not because of censorship, but because of the fear of libel.
Notes included in Bartlett's papers appear to be legal advice regarding
the book. Referring to the suggestion that 'military authorities deliberately suppressed the truth from their chiefs at home', the note warns:

It is this charge of wilful and deliberate suppression of the truth which,
occurring over and over again in this book, makes it so dangerous from a
legal point of view. The Publishers should insist upon its being withdrawn
in toto. However true, its truth COULD NOT BE PROVED.[163]

Were Ashmead-Bartlett's allegations of suppression nonetheless
correct? The attempts of Dawnay to bypass the official channels of communication show that they did have some basis.

Ashmead-Bartlett had a wider purpose beyond the goal of securing
the dismissal of Hamilton and the by-passing of the censorship arrangements. Unusually for a war correspondent, he sought not only to describe
events but to influence them as well. This was a product of his rebel-
liousness and arrogance, and it set him apart from more compliant
correspondents such as Bean and Moseley. Bartlett may have felt his
courageous defiance to be motivated by a sense of patriotism, but much
should also be attributed to an intellectual conceitedness and an instinct
for self-aggrandisement.

Bartlett may have influenced the course of events, though not in the direction he had hoped. His submission to Asquith in June pressed for a clear decision on whether to transfer men and guns from the Western Front, and he pushed for them to be used at Bulair.[164] This did not happen. Indeed, Nevinson later suggested that Ashmead-Bartlett's actions had had the opposite effect to that intended:

> It seems to me that his action was likely to result in dubitation about the whole campaign, hesitation to send adequate and powerful reinforcements to Sir Ian, and a general tendency to regard the Dardanelles as a side-show, instead of an enterprise that ought to be pushed through with the utmost vigour.[165]

Whether it was Bartlett or Dawnay who was the primary influence in securing the recall of Hamilton is also open to doubt. Bartlett even failed to convince the newspaper which serialised *The Uncensored Dardanelles* of his point of view. Liman von Sanders's then recently published memoirs may have played a part in this.[166] In the editorial in the *Daily Telegraph* which concluded the serialisation of Bartlett's book the author is praised, but it is Hamilton's viewpoint that is accepted:

> In another column, Captain Liddell Hart points out how frequently by the enemy's confession, Sir Ian Hamilton came within an ace of success. Further, the consequences of that effort, and their immense potential effect on the whole war, as indicated by Liman von Sanders, are an indirect tribute to Sir Ian Hamilton's vision of the goal and his unshakeable faith in its pursuit. The greater blame for the failure lies therefore on those who, hostile to or half-hearted about the enterprise, denied him the means early enough to ensure its attainment.[167]

In addition to his searing criticisms, Bartlett's memoirs and his war dispatches contained elements of the heroic–romantic myth: faith in the potential of the Eastern strategy and the heroism of the men, for example. It was those positive aspects of the campaign and not Bartlett's criticisms which remained uppermost in the melancholy, yet romantic, perceptions of Gallipoli.

How did other correspondents view Bartlett's interpretation of their role? Bean thought that Bartlett had been wrong to criticise the campaign while he was in London in June: 'It seemed to be typically and exactly the thing that a War Correspondent ought not to do; but I am bound to say I think he's a competent man, though certainly inaccurate.'[168] Bean seems to have understood Bartlett's motivation, though he himself eschewed so proactive a role as a journalist. He wrote to

Murdoch: 'I believe in telling the simple facts, neither more nor less, and letting the truth do its work. I believe it pays in the end even when it doesn't seem to score at the moment. I quite see the point of view of others.'[169] The Hamilton loyalist Moseley also argued that Ashmead-Bartlett should not have made criticisms, that he had forgotten his proper role with unfortunate results:

> The duty of War Correspondents is to record facts and impressions of what they actually see. In the Dardanelles campaign there appears to have been a tendency on the part of one or two correspondents to regard themselves as mentors to the Commander-in-Chief. Mr Ashmead-Bartlett, in particular, was a culprit in this respect. He evidently had ideas of his own as to how the campaign should have been run, and as they differed from the plans of those who were actually responsible, he permitted himself to take a distorted and pessimistic view of the whole operations. It is regrettable, in my view, that the whole of the London Press should have been fed from this jaundiced source.[170]

Compton Mackenzie, by contrast, saw an opportunity missed. He echoed Hamilton's view that correspondents could secure better support for a campaign. Coming from Mackenzie, this was more a call for criticism to be effective and subtle than for no criticism at all:

> Could we indeed have had these correspondents! half a dozen Nevinsons for example, who would have apprehended the meaning of the drama that was being played and each linked action of which is so lucidly set out in Aspinall's pages fourteen years later. And had we had them, could they but have been granted the eloquence to persuade Government, Press and Public to regard the success of the military operations at Gallipoli as vital to the ending of the War in the right way![171]

But Mackenzie's opinion was not one commonly held. Philip Gibbs, for example, working at the Western Front, later described his own role as a war correspondent thus: 'My duty then was that of a chronicler, not arguing why things should have happened so, nor giving reasons why they should not happen so, but describing faithfully many of the things I saw, and narrating the facts as I found them, as far as the Censorship would allow.'[172] He added that 'some of us wrote the truth from first to last as far as the facts of war go apart from deeper psychology, and a naked realism of horrors and losses, and criticisms of facts, which did not come within our liberty of the pen'.[173]

Phillip Knightley has praised Ashmead-Bartlett's decision to break the censorship rules, although he identified Keith Murdoch as the more important figure in the drama. He argues that if the correspondents at the Western Front had shown similar courage and enterprise 'the war might not have continued on its ghastly course'.[174] However, Knightley's argument that there was 'a great conspiracy'[175] to prevent the truth from being known at home is both too simplistic an interpretation of the motivations of all the correspondents and all those engaged in censorship, while it overlooks other sources of information, such as soldiers' letters, conveying news from the front and it assumes a direct correlation between bad news and demoralisation.

Ashmead-Bartlett's behaviour highlights the difficulties inherent in the position of the war correspondent. Hamilton once referred to Bartlett as a 'quasi-civilian',[176] and indeed the role of war correspondent did cause these men to be part-military and part-civilian: they answered to both commanders and censors, and to their employers in the press. A correspondent like Bean further highlights their singular role through his working methods. He was officially based at GHQ, but spent his days at the frontline with the citizen soldiers of Australia. The journalists' portrayal of war reflects that position. The journalists' response sits astride both the official accounts and the soldiers' personal narratives. Their dispatches elaborated on the dry military details, adding colour, though always in a restrained manner under the influence of censorship. Yet in recreating elements of the experience of war they have much in common with the soldiers' own descriptions. Where they differed was in the risks of death each faced.

Notes

1 Ashmead-Bartlett's diary, 25 March 1915, Mitchell Library, State Library of New South Wales, Sydney, Ellis Ashmead-Bartlett Papers, ML A1583 (hereafter abbreviated as Sydney, ML A1583).

2 General A. J. Murray, commander-in-chief, Egyptian Expeditionary Force, 'Report on press representatives, 23 August 1916', PRO, London, CAB 19/30.

3 *Ibid.* Malcolm Ross's son, Noel, had worked for *The Times*; he supplied his father with an account of the Anzac landing in which he was wounded, Australian War Memorial, Canberra (hereafter AWM), Bean Papers, AWM 38 3DRL 8042, item 3. Together they published *Light and Shade in War* (London, 1916), which reproduced articles about the New Zealand forces, focusing mainly on Gallipoli.

4 Ashmead-Bartlett's diary, 14 July 1915, Sydney, ML A1583, p. 123.

5 *Ibid.*, 19 August 1915, Sydney, ML A1583, p. 163.

6 *Ibid.*, 14 July 1915, Sydney, ML A1583, p. 123.
7 General Sir Ian Hamilton, 'Report on press representatives, 12 October 1915', PRO, London, CAB 19/30.
8 Sydney Moseley, *The Truth About the Dardanelles* (London, 1916).
9 Sydney Moseley, *The Truth About a Journalist* (London, 1935), pp. 104–5.
10 Ernest Scott, *Australia During the War*, vol. 11 of the Official History of Australia in the War of 1914–1918 (Sydney, 1937), p. 216.
11 'City journalist at Dardanelles. "Aberdeen Gully". Thrilling experiences of ambulance man', *Evening Express*, Aberdeen (10 July 1915), National Library of Australia, Canberra, Ashmead-Bartlett Papers, mfm M2585 (hereafter Canberra mfm M2585, etc.). The originals of these papers are held at the Institute of Commonwealth Affairs, London.
12 Kevin J. Fewster, 'Expression and suppression: aspects of military censorship in Australia during the Great War', unpublished PhD thesis (University of New South Wales, 1980), p. 82.
13 Scott, *Australia During the War*, p. 216.
14 N. P. Hiley, 'Making war: the British news media and government control, 1914–1916', unpublished PhD thesis (Open University, 1985), p. 185. Ashmead-Bartlett's contemporaries appear to refer to him as both Ashmead-Bartlett and Bartlett.
15 G. Ward Price (Dardanelles, 18 December), 'Our army in the Dardanelles. Guns and weather. Test of endurance', *Daily Telegraph*, 28 December 1915.
16 This is according to Ashmead-Bartlett in a draft article, 'Life and scenes at Gallipoli on land and sea', Canberra, mfm M2583, C6/28/7.
17 Kevin Fewster, 'Ellis Ashmead-Bartlett and the making of the Anzac legend', *Journal of Australian Studies*, 10 (June 1982). The idea was also put forward by Ken Inglis in 'The Australians at Gallipoli – 1', *Historical Studies*, 14:54 (April 1970), and was first suggested by C. E. W. Bean in an article written at Bartlett's death, *Sydney Morning Herald*, 9 May 1931.
18 Bean's diary, 2 October 1915, Bean Papers, AWM 38 3DRL 606, item 17.
19 Ashmead-Bartlett's diary, 28 September 1915, Sydney, ML A1583, p. 185.
20 Bean to Trumble, 10 March 1916, Bean Papers, AWM 38 3DRL 6673, item 270.
21 Permit to leave New Zealand, Canberra, mfm M2582.
22 'Celebrities at home. Mr Ellis Ashmead-Bartlett', *The World*, 28 December 1915, Canberra, Mfm M2586.
23 Fewster, 'Ashmead-Bartlett', pp. 28–9. Details taken from the Introduction to the catalogue of Ellis Ashmead-Bartlett's Papers, Institute of Commonwealth Studies, London.
24 Fewster, 'Ashmead-Bartlett', p. 23.
25 Henry W. Nevinson, *Last Changes, Last Chances* (London, 1928), p. 35.
26 Alan Moorehead, *Gallipoli* (Ware, Hertfordshire, 1997), p. 255.
27 This is according to Hamilton, as cited in Compton Mackenzie, *Gallipoli Memories* (London, 1929), p. 106.

28 Examples of his photographs are scattered throughout the Press cuttings in Canberra, mfm M2585.

29 Ashmead-Bartlett to the editor of *The Sphere*, 11 July 1915. Bartlett promised to try to pick up some sketches, not to draw them himself. The editor had promised to pay 'what you think fair'; editor of *The Sphere* to Ashmead-Bartlett, 7 May 1915, Canberra, mfm M2582, B/3/65.

30 Ashmead-Bartlett's diary, 7 June 1915, Sydney, ML A1583, p. 90.

31 *Ibid.*, 10 June 1915, Sydney, ML A1583, p. 91.

32 *Ibid.*, 12 June 1915, Sydney, ML A1583, p. 103. This film became *Heroes of Gallipoli* (Australia, 1920); see Roger Smither (ed.) *Imperial War Museum Film Catalogue*, (Trowbridge, 1994), 1, p. 373.

33 Ashmead-Bartlett's diary, 14 October 1915, Sydney, ML A1583, p. 192. Henry Nevinson also undertook some lecturing in October 1915 but not, it seems, on the huge scale of Ashmead-Bartlett: General A. J. Murray, 'Report on press representatives', 23 August 1916, PRO, London, CAB 19/30.

34 Ashmead-Bartlett to Mr Christy, 24 October 1915, Canberra, mfm M2582 B/3.

35 Agreement with J. & N. Tait, Melbourne, Australia and London, 4 December 1915, Canberra, mfm M2582, C1/5/41.

36 W. H. Ifould, principal librarian, Public Library of New South Wales, to Messrs Angus and Robertson Ltd, 5 April 1916, Sydney, ML A1583, p. 6.

37 Ellis Ashmead-Bartlett, *Ashmead-Bartlett's Despatches from the Dardanelles: An Epic of Heroism* (London, 1916). This is the copy held by the British Library; however a review in the *Daily Telegraph* suggests that this book was first published around 13 September 1915: see 'Mr Ashmead-Bartlett's despatches. "An epic of heroism" ', *Daily Telegraph*, 13 September 1915, Canberra, mfm M2586.

38 E. Ashmead-Bartlett, *Some of My Experiences in the Great War* (London, 1918).

39 E. Ashmead-Bartlett, *The Uncensored Dardanelles* (London, 1928).

40 Ashmead-Bartlett to Hughes Massie (his agent), 26 August 1915, Canberra, mfm M2582, B/3/124.

41 The greatest difficulty of landing at Bulair was that it was the obvious option and therefore heavily defended. This is discussed in an unsigned review of Bartlett's book, 'An uncensored war correspondent', edited by G. P. Dawnay, in *The Army Quarterly*, 16 (April–July 1928), pp. 323–7. Ashmead-Bartlett claimed that the Turkish commander's memoirs confirmed the veracity of Bartlett's account of his strategy, but Liman von Sanders's *Five Years in Turkey* (Annapolis, 1927) shows that he identified three key points on the peninsula – Bulair, Gaba Tepe and Sedd el Bahr – and concentrated his forces accordingly. Hamilton landed his forces at the latter two points, and von Sanders was at first loathe to take troops away from Bulair. Dawnay's role at Gallipoli is discussed later in this chapter.

42 Cyril Falls, *War Books* (London, 1989 [1930]) p. 178.

43 Fewster, 'Ashmead-Bartlett', p. 28. See also John Robertson, *The Tragedy and Glory of Gallipoli: Anzac and Empire* (London, 1990), p. 255, and an interview with Ashmead-Bartlett, 'Ashmead-Bartlett. Arrival in Sydney. Eulogy of the Anzacs. "Finest in the world" ', *Sydney Morning Herald*, 12 February 1916.

44 Moseley, *The Truth About the Dardanelles*, p. 254.

45 Evidence of Ashmead-Bartlett, Thursday 3 May 1917 (day 75), Dardanelles Commission, Canberra, mfm M2586 F5/2, p. 1408.

46 Ashmead-Bartlett's diary, 22 April 1915, Sydney, ML A1583, p. 30.

47 Hamilton, 'Statement on evidence of witnesses: Ashmead-Bartlett', Liddell Hart Centre for Military Archives, Kings College, London, Hamilton Papers, 8/2/24; This was a document submitted to the Dardanelles commissioners.

48 Ashmead-Bartlett's diary, 2 May 1915, Sydney, ML A1583, p. 52.

49 Mackenzie, *Gallipoli Memories*, p. 200.

50 Ellis Ashmead-Bartlett's articles from the Dardanelles appeared in the *Daily Telegraph* on 24 and 26 April; 6, 7, 8, 11, 18 and 19 May; 23 June; 9, 15, 20 and 27 July; 6, 25 and 26 August; 3 and 4 September; 19, 26 and 30 October; and 2 November 1915.

51 'Notes of the day. The Dardanelles', *The Globe*, 25 August 1915, Canberra, mfm M2585.

52 *Gallipoli Correspondent: The Frontline Diary of C. E. W. Bean*, ed. Kevin Fewster (Sydney, 1983), diary entry for 2 October 1915, p. 164.

53 'Great attack on the Dardanelles. Fleets and armies. Allied troops land in Gallipoli. Success of operations. Large forces advance', *Daily Telegraph*, 27 April 1915.

54 'From our special correspondent, Athens, Thursday, 11.00 a.m. (delayed)' – 'More troops landed. Noteworthy advance', *Daily Telegraph*, 1 May 1915.

55 E. Ashmead-Bartlett (Dardanelles, 24, 26 and 27 April), 'Graphic story from the Dardanelles. Historic scenes. Army disembarked by moonlight. Dashing colonials. Capture of positions. Special cablegrams', *Daily Telegraph*, 7 May 1915.

56 Ashmead-Bartlett's diary, 27 and 29 April 1915, Sydney, ML A1583, pp. 47 and 49.

57 C. E. W. Bean, 'Gallipoli (one)', *Commonwealth of Australia Gazette*, 39 (Monday 17 May 1915), pp. 931–3, Bean Papers, AWM 38 3DRL 8039, item 1. This will be used as the source for Bean's articles; they were published here a few days after they were released to the press.

58 *Australians in Action: The Story of Gallipoli*, Department of Public Instruction (New South Wales, 1915)'; the articles were edited to a considerable extent for inclusion in the pamphlet.

59 Ashmead-Bartlett, *Daily Telegraph*, 7 May 1915. Bean contradicts Bartlett's description in saying that the boats 'hurried inshore': Bean, 'Gallipoli (one)'. All subsequent references to the articles on the landing are to these sources.

60 C. E. W. Bean, 'Sidelights of the war on Australian character', *Royal Australian Historical Society Journal & Proceedings*, 13:4 (1927), p. 210.

61 Fewster, 'Ashmead-Bartlett', p. 20.

62 Ashmead-Bartlett, 'The story of the landing', Canberra, mfm M2584 C7/5/17.

63 Sir Ian Hamilton (GHQ, Mediterranean Expeditionary Force, 20 May 1915), 'Official despatches from the Dardanelles. Sir Ian Hamilton on the operations. Text of the report', *Daily Telegraph*, 7 July 1915.

64 Vice-Admiral John M. De Robeck ('Triad', 1 July 1915), 'Vivid story of Gallipoli landing. Official despatch from Admiral De Robeck. Dashing bravery of the Dominions troops', *Daily Telegraph*, 17 August 1915.

65 Dudley McCarthy, *Gallipoli to the Somme: The Story of C. E. W. Bean* (London, 1983), p. 128. This statement by Bean is taken from an article in *Sydney Morning Herald*, 9 May 1931 (p. 17), written on the occasion of Ashmead-Bartlett's death.

66 Bean's diary, 26 December 1915, Bean Papers, AWM 38 3DRL 606, item 24.

67 Fewster, 'Ashmead-Bartlett', p. 30.

68 An idea popularised in M. Cockerell, P. Hennessy and D. Walker, *Sources Close to the Prime Minister* (London, 1984), p. 89.

69 Bean, 'Gaba Tepe. 12 June', *Commonwealth of Australia Gazette*, 79 (Friday 23 July 1915), p. 1395, Bean Papers, AWM 38 3DRL 8039, item 1.

70 C. E. W. Bean, *The Story of Anzac from the Outbreak of War to the End of the First Phase of the Gallipoli Campaign, May 4, 1915*, vol. 1 of the Official History of Australia in the War of 1914–1918 (St Lucia, Queensland, 1981 [1921]), p. 463.

71 Fewster, 'Ashmead-Bartlett', p. 19.

72 For example, in describing a wounded gunner, Bean wrote: 'His first remark on regaining consciousness was, "Is the gun all right, sergeant?" ': 'Gaba Tepe (twenty two)', 30 July, *Commonwealth of Australia Gazette*, 94 (Monday 16 August 1915), Bean Papers, AWM 38 3DRL 8039, item 1, p. 1595.

73 Paul Fussell, *The Great War and Modern Memory* (London, 1975), p. 178.

74 Bean cable, 'Kaba Tepe [*sic*]', 26 June 1915, Bean Papers, AWM 38 3DRL 8039, item 7.

75 E. Ashmead-Bartlett (Dardanelles, 12 August), 'Battles in the Dardanelles. The new attacks. Heroic exploits of colonial troops. Desperate fighting. Maoris in action. Special cablegram', *Daily Telegraph*, 25 August 1915.

76 Bean's diary, 2 October 1915, Bean Papers, AWM 38 3DRL 606, item 17.

77 C. E. W. Bean, 'Gallipoli (one)'.

78 E. Ashmead-Bartlett (Dardanelles, 23 August), 'The battles in the Dardanelles. Action of Aug. 21. Splendid attacks on Turkish positions. Great British charges. Heroic conduct of the Yeomanry Division. Special cablegram', *Daily Telegraph*, 4 September 1915.

79 Bean's diary, 26 September 1915, Bean Papers, AWM 38 3DRL 606, item 17.

80 *Bulletin*, Sydney, 17 June 1915, Bean papers, AWM 38 3DRL 6673, item 234.

81 Wilson & Mackinnon, Melbourne, to T. Trumble, secretary of defence, 29 September 1915, Bean Papers, AWM 38 3DRL 6673, item 270.

82 *Argus*, 22 April 1916, Bean Papers, AWM 38 3DRL 6673, item 234.

83 See, for example, Keith Murdoch, 'The new Australians. Fierce danger and hardship. Type of the Anzacs. Vain search for "Beachy" ', *Sun*, no date, National Library of Australia, Canberra, Sir Keith Murdoch Papers, MS 2823/2/13, or extracts in Martin Farrar, *News from the Front* (London, 1998).

84 Ashmead-Bartlett (Dardanelles, 14 July), 'Struggle for the Dardanelles. Battle of July 12–13. British advance. Trenches captured. Hand-to-hand fighting. Special cablegram', *Daily Telegraph* (27 July 1915).

85 Ashmead-Bartlett (Dardanelles, 19 August), 'The battles in Gallipoli. Four days' fighting. Desperate bravery of colonial troops. Hand-to-hand conflict. Special cablegram', *Daily Telegraph*, 3 September 1915.

86 Ashmead-Bartlett (Eastern Mediterranean, April), 'Expedition to the Dardanelles. A battleship in action', *Daily Telegraph*, 6 May 1915.

87 Ashmead-Bartlett (Dardanelles, 28 April), 'Allied army at the Dardanelles. Striking scenes. Position well held. Futile Turkish attacks on colonial troops. Special cablegram', *Daily Telegraph*, 8 May 1915.

88 Ashmead-Bartlett (Dardanelles, 10 May), 'Allied armies at the Dardanelles. The first stage. Impregnable position. Overcoming obstacles. Special cablegram', *Daily Telegraph*, 18 May 1915; Ashmead-Bartlett (Dardanelles, 30 June), 'The victory in Gallipoli. Battle of June 28. Graphic story of British heroism. A splendid advance. Fine artillery work', *Daily Telegraph*, 9 July 1915.

89 Ashmead-Bartlett (Dardanelles, 21 May), 'The battles in Gallipoli. Turkish effort. Desperate attack on colonial troops. Totally defeated', *Daily Telegraph*, 23 June 1915.

90 Ashmead-Bartlett's dispatches, *Daily Telegraph*, 18 May, 9 July and 25 August 1915.

91 Ashmead-Bartlett (Eastern Mediterranean, 4 July), 'Battles in Gallipoli. The gully ravine', *Daily Telegraph*, 20 July 1915.

92 Ashmead-Bartlett's dispatch, *Daily Telegraph*, 6 May 1915.

93 Ashmead-Bartlett (Dardanelles, 10 May), 'Allied armies at the Dardanelles. Three days' battle. Furious attacks on Aki Baba Mountain. Turkish resistance. Very slow progress. Special cablegram', *Daily Telegraph*, 19 May 1915.

94 Ashmead-Bartlett, 'Notes taken from the Agamemnon log of the Dardanelles expedition up to March 18th', Canberra, mfm M2584 C7/1/12.

95 Ashmead-Bartlett's diary, 30 June 1915, Sydney, ML A1583, p. 113.

96 Compton Mackenzie, 14 June 1915, telegram to *Daily Telegraph*, Sydney, ML A1585, p. 2.

97 Ashmead-Bartlett, 'Last days of the Majestic', 26 May 1915, Sydney, ML A1584.

98 Ashmead-Bartlett's dispatch, *Daily Telegraph*, 18 May 1915.

99 Hiley, 'Making war', pp. 144–5.

100 Ashmead-Bartlett's diary, 14–20 April 1915, Sydney, ML A1583, p. 26.

101 Hiley, 'Making war', pp. 164–6.

102 Ashmead-Bartlett's diary, 14–20 April 1915, Sydney, ML A1583, p. 24; Ashmead-Bartlett (Eastern Mediterranean, 15 April), 'Expedition to the Dardanelles. Allies' great task', *Daily Telegraph*, 26 April 1915.

103 The military took over control of censorship at the Dardanelles from 13 May 1915, but the journalists were put under the overall control of the War Office only from 10 June. 'No. 66 Censorship of war correspondents' reports', Eastern Mediterranean Squadron temporary memorandum, 13 May 1915, Canberra, mfm M2582 B/3/66; Hiley, 'Making war', p. 173.

104 Nevinson, *Last Changes*, p. 28.

105 Moseley, *Truth About the Dardanelles*, p. 15.

106 Ashmead-Bartlett, *Uncensored Dardanelles*, p. 36.

107 Hiley, 'Making war', p. 178; see also Hamilton to Harry Lawson, 24 July 1915, Hamilton Papers, 7/3/2.

108 Robert Rhodes James, *Gallipoli* (London, 1965), p. 150.

109 Ashmead-Bartlett's dispatch, *Daily Telegraph*, 19 May 1915. A reference to the battle of Leipzig in October 1813, perhaps.

110 'Three days' battle in Gallipoli', *Daily News and Leader*, 19 May 1915, Canberra, mfm M2584.

111 *Pall Mall Gazette*, 20 May 1915, Canberra, mfm M2584.

112 *Truth*, 26 May 1915, Canberra, mfm M2585.

113 Ashmead-Bartlett's diary, 8 May 1915, Sydney, ML A1583, p. 59.

114 Ashmead-Bartlett, 'The general attack on Krithia and Achi Baba, May 6th–8th 1915', Canberra, mfm M2584 C7/10/1–21. It is not clear what this draft chapter was used for – it does not match Ashmead-Bartlett's *Uncensored Dardanelles*. Nor is it clear when it was written, although other comments suggest that it was later on in the war.

115 *Ibid.*, p. 4. In his article he had praised it as 'a perfect example of the classical British attack, carried out over a broad front so as to concentrate the maximum number of men in the firing line for the final assault on the enemy's position with a minimum of loss': *Daily Telegraph*, 19 May 1915.

116 Ashmead-Bartlett, 'The general attack', Canberra, mfm M2584 C7/10/19.

117 Sir Ian Hamilton (GHQ, Mediterranean Expeditionary Force, 26 August 1915), 'Sir Ian Hamilton's stirring despatch. Vivid story of Gallipoli operations. Army in a wilderness. Difficult advances. Fine spirit of the troops', *Daily Telegraph*, 21 September 1915.

118 Ashmead-Bartlett, 'The general attack', Canberra, mfm M2584 C7/10/3.

119 Quoted in Rhodes James, *Gallipoli*, p. 157.

120 Ashmead-Bartlett, *Uncensored Dardanelles*, p. 101.

121 *Ibid.*, p. 158.

122 Bean to GSO 1st Australian Division, 27 June 1915, Bean Papers, AWM 38 3DRL 6673, item 270.

123 Hiley, 'Making war', p. 187.

124 Ashmead-Bartlett diary, 19 May 1915, Sydney, ML A1583, p. 66.

125 *Ibid.*, 26 May 1915, Sydney, ML A1583, p. 77. Hiley notes that *The Uncensored Dardanelles* (pp. 269–77) contains an appendix which is supposed to be the 13 May memorandum, but is actually a later version, the original having been lost on 27 May 1915: 'Making war', p. 167 footnote.

126 H. W. Nevinson's diary, 13 July 1915, Modern Papers Reading Room, Bodleian Library, Oxford, Henry Woodd Nevinson Papers, MS Eng misc e.619/1.

127 Ashmead-Bartlett's diary, 20 May 1915, Sydney, ML A1583, p. 68 (my emphasis).

128 Ashmead-Bartlett, 'My return to England and what happened' (unpublished article?), Canberra, mfm M2583 C6/1/4; a later reference to Versailles suggests that this was written after 1919.

129 *Ibid.*, C6/1/5. It has been impossible to verify this, and Compton Mackenzie later wrote: 'At GHQ Kephalo, we had thought Stanley Wilson an unreliable chatterbox': *My Life and Times: Octave Five 1915–1923* (London, 1966), p. 42.

130 Ashmead-Bartlett, 'Review of the situation in Gallipoli', Sydney, ML A1583, p. 10/227; another copy is filed in A1584 and is signed and dated Ashmead-Bartlett June 1 1915. Ashmead-Bartlett's evidence to the Dardanelles Commission does not mention the encouragement from the King's Messengers, but states that Admiral Limpus at Malta urged him to go to London and tell the truth as to what was happening: Evidence of Ashmead-Bartlett, Thursday 3 May 1917 (day 75), Dardanelles Commission, Canberra, mfm M2586 F5/2, p. 1408.

131 Ashmead-Bartlett's diary, 11 June 1915, Sydney, ML A1583, p. 98; see also note attached to 'Memorandum on the situation in Gallipoli' by George Robertson from whom the Mitchell Library purchased these volumes: Sydney, ML A1583.

132 Ashmead-Bartlett, 'My return to England', Canberra, mfm M2583 C6/1/8.

133 Ashmead-Bartlett, *Uncensored Dardanelles*, p. 133.

134 Mackenzie, *Gallipoli Memories*, pp. 178–9.

135 Hamilton to Kitchener, no. M.F. 289, 3 June 1915, Hamilton Papers, 7/3/1.

136 Kitchener to Hamilton, no. M.F. 5201, 7 June 1915, Hamilton Papers, 7/3/1.

137 Ashmead-Bartlett diary, 30 June 1915, Sydney, ML A1583, p. 114 (my emphasis).

138 Bean to GSO 1st Australian Division, 27 June 1915, Bean Papers, AWM 38 3DRL 6673, item 270.

139 Ashmead-Bartlett's diary, 2 August 1915, Sydney, ML A1583, p. 123; Hiley, 'Making war', pp. 179–80.

140 *Ibid.*, 18 July 1915, Sydney, ML A1583, p. 125.

141 Ashmead-Bartlett to Lawson, 19 July 1915, Canberra, mfm M2582 B/5/53.

142 Ashmead-Bartlett, telegram to *Daily Telegraph* (re. 8 August), 24 August 1915, Sydney ML A1585.

143 Ashmead-Bartlett, telegram (re. 23 August), 15 September 1915, Sydney, ML A1585.

144 Ashmead-Bartlett, telegram, 23 July 1915, Sydney, ML A1585; this article appeared on 27 July 1915.

145 *Ibid.*

146 Ashmead-Bartlett, *Uncensored Dardanelles*, p. 237.

147 Ashmead-Bartlett's diary, Sydney, ML A1583, pp. 184 and 187.

148 *Ibid.*, 3 September 1915, Sydney, ML A1583, p. 173.

149 Evidence of Lieutenant-Colonel, The Earl of Granard, KP, GCVO, 10 July 1917 (day 79), Dardanelles Commission, qq. 27618–40, PRO, London, CAB 19/33.

150 Mackenzie, *Gallipoli Memories*, pp. 96–7.

151 Orlo Williams's diary, 2 September 1915, Imperial War Museum, London, O. C. Williams Papers, diary 2, p. 15.

152 Typescript, possibly extracts from draft biography of Deedes by Gladys Skelton, Imperial War Museum, London, G. P. Dawnay Papers, 69/21/5, 'Miscellaneous speeches and articles 1920–1947'; see also John Presland, *Deedes Bey: A Study of Sir Wyndham Deedes 1883–1923* (London, 1942), pp. 217–26.

153 Dawnay Papers, 69/21/1, 'Dardanelles 1915 – Official correspondence'; Sir Robert Rhodes James's private notes on Dawnay's London visit.

154 Rhodes James, *Gallipoli*, p. 316.

155 Ashmead-Bartlett's diary, 23 August and 9 September 1915, Sydney, ML A1583, p. 180.

156 Presland, *Deedes Bey*, p. 182.

157 Dawnay to his wife, 30 June 1915, Robert Rhodes James's Private Papers.

158 Hamilton to Grimwood Mears, secretary to the Dardanelles Commission, 10 May 1917, Hamilton Papers, 8/1/46.

159 Ashmead-Bartlett to Asquith, 8 September 1915, Sydney, ML A1583, pp. 248, 251.

160 *Ibid.*, p. 252.

161 Ashmead-Bartlett's diary, 15 October 1915, Sydney, ML A1583, p. 196.

162 Ashmead-Bartlett to Churchill, 13 November 1915, Canberra, mfm M2582 B/3/203.

163 'Observations of Book UNCENSORED DARDANELLES', Canberra, mfm M2584 C8/17/2. Conversely, Compton Mackenzie hoped to provoke Ashmead-Bartlett into a libel action against his *Gallipoli Memories*: see Compton Mackenzie, 'The Dardanelles', 29 April 1956, unidentified newspaper, National Library of Australia, Canberra, Alan Moorehead Papers, MS 5654, box 13, folder 107.

164 Ashmead-Bartlett, 'Review of the situation in Gallipoli', Sydney, ML A1583, pp. 17/234–18/235.

165 H. W. Nevinson, 'The Dardanelles controversy', *Observer*, 8 April 1928, Hamilton Papers, 7/3/11.

166 'Book of the day. Defence of the Dardanelles. Liman von Sanders's memoirs', *The Times*, 13 January 1928, Hamilton Papers, 7/3/11, shows that *Five Years in Turkey* was first published in translation in the month before *The Uncensored Dardanelles* was serialised.

167 'Gallipoli', *Daily Telegraph*, 14 February 1928, Hamilton Papers, 7/3/11.

168 Fewster (ed.), *Frontline Diary*, 7 July 1915, p. 138.

169 Bean to Murdoch, 14 June 1916, Murdoch Papers, MS 2823/2/5.

170 Moseley, *Truth About the Dardanelles*, p. 165.

171 Mackenzie, *Gallipoli Memories*, p. 205.

172 Philip Gibbs, *Realities of War* (London, 1929 [1920]), p. 7.

173 *Ibid.*, p. 315.

174 Phillip Knightley, *The First Casualty. From the Crimea to Vietnam: The War Correspondent as Hero, Propagandist, and Myth-Maker* (London, 1978), p. 103.

175 Knightley, *First Casualty*, p. 80.

176 Nevinson, *Last Changes*, p. 32; this may be Nevinson's own phrase.

4

The soldiers' tale: participants' personal narratives

In the years between the launching of the Gallipoli campaign and the outbreak of a second world war more than sixty books were published on the subject. The majority of these were written by men[1] who visited the peninsula in some capacity during the campaign. This chapter considers a selection of the published responses of those participants. Some of them emphasise and exaggerate the romance of the campaign; others do not. None of them condemns the campaign. Their portrayals and some of the reasons for their points of view will be explored.

Veterans' and observers' accounts can be divided into two broad categories. There are those whose simple purpose was to write a personal narrative to bear witness to their role in the campaign; and there are those whose purpose led them to heighten or even distort the reality of the campaign and their experience of it, to romanticise it.

In his survey of Australian war-writing, Robin Gerster suggested:

> Propaganda hacks, misguided ego-trippers, self-styled modern Homers – whatever their various motivations and aspirations, all were to some degree impelled by the same didactic purpose. From 1915 on, every mode of Australian war prose, whether 'factual', 'fictional', 'historical' or 'imaginative', typically functions either overtly or covertly as publicity for the Australian soldier as a twentieth-century embodiment of classical heroic virtue.[2]

While the heroic theme is undoubtedly of great importance, it is perhaps less prevalent than Gerster argues.[3] A very different view has been put forward by Samuel Hynes who has considered war-writing, specifically personal narratives of war experiences, not in terms of a particular nationality, but in terms of a particular point of view, that of the front-line soldier, the one who, says Hynes quoting Tolstoy, did 'the actual killing'.[4]

Although some Gallipoli authors, including Charles Bean, particularly in his commemorative official history, conformed to the didactic purpose of Gerster's thesis, Hynes suggests something quite different: personal narratives

> subvert the expectations of romance. They work at a level below the big words and the brave sentiments, down on the surface of the earth where men fight. They don't glorify war, or aestheticize it, or make it literary or heroic; they speak in their own voices, in their own plain language. They are not antiwar – that is, they are not polemics against war; they simply tell us what it is like. They make war actual, without making it familiar. They bear witness.[5]

Hynes's idea is that there is a coherence to the sum of all the personal narratives written by soldiers who have participated in war. He calls this *the soldiers' tale*. In all its diverse manifestations it explains what war is like and how it feels. The soldiers' story of war is not one of manoeuvres, tactics, strategies, numbers and statistics; it is about the experience of having been there. Hynes writes: 'And so if we would understand what war is like, and how it *feels*, we must turn away from history and its numbers, and seek the reality in the personal witness of the men who were there.'[6]

Sydney de Loghe: *The Straits Impregnable*

Hynes suggests various characteristics that recur in the personal narratives of frontline soldiers. Hynes formulated his ideas in response to memoirs published quite some time after the events they describe, though the particular Gallipoli personal narrative discussed here, *The Straits Impregnable* by Sydney de Loghe, was published in 1917.[7] Even so, it will be seen to conform to Hynes's thesis of the soldiers' tale, as do many of the other similar books that it exemplifies.[8]

'Sydney de Loghe' was the pseudonym of Frederick Loch (1889–1954). He served as a bombardier in 2 Field Artillery Brigade, AIF.[9] Prior to the First World War he had worked as a farmer in Gippsland, and afterwards he married Joice Nankivell and worked in Ireland, Poland and Greece, combining journalism with relief work for refugees. He went on to write at least five more books, three of them novels.[10]

A central theme in Hynes's thesis is that the soldiers' tale is the 'whole story' of war in all its infinite variety; by extension, I would argue, the tales of individual soldiers are replete with complex and sometimes conflicting emotions. This is the case in *The Straits Impregnable*, and the attitudes to war and participation in war therein expressed. Early on in the account, while the author is stationed in Egypt, a grand vision of Australia's role in war is suggested. In the land of Moses and Cleopatra, he asks: 'Which first shall be forgotten – Anzac, or the ancient, ageless Nile?'[11] and he admits: 'I never quite shook off the glamour of that island set in the Aegean.'[12] Yet, later on, the response to noble sentiments is far more sceptical. De Loghe reports a half-hearted argument that took place in a trench, late in the campaign, concerning the men's reasons for enlisting:

> 'What did you join fer, Darkie? Was it the six bob, or a row with yer tart, or was the police after yer?'
> Darkie made no answer. 'Wot was it, Darkie?'
> 'I joined cos I thought a bloke ought ter join.'
> It was like the bursting of an 8.25 shell. Nobody said anything. Nobody moved at all. I looked around for a museum to put the sentiment in.[13]

Hynes's suggestion that personal narratives work at a level below that of the 'big words' is apt here. Similarly, Hynes observes, 'most men do feel war's high excitement and romance, and even its beauty . . . and not only *before* they experience war but *after*'.[14] Thus De Loghe describes the first time he heard the distant sound of guns as 'like a draught of thunder and champagne'.[15] He writes of his approach to the landing:

> The while that firing grew more distinct, until it was no more a muttering, but had become a sullen, weariless booming, soaring up and down, a booming with the power to intoxicate the heart. I listened with soberness befitting a guest at one of Death's At Homes; and yet I was ready to shout too, shout that I was coming, that soon I would be there.[16]

Yet the heroic version of the landing is dismissed in favour of a more realistic account of mistakes and advancing too far – 'But you know it wasn't the great affair it was made out to be', says his friend.[17]

Where Charles Bean emphasised the Anzacs' courage of endurance and the bonds of comradeship, De Loghe presents a more finely nuanced picture. Thus when he writes of his steadfastness there is also a touch of nervousness, which makes his courage the more remarkable and human: 'There was no cover for anybody, and the shrapnel arrived so fast and so near that I found myself pretty jumpy again, to speak the truth. Yet it would have needed a handsome cheque to buy my seat.'[18] In De Loghe's account there is 'beastly' and ignoble death to confront.[19] Yet he tempered the negative aspects of his portrayal. Death is not entirely base and pointless, nor is it simply heroic and inspiring; it is a mixture of the two extremes. Here is his description of the death of a friend, suddenly caught by shrapnel while the two of them were on the beach:

> I looked into Sam's face and an old thought came back to me. Death is not often beautiful. Here was no heroic end; here was no bold gaze, which told of past duties well done. Nothing of that kind, nothing. But, instead, a silly smile where the mouth dropped, and a little blood upon the palate, and a skin turning yellow and blue. Not heroic, my friends; not beautiful [. . .]
>
> Friend Sam, you were rather 'a rotter' – weak and easy to lead. Life owed you more years; but they would have been years without profit. Now you have died at the start of life, and others following will remember your sacrifice and take heart. You could have done no better thing.[20]

In some respects, however, personal narratives such as De Loghe's did not tell the whole story, nor were they designed to. Their concern is the personal experience of war and all the emotions thereby enjoined. They ignore much outside this. As Hynes says: 'War narratives are experience books; they are about what happened, and how it felt. *Why* is not a soldier's question: Tennyson at least got that part of the Charge of the Light Brigade right: "Theirs not to reason why".'[21] They are not concerned primarily with the politics, the strategy or the tactics of the campaign; those are the concerns of history books. Personal narratives embrace, above all, the personal implications of these things. Therefore they begin when their authors' own war begins – enlistment, embarkation or training – and end their coverage of Gallipoli when they leave the peninsula. We are told that De Loghe enlisted under the name of Lake and that he was an artilleryman. That his rank and assignment are difficult to ascertain is typical of the soldiers' tale. These details are not vital to the recounting of the experience. Nor does he give technical details about his work. In keeping with this focus purely on the personal, the political wranglings over ammunition supply are important to De Loghe's narrative only for the resulting frustration of his colonel at the scant resources – 'They're limited to a round a day or something! Good God! Why don't we shoot off all we've got, and then pack up the guns and send them home, and go to Hell like gentleman!' he is reported as having said.[22] Similarly, it is seldom clear in any personal narrative exactly when or where a given action occurs.

Perhaps the most notable omission from 'the whole story' is that De Loghe does not describe his own involvement in the essential task of soldiering: killing. This might be ascribed to his role as an artilleryman, but the omission is repeated in other Gallipoli personal narratives. Hynes notes the same phenomenon and ascribes it to the morals of civilian soldiers: 'war narrators seem to have felt a reluctance, a moral fastidiousness, before the act of taking a life. These civilian soldiers seem to hold back from confessing to the essential act that a soldier *must* perform but that a civilian must *not*.'[23]

De Loghe displays other characteristics that are typical of soldiers' personal narratives. He begins with the assertion: 'This Book, Written in Australia, Egypt and Gallipoli, is true.' Unlike other accounts of war by journalists, historians or novelists, as Hynes notes, those by ordinary soldiers often seem to betray a need to declare the veracity of their own version and assert their authority as a participant and witness.[24] And rather than attempting to give a faithful account of the entire campaign, the emphases of each personal narrative, as might be expected, vary with the differing experience of each man. Therefore, some give greater weight to the unpleasant living conditions on the peninsula (see figure 5) – this is particularly true of men who arrived after the main battles had taken place – whereas others are most notable for vivid descriptions of entering battle or being wounded. Indeed the greatest strength of personal narratives is that they provide, through their very individual view of battle, an original and authentic alternative to the clichés of thrilling charges. De Loghe describes scrambling through the open to deliver a message,[25] but not any direct involvement in fighting. To borrow an example from another narrative, however, is to show how different the voice of a soldier in war can be from the stereotype. This is New Zealander Stanley Wright's account of an attack in August:

> It's hotter than hell in this trench with the fierce August sun beating right in. The rum some of us have isn't worth a damn to thirsty bodies. The Corporal suddenly yells, 'Up with you, quick; he's coming!' The balance of the command is drowned in the hurricane of rapid fire that bursts out along the ragged trench line. In this moment of peril the little NCO is everywhere at once, cursing, threatening and encouraging. He yells at me above the din, 'You bloody fool, load!' and suddenly I realize that I've fired the ten shots in the magazine, and am still clicking away with an empty rifle. Just excitement. The attack melts away; with this our confidence grows. Wide awake now we take spells at the periscope.[26]

It is the strangeness of remembered war that sets personal narratives apart from other accounts. Hynes writes: 'In war every kind of monstrosity is possible. And the witness sees it more with fascination than with disgust, arrested by its strangeness. It's a simple but true proposi-

5 Dug-outs of the 2nd and 3rd Australian Field Ambulances at Anzac Cove

tion: in war, death is grotesque and astonishing.'[27] His point is borne out
by De Loghe's description of the death of a marine, part of whose flesh
lands quivering on De Loghe's boot;[28] and by Australian light-horseman
Ion Idriess's account of a young man's death:

> A man was just shot dead in front of me. He was a little infantry lad, quite
> a boy, with snowy hair that looked comical above his clean white singlet. I
> was going for water. He stepped out of a dugout and walked down the path
> ahead, whistling. I was puffing the old pipe, while carrying a dozen water-
> bottles. Just as we were crossing Shrapnel Gully he suddenly flung up his
> water-bottles, wheeled around, and stared for one startled second, even as
> he crumpled to my feet. In seconds his hair was scarlet, his clean white
> singlet all crimson.[29]

Some of the strangest experiences were those of the wounded. De Loghe
was not wounded, so this example is taken from Newfoundlander John
Gallishaw's account:

> Just then I felt a dull thud in my left shoulder blade, and a sharp pain in
> the region of my heart. At first I thought that in running for cover one of
> the men had thrown a pick-ax that hit me. Until I felt the blood trickling
> down my back like warm water, it did not occur to me that I had been hit.
> Then came a drowsy, languid sensation, the most enjoyable and pleasant I
> have ever experienced. It seemed to me that my backbone became like pulp,
> and I closed up like a concertina.[30]

Hynes labels the literary style of the personal narratives 'battlefield
gothic'. He claims that soldiers tend to be unaffected by literary trends
and instead report their wars 'in a plain, naming vocabulary, describing
objects and actions in unmetaphorical terms, appealing always to the
data of the senses'.[31] He rejects the label 'realism' as unsuitable to the
material, choosing to develop his use of 'gothic'. This term is more often
used to describe nineteenth-century novels with supernatural or horri-
fying events: gothic as a genre deals especially with the physicality of
horror, dwelling, for example, on blood and gore.

Robin Gerster praises *The Straits Impregnable* as 'a perceptive and
stylistically satisfying treatment of one man's war', and accepts it as one
of the 'very few wartime narratives by Australian soldiers [that] managed
to add to the proliferating bushman–warrior legend and at the same time
give a balanced account of the fighting'.[32] Yet the subtleties of its
portrayal do not seem to make it *primarily* intent on 'big noting'
the Australians at Gallipoli. It seems more likely that De Loghe was
attempting to bear witness to his own experiences, as Hynes suggests.

This becomes clearer if *The Straits Impregnable* is compared to De Loghe's later account of Gallipoli in which there is direct evidence of his purpose.

De Loghe, writing under his real name F. S. Loch, prepared a novel with the title 'Turn'd, but Not Torn' in about 1934.[33] This novel has much in common with his earlier work. It follows John Erskine from his job on a sheep station through his experience at Gallipoli as an artilleryman. Like *The Straits Impregnable*, it gives something of the experience of the campaign, showing for example the strangeness of death,[34] and giving a vivid description of being buried alive by a shell blast.[35] But it also gives far more strategic explanations,[36] specific names of formations and battles,[37] and casualty figures,[38] and it describes Hamilton, even quoting his message rejecting the option of evacuation on the first night: 'Dig, dig, dig'.[39] What is more, each chapter begins with an epigraph from literary sources such as the *Iliad*, one of these providing the book's indomitable title,[40] and the book concludes with a reflection on the nobility of the campaign:

> And Erskine reflected, staring round, that the valley was almost a pleasant place in the winter sunlight. If he lived to look back at it in retrospect, would he recall it as not altogether a terrible home? Would the sun of memory seem benigner, the sea more refreshing, the wrinkles in the hills more secure from enemy fire than now in his fresh and bleeding recollection? And the pitiless musketry fire that had met him during eight months from trenches held by a stubborn and chivalrous foe, men belonging to a historic empire as did he; would he in retrospect call out to that enemy across the growing gap of time, saying neither you nor I may have known it then, but we were each the touchstone lifting the other for a period out of the slough of every-day to a spiritual splendour. Those vigils and those fasts we demanded of one another were the pastures of the spirit and have stamped today's pattern on us.[41]

The clue to this ringing passage is provided by the letter which accompanied the manuscript's sumnission to the Australian War Memorial, in which he explained what motivated him to write the novel:

> My reason for writing the book was a letter written by an ex-officer, a German, who was serving in some rather lowly position in an American hotel. He wrote, in spite of his own unfortunate circumstances, indignantly against the spirit of Remarque's book 'All Quiet on the Western Front' and I myself felt he had a right to feel anger against the self-pity that appears on every page. His letter made me wish to write a book giving some idea of the Australian spirit in the war, which was never one of self-pity. To mix

accurate history and fiction is not easy, and my book possibly falls between two stools but I have tried to make it truthful both as regards actual statement of fact and as to the daily atmosphere of a very tremendous time.[42]

The contrasts between Loch's two accounts of Gallipoli may be described thus: *The Straits Impregnable* is a personal narrative bearing witness to his role in the campaign, while 'Turn'd but Not Torn' brings some romance and strategic explanation in order to assert the nobility of the campaign.

John Graham Gillam

Loch/De Loghe was not the only Gallipoli veteran to write both a personal narrative and a novel based on his experiences. Major John Graham Gillam published *Gallipoli Diary* in 1918 and *Gallipoli Adventure* in 1939.[43] As a supply officer in the 29th Division, he was not one of Hynes's soldiers who did the actual killing, but his personal narrative nonetheless has much in common with the soldiers' tale. His narrative is concerned mostly with how he passed his days and with his expectations and reactions; but his work as a supply officer is scarcely mentioned. Gillam's Preface confirms that his purpose was to bear witness:

> I am no John Masefield, and do not seek to compete with my betters. Those who desire to survey the whole amazing Gallipoli campaign in perspective must look elsewhere than in these pages. Their sole object was to record the personal impressions, feeling, [sic] and doings from day to day of one supply officer to a Division whose gallantry in that campaign well earned for it the epithet 'Immortal'.[44]

Thus his narrative displays various features of the soldiers' tale. It is written in the style of battlefield gothic and features several examples of the strangeness of war, such as a religious service conducted in dangerous conditions. (He noted: 'It is a lovely morning, and as the soldiers sing the hymns with lusty voices, an accompaniment is provided by the screaming of shells overhead.'[45]) In the Preface he does not make the customary claim to truthfulness – indeed a sense of the inadequacy of his text may have led him to include some supplements in the form of a few passages by a friend 'describing, so far as words can, the exquisite loveliness of the Peninsula'.[46] In doing so, his may be compared with Oswin Creighton's personal narrative which also featured some inserted supplementary descriptions.[47] These were three accounts of the landing written by participants. Reverend Creighton, chaplain to the 29th Division, had observed them only from a distance – the additions to his text were necessitated by deficiencies in his experience of war rather than by shortcomings as a writer. This implicit privileging of the man who was there, and particularly the man who was part of it, is at the heart of the phenomenon already noted, whereby the soldiers' tale stakes an absolute claim to the authority of the ordinary man's witness. Gillam concurs:

> If it were possible for all ranks, from OC to private, in an army fighting in any certain campaign to keep an accurate diary of all they do and see, then there could be published a perfectly true record of the development and history of that campaign, so it is not possible, and never will be, for the truth of all happenings in that campaign to be known. And it never will be in any campaign. Hundreds of deeds, gallant, tragic, cowardly, and foolish, occur which are never, and can never be recorded. When the daily Press, arm-chair critics in clubs, etc., criticize any statesman or Army Staff, they are simply talking hot air, for how is it possible for them to judge, when their source of information is as unreliable as a 'W' Beach rumour? So why waste words? Much better go and do something useful, or shut up and go and hide. War is like a big game. This war we must win – or we shall lose.
>   If we lose, it is on too huge a scale to be through any man's fault – it will be Destiny.[48]

Major Gillam was no frontline soldier – however fine a distinction that may have been in a cramped theatre such as Gallipoli with its constant risk of death from enemy shells and snipers – and his slightly detached role is reflected in some facets of his work. Thus he is an onlooker who describes the sun glistening on bayonets during battle,[49] rather than the sensation of going over the top. He steps back to contrast modern and ancient warfare in this classically-infused location.[50] And, most notably, his detached position enables him to make comments on the campaign's progress and strategy – for example, he concludes in late August that the conquest of the peninsula is now impossible.[51] Strategic comments such as this are typical of the other senior officers' narratives – it was, after all, their business to take more of an overview of a campaign. Indeed, other senior officers' narratives are dominated by considerations of their military duties at the expense of any sense of the individual's personality or emotions.[52]

When Gillam chose to return to the subject of Gallipoli, he included more comments on the strategic value of the campaign and the reasons for its failure. Therefore his characters make observations concerning the foolishness of forewarning the Turks,[53] and they praise Churchill's vision ('It's certainly a brilliant scheme'[54]) while lamenting the fact that he was not in supreme control. Perhaps this last comment reflects the changed fortunes of Churchill's reputation by 1939. In outlining Suvla and the supporting operations elsewhere, the brilliant potential of the overall campaign is explained –'the war definitely over by Christmas; and peace for all time. Was such a prospect fantastic? If so, the whole campaign was without justification.'[55] Although this last comment might be interpreted as a denunciation of the campaign's achievement, and however tempting it may be to conclude that the melodramatic–romantic storyline of the novel could not possibly be intentionally anything but ironic, this would not seem to be consistent with the rest of the book, nor with his earlier account. On the contrary, it is suggested that the book's purpose was to defend the campaign. Admittedly, without an explanatory introduction or extant private papers, Gillam's purpose in writing his novel can only be guessed at. But it may be that Gillam wished to revisit his memories and thereby explain and justify the failed strategy. Perhaps a novel held the prospect of a wider readership – it certainly enabled him to include key events of the campaign: the April landing;[56] the armistice;[57] the sinking of the *Triumph*[58] and the evacuation.[59] He thus tells the story of a man whose life is ruined by the revelation, on the eve of war, that he was born both illegitimate and of German parentage. He subsequently ruins his opportunity to propose to his true love Bridget and takes up with a woman of a lower class, Mildred; and, cad that he is, he fails to marry her. What it does lack is any romance of battle[60] and the only classical reference comes in observing the *River Clyde*: 'a reminder that the conjuring trick of the Horse of Troy was a joke which could not be successfully played twice'.[61]

In each of these pairings of personal narratives and novels, the limited perspective and the unadorned language of the experiential narrative have been highlighted by the later fictionalised account which makes broader strategic judgements or romantic allusions for a didactic purpose. Yet, some frontline personal narratives share these novels' didactic purpose – meaning that they do not conform to Hynes's thesis. Take, for example, Oliver Hogue's account of his own experience in the Australian 2nd Light Horse Brigade *Trooper Bluegum at the Dardanelles* (1916). There, the nuances and conflicting emotions of *The Straits Impregnable* are absent and in their stead is a cheerful picture of humorous heroes who 'showed the world that Australians could live and fight and die like Britishers'.[62] At Lone Pine, Hogue tells us, it

> made one's blood flow faster and tingle with pride to see the magnificent way our young Australians played the great game of war. Hemmed in and

cooped up in the trenches for weary weeks, they had at last been let loose upon the enemy at Lone Pine. Like hounds from the leash they charged across the bullet-swept area between the contending armies. The Turkish lines spat fire from every loophole, and machine-guns seemed to revel in murderous music. On swept the line, thinned but dauntless. Heroes fell on every side. Enfilading volleys swept across the side. To us on the right the men seemed to falter for a space; but it was only to hack their way through the maze of barbed wire. Then they scrambled over the sandbags, their last obstacle, and bayoneted the Turks by scores. One wild mêlée on the parapet – thrust, lunge, and parry – then the trenches were ours.[63]

This is not the confused story of a man describing his own sensations and experiences in the surrounding battle, but the creation of a tale of heroic larrikins. Indeed, Hogue's book is subtitled 'Descriptive Narratives of the More Desperate Engagements on the Gallipoli Peninsula'. This was one of two books that Hogue (1880–1919) published during the war on the basis of articles he had originally written for the *Sydney Morning Herald*, for which he had previously worked. Hogue was not therefore driven by a need to bear witness to extraordinary events in his life; rather he was continuing his professional work as a journalist.[64] He wrote propaganda in the same vein as that of the journalists based in Shepherd's Hotel, Cairo. Robin Gerster refers to Hogue and another Gallipoli veteran R. Hugh Knyvett as 'cheerful wartime liars'.[65] Knyvett, an intelligence officer with the 15th Australian Infantry, published *'Over There' with the Australians* in 1918 in New York. His account hoped to encourage 'this great American democracy' to 'speed in sending them [Australian soldiers] succor as though . . . the bestial Hun were even now, with lust dominant, smashing at your own door'.[66] Knyvett's account asserts the romance of Gallipoli and the prowess of the Anzacs; he rejects criticism of the campaign and seems proud of the Wasir riot in Egypt as a justified act of cleansing in a 'vile spot'.[67] As such, he provides not a more finely nuanced picture of the Anzac legend, but one of the most extreme versions of it. Books such as those by Hogue and Knyvett epitomise Robin Gerster's thesis that Australian military narratives are dominated by a boastful 'glory syndrome': the urge to 'big note'.[68]

Ernest Raymond: *Tell England*

What writers like Hogue and Knyvett provide is a simplified version of events, one that feeds into the war myth of the Anzac legend. Hynes explains the difference between war myths and the soldiers' tale thus:

> By 'myth' I don't mean a fabrication or fiction; I mean rather the simpli-
> fied narrative that evolves from a war, through which it is given meaning:
> a Good War, a Bad War, a Necessary War. Myths seem to be socially neces-
> sary, as judgments or justifications of the terrible costs of war, but they take
> their shape at the expense of the particularity and ordinariness of experi-
> ence, and the inconsistencies and contradictions of human behavior. The
> myth of a war tells what is imaginable and manageable; the soldiers' tale,
> in its infinite variety, tells the whole story.[69]

My argument here is that there is a British equivalent to the Anzac
legend: the heroic–romantic myth. Just as De Loghe/Loch's novelisa-
tion of his Gallipoli experience provided a romanticised, simplified
version of events, so one of the more excessive expressions of the
heroic–romantic myth was a hugely popular novel: Ernest Raymond's
Tell England (1922) sold 300,000 copies by the end of 1939, thereby
demonstrating the resonance of the myth as well as the popularity of
melodrama.[70] Raymond had been the chaplain to the East Lancashire
Territorials of 42nd Division.[71] *Tell England* is an intensely romantic
work, one that now seems chauvinistic and bombastic. Some contemporary critics dismissed it as 'laughable when it is not revolting by reason
of its sticky sentimentality'.[72] Its theme is the adventure of war and the
glorious selflessness and spiritual beauty of living and dying honourably
in the name of patriotism.

The novel follows two boys, Rupert Ray and Edgar Doe, from a board-
ing school worthy of Henry Newbolt to their participation in the late
stages of the Gallipoli campaign. Much of the plot focuses on the influence of Padre Monty as he prepares them for battle and for death. He
portrays their voyage as a knight's vigil in which their aim is to enter
battle pure and white. For it is nothing less than a crusade to rescue Constantinople for Christendom. Before the boys depart for the East they are
told:

> 'You're not over-religious, I expect, but you're Christians before you're
> Moslems, and your hands should fly to your swords when I say the Gal-
> lipoli campaign is a New Crusade. You're going out to force a passage
> through the Dardanelles to Constantinople. And Constantinople is a sacred
> city. It's the only ancient city purely Christian in its origin, having been
> built by the first Christian Emperor in honour of the Blessed Virgin. Which
> brings us to the noblest idea of all. In their fight to wrest this city from
> the Turk, the three great divisions of the Church are united once more. The
> great Roman branch is represented by the soldiers and ships of France:
> the Eastern Orthodox branch by the Russians, who are behind the fight:

the great Anglican branch by the British, who can be proud to have started the movement, and to be leading it. Thus Christendom United fights for Constantinople, under the leadership of the British, whose flag is made up of the crosses of the saints. The army opposing the Christians fights under the crescent of Islam.'[73]

The boys join up enthused with Rupert Brooke-style notions of their good luck to be able to fight and die for England. The idea of heroic patriotism is continued throughout the story. At the end, the surviving boy is encouraged by the padre to 'tell England' the story of the peninsula. This phrase is taken from the epitaph on a friend's grave:

> Tell England, ye who pass this monument,
> We died for her, and here we rest content.[74]

Raymond took this idea from Simonides's epitaph on the Spartans who fell at Thermopylae.[75] A keen sense of the classical associations of the area suffuse the novel. This is confirmed by Raymond in his autobiography. He was sent to six fronts during the war, but it was Gallipoli that held a special glamour and tragic beauty for him. This he attributed to its classical setting and the campaign's 'Attic shape' of a Greek tragedy.[76] Raymond's characters consider life on the peninsula to be 'crowded, glorious living', and the thought of approaching death 'a terribly wonderful thing'.[77] Save for a brief mention of the flies, the hardships of life on the peninsula are absent from the novel. The romanticism of the novel is epitomised by this climactic battle scene: 'Doe stopped, and staggered slightly backwards. His cap fell off, and the wind blew his hair about, as it used to do on the cricket-field at school. He recovered an upright position; he smiled very clearly – then folded up, and collapsed.'[78] Edgar Doe's selfless heroism and its resulting fatal wound are portrayed as his finest achievement. This is clean, exciting and heroic warfare in which the individual makes a difference.

It can be seen that Raymond's novel uses many of the central ideas of the heroic–romantic myth of Gallipoli. Why did he write in this manner? The nature of Raymond's participation in the campaign perhaps facilitated a predisposition to romanticise Gallipoli. Certainly, he arrived at the peninsula in the later stages of the campaign and therefore did not witness the carnage of the landings, hearing of them instead as heroic tales. But the greater part of the explanation is probably to be found in that predisposition towards sentimentality. Even in his autobiography, written in 1968, and despite his embarrassment at 'the naive romanticisms, the pieties, the too facile heroics and too uncritical patriotism',[79] Raymond's description of the campaign is still heavily influenced by his earlier attitude.

The decision to write a novel using his own experiences must also have played its part. A fictionalised account brings the freedom to embellish and elaborate on elements that might otherwise be downplayed. Michael Moynihan makes this point in his study of chaplains in the war:

> In most padres' accounts of their experiences at the front, there is a tendency to concentrate on events and to take for granted the spiritual aspects of their ministrations. Raymond's is no exception. Religion scarcely figures in the section of his autobiography covering his years as a padre. But in the ostensibly fictional *Tell England* he could let himself go, without inhibition.[80]

Cyril Falls made a similar point about the licence of a novel writer in explaining Raymond's phenomenal success:

> The reasons are clear; they are a combination of several qualities dear to the British middle-class reader – a lively story, not too obscure humour, sentiment laid on with a trowel but by a refined and gentlemanly hand, and a strong dash of religion. If this is not the War as it was it certainly was the War as it ought to have been.[81]

It is interesting to note that in other fictional accounts also there can be found Gallipoli as it should have been. For example, two accounts written for children so embellish their stories that their heroes are captured by the Turks but escape and manage to get on board an English submarine that makes its way through the narrows.[82] Finally, Stuart Sillars has suggested that *Tell England*'s popularity lay in its assertion of the continuity of an idealised England and the power of that ideal to console the bereaved.[83] This motif is echoed in Rosa Maria Bracco's study of a broader selection of middlebrow fiction in the inter-war years.[84] The consoling power of a romantic myth is a driving force behind many of the narratives considered in this book.

Another novel, set partly in Gallipoli, gives a somewhat romanticised portrayal of the peninsula. In this case, the author's didactic purpose is particularly clear and important. A. P. Herbert was battalion scout officer, in charge of the 12th Platoon, C Company, Hawke Battalion, in the Royal Naval Division on Gallipoli.[85] He wrote *The Secret Battle* in 1917, and later became an Independent MP for Oxford University from 1935 to 1950.[86] His biographer writes that *The Secret Battle* was 'com-

pulsively written under the duress of frightful memories.'[87] It is a strin-
gent attack on the courts martial procedures of the British Army. It was
based on the case of a sub-lieutenant in the Nelson Battalion of the Naval
Division.[88] Herbert presents an eager young officer, Harry Penrose,
whose nerve is slowly worn away. Ultimately an incident in France leads
to Harry being executed for cowardice. The book concludes: 'That is the
gist of it; that my friend Harry was shot for cowardice – and he was one
of the bravest men I ever knew.'[89] The purpose of the novel is therefore
to make the reader understand something of the strains of war and
thereby to engender sympathy for the men subject to the unjust procedures of the army. The romantic portrayal of Gallipoli in the early stages
of the story (for example, Herbert writes: 'The Romance of War was in
full song. And scrambling down the cliff, we bathed almost reverently in
the Hellespont'[90]) is therefore vital in conveying the changes that come
over Harry. Later, in France, the narrator underlines this change:

> No one but myself would have said that this was not the same Harry of a
> year ago; for he was fit and fresh and bubbling over with keenness. Only
> myself, who had sat over the Dardanelles with him and talked about Troy,
> knew what was missing. There were no more romantic illusions about war,
> and, I think, no more military ambitions. Only he was sufficiently rested
> to be very keen again, and had not yet seen enough of it to be ordinarily
> bored.[91]

A. P. Herbert assisted in the writing of the script when Anthony Asquith
made *Tell England* into a film.[92] The cinematic version played down some
of the romance, and its final scenes conveyed something of the sense of
disenchantment with the war prevalent at the time.[93]

Compton Mackenzie's 1929 *Gallipoli Memories*[94] responded directly to
some of the criticisms of the day. Towards the close of his account, he
fulminates: 'And I have lived to hear Rupert Brooke sneered at for a
romantic by the prematurely weaned young sucking-pigs of the next generation.'[95] And, indeed, Mackenzie clearly shared many of the romantic
attitudes that were common among members of GHQ. His appreciation
of the manly beauty of the Anzacs is widely known,

> There was not one of those glorious young men I saw that day who might
> not himself have been Ajax or Diomed, Hector or Achilles. Their almost
> complete nudity, their tallness and majestic simplicity of line, their rose-
> brown flesh burnt by the sun and purged of all grossness by the ordeal
> through which they were passing, all these united to create something as
> near to absolute beauty as I shall hope ever to see in this world.[96]

As he left the peninsula, he was still moved by its classical associations and by the recent burial of Brooke.[97] Yet his account is more complex in tone than this.

Mackenzie, who was already a well-known novelist in 1915, worked as an intelligence officer attached to GHQ during the Gallipoli campaign. His book is an engaging personal narrative of the campaign. His aim in writing was the 'recapturing [of] the emotions and excitements and embarrassments of one insignificant individual against the background of that heroic tragedy'.[98] Unlike the works of Ernest Raymond or A. P. Herbert, therefore, Compton Mackenzie's response to Gallipoli has some things in common with the narratives of Hynes's soldiers' tale. In particular, Mackenzie conveys the strangeness of war. He is often driven to bizarre comparisons: GHQ and the Mad Hatter's Tea-Party[99] or the shores of Gallipoli and Margate on an August Bank Holiday.[100] His adventures in counter-intelligence are particularly absurd. In his autobiography he described himself at Gallipoli as 'a mere butterfly in a graveyard',[101] and this captures the tone of his narrative. His comments frequently shift swiftly from the comic to the tragic. On the same page that he likens the armistice to a sports day, for example, he gives a graphic account of that day:

> Looking down I saw squelching up from the ground on either side of my boot like a rotten mangold the deliquescent green and black flesh of a Turk's head. [. . .]
>   I cannot recall a single incident on the way back down the valley. I only know that nothing could cleanse the smell of death from the nostrils for a fortnight afterwards. There was no herb so aromatic but it reeked of carrion, not thyme nor lavender, nor even rosemary.[102]

This is the kind of vivid portrayal that comes only from an eyewitness. However, his battle descriptions reflect his remoteness from the action. He describes them as a distant observer[103] or in terms of the frustrating wait for news, as in his picture of Aspinall drawing doodles as they wait, exasperated, for details of the Suvla landings.[104] Indeed, Mackenzie is most interesting for the portrait of GHQ that he provides. His experience of the campaign was largely spent meeting and working with important figures on the staff. His responses to them and to the concerns of GHQ – politics, strategy and leadership – take up much of his narrative.

Mackenzie provides a strange mixture of the soldiers' tale, the heroic–romantic myth and the ironic. His narrative is absurd, romantic and tragic, though it is the first of these that predominates. For example, he chooses the absurd strangeness of the soldiers' tale over the romantic in his selection of an account of the landing: 'All he knew was that he had jumped out of a bloody boat in the dark and before he had walked five bloody yards he had had a bloody bullet in his foot and had been pushed back to bloody Alexandria, almost before he bloody well knew he had left it.'[105]

Various explanations may be suggested for Mackenzie's portrayal of the campaign. As a popular novelist, he had a well-developed sense of the ridiculous and an engaging writing style, providing polished professionalism rather than the 'direct and undecorated'[106] view we usually get from the soldiers' tale. The number of years that passed between the campaign and the writing of the book may have contributed to the occasionally ironic tone, yet he explicitly rejects the disillusionment that was current at the time. In doing so he claims to be faithfully reflecting the manner in which the campaign was perceived: 'My object has been to recapture the spirit in which I passed through a memorable experience. This must be my excuse for not displaying as much moral indignation as the mood of the moment expects from a writer about the War.'[107] And it does seem that his friends and colleagues at GHQ felt he had successfully recaptured its spirit. Walter Braithwaite wrote to him: 'I don't know that I have ever read a book that so brought back to my mind a true atmosphere of a time and place.'[108] This reflects not only the particular and remote view of GHQ, but also the welcome given to an antidote to the growing suggestion that the war had been futile. Orlo Williams told Mackenzie: 'Everybody speaks of it with rapture,'[109] and this may be relief from the tide of disillusionment, and further proof of Bracco's suggestion of the resilience of the view that the war had been worthwhile.[110] Compton Mackenzie propagated an essentially romantic view of the campaign and continued to insist on its nobility and vision.[111] That such arguments were a tonic to participants is suggested by an anecdote which both shows Mackenzie's continuing sympathy and, unusually, reveals that Hamilton was not always as indomitably optimistic as he sometimes seems. Mackenzie had said in a 1956 radio broadcast:

> Ian Hamilton himself had to bear for a long time sneers at his leadership by that common cry of scribes who thought they were writing in the fashion of public opinion.
>
> I can suggest something of what he had been enduring by a story I have never told before. When my book 'Gallipoli Memories' was published in 1929 I sent him a copy, and for over six weeks I heard not a word from him.

Then he wrote me a kind letter, and soon afterwards Lady Hamilton asked me to lunch. She told me that when my book reached him the General had taken it up to his room but that day after day had gone by without his opening it. At last she had read the book herself and had then urged her husband to read it. 'And next morning,' she told me, 'Ian came down to breakfast, humming.' That was a proud moment for me. The Gods who had been so ruthless with Ian Hamilton relented and he was granted years to outlive most of his detractors and best of all to be loved and respected by the younger generation.[112]

Histories

Hynes has contrasted personal narratives with 'history and its numbers',[113] but some participants in the campaign chose to remove themselves entirely from their narratives of Gallipoli and to write a history of the campaign. These histories are of two broad types: unit histories and more generalised accounts. The focus here is on two general histories of the campaign: Henry Nevinson's *The Dardanelles Campaign* (1918) and Phillip Schuler's *Australia at War* (1916), but a few comments about unit histories may be usefully made.[114] Keith Grieves has noted of early regimental histories of the war that 'they emerged in the context of remembrance not as quests for objective truths',[115] and that 'the accounts met private rather than public needs foremost'.[116] In their particular way, unit histories bore witness, but that witness was to the *fact* of an individual's or a unit's participation in war, rather than to the *experience* of that participation. This aim of remembrance thus manifested itself, for example, in an appendix featuring individual photographs and biographical details of members of the Dublin Pals in Henry Hanna's record thereof.[117]

There are several obvious differences between personal narratives and unit histories. Where the authors of personal narratives tend to rely on their eyewitness evidence, all of the authors of unit histories have attempted to do some research, and they refer to and quote from other works on the campaign. Rather than concentrating on the nature of the experience, the histories tend to give factual accounts of those military aspects of the campaign which had featured their particular unit. The regimental accounts are full of names, dates and places. Their participant authors do not tend to give a broader overview of the strategy of the campaign, but they do give details of the origins of the units. Such features also stem from the purpose of remembering the men of the unit. Divisional histories provide an even greater contrast to the soldiers' tale. They relate the campaign from the top down and cover only the

important actions that involved the division, being careful to explain the
context and the plan of action to make their narrative comprehensible.
These differences between regimental and divisional histories stem from
the size of the unit: the smaller the unit the more personal the history.
This tendency was also seen in chapter 2 in the contrasting styles of
British and Australian official histories; it can be seen, too, in the narratives of the senior officers attached to those larger formations.

Schuler's and Nevinson's histories represent early articulations of their
respective country's myths of Gallipoli. Both men were journalists.
Henry Nevinson was a distinguished war correspondent who had
worked for the *Manchester Guardian*. He reached the peninsula on
14 July to cover the campaign for the provincial press. Compton
Mackenzie later recalled their first encounter at Gallipoli:

> The impression Nevinson made on me that day has never faded from my
> mind. He was then either on the edge or just past sixty, a splendid figure
> of a man with fearless eyes that might have belonged to a poet or to a
> general, dignified, courtly, immensely experienced, slightly austere, and
> above all the very personification of absolute integrity.[118]

Phillip Schuler worked for *The Age*, Melbourne, and had visited the
peninsula in August. Schuler's narrative, *Australia in Arms: A Narrative
of the Australasian Imperial Force and Their Achievement at Anzac* (1916)
shares some characteristics with the unit histories. It, too, is very detailed
in its descriptions and careful to identify places, times, brigades and commanders. And while Schuler's scope is much broader, he nonetheless
limits his coverage to a specific group of soldiers. Schuler took care to
explain that the British and French forces were equally heroic and that
his concentration on the part of the Australians was 'because it was the
only one of which I had full knowledge'.[119] But the tone of Schuler's work
is distinctive. He clearly set out to 'big-note', focusing throughout on the
heroism of the men. After his description of the light horsemen at the
Nek, he quotes from Tennyson's *Charge of the Light Brigade*. He concludes with a ringing summary of the most positive elements of the
Anzac legend:

> In one day – 25th April – Australia attained Nationhood by the heroism of
> her noble sons. 'Anzac' will ever form the front page in her history, and a
> unique and vivid chapter in the annals of the Empire. The very vigour of
> their manhood, the impetuosity of their courage, carried slopes that after-
> wards in cold blood, seemed impregnable. And they held what they won,
> and proved themselves an army fit to rank alongside any that a World
> Empire has produced. [. . .]

They gained a respect for themselves and for discipline. They formed for the generations of new armies yet unborn on Australian soil, traditions worthy of the hardy, freeborn race living under the cloudless skies of the Southern Cross. Open-hearted, ever generous, true as gold, and hard as steel, Australia's first great volunteer army, and its valorous deeds, will live in history while the world lasts.[120]

Henry Nevinson's version was also a romanticised account of the campaign. His history is broader in scope than Schuler's: in addition to detailed descriptions of battles involving the British and the Anzacs, it portrays the characters of GHQ, praises the overall strategy of the campaign and criticises the politicians in London who did not give the campaign its due priority. It is a strong defence of General Sir Ian Hamilton. The tone of Nevinson's work is established in his Preface, in which he quotes Thucydides and notes that the Dardanelles Straits were the scene of the Trojan dramas.[121] He goes on to explain his view of the campaign:

It is as an episode of a vanished past that I have attempted to represent it – a tragic episode enacted in the space of eleven months, but marked by every attribute of noble tragedy, whether we consider the grandeur of theme and personality, or the sympathy aroused by the spectacle of heroic figures struggling against the unconscious adversity of fate and the malign influences of hostile and deceptive power.[122]

That Nevinson should espouse so many elements of the heroic–romantic myth of Gallipoli is unsurprising. He consciously set out to emulate Masefield. When Nevinson purchased a copy of *Gallipoli* he noted in his diary: 'Read it all day: with rather bitter envy: for I could have written it quite as well, though perhaps with less enthusiasm.'[123] Nevinson had a long conversation with Masefield on the matter, in which it transpired that Masefield had originally suggested to the Government that the journalist should write about the campaign, but Masefield's fame in America – the primary target for the propaganda – was the deciding factor.[124] Both Masefield and Hamilton urged Nevinson to write his own book on the campaign. Hamilton lent his diaries and Dardanelles Commission evidence to support Nevinson's research.[125] Nevinson talked to various interested parties, including Churchill[126] and Masterton Smith[127] (the permanent secretary to the first lord of the Admiralty and a Churchill loyalist) – such interviews help explain Nevinson's defence of the Dardanelles strategy. Colonel Leslie Wilson appears to have been the only one of Nevinson's interviewees who was hostile to Hamilton.[128] Hamilton's influence extended even to making corrections to Nevinson's draft. But this influence should not perhaps be exaggerated. Nevinson's portrayal of the campaign reflected his own impressions, too. When he later wrote his autobiography he repeated his defence of the campaign, with only a small reduction in the romantic elements of his account.[129]

Conclusion

In discussing war narratives Samuel Hynes has in mind three different styles of writing: the soldiers' tale; the myth of a war; and historical reconstruction. Hynes's notion of the soldiers' tale has been a useful tool in discussing soldiers' personal narratives of Gallipoli. Some of the front-line soldiers' narratives fitted Hynes's characteristics perfectly; but when a narrative's author was removed – in terms of time or space – from the frontline, the narrative's focus spread beyond the purely personal and experiential. What is more, when authors sought to elevate the campaign's reputation for a particular reason, usually to commend it to others, they turned to the high diction of the heroic–romantic myth and the Anzac legend.

When an author's intention was to write a history of the campaign – what Hynes defines as a factual and de-personalised account – there are discernible elements of both the soldiers' tale and the myths of Gallipoli. The soldiers' tale's essential characteristic of bearing witness to a campaign is essentially similar to the unit histories' aim of remembrance. But while the soldiers' tale remembers the *experience*, the histories remember the *participation*. As the size of the unit grows, the emphasis shifts from remembering the participation of a particular individual to remembering a particular battalion or regiment or division. With this shift comes a decline in the number of characteristics shared with the soldiers' tale and, sometimes, an increased use of the romantic elements of the myth of Gallipoli. A similar phenomenon was seen in relation to Bean's official history of the campaign. His account, however, was even more romantic, in its way, since he was not simply remembering the participation of the Anzacs but commemorating their achievements for the nation.

The histories are also similar to the official responses to Gallipoli in that they view it from the top down; but, by contrast, they have greater freedom to include romantic elements in their portrayals. Those personal narratives that describe the campaign from the opposite perspective – from the bottom up – give not a contradictory version of events, but a complementary one. They provide the details that are lost in the grand overview of the distant observer, or the romance that is almost squeezed out of the official responses to the campaign. Ultimately, however, the nuances and contradictions of the narratives which fit Hynes's soldiers' tale are too complex and their focus is too confused and parochial, so that it is the simplified and more palatable romantic myths that are remembered.

Notes

1 May Tilton's *The Grey Battalion* (Sydney, 1933) was written by a nursing sister with the AIF who was stationed in Egypt and was never near the frontline.

2 Robin Gerster, *Big Noting: The Heroic Theme in Australian War Writing* (Melbourne, 1987), p. 5.

3 This point is made in several reviews: John Barret in *Journal of Australian Studies*, 23 (November 1988), pp. 106–8; Richard White in *Australian Historical Studies*, 23:92 (April 1989), pp. 323–4; Adrian Caesar in *Journal of the Australian War Memorial*, 14 (April 1989), pp. 58–9.

4 Samuel Hynes, *The Soldiers' Tale: Bearing Witness to Modern War* (New York, 1997), p. xii.

5 *Ibid.*, p. 30.

6 *Ibid.*, p. xii. Hynes uses the term 'history' to describe factual accounts of the past that detail and explain particular events. He does so to differentiate between such accounts and personal narratives with their focus on one individual's experience. Hynes does not imply that personal narratives are the opposite to the factual accounts of 'history', i.e. that they are fictional, but that they are divorced from contextualising details like dates or tactics.

7 Sydney de Loghe (F. S. Loch), *The Straits Impregnable* (London, 1917).

8 Other personal narratives of Gallipoli by men who served as frontline soldiers published during the inter-war years are: Capt. R. W. Campbell, *The Kangaroo Marines* (London, 1915) and 'Anzac', *On the Anzac Trail: Being Extracts from the Diary of a New Zealand Sapper* (London, 1916); Oliver Hogue, *Trooper Bluegum at the Dardanelles: Descriptive Narratives of the More Desperate Engagements on the Gallipoli Peninsula* (London, 1916); John Gallishaw, *Trenching at Gallipoli: A Personal Narrative of a Newfoundlander with the Ill-Fated Dardanelles Expedition* (New York, 1916); Juvenis, *Suvla Bay and After* (London, 1916); Trooper L. McCustra, *Gallipoli Days and Nights* (London, 1916); E. Y. Priestman, *With a B-P Scout in Gallipoli: A Record of the Belton Bulldogs* (London, 1916); Captain David Fallon, MC, *The Big Fight (Gallipoli to the Somme)* (London, 1918); Captain R. Hugh Knyvett, *'Over There' with the Australians* (New York, 1918); Hector Dinning, *By-Ways on Service: Notes from an Australian Journal* (London,

1918); E. F. Hanman, *Twelve Months with the 'Anzacs'* (Brisbane, 1918); Eric Partridge, *Frank Honywood, Private: A Personal Record of the 1914–1918 War* (Melbourne, 1987 [1929]); S. F. Hatton, *The Yarn of a Yeoman* (London, 1930); Stanley Sherman Wright, *Of That Fellowship: The Tragedy, Humour and Pathos of Gallipoli!* (London, 1931); Ion L. Idriess, *The Desert Column* (Sydney, 1932).

  9 Australian War Memorial, Canberra (AWM) catalogue.

10 William H. Wilde, Joy Hooton and Barry Andrews (eds) *The Oxford Companion to Australian Literature* (Melbourne, 1994), p. 474.

11 De Loghe, *Straits Impregnable*, p. 82.

12 *Ibid.*, p. 94.

13 *Ibid.*, pp. 238–9.

14 Hynes, *Soldiers' Tale*, p. 27.

15 De Loghe, *Straits Impregnable*, p. 105.

16 *Ibid.*, p. 106.

17 *Ibid.*, p. 210.

18 *Ibid.*, p. 128.

19 *Ibid.*, pp. 188–9.

20 *Ibid.*, pp. 206–7.

21 Hynes, *Soldiers' Tale*, p. 11.

22 De Loghe, *Straits Impregnable*, p. 222.

23 Hynes, *Soldiers' Tale*, p. 66. Joanna Bourke's *An Intimate History of Killing: Face-to-Face Killing in Twentieth-Century Warfare* (London, 1999) considers men's experiences of killing and provides many examples of soldiers discussing these experiences.

24 Hynes, *Soldiers' Tale*, p. 1.

25 De Loghe, *Straits Impregnable*, p. 158.

26 Wright, *Of That Fellowship*, pp. 82–3.

27 Hynes, *Soldiers' Tale*, p. 20.

28 De Loghe, *Straits Impregnable*, p. 189.

29 Idriess, *Desert Column*, p. 25.

30 Gallishaw, *Trenching at Gallipoli*, p. 180.

31 Hynes, *Soldiers' Tale*, p. 25.

32 Gerster, *Big Noting*, p. 50.

33 Frederick Sydney Loch, 'Turn'd, but Not Torn' (*c.*1934), AWM, MSS 1367.

34 *Ibid*, p. 134.

35 *Ibid.*, p. 285.

36 *Ibid.*, pp. 41, 310.

37 *Ibid.*, pp. 115, 171.

38 *Ibid.*, p. 192.

39 *Ibid.*, pp. 42, 115.

40 'Or for a little time we'll lie / As robes laid by; / To be another day re-worn, / Turn'd, but not torn' (Herrick), *ibid.*, p. 343.

41 *Ibid.*, p. 345.

42 Sydney Loch to an official at the Australian War Memorial, 26 November 1935, AWM, MSS1367.

43 Major John Graham Gillam DSO, *Gallipoli Diary* (London, 1918) and John Gillam, *Gallipoli Adventure* (London, 1939).

44 Gillam, *Diary*, p. 7.

45 Gillam, *Diary*, p. 89.

46 *Ibid.*, p. 7.

47 Reverend O. Creighton, CF, *With the Twenty-Ninth Division in Gallipoli: A Chaplain's Experiences* (London, 1916).

48 Gillam, *Diary*, p. 201.

49 *Ibid.*, p. 120.

50 *Ibid.*, p. 70.

51 *Ibid.*, p. 216.

52 Other personal narratives published by senior officers in the Gallipoli campaign include, Lieutenant-Colonel C. H. Weston, *Three Years with the New Zealanders* (London, 1918); General Sir Ian Hamilton, *Gallipoli Diary* (London, 1920); Major C. B. Brereton, *Tales of Three Campaigns* (London, 1926); Lieutenant-General Sir William Marshall, *Memories of Four Fronts* (London, 1929); General Sir Alexander Godley, *Life of an Irish Soldier* (London, 1939); Field Marshal Lord Birdwood, *Khaki and Gown: An Autobiography* (London, 1941).

53 Gillam, *Adventure*, pp. 76 and 82.

54 *Ibid.*, p. 86.

55 *Ibid.*, p. 217.

56 *Ibid.*, p. 100.

57 *Ibid.*, p. 132.

58 *Ibid.*, p. 176.

59 *Ibid.*, p. 252.

60 *Ibid.*, pp. 126, 144, 209.

61 *Ibid.*, p. 120.

62 Hogue, *Trooper Bluegum*, p. 281.

63 *Ibid.*, p. 199.

64 *Love Letters of an Anzac* (1916) was also a collection of the articles he wrote for the *Herald*. He served at Gallipoli and in the desert campaigns, but died in the influenza epidemic of 1919: Wilde *et al.* (eds) *Oxford Companion to Australian Literature*, p. 375.

65 Gerster, *Big Noting*, p. 117.

66 Knyvett, 'Over There', p. 11. One of the key mythologising accounts of Gallipoli, John Masefield's *Gallipoli* (1916), was also written with the American market in mind.

67 Knyvett, 'Over There', p. 91.

68 *Ibid.*, p. 3.

69 *Ibid.*, p. xiii.

70 Ernest Raymond, *Please You, Draw Near: Autobiography 1922–1968*

(London, 1969), p. 69. *Tell England* had reached its fortieth edition by 1973; Raymond went on to write several dozen books.

71 Other Gallipoli chaplains' narratives are the aforementioned Creighton, *With the Twenty-Ninth Division*; and William Ewing, MC, DD, *From Gallipoli to Baghdad* (London, 1918) and Reverend H. C. Foster, MA, *At Antwerp and the Dardanelles* (London, 1918). The only narrative by an AIF chaplain that I have found, K. T. Henderson, MA, CF, *Khaki and Cassock* (Melbourne, 1919), does not touch on the Gallipoli campaign.

72 Michael Moynihan (ed.) *God on Our Side* (London, 1983), p. 81.

73 Ernest Raymond, *Tell England: A Study in a Generation* (London, 1922), p. 180.

74 *Ibid.*, p. 273.

75 Ernest Raymond, *The Story of My Days: An Autobiography 1888–1922* (London, 1968), p. 141.

76 Raymond, *Tell England*, p. 127.

77 *Ibid.*, p. 275.

78 *Ibid.*, p. 290.

79 Raymond, *The Story of My Days*, p. 179.

80 Moynihan (ed.) *God on Our Side*, p. 82.

81 Cyril Falls, *War Books* (London 1989 [1930]), p. 293.

82 Percy F. Westerman, *The Fight for Constantinople: A Story of the Gallipoli Peninsula* (London, 1915), and T. C. Bridges, *On Land and Sea at the Dardanelles* (London, 1915). Another account, probably fictionalised, includes a failed romance with a nurse and an escape from imprisonment by the Turks: *Peninsula of Death – as Told to W. J. Blackledge by Digger Craven* (London, 1937). On the theme of imprisonment, R. F. Lushington was captured so swiftly that almost his entire personal narrative concerns his imprisonment: R. F. Lushington, *A Prisoner with the Turks 1915–1918* (London, 1923). Another novel, George Blake's *The Path of Glory* (London, 1929), does not present an idealised picture of Gallipoli; rather it has several of the features of the soldiers' tale, such as confused battle descriptions and strange incidents. It is not clear whether Blake participated in the campaign.

83 Stuart Sillars, *Art and Survival in First World War Britain* (London, 1987) pp. 135–42.

84 Rosa Maria Bracco, *Merchants of Hope: British Middlebrow Writers and the First World War 1919–1939* (Oxford, 1993).

85 Sir Alan Herbert, CH, *A. P. H. His Life and Times* (London, 1970), pp. 3 and 40. He should not be confused with Aubrey Herbert, intelligence officer with the New Zealand Division, organiser of the only armistice during the campaign and Conservative MP for South Somerset from 1911. His memoir of the campaign is *Mons, Anzac and Kut* (London, 1919).

86 Robin Young, 'The man with no party has class act to follow', *The Times*, 3 May 1997, p. 11.

87 Reginald Pound, *A. P. Herbert: A Biography* (London, 1976), p. 55.

88 *Ibid.*, p. 53. The specific case is thought to be that of temporary Sub-Lieutenant Edwin Dyett, Nelson Battalion, 63rd (RN) Division. The details of this case, which differ from Herbert's version, are given in Anthony Babington, *For the Sake of Example* (London, 1993), and in Leonard Sellers, *For God's Sake Shoot Straight* (London, 1995).

89 A. P. Herbert, *The Secret Battle* (Oxford, 1982 [1919]), p. 130.

90 *Ibid.*, p. 12.

91 *Ibid.*, p. 69.

92 Andrew Kelly, *Cinema and the Great War* (London, 1997), p. 75.

93 Keith Grieves, 'Remembering an ill-fated venture: personal and collective histories of Gallipoli in a southern English community 1919–1939' in Jenny Macleod (ed.) *Gallipoli: Making History* (forthcoming).

94 Compton Mackenzie, *Gallipoli Memories* (London, 1929).

95 *Ibid.*, p. 394.

96 *Ibid.*, p. 81.

97 *Ibid.*, p. 400.

98 *Ibid.*, p. 29.

99 *Ibid.*, p. 35.

100 *Ibid.*, p. 163.

101 Compton Mackenzie, *My Life and Times: Octave Five 1915–1923* (London, 1966), p. 16.

102 Mackenzie, *Gallipoli Memories*, pp. 82–3.

103 *Ibid.*, p. 33.

104 *Ibid.*, p. 374.

105 *Ibid.*, p. 20.

106 Hynes, *Soldiers' Tale*, p. xv.

107 Mackenzie, *Gallipoli Memories*, p. x.

108 Sir Walter Braithwaite to Sir Compton Mackenzie, 20 November 1929, TLS, Harry Ransom Centre (HRC), University of Texas at Austin, Compton Mackenzie Papers. Similarly appreciative letters were written to Mackenzie by Edward Marsh, Guy Dawnay, Orlo Williams and General Sir Ian Hamilton.

109 Orlo Williams to Compton Mackenzie ('Monty'), 12 January 1930, HRC, Austin, TX, Compton Mackenzie Papers.

110 Bracco, *Merchants of Hope*.

111 For example, Compton Mackenzie, 'The Dardanelles', 29 April 1956, unidentified newspaper, National Library of Australia, Canberra, Alan Moorehead Papers, MS 5654, box 13, folder 107.

112 '3.5.56 European Service, General News Talk, Weekly Book Summary No 645: "Gallipoli" by Alan Moorehead, reviewed by Sir Compton Mackenzie', Alan Moorehead Papers, MS5654, box 13, folder 107.

113 Hynes, *Soldiers' Tale*, p. xii.

114 See also Helen McCartney, 'Unit histories: Gallipoli and after' in Jenny Macleod (ed.) *Gallipoli: Making History* (forthcoming).

115 Keith Grieves, 'Making sense of the Great War: regimental histories, 1918–23', *Journal of the Society for Army Historical Research*, 69:277 (spring, 1991), p. 14.

116 *Ibid.*

117 Henry Hanna, KC, *The Pals at Suvla Bay (Being the Record of 'D' Company of the 7th Royal Dublin Fusiliers)* (Dublin, 1916). Other unit histories of Gallipoli include: E. Pebody, *Experiences in the Dardanelles of the 1st/5th Beds. Regiment TF* (Olney, 1916); Gerald B. Hurst, *With Manchesters in the East* (Manchester, 1918); Bryan Cooper, *The Tenth (Irish) Division in Gallipoli* (London, 1918; Blackrock, Co. Dublin, 1993); Douglas Jerrold, *The Royal Naval Division* (London, 1923); Capt. Stair Gillon, *The Story of the 29th Division: A Record of Gallant Deeds* (London, 1925); Lt-Colonel R. R. Thompson, MC, *The Fifty-Second (Lowland) Division 1914–1918* (Glasgow, 1923). Another two unit histories I have found were not written by participants: F. P. Gibbon, *The 42nd (East Lancashire) Division 1914–1918* (London, 1921); and James Cowan, *The Maoris in the Great War: A History of the New Zealand Native Contingent and Pioneer Battalion* (Auckland, 1926). Although, strictly speaking, brigades, divisions and corps are formations, for ease of expression their histories will be referred to as unit histories.

118 Compton Mackenzie, 'A great man', *Evening News*, 16 March 1945, Bodleian Library, Oxford, Henry Woodd Nevinson papers, MS Eng misc c.497/2, Press cuttings.

119 Phillip Schuler, *Australia in Arms: A Narrative of the Australasian Imperial Force and Their Achievement at Anzac* (London, 1916) p. 10.

120 *Ibid.*, pp. 291–2. Schuler produced a distilled version of these sentiments in a collection of photographs: P. F. E. Schuler, *Pictures of the Battlefields of Anzac: On Which the Australasians Won Deathless Fame* (Melbourne, 1916). There were several similar brief histories of the campaign produced in Australia during the war. They were written by non-participants in the campaign and share a breathless high diction and have a similar tone: S. Bennett, *Gallipoli: The Heroic Story of the Australasians at Anzac: Complete Official and Other Accounts – Illustrated* (Sydney, 1916); Dr J. W. Springthorpe, *The Great Withdrawal: Story of a Daring Plan. Last Days at Anzac. How Our Soldiers Left. A Vivid Narrative* (Melbourne, 1916); Lt the Honourable Staniforth Smith, *Australian Campaigns in the Great War* (Melbourne, 1919). E. C. Buley, *Glorious Deeds of Australasians in the Great War* (London, 1915); and A. St John Adcock, *Australasia Triumphant! With the Australians and New Zealanders in the Great War on Land and Sea* (London, 1916).

121 Henry W. Nevinson, *The Dardanelles Campaign* (London, 1918), p. vii.

122 *Ibid.*, p. ix.

123 Nevinson's diary, September 16, 1916, H. W. Nevinson Papers, MS Eng misc e.620/1.

124 *Ibid.*, December 25, 1916.

125 *Ibid.*, February 6, 1917, H. W. Nevinson Papers, MS Eng misc e.620/2.
126 *Ibid.*, May 8, 1917.
127 *Ibid.*, May 15, 1917.
128 *Ibid.*, November 15, 1917.
129 Henry W. Nevinson, *Last Changes, Last Chances* (London, 1928), pp. 29–66.

5

The commander's response: General Sir Ian Hamilton's *Gallipoli Diary*

In 1920 General Sir Ian Hamilton published the two volumes of his *Gallipoli Diary*.[1] It was the summit of his attempts to portray the campaign in a positive light. It is an unusual and skilful senior officer's memoir. Not only does it seek to bear witness to the commander's experience, but it does so in a highly romanticised way, developing the heroic–romantic myth of Gallipoli. This chapter explores the motivation for and the construction of the commander's response.

Hamilton's character and career

At the outbreak of the First World War, Ian Hamilton had been a widely experienced and decorated soldier. He had twice been considered for the Victoria Cross – rejected once because of his junior rank and again, later, because of his seniority.[2] He had acted as Kitchener's chief of staff during the Boer War and in November 1914 Kitchener suggested to Joffre that Hamilton should replace French as commander of the British Expeditionary Force in France.[3] On 13 March 1915 he was appointed commander-in-chief of the MEF and hastily despatched to the Dardanelles. He was dismissed seven months later, and he never again held an important command. During his retirement he remained a public figure, working extensively for the British Legion, unveiling war memorials, attending commemorative dinners, and writing books and prefaces.

Hamilton was a loquacious communicator, charming and intellectual. He published numerous books during his lifetime. He wrote imaginatively on military problems and even his poetry was published.[4] His obituary in *The Times* noted:

> His intellectual gifts, his personal charm, his vivid imagination, his wit, his versatility, his forthrightness of tongue, and his power with the pen made

a remarkable impression upon his fellow-countrymen. This was perhaps heightened by the fact that he was inclined to take extremely liberal, if not what are called 'Leftish', views.[5]

Hamilton was a Liberal, but held no sympathy for collectivism. He opposed compulsory service – a stand which put him in opposition to his former commander Lord Roberts during the pre-1914 controversy. He was mooted as a candidate for the House of Lords by the Liberals during the constitutional crisis of 1910.[6] He refused Ramsay Macdonald's request to be secretary of state for war in the first Labour Government.[7] He did, however, come to sympathise with the stance taken by pacifists of the inter-war period. Henry Nevinson, the highly regarded war correspondent, became a friend of Hamilton; he described this unusual general's sanguine and chivalrous nature thus:

> Undoubtedly he was deeply tinged with the 'Celtic charm' – that glamour of mind and courtesy of behaviour which create suspicion among people endowed with neither. Through his nature ran a strain of the idealistic spirit which some despise as quixotic, and others salute as chivalrous, while, with cautious solicitude, they avoid it in themselves.[8]

The purpose of *Gallipoli Diary*

Given his established pattern as an author, it is not surprising that Hamilton wrote on the Gallipoli campaign. Moreover, his reasons for putting pen to paper in that regard were more compelling than usual. The campaign had been the greatest event of his career – and its greatest failure. It had ruined him and tarnished his reputation. He worked assiduously, therefore, to clear his name and that of the campaign with which he was most closely associated.

Hamilton's attempts to influence the Dardanelles Commission were considered in chapter 1. The findings of that commission proved to be highly unsatisfactory. The commission's scope was strictly limited, dealing only with a narrow range of concerns and drawing only limited conclusions. Furthermore the publication of its reports was delayed and its evidence remained secret. Hamilton's exculpation therefore remained elusive. Hamilton expressed his frustration at this situation in the following passage, written soon after the war but posthumously published in *The Commander*:

> If there are those who doubt or wish to refute these contentions about the real reasons behind the limitations imposed on our fighting in the

Dardanelles and our subsequent evacuation; if there are those who feel it was not as much the influence of outsiders toying with power they had no right to as the failing nerve of the politicians, then let me put this question to them. Why has the Report of the Royal Commission on the Dardanelles not been published with all the detailed evidence – taken from every conceivable witness – it contains? Not one line of it has been produced for the public to see. Where is the Official History of the Dardanelles, begun by a tried historian whose accuracy, impartiality and good faith are proverbial, the Honourable John Fortescue? No! 'The melancholy drama which, under the title of the "glorious retirement from Gallipoli", was to make its Don Quixote progress through the journalistic forest of the Entente press' – the words are not mine – must be kept secret while I and others are alive to refute with the living word the glib excuses which the Government of the day has made for their actions.[9]

For Hamilton's purposes, therefore, the report of the Dardanelles Commission was a failed narrative. *Ian Hamilton's Final Despatch* and *Ian Hamilton's Despatches from the Dardanelles* had been published in 1916 and 1917, but these were bland and essentially technical narratives which failed to counter the generally held impression that he was to blame for the failure at Gallipoli. Hamilton therefore sought to address a wider audience with his *Gallipoli Diary*.

The idea that the *Diary* was a riposte to the Dardanelles Commission is tacitly confirmed by its Preface in which Hamilton described his reasons for publishing. He explained that he began to keep a diary in the wake of the South African War and the subsequent royal commissions. During those commissions, through 'constant observation of civilian Judges and soldier witnesses', he realised that the 'unaided military memory' is 'fallible' and that '[t]he winner is asked no questions – the loser has to answer for everything'.[10] These comments are remarkably pertinent to his experience also of the Dardanelles Commission. Diaries were Hamilton's means of self-defence in the wake of war.

It was seen chapter 4 that, even as the Dardanelles Commission was sitting, Hamilton had persuaded Henry Nevinson to write a sympathetic account of the campaign. While Hamilton waited impatiently for the commission's reports to be published, he worked on his own narrative. It would prove to be the peak of his attempts to influence perceptions of his campaign. This scheme had great potential for success, not just because of his privileged position as the campaign's commander-in-chief, but because accounts of the campaign were still relatively scarce. Ian Beckett has noted that, in a situation where access to official documents is strictly controlled, the earliest knowledgeable participant to publish 'had considerable impact in establishing some of the post-war controversies'.[11] Nor was Hamilton alone in using his own diary to convey his point of view. For example, Haig's unpublished diary was circulated in defence of his own conduct of operations.[12]

Hamilton sought to demonstrate that the campaign had not been a disaster and that he was not primarily responsible for its failure. He therefore constructed a narrative that portrayed the campaign in the best possible light. This entailed the fullest demonstration of the heroic–romantic myth of Gallipoli. As I explained in the Introduction, there are three strands to this myth. First there is the romantic and glamorous strand: in Hamilton's writing this was derived from a roman-tic view of warfare and the campaign's classical setting, and it was rein-forced by a careful suppression of the more horrific elements of warfare. The second strand is that of honour and heroism: Hamilton stressed the chivalrous virtues, and the honour and gallantry of the men. In part this rested on the assertion that the failure of the campaign was not the fault of those who fought on Gallipoli. This idea leads to the concerns of the third strand, strategy and politics, in particular the suggestion that failure resulted from the mistakes of politicians in London – and of Kitchener, especially. This subtext runs throughout the *Diary*. Such implied criti-cism of Kitchener was daring given the popularity and, indeed, the awe in which Kitchener was held by the public. Yet it was the most impor-tant of the three strands for Hamilton, in that it was crucial to vindicat-ing the commander and his campaign. This explanation of failure served also to make the campaign more poignant and to highlight the tantalis-ing opportunity lost in defeat: the chance to foreshorten the war. In developing the heroic–romantic myth of Gallipoli, particularly in criti-cising his former boss, it will be seen that Hamilton was composing a narrative that had not been possible within the constraints of the Dardanelles Commission or in his despatches during the campaign.

Hamilton's prefacing description of the generally held impression of the campaign suggests that the heroic–romantic myth of Gallipoli was already well established:

> [O]nly the vastness of the stakes; the intensity of the effort and the grandeur of the sacrifice still stand out clearly when we, in dreams, behold the Dardanelles. Why not leave that shining impression as a martial cloak to cover the errors and vicissitudes of all the poor mortals who, in the words of Thucydides, 'dared beyond their strength, hazarded against their judg-ment, and in extremities were of an excellent hope?'[13]

Hamilton accordingly claimed to have 'no complaints' that he needed to express, and he illustrated this contentment by praising works by Masefield, Nevinson and Callwell as 'each essentially true'. But 'on the top of these' he singled out the report of the Dardanelles Commission and Sir George Arthur's biography of Kitchener which gave the secretary of state's side of the story; the implication being that those works were not 'essentially true'. Hamilton also wrote that he wished to face his critics rather than to have his work published posthumously: he portrayed publication as a matter of honour. Furthermore he wanted his comrades to confirm his judgements: 'Before I go I want to have the verdict of my comrades of all ranks at the Dardanelles, and until they know the truth, as it appeared to me at the time, how can they give that verdict?'[14]

Hamilton's construction of *Gallipoli Diary*

Why did Hamilton choose to present his recollections as a diary? The question is a pertinent one since it is widely acknowledged that *Gallipoli Diary* was not a faithful reproduction of a record kept during the course of the campaign. This became a matter of controversy in 1956 following the publication of Alan Moorehead's account of the campaign. Hamilton's secretary Mary Shield objected strongly to the suggestion that Hamilton had found the time to write 5,000 words in his diary during the first landings.[15] She and others wrote to *The Times*. Moorehead's draft response was this:

> The point of course is that your correspondents' argument lies not with me but with the General and in defending him they condemn him. They are saying quite bluntly that Hamilton was telling an untruth when he wrote that he compiled his diary 'red-hot amidst tumult'. And so it is surely their word agst his.[16]

Moorehead concluded that Hamilton had made jottings on the spot. Hamilton's niece Janet Leeper wrote to Moorehead: 'the *Gallipoli Diary* was after all not a diary but a work of art, as one of the Critics said on the BBC. I think he took four years to write it.'[17] It seems that what Hamilton had produced was a memoir in diary form based on a few comments noted down each day.[18]

This deception was clearly useful to Hamilton. He wrote to a correspondent in 1920, explaining: 'it was a record taken down on the spot. I don't mean to say that there have been no cuttings out of repetitions and redundancies, or improvements in ways of saying things, but essentially the Diary is there as it was at the time and cannot in its body be changed.'[19] Hamilton therefore used the diary format to defend his narrative as the truth as he saw it – thus avoiding the need to declare the veracity of his narratives as other soldiers' narratives do. Hamilton used the diary form to privilege his opinions and defend himself from criticism and accusations based on hindsight. It was also a convenient format for portraying the development of events. It enabled Hamilton to explain his views and sentiments unencumbered by the need to go into the details of developments on the ground. It differed, therefore, from both his official dispatches and the narratives of other senior officers.

Hamilton had given far more detailed accounts of the military manoeuvres undertaken in his official dispatches, accounts which lack the confusion of the *Diary*'s emerging picture. The dispatches are notable for their sober language, their tendency to frankly admit casualty figures and their lack of other distracting details. However, the tone of *Gallipoli Diary* is not attributable simply to its status as a personal narrative rather than an official document. Nor can it be accounted for by Hamilton's position in the force – comparison with personal narratives by other senior and middle-ranking officers at Gallipoli demonstrates how unusual was his *Gallipoli Diary*.[20]

Senior officers' attempts to bear witness to their personal experiences were largely unsuccessful. They failed to distinguish their own views from those expressed in their official work. Their particular role in the campaign – which required an attention to tactics and assessments of their progress – and their necessary remoteness from the frontline indelibly marked the way they wrote. But there is a further reason for their particular style. All these men were professional soldiers. Their experiences and attitudes do not make for engaging personal narratives for the non-military reader. As Samuel Hynes explains:

> They make good soldiers, but they are by and large no good for war memoirs; they stand too close to the center of war's values, and whether they mean to or not, they act out the mottoes on the flags and the slogans on the posters. What suits memory best is a war life lived close to the action but at some distance from the values, by a man who is by nature or circumstances an outsider, who can be a witness as well as a soldier, who has felt war but doesn't love it.[21]

These senior officers' close identification with the military and its values can be seen in their writing style. It is distinct from battlefield gothic, it cannot shake off the influence of the battalion diary or the commanders' dispatch.

There is, however, an exception to the senior officers' style besides Hamilton: Sir John Monash. *War Letters of General Monash*[22] was published posthumously in 1934, having been edited by his daughter and son-in-law,[23] and then by official historian F. M. Cutlack, who had worked on Monash's staff in France. Far more so than senior officers' personal narratives, Monash's letters to his wife and family during the war give a much stronger sense of the man and his preoccupations, though naturally centring on his evaluations of strategy, tactics, hospital arrangements, and so forth. They also show his self-regard[24] and his strong appreciation of the Australian troops,[25] even though his editors sought to remove the excessively egotistical comments as well as his derogatory comments regarding the British troops.[26] Perhaps because they are letters written to family members and because they were written by a highly educated citizen soldier, this narrative escapes the dry language of the dispatch (though it could not be described as battlefield gothic). The letters may be seen as acting primarily to bolster the Anzac legend and to boost the general's own reputation, already unrivalled in Australia.[27]

Hamilton's *Gallipoli Diary* was similarly unusual and promotional. Although he was a professional soldier, Hamilton had long proved his intellectual ability to step outside military orthodoxy – in both style and opinion – and his narrative is therefore unlike most senior officers' narratives. At the same time, his narrative does not echo the soldiers' tale. Hamilton's purpose was not simply to bear witness but to elevate the reputation of the campaign. This was a task to which he was temperamentally well suited. The creative facets of his personality that had aroused the suspicion of his peers would now come into full play in his rehabilitation. The diary form was the repository for this unfettered self-expression; the diary is therefore the perfect format for self-explanation and so for self-justification, for the expression of a romantic temperament and therefore of the heroic–romantic myth of Gallipoli.

How did Hamilton construct this exculpatory narrative? In his papers there is a portion of manuscript that offers some clues.[28] It is certainly not a part of the original diary kept during the campaign: it shows that certain alterations had been made prior to publication. These were not merely inconsequential changes to grammar or syntax. The changes included the editing and modification of criticisms of individuals, and were such as to temper the tone of the writing. A 1919 letter to Churchill suggests the reasoning by which such changes were made:

Looking over some of my own old letters to my wife I found I heard a rumour of your resignation the previous evening, the 21st and my comments on it in the letter are better put than in the diary when de Robeck brought over the Reuter next day. In the letter to my wife there was a remark about the alarm amongst the sailors lest Fisher should come back as First Lord but the old boy has been so decent to you that I have thought it better left out.[29]

This again suggests that the *Diary* was in part a weapon to be used against critics. Other additions to the *Diary* included the insertion of battle descriptions. More importantly, he inserted the text of many of his cables. Such is their quantity that they account approximately for more than one quarter of the published two-volume *Diary*. It will be seen that these cables were a vital part of Hamilton's self justification.

Gallipoli Diary and the romance of war

The alterations to the manuscript were made in order to express Hamilton's viewpoint in the most convincing way. Hamilton's distinctive writing style is a central factor in making *Gallipoli Diary* a persuasive portrayal of a worthwhile and well-conducted campaign. His manner of self-expression was perfectly suited to building a heroic–romantic portrait of Gallipoli. Hamilton's writing style was a product of his education and attitudes. His prose, at the age of 67, demonstrates the influence of a traditional Victorian public-school education.[30] It is ornate and embellished, particularly in its classical allusions; battlefield gothic it certainly is not.

The style and sentiment of his work echoes nineteenth-century modes of war literature, those of the middle-brow writers of the Great War (studied by Rosa Maria Bracco[31]) who continued to assert the presence in war of inspirational human values rather than emulate the ironic voice of disillusionment and alienation. Indeed, Hamilton explicitly distanced his view of war from those conveyed by the latter style of writing:

> There are poets and writers who see naught in war but carrion, filth, savagery and horror. The heroism of the rank and file makes no appeal. They refuse war the credit of being the only exercise in devotion on the large scale existing in this world. The superb moral victory over death leaves them cold. Each one to his taste. To me this is no valley of death – it is a valley brim full of life at its highest power.[32]

In any case, the description of war in terms of 'savagery and horror' would not have served Hamilton's purpose regarding Gallipoli. In later years, however, Hamilton praised the disillusionment of the war book *All Quiet on the Western Front*:

> There was a time when I would have strenuously combated [*sic*] Remarque's inferences and conclusions. Now, sorrowfully, I must admit, there is a great deal of truth in them. Latrines, rats, lice; smells, blood, corpses; scenes of sheer horror as where comrades surround the deathbed of a young *Kamerad* with one eye on his agonies, the other on his new English boots; the uninspired strategy; the feeling that the leaders are unsympathetic or stupid; the shrivelling up of thought and enthusiasm under ever-growing machinery of attrition war; all this lasting too long.[33]

It is remarkable that any general should comment in this way: such notions served to bolster the general revulsion against war and its leaders. Perhaps Hamilton's ability to think this way lay not only in the independence of his thought but in his isolation from the Western Front. Perhaps the worse the Western Front seems, the more tragic and romantic seems Gallipoli, a campaign of inspired strategy and sympathetic leadership which might have curtailed the war.

Hamilton gave expression to these jaded views only later: in *The Soul and Body of an Army* (1921) he commended the spirit of patriotism of the men and concluded: '*Dulce et decorum est pro patria mori*' without a trace of Wilfred Owen's irony.[34] Similarly, in *Gallipoli Diary*, Hamilton's romantic view of warfare is clear. He saw value in war, believing that it brought out the virtue in men, and hastened reform and change in nations: social Darwinist notions. Witnessing the discipline of the crew of a sinking ship, he commented:

> On the deck of that battleship staggering along at a stone's throw was a vindication of war in itself; of war, the state of being, quite apart from war motives or gains. Ten thousand years of peace would fail to produce a spectacle of so great virtue [. . .]
>
> Only by intense sufferings can the nations grow, just as the snake once a year must with anguish slough off the once beautiful coat which has now become a strait jacket.[35]

Hamilton the soldier thrilled to the sight of naval battle. He went on to suggest that the submarine, like the aeroplane, retained war's spirit of adventure: 'The exploits of the submarine give a flat knock-out to Norman Angell's contention that excitement and romance have now gone out of war.'[36] The romance of war was also reinforced by the brief role in the campaign of Rupert Brooke. The poet died on the eve of the landing (from the unromantic cause of septicaemia), but, before he fell ill, Hamilton had invited him to join his personal staff: 'Young Brooke replied, as a *preux chevalier* would naturally reply, – he realised the privileges he was foregoing, but he felt bound to do the landing shoulder-to-shoulder with his comrades. He looked extraordinarily handsome, quite a knightly presence.'[37] Despite this romantic view of warfare, however, it should be noted that Hamilton retained a very humane sympathy for the men in the thick of the fighting. For example, on the night after the landings he wrote: 'What of those men fighting for their lives in the darkness. I put them there. Might they not, all of them, be sailing back to safe England, but for me?'[38] Even in this there are literary and therefore romanticising overtones: in Shakespeare's *Henry V*, on the eve of battle the king ponders and then denies his responsibility for his soldiers' deaths.[39]

Hamilton also built up the general sense of the romance of the campaign through his many references to its setting. His allusions to the days of Troy invest his attempt to capture Constantinople with an air of grand adventure and heroic struggle. Descriptions of the beauty of the peninsula – rising out of the clear blue sea under bright sunshine – with its sprinkling of wild flowers, also provide a powerful contrast to images, in other works, of the muddy bleakness of the Western Front. Hamilton dwells on these themes most frequently at the beginning of the campaign. The following passage was inspired by his first sight of the Dardanelles:

> No other panorama can touch it. There, Hero trimmed her little lamp; yonder the amorous breath of Leander changed to soft sea form. [. . .] Against this enchanted background to deeds done by immortals and mortals as they struggled for ten long years five thousand years ago, – stands forth formidably the Peninsula. Glowing with bright, springtime colours it sweeps upwards from the sea like the glacis of a giant's fortress.[40]

However, perhaps the most important aspect of this romantic strand is Hamilton's subtle and continuous project to minimise the horrors of warfare on the peninsula. This can be seen in his portrayal of living conditions and battles, and in the casualty statistics. References to the tough living conditions of the men are infrequent, even though, once Hamilton left the relative luxury of life on board ship, he shared some of the men's discomforts at the ill-sited HQ on Imbros. He remarks only briefly on major irritations, such as the heat or the swarms of flies. Similarly, although he remarked on the need for stamina in potential new senior officers for the force, the strains of living and fighting which necessitated it were not spelt out. The following example where he did describe conditions in detail is followed by a colourful assertion as to the men's morale, thereby imnplying that such trying conditions were relatively insignificant. Having inspected the 29th Division on 12 May, he wrote:

> Spent over an hour chatting to groups of Officers and men who looked like earth to earth, caked as they were with mud, haggard with lack of sleep, pale as the dead, many of them slightly wounded and bandaged, hand or head, their clothes blood-stained, their eyes blood-shot. [. . .] This sounds horrible but the hearty welcome extended to us by all ranks and the pride they took in their achievements was a sublime triumph of mind over matter. Our voluntary service regulars are the last descendants of those rulers of the ancient world, the Roman Legionaries.[41]

Occasionally the *Diary* hints at the sickness that was such a problem at Gallipoli, but again Hamilton tended not to dwell on its implications. On 12 July, he wrote that he was 'too bad with the universal complaint to venture many yards from camp';[42] he then went on to describe a full day's work.

Similarly, Hamilton tended to avoid giving explicit descriptions of suffering and killing. Consider his description of a bayonet attack: 'Bayonets sparkled all over the wide plain. Under our glasses this vague movement took form and human shape: men rose, fell, ran, rushed on in waves, broke, recoiled, crumbled away and disappeared.'[43] The reader remains detached from the action, in part because the writer, too, is removed from the action. Yet a bayonet attack would have been vicious, ugly and bloody; Hamilton has softened its horror and deflected its impact. The style of Hamilton's description is in keeping with that of other participants' narratives who were distant from the frontline. Only direct participants in an action managed to vividly convey the nature of the experience. However, a comparison of the diary–manuscript and the book shows that Hamilton's portrayal is not simply a product of his detached position. It reveals a willingness, on occasion, to edit the text so as to achieve a more optimistic note. On 7 May, Hamilton dictated letters to ease the tension of waiting for news from the battlefield. The diary items he quotes in the book contain news both of good progress by Hunter-Weston and of Turkish reinforcements. In addition, however, the manuscript includes a letter to Maxwell which says: 'There is a bloody battle in full flame at this moment so it is a strange opportunity for correspondence . . . We are going at a very ugly looking fence here.'[44] This sombre analysis has been discarded, thereby lightening the tone of the passage in the published version.

Furthermore, Hamilton avoided bald casualty statistics. All too often he wrote of 1,000 or more Turks being killed, without stating the corresponding number of casualties among his own troops. Where he did, the information might follow positive news of a victory, or he might say that most of his troops' casualties had suffered only light wounds. British losses almost always seem to be lighter than the Turks', although in fairness it should be noted that overall this is probably statistically accurate.[45] A comparison of Hamilton's reporting of casualties as between his dispatches and the *Diary* is telling. Consider his description of the Turk's attack at Anzac of 18 May. After some details of the course of events in the dispatch, Hamilton concluded:

> The enemy's casualties were heavy, as may be judged from the fact that over 3,000 dead were lying in the open in view of our trenches. A large proportion of these losses were due to our artillery fire. Our casualties amounted to about 100 killed and 500 wounded, including nine officers wounded.[46]

This may be compared to the account given in *Gallipoli Diary*: some of the same aspects of the fighting are described, but the tone is different. Cold statistics have been replaced by the jubilant but vague cry of a warrior:

> Tidings of great joy from Anzac. The whole of the enemy's freshly-arrived contingent have made a grand assault and have been shattered in the attempt [. . .]
> A few more shells and they would have been swept off the face of the earth. As it is we have slaughtered a multitude.[47]

The phrasing is redolent of high diction with biblical overtones.[48] The best indication in the *Diary* of the severe losses comes from Hamilton's repeated calls for reinforcements. Yet it still comes as a shock to read his cable to Kitchener of 23 August stating: 'The total casualties including sick since 6th August amount to 40,000, and my total force is now only 85,000, of which the fighting strength is 68,000.'[49]

Gallipoli Diary and heroism in war

Against this romantic backdrop, Hamilton portrayed the honour and heroism of his men. This is the second strand of the heroic–romantic myth. He detailed their best attributes, their morale and their motives, and he described units and individuals as positively as possible. For example, in recounting General D'Amade's departure, Hamilton discarded his manuscript description of a man at breaking point, but retained his tribute to D'Amade as 'a most charming, chivalrous and loyal soldier'.[50] Even more telling is his description of a setback on 8 June. New Turkish divisions had made a footing in the lines of the East Lancashires, but Hamilton was quick to assert that this would soon be overcome. The manuscript draft reveals the reason for this problem in strongly critical tones: 'Bad generalship (Doran) is at the bottom of this *contretemps*. Why French failure should be thought good enough for Gallipoli, I cannot think.'[51] However Hamilton chose not to publish such a harsh and per-sonalised attack.

Concomitant to this avoidance of criticism is Hamilton's glowing assessment of his men's motivation for fighting. He wrote of the Anzacs: 'They are not charging up into this Sari Bair range for money or by com-pulsion. They fight for love – all the way from the Southern Cross for love of the old country and of liberty.'[52] Charles Bean's assessment was different. In more sober language, he ascribed their motivation to 'the mettle of the men themselves', to love of their own country and their mates.[53] Hamilton was also keen to assert the fighting spirit of his men. This apparently remained strong even among the wounded. The com-ments of some experienced nurses he encountered were paraphrased thus:

> Never a day passed, so they said, in France, but some patient would, with tears in his eyes, entreat to be sent home. Here at Mudros there had never been one single instance. The patients, if they said anything at all, have showed impatience to get back to their comrades in the fighting line.[54]

On occasion, Hamilton did describe men's exhaustion and shaken spirit – for example, following an inspection of the Plymouth Battalion on 12 May. These men had seen some hard fighting, and Hamilton wrote candidly of its effect on them: 'The faces of Officers and men had a crushed, utterly finished expression: some of the younger Officers espe-cially had that true funeral set about their lips which spreads the con-tagion of gloom through the hearts of the bravest soldiers.' However Hamilton still managed to pluck a positive point from this, 'They have nerves, the defects of their good qualities [. . .] No one fights better than they do – for a spell – and a good long spell too. But they have not the invincible carelessness or temperamental springiness of the old lot – and how should they?'[55] Only at the very end of his campaign did Hamilton report, without making compensatory comments, that morale was suf-fering. Having inspected the 29th Division on 30 September he wrote: 'The men were in rags and looked very tired. This is the first time in the campaign our rank and file have seemed sorry for themselves.'[56] Perhaps by pointing to such failings in his men – men who had been over-stretched – Hamilton is making a point about the paucity of the resources with which he had been forced to work. He is able to praise the men's effort while implying a criticism of London.

Hamilton's portrayal of the fine nature of his men was counter-pointed by his disdainful attitude towards the Turks. A similar underes-timation of the Turks had influenced the original decision to launch the expedition. Hamilton's description of a battle was modified between manuscript and book to play down the valour of the Turkish men. In the manuscript, the Turks were said to have attempted to hold their trench with 'true heroism',[57] while in the book they merely 'stuck it out bravely'[58] – a subtle but important difference. Hamilton seemed to regret that decent men's lives were to be wasted in the killing of such inferior beings: 'Here are the best the old country can produce; the hope of the progress of the British ideal in the world; and half of them are going to swap lives with Turks whose relative value to the well-being of human-ity is to theirs as is a locust to a honey-bee.'[59]

There was a racial basis to his opinions. He attributed the strength of the Turks to the Teutonic influence: 'German thoroughness and fore-thought have gripped the old go-as-you-please Turk'.[60] He thought his Anglo-Saxon men to be morally and martially superior:

> Let me bring my lads face to face with Turks in the open field, we *must* beat them every time because British volunteer soldiers are superior individu-als to Anatolians, Syrians or Arabs and are animated with a superior ideal and an equal joy in battle [. . .]
>
> To attempt to solve the problem by letting a single dirty Turk at the Maxim kill ten – twenty – fifty – of our fellows on the barbed wire – ten – twenty – fifty – *each of whom is worth several dozen Turks*, is a sin of the Holy Ghost category.[61]

Such racialist views – like his similar social Darwinist ideas, typical of the time and his generation – are also demonstrated by Hamilton's dismis-sive comments on the fighting prowess of the Senegalese troops in the French contingent.[62] Towards the end of the fighting, however, Hamil-ton was forced to modify his view of the Turks. While he still believed that the Turks could be beaten, he did accept that his enemy was 'a for-midable fellow to turn out of his trench'.[63]

In addition to describing his comrades in a positive light, Hamilton presented a virtuous image of himself. It is clear from the text that he was an honourable, chivalrous, imaginative and inspiring general who bore his fate with grace and stoicism. He was above all an optimist. That such a strong sense of the man can be derived from the book is in part a function of the diary format, which encourages introspection and comment, but also a tribute to Hamilton's communication skills. The individuality of *Gallipoli Diary* is matched only by Compton Mackenzie's memoirs among the other Gallipoli narratives.

Gallipoli Diary and strategy

Hamilton's optimism served to perpetuate the idea of the campaign's potential. Throughout Hamilton retained his faith that victory was near and remained convinced that the seizure of Constantinople was possible. It is at this point that the second and third strands of the heroic–romantic myth begin to overlap. While promoting himself and the achievements of his campaign, Hamilton was also projecting certain ideas about the strategy and the reasons for its failure. These were that the strategy was a sound and imaginative idea and that failure resulted from mistakes made in London, particularly by Kitchener. Thes ideas were present throughout the *Diary* and were vital to the vindication of Hamilton and his campaign.

There are numerous examples of Hamilton's optimistic nature. He seems to have found the positive in every situation: the Turks lost more, we seized prisoners, we took a certain number of trenches. He always had a relatively palatable explanation for set-backs: we had to fall back only because of fatigue, lack of high explosives, shrapnel and so on. Such explanations did not denigrate the honour of his men but they did quietly and continually push the idea that London had failed the campaign. An example of Hamilton's optimism was his encounter with Lord Brassey on 15 August. He shocked Hamilton by his talk of defeat and the hopelessness of the task:

> The dear old man gave me a warm greeting, but also something of a shock by talking about our terrible defeat: by condoling and by saying I had been asked to do the impossible. I have *not* been asked to do anything impossible in taking Constantinople. The feat is perfectly feasible. For the third time since we began it trembled in the balance a week ago. Nor is the capture of Suvla Bay and the linking up thereof with Anzac a defeat: a cruel disappointment, no doubt, but not a defeat; for, two more such defeats, measured in mere acreage, will give us the Narrows.[64]

This expression of faith came after the Suvla landings, but from that first week in August onwards it is possible to detect a wavering in Hamilton's spirit. Of course, before that there are moments in the *Diary* of frustration, irritation or disappointment, but with the dwindling hope of Suvla a rising panic is palpable. Hamilton's disquiet grew as he attempted to intervene at Suvla: Stopford the local commander was reluctant to drive on and take risks, and an air of complacency prevailed while the advantage of surprise was lost. Hamilton became disconsolate:

> We were holding our own; the Welsh Division are coming in this morning; but we have not sweated blood only to hold our own; our occupation of the open key positions has been just too late! The element of surprise – wasted! The prime factor set aside for the sake of other factors! Words are no use.[65]

'Words are no use' – that was the ultimate expression of dejection for a man like Hamilton. His sense of doom and foreboding grew further. On 2 September, he reports a nightmare of the night before: 'I was lying in my little camp bed, and yet I was being drowned, held violently under the Hellespont.'[66] But even after the final failure of the offensive in late August and his recall he retained his optimistic belief in the potential of the campaign and the possibility of victory: 'Whenever I get home I shall do what I can to convince K[itchener] that the game is still in his hands if only he will shake himself free from slippery politics; come right out here and run the show himself. Constantinople is the only big big hit lying open on the map at this moment.'[67]

Hamilton's optimism is an important element in the myth of Gallipoli. During the campaign it was also an important part of his leadership style and in the maintenance of morale: a commander, he noted, 'may still help to win the battle by putting a brave face upon the game when it seems to be up. By his character he may still stop the rot and inspire his men to advance once more.'[68] But this was a double-edged sword: it simultaneously damaged the campaign as a whole. Hamilton's cables lulled the politicians into a false impression of developments at Gallipoli. The actions of the pessimistic Ashmead-Bartlett during his return to London in June therefore caused disquiet amongst them. Hamilton received a questioning letter from an unidentified friendly statesman[69] following the establishing of the Dardanelles committee. In his reply on 29 July, Hamilton considered the interplay of personality and the interpretation of events as presented in cables:

I am not quite sure that I clearly understand your meaning about cabling home the exact truth. Is there any occasion on which I have failed to do so? I should be very sorry indeed to think I had consciously or unconsciously misled anyone by my cables. There is always, of course, the broad spirit of a cable which depends on the temperament of the sender. It is either tinged with hope or it has been dictated by one who fears the worst. If you mean that you would prefer a pessimistic tone given to my appreciations, then I am afraid you will have to get another General.[70]

Although Hamilton denied that he had been misleading, his chief cipher officer, Orlo Williams, confirmed Robert Rhodes James's opinion that Hamilton's letters and telegrams were 'notably, and fatally, inconsistent'.[71] In a 1929 article, Williams used the example of a telegram drafted on 9 May that stressed the need for more reinforcements and armaments, the lack of which was precluding further progress. This telegram was redrafted the next morning with assurances of prospective success and strong morale, as befitted Hamilton's optimistic mood. Williams commented on the revised telegram:

This last remark, true of himself, was quite untrue of the troops, as even I well knew: their confidence, especially in those who framed their orders, had received a rude shock and was never afterwards quite regained. But it was typical of Sir Ian Hamilton, both now and later, that he would dilute cogently drafted reports with literary palliatives and comforting trimmings that were justified less by facts than by his own personal convictions.[72]

The tension regarding cables was felt on both sides at Hamilton's GHQ. Hamilton complained in his manuscript of his officials' attempts to alter his cables, seemingly because it made them dull:

I wrote cables, which I may at least say they are descriptive as far as official phraseology will admit, and they are turned by some miserable people somewhere into horrible bureaucratic *clichés* or dead languages, i.e. – we have made an appreciable advance; the situation remains unchanged; and similar god-damned phrases. Enough themselves to turn the most interesting news into soporifics.[73]

Hamilton's objection was really that the bureaucratic clichés punctured the romance of war, revealing something more like the stark truth that his flowing phrases tended to obscure.

Another of Hamilton's attributes reinforced the damaging effects of his optimism on his cables. This was his chivalrous view of warfare and code of honourable behaviour. Such chivalry contributes to the heroic strand of the Gallipoli myth, but, since it inclined Hamilton towards a deferential attitude to his seniors, it too played a part in his defeat. Hamilton's tactics and success were constrained by a shortage of men, and in particular, a shortage of arms. The difficulties of his negotiations with London for further supplies were intricately bound up with his deferential relationship with Kitchener. Hamilton had served as Kitchener's chief of staff in South Africa and held him in the highest regard. Hamilton stifled his own ability to influence politics in London because of his regard for propriety in communicating with superiors. He therefore limited himself to corresponding solely with Kitchener and the War Office, thus precluding communication with Asquith or Churchill. He informed Churchill of his decision on 12 March: 'I must not in loyalty tell you too much of my War Office conversation, but I see I shall need some courage in stating my opinions, as well as in attacking the enemy; also that the Cabinet will not be quite eye to eye whatever I may have to say!!'[74] Closing this avenue may well have damaged his operations, for to have kept his eloquent and dynamic friend better informed could have influenced important supply decisions. On several occasions Hamilton expressed his frustration at not being able to contact Churchill and the Admiralty in order to secure, for example, high-explosive shells or aeroplanes.[75] The sense of loss at Churchill's resignation was reinforced by Hamilton's prescient likening of his friend to Pitt.[76]

Having limited himself to communicating solely with Kitchener, Hamilton compounded the situation by not pressing his views sufficiently hard. One result of this was the imposition on his command of Stopford. Hamilton's deference towards Kitchener prevented him from insisting on his own choice of commander for the landings at Suvla or from rejecting Stopford – a man wholly unsuited to the task who was chosen only on grounds of his superiority. In the manuscript, Hamilton commented on these difficulties. He felt he could have argued with a civilian but not with a soldier:

> A Field Marshal Secretary of State for War has his drawbacks. Imagine Brodrick in the South African War nominating the Column Commanders. K. would not have stood it for five minutes. Nor would Lord Bobs. But when the head of the Army under the King and constitution happens also to be head of the Army as a soldier . . . ?[77]

More importantly, having promised to undertake an operation with a specified contingent of men and supplies, Hamilton felt honour-bound to attempt to stand by this, even though the nature of the operation had fundamentally changed. He also took it on himself to understand the constraints placed on Kitchener by domestic politics and operations elsewhere. This added a further disincentive to demand more reinforcements. Yet it was his place to request what was necessary, leaving the decision as to what was possible to Kitchener. Hamilton was concerned not to ask for too much: 'Nothing easier than to ask for 150,000 men and then, if I fail say I didn't get what I wanted, but the boldest leaders, Bobs, White, Gordon, K., have always "asked for more" with a most queasy conscience.'[78] Hamilton did not want to cry wolf as a matter of honour. Furthermore, he struggled to strike a balance between persuading the politicians of his need for more of everything and his fear of frightening them away from the whole scheme. Therefore, for example, when he was presented with a golden opportunity for candour, Hamilton instead humoured Kitchener. He cabled privately on 19 May: 'You need not be despondent at anything in situation. Remember that you asked me to answer on the assumption that you had adequate forces at your disposal, and I did so.'[79]

Hamilton's chivalrous attitudes are also apparent in his dealings with his subordinate commanders. Here, too, it damaged the progress of the campaign. Having accepted each officer, his attitude – which mirrored that of many commanders on the Western Front – seems to have been that once his orders had been given he must trust them and leave them to get on with the task in hand.[80] The same attitude led him to persevere in capturing Gallipoli – he had taken on the task and had been trusted to do so, therefore even though the situation had changed he felt honour-bound to carry on. His inactivity at the initial landings resulted from his perception of the detached role of the commander. For example, when he sensed an opportunity at Y beach, he was only tentative in his wire to Hunter Weston: 'Would you like to get some more men ashore on "Y" beach?'[81] Only in a dire emergency did he forcibly intervene and give his 'Dig, dig, dig' order to the Anzac commanders pondering evacuation.[82] This self-imposed impotence was repeated during the Suvla landings. Although concerned about his new landing and having received only scant information, he responded to the commander of the IX Corps: 'You and your troops have indeed done splendidly. Please tell Hammersley how much we hope from his able and rapid advance.'[83] Hamilton should have replied in far blunter terms demanding information and progress. He was far too slow to act on his private misgivings, to assert himself and to relieve Stopford of command. Similarly, it has been suggested that Hamilton was unable to impose his will on his staff, to the detriment of the campaign. Bean wrote of this situation in his diary: 'It is rather a fault of character than of intellect that has caused him to fail. He has not the strength to command his staff – they command him; especially Braithwaite; his chief of staff, with whom he is on the worst of terms, I believe has commanded this expedition.'[84] Bean went on to reveal more of this disastrous interplay of Hamilton's deference and optimism: 'Hamilton has not the strength to give those with whom he is surrounded a straight out blow from the shoulder – however much the situation demands it. To mix the metaphor – he has an unlucky ability for gilding the pill.'[85]

Hamilton 'gilded the pill', not only in commanding his subordinates or corresponding with his superiors, but in formulating his later criticism. This resulted partly from the very difficult position in which he found himself. He wanted to show that he had been let down by London and by Kitchener, but he probably felt that it was dangerous to openly attack such an important and revered figure. He probably also felt some loyalty to his former chief. This chivalry was a further brake on criticism. Hamilton's solution came in two parts. First, he published a very full description of his preparations for the landing that amounted to approximately one-fifth of the *Diary*'s length. This demonstrated how difficult the task of landing on the peninsula was, how inadequate were the War Office preparations and how hastily he was expected to depart from London. In the course of this explanation he mentions his reasons for temporarily leaving behind in Egypt his administrative and supply staff (the A and Q branches), portraying this as a sensible arrangement and thereby rebutting a criticism of the Dardanelles Commission.[86] In the course of this description of his preparations, Hamilton did not explicitly criticise Kitchener, but he did express regret that sufficient planning, which could have greatly improved the situation, had not been possible.[87] This section establishes the idea that the campaign was ill-served by the War Office and that the very achievement of landing on the peninsula was extraordinary.

The second of Hamilton's means of explaining failure without engaging in explicit criticism was to insert the text of many of the cables and letters that passed between himself and London. In a manner reminiscent of his stance welcoming the fullest possible disclosure of documents for the Dardanelles Commission, Hamilton allowed the cables to tell their own story. They provided copious evidence of Hamilton's attempts to secure more men and armaments. These are supplemented by two appendices on the artillery situation which confirm his criticisms.[88] The result was the creation of the impression that Hamilton was continuously being rebuffed by a short-sighted War Office without the need to complain at length and with ill grace in the text of the *Diary*.

It should be noted that, having demonstrated the extreme provocations that he had encountered, Hamilton often did express his exasperation. On 5 May, for example, having received a cable urging him to push on while the War Office reconsidered the situation, his response concluded: 'it's not the advice that riles me: it's the fact that people who have made a mistake, and should be sorry, slur over my appeal for the stuff advances are made of and yet continue to urge us on as if we were hanging back'.[89] That Hamilton pressed for more on many occasions – and that the War Office were wrong to put him in such a position – does not contradict the point stated earlier, that Hamilton did not press sufficiently hard. He admitted as much in 1921:

> With too rare exceptions I was mealy mouthed in my cables and kept my outspokenness for my diary. It was wrong. Yet K. was so formidable – so enormous a Personage that there is a certain excuse. Through the Diary I am always struggling up against his Colossus who overshadows my whole horizon – and that is what has led so many reviewers to think I am *attacking* K. who really was looming too big in my mind.[90]

Yet, despite the continuous subtext in the *Diary* blaming Kitchener, Hamilton tried to deny that it was his aim to belittle the secretary of state. In a footnote attributed to 1920, he wrote:

> [A]ll the time I was conscious, and am still more so now, of K.'s greatness. Still more so now because, when I compare him with his survivors, they seem measurable, he remains immeasurable.
>
> I wish very much I could make people admire Lord K. understandingly . . . K. was an individualist. He was a Master of Expedients; the greatest probably the world has ever seen.[91]

Perhaps these sentiments explain why Hamilton in revealing Kitchener's mistakes and weaknesses, tended to portray him as a great man in the wrong job, who was surrounded by dangers. He later explained his view of Kitchener in *The Commander*. Commenting on Lord Esher's *The Tragedy of Lord Kitchener*, he wrote:

> I would only add to his description of K. struggling to raise a national army – in which he succeeded so well – and, above all, struggling to keep his head above water as a member of the War Cabinet and the Head of the War Office, by saying this: what Lord Esher, and more so, many others have failed to realize is that K. was utterly out of his depth. K. wanted to be a Supreme Commander and wasn't in a position to be one.[92]

An illustration of this in the *Diary* is Hamilton's concerned response to a despondent cable from the War Office on 21 May. Hamilton noted that it had been written on the day of Churchill's and Fisher's resignations. He wrote warily of the sinister politicians Kitchener faced – in the book they were 'masked figures'; in the manuscript they had been, worse still, 'dirk and stiletto men'.[93] Hamilton suggested that Kitchener was not at his best in such a situation. Rather his strength lay in his ability to focus on the task in hand and to act immediately on it: 'But to-day, though he sees, the power of believing in his own vision and of hanging on to it like a bulldog, seems paralysed.'[94] Hamilton blamed not only the politicians around Kitchener but in his manuscript the poor calibre of his staff:

> [A]s surely as Samson's force lay in the length of his hair, so did his, K.'s, in the strength of his Staff; in his magic gift of making his immediate entourage into a band of devoted slaves. And those old slaves of his were really capable fellows. Now, I fear, K. begins to think he did it all: – peace with the Boers, victory over the Viceroy. So in a sense he did, but only by working his vague, sometimes childish thoughts through the mill of the brains of his intimates.[95]

Hamilton sought to defend his personal honour by portraying his optimistic and chivalrous nature and by demonstrating that he had done all he could to ensure the success of the campaign. In so doing, he incidentally revealed how those virtues were also personal failings. The honour of the campaign and its participants (i.e. strand two of the myth) is intricately bound up with the reasons for its failure – responsibility for which lay with Kitchener, the War Office and the politicians – and also the proximity of victory and the potential implications of success. Thus in addition to establishing the culpability of Kitchener and the War Office, and his optimistic assertions of near-success, Hamilton pushed his 'Easterner' view of the potential consequences of the capture of Constantinople. Hamilton was most outspoken in his expression of these ideas in *The Commander*, a book published posthumously:

> [T]he one venture in combined operations that we tried was the Dardanelles: a venture that was given less than half support; where the stores were loaded in the wrong order; where shipments of shells were sometimes of the wrong calibre; and where every scrap of material was begrudged. When, in spite of all this, the venture – this 'sideshow' – was about to pay a real dividend for the lives it had cost, the Government lost their nerve and put paid to our last hope of ending the war in 1916.[96]

In the *Diary*, Hamilton implanted this idea from the very beginning by quoting Kitchener's final words to him: 'If the Fleet gets through, Constantinople will fall of itself and you will have won, not a battle, but the war.'[97]

The response to *Gallipoli Diary*

Gallipoli Diary was published in May 1920 and was widely reviewed.[98] While some reviewers criticised Hamilton's conduct, most accepted his basic argument, that he was ill-served by the Government. These extracts from the unsigned review in the *Daily Express* can be taken as broadly representative of the general tone:

> As in his 'Staff Officer's Scrap Book', General Hamilton reveals himself as perhaps the greatest journalist who ever wore uniform. His literary style is almost wholly free from any reproach, his descriptive reporting is magnificent in its imaginative realism, and his judgments of men and things are shrewd, humorous, and always chivalrous. A man to love, a commander to inspire affection, a chief to deserve the loyalty with which he defends subordinates and – and always the ready writer [. . .]
>
> Sir Ian reveals very fully the incompetence of Whitehall and the handicaps of his task. He drives new nails into new coffins. He explains the tragic limitations, while he eulogises the merits, of Lord Kitchener's last phase. He shows in sharpest outline the repetition in Gallipoli of all the administrative blunders that made the Crimea horrible and of many tactical absurdities which made the Boer war deadly [. . .]
>
> This is essentially a book to read both for the pleasure of reading so well-made a book and as an exercise in the revelation of human agonies. It has its value as a side-light on the great war and its conduct.[99]

The *Diary* served to stir up the Murdoch controversy once more, and this was the focus of the reviews in Australia. This had been Hamilton's aim. He wrote to Churchill prior to the book's publication:

> One line before you read the Diary. I have thought it best to have the story printed quite complete but that does not necessarily mean that I intend to publish all that is now contained therein. For instance, I don't think I shall publish Granard's letter for he behaved quite decently afterwards and said he was sorry. As to the wickedness at the end which bust up the show there I am quite prepared to face libel action or anything else so that I can have the truth out.[100]

Hamilton received many private letters of congratulations on *Gallipoli Diary*. These would seem to suggest, in combination with the newspaper reviews, that publication of the *Diary* struck a chord with many and helped to alter opinion on the Gallipoli campaign. Three examples will illustrate this point. General Beauvoir de Lisle, who had been GOC, 29th Division, wrote to him:

> I knew you had great difficulties with the WO, but until I read your book I never realised a fraction of what these difficulties were. Had the WO supported you adequately, it is difficult to appreciate what the result might have been. I often think however that the wearing down of the Turkish Regular Army on the Gallipoli Peninsula assisted the Allied Cause more than any temporary success would have done. I say temporary, because the capture of Achi Baba or Chunuk Bair would have brought down heavy German reinforcements to check further progress. As it was, both Jerusalem and Baghdad were gained on the shores of the Gallipoli Peninsula.[101]

Capt. W. Henry Williams wrote: 'Though we failed time after time to achieve our objective we are now greatly encouraged by the masterly and courageous evidence from you that the failure was not the fault of those who did the fighting.'[102]

Reverend Henry Hall, chaplain to the 29th Division at Gallipoli and Vicar of Holy Trinity Church, Eltham wrote: 'Anyhow your book gave me an illustration in last evening's sermon for the "right spirit". I told my people of the . . . glory and sadness of your book – and that we who served under you loved and honoured you chiefly for your "spirit" and chivalry.'[103]

Despite such reactions to *Gallipoli Diary*, however, it has been suggested by both Edward Spiers[104] and John Robertson[105] that the real turning point in the public perception of Gallipoli came with the publication of Winston Churchill's *The World Crisis 1915*.[106] Like his friend Hamilton, Churchill had been working hard, since the Dardanelles Commission and before, to defend his role in the campaign. His motives in doing so are clear: in his Preface he wrote: 'Upon me more than any other person the responsibility for the Dardanelles and all that it involved had been cast.'[107] He, too, was seeking to clear his reputation and secure his career. He made speeches in Parliament, wrote newspaper articles concerning the war and, from the winter of 1919–20, worked on his memoirs.[108] Churchill also hoped for a handsome profit, extracting a promise from his literary agents that he would receive not less than £20,000 from the sales and serialisation of his memoirs.[109]

In much the same way as Hamilton had reproduced telegrams and cables in his account, Churchill made extensive use of contemporary documents to bolster his argument. As with Hamilton's openness when before the Dardanelles Commission, this was in keeping with early attempts to secure the publication of the relevant documents prior to the appointment of the commission. Churchill used documents acquired during his time as first lord of the Admiralty and corresponded with many friends and former colleagues in order to secure minutes, memoranda and letters that he was missing. He also put the matter to the Cabinet on 30 January 1922, in order to secure permission to publish secret documents so that he might defend himself properly.[110]

Churchill was not only continuing a line of argument he had maintained since the Dardanelles Commission: he was recycling the very words he used before the commission, inserting them directly into his narrative in *The World Crisis*. For example, his description of Kitchener's immense prestige and authority in Cabinet is initially repeated verbatim.[111] But the book inserts a long passage of criticism before concluding with a repetition of his tribute to Kitchener's courage and unvarying kindness, as in his evidence. In particular, Churchill attacks Kitchener's resistance to plans to lighten his administrative load, and the weakness of Kitchener's colleagues and subordinates in not standing up to him, which meant that Kitchener never resolved his strategic indecisiveness between East and West.

This last was part of an argument Churchill pressed repeatedly, and one in which he echoed Hamilton's arguments. In particular, he produced a robust defence of the Eastern strategy that he had worked so hard to implement in government and for which he had subsequently received so much criticism: 'It must, however, be observed that whereas the Turkish shortage of ammunition arose from causes beyond their control, the British shortage sprang solely from the lack of decision in the distribution of the available quantities between the various theatres of war.'[112] Churchill later fought to allow a discussion of the implication of strategic decisions to be included in Aspinall's official history. Churchill repeatedly emphasised the damaging effect of the piecemeal dispatch of men and ammunitions, for which he blamed Kitchener and the authorities in London. Describing the preparations for the August operations, Churchill wrote: 'There is no principle of war better established than that everything should be massed for the battle [. . .] This high prudence cannot be discerned in Lord Kitchener's preparations at this time.'[113] Churchill revealed that Kitchener had come close to being removed from the War Office in May 1915, but that the vehement public response to an attack on Kitchener by Northcliffe forced a sharp change of plan, and he was instead invested with the Order of the Garter.[114] By contrast, Churchill was sacked from the Admiralty and all the blame was thereby unfairly placed on his shoulders. Churchill constructed a virtuous picture of himself in that situation, one of dignity in the face of such humiliation when in fact he had tried to cling to office through a series of letters to Asquith.[115] He contrasted the pettiness of his colleagues' politicking in May with his own attempt to focus on Gallipoli, and how, on his final resignation in November, he left politics behind to fight in France.[116]

Churchill couched his argument in a particularly powerful expression of the other facets of the heroic–romantic myth. The following description of the attack led by Doughty-Wylie on 26 April conveys something of Churchill's eloquence:

> When the cannonade ceased the English and Irish soldiers mingled together, animated by a common resolve, issued forth from the shattered houses of Sedd-el-Bahr, and in broad daylight by main force and with cruel sacrifice stormed the redoubt and slew its stubborn defenders. The prolonged, renewed, and seemingly inexhaustible efforts of the survivors of these three battalions, their persistency, their will power, their physical endurance, achieved a feat of arms certainly in these respects not often, if ever surpassed in the history of either island race.[117]

Such is the power of Churchill's description, however, that, unlike other writers, he had no need to use classical allusion. Lord Sydenham, a contemporary of Churchill, later warned of his dazzling rhetoric's potential to distort: 'The very attractiveness of Mr. Churchill's writing of itself constitutes a danger; for the layman may well be led to accept facile phrase and seductive argument for hard fact and sober reasoning.'[118]

Robin Prior has managed to look beyond Churchill's facile phrases and has meticulously dissected his work.[119] He notes that Churchill quoted misleadingly from his contemporary correspondence, for example omitting the key sentence from a letter to Fisher of 4 January 1915: 'Germany is the foe and it is bad war to seek cheaper victories and easier antagonists.'[120] Prior demonstrates how Churchill glossed over logistical considerations and other difficult issues,[121] invoked fate to explain away failure[122] and, in particular, how he amended his work to shift the blame away from Hamilton and on to Kitchener.[123]

According to Prior, whereas Churchill argued that Kitchener was torn between two clear-cut strategic views, in fact Kitchener chose the Western Front: loss there meant overall defeat. This choice did not preclude action elsewhere, but it meant that the troops sent to Gallipoli were limited to those considered to be surplus to the needs of the Western Front. Prior asserts that Churchill failed to recognise this and he was thus 'led to condemn as vacillation what was a perfectly consistent policy'.[124] Churchill also constructed his account so as to avoid embarrassing Hamilton regarding the plan for the April landings and the battle of late August.[125] This was due, in part, to the fact that Churchill was relying on Hamilton and Aspinall for information on the military campaign and therefore did not realise some of the mistakes that had been made.[126] It may also account for the sketchy nature of his account of military aspects of Gallipoli.[127] Churchill's treatment of Fisher was more mixed. In some respects his misleading account worked to the admiral's detriment, in that Churchill failed to show the important questions Fisher asked as to the campaign's potential for success and Fisher's lack of faith in Hamilton. But he also protected Fisher – just as he had done at the Dardanelles Commission – for example, amending his work to show Fisher to have been on the verge of collapse rather than incapable of performing duties. As Prior notes, this was to some extent self-serving:

> No doubt Churchill decided to conceal the full truth about Fisher's state to protect the reputation of the old Admiral, but it must be admitted that this also had the effect of concealing the magnitude of Churchill's mistake in re-installing him at the Admiralty and later pleading with him to come back.[128]

Churchill's *World Crisis* is undoubtedly one of the most influential accounts of Gallipoli. Its comparatively minor role in this consideration has been prompted by the fine work of Robin Prior. Moreover, that General Sir Ian Hamilton's *Gallipoli Diary* deserves this chapter's focus is justified, for it is the final piece of evidence on Hamilton's various attempts to manipulate perceptions of Gallipoli, and one which certainly had an important impact. As has been noted, Hamilton influenced his friend Churchill, and was also a close friend of John Masefield, another prominent defender of Gallipoli. He encouraged Henry Nevinson to write what, for some years, was considered one of the main texts on the campaign. He worked hard to influence the Dardanelles Commission and the official history. In his *Gallipoli Diary* he produced one individual's view of the campaign: it is the commander's response. Its format brought to the author a freedom of expression denied to him in the context of the official responses. It is therefore distinctly different from his *Despatches*: his literary skill and his purpose distinguished it from the narratives of other senior officers. Hamilton's purpose was not simply to bear witness to his own experience of the campaign, but to elevate the reputation of the campaign. He therefore gave expression to the romance and heroism of the campaign, and he offered an unfettered explanation of its conduct. This was his reply to his critics and his own apologia as well.

Notes

1 General Sir Ian S. M. Hamilton, *Gallipoli Diary*, 2 vols (London, 1920).
2 General Sir Ian Hamilton, *Listening for the Drums* (London, 1944), p. 93.
3 Ian B. M. Hamilton, *The Happy Warrior: A Life of General Sir Ian Hamilton GCB, GCMG, DSO by His Nephew* (London, 1966), p. 268. See also John Lee, *A Soldier's Life: General Sir Ian Hamilton 1853–1947* (London, 2000); and Celia Lee, *Jean, Lady Hamilton 1861–1941: A Soldier's Wife. A Biography from Her Diaries* (London, 2001).
4 Hamilton's twenty publications, dating from 1884, include: *A Staff Officer's Scrap Book* (London, 1905); *Compulsory Service* (London, 1910); *National Life and National Training* (Birmingham, 1912); *Ian Hamilton's Final Despatch* (London, 1916); *Ian Hamilton's Despatches from the Dardanelles* (London, 1917); *The Millennium* (London, 1919); *Gallipoli Diary* (London, 1920); *The Soul and Body of an Army* (London, 1991; first published 1921); *The Friends of England: Lectures to Members of the British Legion* (London, 1923); with Victor Sampson, *Anti-Commando* (London, 1931); *When I was a Boy* (London, 1939); *Jean – a Memoir* (London, 1942); *Listening for the Drums* (London, 1944); *The Commander*, ed. Anthony Farrar-Hockley (London, 1957). He contributed introductions and forewords to at least nine books.
5 *The Times*, 13 October 1947, p. 8.
6 Keith Grieves, 'C. E. Montague, Manchester and the remembrance of war, 1918–25', *Bulletin of the John Rylands University Library of Manchester*, 77:2 (summer 1995), p. 92.
7 Ian B. M. Hamilton, *The Happy Warrior*, p. 445.
8 Henry W. Nevinson, *The Dardanelles Campaign* (London, 1918), p. 66.
9 Hamilton, *The Commander*, pp. 23–4; the reference to Fortescue suggests Hamilton wrote this passage before Fortescue's resignation in December 1919.
10 Hamilton, *Gallipoli Diary*, 1, p. v.
11 Ian Beckett, 'Frocks and brasshats' in Brian Bond (ed.) *The First World War and British Military History* (Oxford, 1991), p. 92.
12 Keith Simpson, 'The reputation of Sir Douglas Haig' in Bond (ed.) *The First World War and British Military History*, pp. 141–4.
13 Hamilton, *Gallipoli Diary*, 1, p. vii.
14 *Ibid.*, pp. viii–ix.

15 Mary Shield to Alan Moorehead, 26 April 1956, National Library of Australia, Canberra, Alan Moorehead Papers, MS 5654, box 13, folder 107.

16 Handwritten, no date, Moorehead Papers, box 13, folder 10; Moorehead lists John North and John Graham Gillam as other correspondents.

17 Janet Leeper to Moorehead, 19 June 1956, Moorehead Papers, box 13, folder 107.

18 When amassing evidence for the Dardanelles Commission, Hamilton drew together a table of information that tallies with the appointments' diary kept by Sergeant Major H. G. Stuart during the campaign (Hamilton Papers, 7/4/9), which Hamilton referred to as his 'personal diary' (Hamilton Papers, 8/2/22). Information courtesy of Kate O'Brien, Military Archivist at the Liddell Hart Centre for Military Archives, King's College, London.

19 Hamilton to Colonel Blair, 20 September 1920, Hamilton Papers, 7/10/12.

20 Lt-Col. C. H. Weston, _Three Years with the New Zealanders_ (London, 1918); Major J. G. Gillam, _Gallipoli Diary_ (London, 1918); Major C. B. Brereton, _Tales of Three Campaigns_ (London, 1926); Lt-General Sir William Marshall, _Memories of Four Fronts_ (London, 1929); General Sir Alexander Godley, _Life of an Irish Soldier_ (London, 1939); Field-Marshal Lord Birdwood, _Khaki and Gown: An Autobiography_ (London, 1941). Brudenell White did not publish a personal narrative, but he did give a lecture on the war: Major-General Sir C. B. B. White, _Some Reflections Upon the Great War_ (Sydney, 1921).

21 Samuel Hynes, _The Soldiers' Tale: Bearing Witness to Modern War_ (New York, 1987), p. 28.

22 F. M. Cutlack (ed.) _War Letters of General Monash_ (Sydney, 1934); the book was serialised in Keith Murdoch's _Herald_ (Melbourne) in November and December 1934, earning Monash's relatives at least £950: 'Extract from Sir Keith Murdoch's letter' attached to letter from Bennett to Murdoch, 20 September 1934, National Library of Australia, Canberra, Sir John Monash Papers, MS 1884, folder 1623. They were also serialised in the _Advertiser_ (Adelaide), _Sun_ (Sydney), and _Daily News_ (Perth).

23 Dr Gershon Bennett to F. M. Cutlack, 27 October 1934, Monash Papers, folder 1624.

24 Cutlack (ed.) _War Letters_, pp. vii, 40, 62.

25 _Ibid._, pp. 18, 34, 39, 40, 46, 65.

26 Cutlack to Bennett, 21 November (no year given), Monash Papers, folder 1623; Cutlack to Murdoch, 11 October 1934 and Bennett to Cutlack, 18 November 1934, Monash Papers, folder 1624; 'Correspondence and copies of war letters 1–94, December 1914–May 1915', Monash Papers, folder 955. Reviews of the _War Letters_ tended to regret that they were not edited to a greater extent. 'Australia at war. The letters of Sir John Monash', _West Australian_ (Perth), 20 December 1934; 'General Monash', _The Age_ (Melbourne), 22 December 1934, AWM, Canberra, Press cuttings, Biography, Monash.

27 Articles published on his death included: 'World leader of men. Sir John

Monash. Brilliant deeds during war recalled. Wonderful career', *Sun* (Sydney), 8 October 1931, AWM, Press cuttings, Biography, Monash, p. 51.

28 'Part II, diary of Sir Ian Hamilton' covers 5 May–30 July 1915, Hamilton Papers, 7/10/3.

29 Hamilton to Churchill, 29 December 1919, Churchill College, Cambridge, Churchill Archives Centre, Churchill Papers, CHAR 2/106/174–5.

30 Hamilton attended Cheam and Wellington before joining the army in 1873.

31 Rosa Maria Bracco, *Merchants of Hope: British Middlebrow Writers and the First World War 1919–1939* (Oxford, 1993).

32 Hamilton, *Gallipoli Diary*, 1, p. 258.

33 Hamilton to Huntington [a publisher], 2 April 1929, reproduced in 'The end of war? A correspondence between the author of *All Quiet on the Western Front* and General Sir Ian Hamilton GCB, GCMG' in *Life and Letters*, 3: *July 1929 to December 1929*, p. 403.

34 Hamilton, *Soul and Body*, pp. 302–3.

35 Hamilton, *Gallipoli Diary*, 1, p. 34.

36 *Ibid.*, p. 234. In 1930 at a party celebrating the twenty-first anniversary of *The Great Illusion*, however, Hamilton urged Angell to write a sequel: 'A noted book comes of age', *Daily Chronicle*, 21 March 1930, Hamilton Papers 17/52.

37 *Ibid.*, p. 71.

38 *Ibid.*, p. 141.

39 William Shakespeare, *Henry V*, Arden Shakespeare, 3rd series (London, 1996), Act 4, sc.1, lines 147–84.

40 Hamilton, *Gallipoli Diary*, 1, p. 28.

41 *Ibid.*, pp. 220–1.

42 Hamilton, *Gallipoli Diary*, 2, p. 6.

43 Hamilton, *Gallipoli Diary*, 1, p. 211.

44 *Ibid.*, p. 208 and Hamilton Papers, 7/10/3, p. 250.

45 An article in the *Daily Telegraph* of 22 September 1922 stated that, according to Liman von Sanders, the commander of the Turkish Army, British dead numbered 20,000, while Turkish dead numbered 60,000; other casualty estimates vary, but seem to agree that the Turks suffered the greater casualties.

46 Hamilton, *Despatches from the Dardanelles*, p. 77.

47 Hamilton, *Gallipoli Diary*, 1, p. 238–9.

48 Although there are no direct matches, several passages in the Bible reflect something of the tone of this passage: Ezekiel 26:15 and 32:25; Jeremiah 19:6; 1 Samuel 6:19. I am grateful to Reverend Elliot Vernon for these references; see Paul Fussell's discussion of the language used to dignify and ennoble warfare in his *The Great War and Modern Memory* (London 1975), pp. 21–2.

49 Hamilton, *Gallipoli Diary*, 2, p. 136.

50 Hamilton, *Gallipoli Diary*, 1, p. 222 and Hamilton Papers, 7/10/3, p. 266a.

51 *Ibid.*, p. 284 and Hamilton Papers, 7/10/3, p. 181.

52 Hamilton, *Gallipoli Diary*, 1, p. 128.
53 C. E. W. Bean, *The Story of Anzac from the Outbreak of War to the End of the First Phase of the Gallipoli Campaign, May 4, 1915*, vol. 1 of the Official History of Australia in the War of 1914–1918 (St Lucia, Queensland, 1981 [1921]), p. 607.
54 Hamilton, *Gallipoli Diary*, 2, p. 169.
55 Hamilton, *Gallipoli Diary*, 1, p. 221.
56 Hamilton, *Gallipoli Diary*, 2, p. 230.
57 Hamilton Papers, 7/10/3, p. 254.
58 Hamilton, *Gallipoli Diary*, 1, p. 209.
59 *Ibid.*, p. 207.
60 *Ibid.*, p. 23.
61 *Ibid.*, pp. 304–5.
62 *Ibid.*, p. 106.
63 Hamilton, *Gallipoli Diary*, 2, p. 212.
64 *Ibid.*, pp. 105–6.
65 *Ibid.*, p. 71.
66 *Ibid.*, p. 163.
67 *Ibid.*, p. 273.
68 Hamilton, *Gallipoli Diary*, 1, p. 141.
69 The manuscript identifies him as Lord Selborne: Hamilton Papers, 7/10/3, p. 262i.
70 Hamilton, *Gallipoli Diary*, 2, p. 39.
71 Robert Rhodes James, 'General Sir Ian Hamilton' in Field Marshal Sir Michael Carver (ed.) *The War Lords: Military Commanders of the Twentieth Century* (London, 1976), p. 92.
72 Orlo Williams, 'The Gallipoli tragedy: part I', *The Nineteenth Century and After*, 106 (July–December 1929), p. 93.
73 Hamilton Papers, 7/10/3, p. 208b.
74 Hamilton to Churchill, 12 March 1915, Martin Gilbert, *Winston S. Churchill*, 3: *Companion Part I, July 1914–April 1915* (London, 1972), p. 683.
75 Hamilton, *Gallipoli Diary*, 1, pp. 161 and 287.
76 *Ibid.*, p. 240.
77 Hamilton Papers, 7/10/3, p. 192. William St John Brodrick was the secretary of state for war until 1903; Lord Roberts replaced Buller as commander-in-chief in South Africa with Lord Kitchener as his chief of staff in late 1899.
78 Hamilton, *Gallipoli Diary*, 1, p. 228.
79 *Ibid.*, p. 238.
80 John Bourne, 'British Generals in the First World War' in G. D. Sheffield (ed.) *Leadership and Command: The Anglo-American Military Experience Since 1861* (London, 1997), pp. 93–116.
81 Hamilton, *Gallipoli Diary*, 1, p. 133.
82 *Ibid.*, p. 144.
83 Hamilton, *Gallipoli Diary*, 2, footnote p. 59.

84 K. Fewster (ed.) *Gallipoli Correspondent: The Frontline Diary of C. E. W. Bean* (Sydney, 1983), pp. 169–70. Hamilton gives no indication in his book that his relations with Braithwaite may have been strained; nor have I been able to locate any such allusions in his papers; nonetheless this allegation is made quite frequently by contemporaries.

85 *Ibid.*, p. 170.

86 Hamilton, *Gallipoli Diary*, 1, p. 80.

87 *Ibid.*, p. 47.

88 Hamilton, *Gallipoli Diary*, 2, Appendix I: 'Statement on artillery by Brigadier-General Sir Hugh Simpson Baikie, ex-commander of the British Artillery at Cape Helles'; Appendix II: 'Notes by Lieutenant-Colonel Charles Rosenthal, commanding 3rd Australian Field Artillery Brigade, 1st Australian Division, relating to artillery at Anzac, from 25 April to 25 August 1915'.

89 Hamilton, *Gallipoli Diary*, 1, p. 198.

90 Hamilton to Spenser Wilkinson, 27 May 1921, Hamilton Papers, 13/113.

91 Hamilton, *Gallipoli Diary*, 1, p. 238.

92 Hamilton, *The Commander*, pp. 129–30.

93 Hamilton, *Gallipoli Diary*, 1, p. 240 and Hamilton Papers, 7/10/3, p. 154a.

94 Hamilton, *Gallipoli Diary*, 1, p. 279.

95 Hamilton Papers, 7/10/3, p. 155.

96 Hamilton, *The Commander*, pp. 139–40.

97 Hamilton, *Gallipoli Diary*, 1, p. 16.

98 A Press cuttings book concerning *Gallipoli Diary* is to be found in Hamilton's Papers, file 33/2.

99 'Ian Hamilton's defence – diary of a tragic campaign', *Daily Express*, 17 May 1920, Hamilton Papers, 17/43, p. 8.

100 Hamilton to Churchill, 15 December 1919, Churchill Papers, CHAR 2/106/152.

101 General Sir Beauvoir de Lisle to Hamilton, 31 May 1920, Hamilton Papers, 7/10/12.

102 Capt. W. Henry Williams to Hamilton, 17 May 1920, Hamilton Papers, 7/10/12.

103 Henry A. Hall to Hamilton, 24 May 1920, Hamilton Papers, 7/10/12. Reverend Hall's work in commemorating Gallipoli at Holy Trinity Church, Eltham, is discussed in the final chapter.

104 Edward Spiers, 'Gallipoli' in Bond (ed.) *The First World War and British Military History*, pp. 168–70.

105 John Robertson, *Anzac and Empire: The Tragedy and Glory of Gallipoli* (London, 1990), p. 271.

106 W. S. Churchill, *The World Crisis 1915* (London, 1923).

107 *Ibid.*, p. 10.

108 Martin Gilbert's *Winston S. Churchill*, 4: *1916–1922* (London, 1975) describes the early stages of Churchill's memoir writing in ch. 41.

109 *Ibid.*, p. 751.

110 *Ibid.*, p. 757; this move was prompted by the false picture conveyed in Lord Esher's *The Tragedy of Lord Kitchener* (1921).

111 Evidence of Right Hon. Winston Spencer Churchill, MP, Thursday 28 September 1916 (day 5), Dardanelles Commission, q. 1195, PRO, London, CAB 19/33; *The World Crisis 1915*, pp. 172–3. I am grateful to Sir Martin Gilbert for pointing this out to me.

112 Churchill, *World Crisis*, p. 417.

113 *Ibid.*, p. 429.

114 *Ibid.*, pp. 370–1.

115 Robin Prior, *Churchill's 'World Crisis' as History* (London, 1983), p. 144.

116 Churchill, *World Crisis*, p. 497.

117 *Ibid.*, p. 324.

118 *The World Crisis by Winston Churchill: A Criticism by Colonel The Lord Sydenham of Combe, Admiral Sir Reginald Bacon, General Frederick Maurice, General Sir W. D. Bird and Sir Charles Oman* (London, 1928), p. 6.

119 Other considerations of Churchill's memoirs and work as a historian include: Malcolm Muggeridge 'Churchill the biographer and historian' in Charles Eade (ed.) *Churchill by His Contemporaries* (London, 1953), pp. 343–52; Herbert Leslie Stewart, *Sir Winston Churchill as Writer and Speaker* (London, 1954); Maurice Ashley, *Churchill as Historian* (London, 1968); F. W. Deakin, *Churchill the Historian*, Churchill Memorial Lecture (Zurich, 1968); Ian Beckett, 'Frocks and brasshats' in Bond (ed.) *The First World War and British Military History*, pp. 89–112; Robert Blake, 'Winston Churchill as historian' in Wm Roger Louis (ed.) *Adventures with Britannia: Personalities, Politics and Culture in Britain* (London, 1995), pp. 41–50; John Ramsden, *'That Will Depend on Who Writes the History'. Winston Churchill as His Own Historian*, Inaugural Lecture at Queen Mary and Westfield College, London, 22 October 1996 (London, 1997).

120 Prior, *Churchill's 'World Crisis'*, p. 71.

121 *Ibid.*, pp. 139, 167, 277.

122 *Ibid.*, p. 279.

123 *Ibid.*, p. 140.

124 *Ibid.*, pp. 82–3.

125 *Ibid.*, pp. 138 and 169.

126 *Ibid.*, p. 139. Hamilton and Aspinall also read proofs of *The World Crisis* and corresponded with Churchill about them: Churchill Papers, CHAR 8/45/11, 17, 20.

127 Prior, *Churchill's 'World Crisis'*, p. 277.

128 *Ibid.*, pp. 136–9; see also Geoffrey Penn, *Fisher, Churchill and the Dardanelles* (London, 1999).

6

Post-participant historiography of Gallipoli

The most important and influential participants' accounts of the campaign were published in the inter-war years. (One notable exception was Maurice Hankey's *The Supreme Command*,[1] which was delayed on grounds of official secrecy and was not, in any case, primarily concerned with Gallipoli.) Subsequent portrayals are interesting for a number of reasons: they offer a means to explore the influence of the Anzac legend and the heroic–romantic myth; they show how later generations have viewed the campaign in the context of changing attitudes; and they illustrate the way in which the story of an event must be told and re-told if it is to remain current. This chapter considers a selection of modern Gallipoli books in order to show the evolving continuities in histories subsequent to the phase of participant writings.

John North's *Fading Vision*

The power of the heroic–romantic myth of Gallipoli is demonstrated by the example of John North. North was a qualified barrister who published several novels in the 1920s.[2] A veteran of the Western Front, North became obsessed by Gallipoli during a visit to the peninsula in 1926; thereafter he read every book he could find on the subject, and revisited the peninsula on several occasions. His book *Gallipoli: The Fading Vision* was published to coincide with the twenty-first anniversary of the decisive naval encounter of 18 March 1915.[3]

What had captured North's imagination, he tells us at the beginning of his book, was a sense of the campaign's glamour. A conversation with a friend in 1934, however, helped to change his view. North recalled:

> Not long before I sailed a Gallipoli friend asked me why in heaven's name I kept on returning to that scene of *senseless horror and sacrifice*; and these

four words had stuck in my mind. Was it possible that they did indeed sum up the simple truth about a campaign which had hitherto attracted me because of the tragic immensity of its theme? Had the classical setting for the campaign made it difficult to turn an objective eye upon the campaign itself? I went back to the books I had not opened for nearly four years; I proceeded steadily to read them through; and as steadily my mood of disillusion deepened.[4]

North argued that the classical associations of the area obscured the true story of the campaign. He therefore promised of his book: 'All classical opiates will, therefore, be absent from this volume; the snows of Ida will go unsung.'[5]

North appeared to be rejecting the heroic–romantic myth as a 'fading vision', but in fact he discarded merely its most overtly romantic aspects:

> Nevertheless I still cherish a conviction that the reader may find the story of Gallipoli not to be dependent on an entirely false glamour for the attention and the admiration it has secured in the past. The story, indeed, must always be deserving of an adjective that has never been more abused than in its association with this campaign: but in so far as it relates the triumph of human endurance over suffering and peril that story is epic.[6]

It is without irony that North dedicated his book 'to all those who had the good fortune to serve in Gallipoli'.[7] His conclusion reveals that he remained deeply affected by the aura that surrounds Gallipoli. He seemed to acknowledge that the myth has elevated Gallipoli to more than simply a strip of land:

> Even those who return to the Peninsula to keep an appointment with the dead intrude upon its loneliness, its emptiness, its shattering silence. However, perhaps it is not upon Gallipoli that they intrude. Gallipoli is no longer a narrow neck of land set in the blue or the grey of the sea. If it is anything at all, it is a country of the mind.[8]

Therefore, although North appeared to see through those who add to the romance of the campaign, his writing nonetheless served to add to the dignified tragedy of the campaign. This description of the Anzacs, for example, is elegiac in tone:

> These twenty thousand men were called upon to fight strenuously and heroically to defend their cavelike existence on the slopes of those hills which they were to consecrate by such a 'sum of bravery' that there must for ever reside in the name of Anzac a magic and a splendour to uplift all

hearts. The Anzac that has come down to history is the domestic human story of this unique community of men, leading an utterly self-contained existence on a desert strip of land. In the broad canvas of the campaign they enter the picture when the main thrust towards the Narrows was transferred from Helles to the Anzac front. Not until then were they given an opportunity of entering into possession of those hills that would have represented for them the gates of freedom and the way of victory. This opportunity they were unable to seize. It is a supreme irony of history that the glamorous story of Anzac should move to final disaster immediately it joins the main narrative of the campaign.[9]

It seems clear that North had absorbed both the Anzac legend and Hamilton's portrayal of events. Like Nevinson, North's own opinion was doubtless reinforced by the co-operation of Hamilton who offered the use of his 'actual rough diary' and probably his corrected drafts of the book.[10] A magazine article on Hamilton by North, entitled 'The last of the Bayards', explained that North was a regular visitor to the Hamilton household,[11] and his portrayal added lustre to Hamilton's image as a loyal and imaginative general of great destiny.[12] Paraphrasing William Blake's *Jerusalem*, North wrote:

> But the Commander-in-Chief never lost faith, nor ceased from mental fight, nor let his sword sleep in his hand; nor did he put the blame for failure on some 'implacable and malign destiny'. No support will be found in *Gallipoli Diary* for the easy doctrine that 'the hostile gods were marshalled against the Mediterranean Expeditionary Force', or that the gods 'ordained' that it should fail. 'Nothing happens without a cause,' wrote the Greek philosopher, 'but everything for a reason and by necessity.' *Gallipoli Diary* touches the heights of the human spirit, and is aflame with a dazzling clearness of vision and apprehension that can leave no doubt that the expedition to Gallipoli was led by a commander under whom men could be proud to serve.[13]

North also followed Hamilton, and others, in emphasising the third strand of the British heroic–romantic myth, regarding strategy. He praised Churchill's vision of the strategic potential of Gallipoli.[14] He even claimed that the peninsula should not have been evacuated because of the damage this did to the empire.[15] Furthermore, like the Dardanelles Commission, he identified the reason for Gallipoli's failure as its leaders, especially those in London. He suggested that 'some useful purpose may be served by contrasting the sufferings and the heroisms of the "simple soldier" with the almost superhuman inadequacy of his political and military leaders – particularly on the home front'.[16] His criticism of the military and particularly the naval leadership at the Dardanelles provoked Aspinall-Oglander to write what proved to be the only scornful review of *The Fading Vision*.[17] His reaction may, however, have been provoked by North's dismissal of the evacuation that Aspinall, its planner, considered a personal triumph. But the disproportionate attention to North's treatment of De Robeck was also necessitated by Aspinall's precarious social position on the Isle of Wight, where the admiral's family was influential.[18]

Where North diverged from many other earlier accounts of Gallipoli was in his overt depiction of the campaign as a failure. Yet even that was tempered by his admiration for the campaign and, in particular, for the heroism of the men. He wrote:

> It is the mere magnificence of the bungling that gives cause for astonishment; and on this point let it be said that in face of so immense and so grievous a failure as Gallipoli, the voice of direct and deliberate criticism must be discomfited. Let it also be said that the reproach in memory would have been deeper still had the enterprise never been attempted. These protagonists, then, without any exception whatsoever, failed, whether excusably or otherwise. The only figures in the canvas of the campaign who never failed were the men. Never in the whole history of the campaign did they fail to go forward when the order was given, although it must now be obvious that on nine out of ten occasions that order meant the most rudimentary form of self-destruction [. . .]
>
> If it is still possible to think of this story of unrelieved failure as 'splendid', it is only because the men redeem it. If they failed at arms, they did not fail in death.[19]

Even so, the heroic–romantic myth continued to have the effect of distracting attention from the defeat. Harold Nicolson's review commented: 'His account is so restrained, so inevitable and so well-written that the reader is left with the impression of a noble enterprise rather than with the impression of a sorry failure.'[20]

John North's work is symptomatic of two trends in the later historiography of Gallipoli. The first is the decline, apparent from the 1930s, of the extravagantly romantic response to the campaign. Where contemporary authors often linked the campaign to its classical surroundings, for example, later authors have tended merely to note that this link had often been made. The second trend is the continuing fascination that the campaign holds. These trends are illustrated by Alan Moorehead's *Gallipoli* (1956).[21]

Moorehead, Rhodes James, Nolan and Johnston

Gallipoli is a compelling and entertaining tale of the campaign, with its vivid pen portraits of many characters, including the Turkish leaders, and its eye for an interesting story. Its telling juxtaposition of the parallel events in London, Constantinople and on either side of the frontline on the peninsula are revealed by hindsight and by Moorehead's access to the official archives in Ankara.[22] Moorehead eschewed elevated, ennobling language and the poetic touches of Masefield or Hamilton, but nonetheless told an absorbing story that perpetuated the Anzac legend and the heroic–romantic myth. The following is a good example of a modern reference to Gallipoli's classical past which points to its romantic potential in a low-key way. In discussing Liman von Sanders's disposal of his forces prior to the April landings, Moorehead wrote:

> This arrangement might have been sound enough at the time when Xerxes crossed from east to west in his advance on Europe, but to Liman's mind it was precisely calculated to lead to the complete annihilation of the Army as soon as an enemy attacked from the south.[23]

Gallipoli, however, still sparked off flights of hyperbole in reviewers of the book. For example:

> To many of my generation, the Second World War generation, the thought of Gallipoli, during many years of our boyhood and youth, exercised an especial and powerful fascination. It was the great, sad and stirring myth in whose shadow we grew up. The enormous, slaughterous battles of the Western Front sickened and horrified me (they still do); contemplation of them left my spirit bruised and dazed; but I thought (I still think) that I could understand Gallipoli. It blended the classical and romantic in my small but ever-to-be enlarged store of experience; Virgil and Euripides taught me something about it: Thucydides more; it ranged itself in my imagination with Thermopylae and Marathon, and the dire, doomed Athenian expedition to Sicily. The poets and the novelists whom I most admired wrote about Gallipoli. They all seemed to have fought there. More than one had died there. In my time, I suppose, I have read almost everything that has been written about Gallipoli.[24]

Only one reviewer railed at the classical references and the romanticisation of Gallipoli and of war. Norman Podhoretz fulminated in the *New Yorker*:

> He tells the whole story with an eye on its dramatic value and an awareness of the workings of destiny on the ambitions of men, for his purpose,

I suspect is not only to relate what 'really' happened at Gallipoli but to create a Gallipoli as worthy of an epic poem as the Trojan. At that, 'The Iliad' is no further from Mr. Moorehead's mind when he writes of Gallipoli than it was from the minds of some of the men who fought there, in particular the commander-in-chief, General Sir Ian Hamilton. [. . .]

At moments, his book sounds like a eulogy of a dead world; at others, like a desperate insistence that the corpse still has life in it. But to most of his readers, I think, it will be clear that Gallipoli was no Trojan War. It was a cruel joke played by history on the illusions of men who had not yet had time to notice that they were living in the twentieth century.[25]

Podhoretz's righteous and venomous rebuttal notwithstanding, Moorehead's book fuelled a renascence of the continuing fascination of Gallipoli. The book's success was not immediate: Moorehead had some trouble securing an American publisher and travelled to the United States following its publication in Britain, in April 1956, to push his case. On his return, however, he found he had become the talk of the literary world.[26] Indeed, in November 1956 he was awarded both *The Sunday Times* Prize for Literature and the first Duff Cooper Prize.[27] A programme based on the book was shown on the first night of broadcasting by ITV.[28]

It may have been that the coincidence of the publication of Moorehead's book with a new British failure in the Mediterranean in the autumn of 1956 – Suez – accounted in part for its interest. The contemporaneous anti-Soviet uprising in Hungary, in October 1956, will have added further piquancy to Moorehead's argument, since his approval of the strategic vision of Gallipoli extended so far as to allow his claim that 'if the Allies had succeeded in penetrating the Dardanelles in 1915 or 1916 the Russians would not have signed a separate peace, and that the revolution might not have followed, not at all events so soon, or possibly so drastically'.[29]

However, the key event informing Moorehead's work on Gallipoli and the response it received was the Second World War. Moorehead had been a successful war correspondent, particularly in North Africa, and that experience lent him both the authority to comment on an earlier war and the journalistic skill to present it in an attractive fashion.[30] In Dunkirk, the war provided an example of an evacuation that led to later victories and also perhaps honed the British penchant for appreciating a gallant defeat. Furthermore, the war had featured a whole series of amphibious operations leading up to D-Day that not only drew on the practical experience gained at Gallipoli, thereby making that campaign more worthwhile, but vindicated the very idea of amphibious operations.[31] The Second World War brought fame to the campaign's participants, such as Clement Attlee and Field Marshal Slim, adding a little extra distinction to its story.[32] However, the most important impact of the Second World War was the rehabilitation of Winston Churchill's reputation as an imaginative strategist and a war leader without parallel. This cast a different light on his early efforts at Gallipoli. Moorehead warmly endorsed both Churchill's strategy and his work to restore that reputation through *World Crisis*.[33] He has Churchill's ringing assertion 'The terrible "Ifs" accumulate'[34] as an epigraph to one of his chapters, and later implicitly suggests a further terrible if: if only Brigadier-General John Monash's 'quite exceptional ability' had been recognised, he 'would have been the ideal commander for the Suvla operation'.[35]

Moorehead's portrayal was heavily influenced by Roger Keyes's and Cecil Aspinall-Oglander's passionate commitment to the possibilities of the Gallipoli campaign. Keyes's opinions are powerfully presented by Moorehead in describing crucial moments, such as the later stages of the naval attack of 18 March 1915, from the commodore's point of view. This focus on the most energetic, optimistic and bellicose officer in the Navy also provided a dramatic contrast to the cautious decisions taken, and his view becomes all the more tantalising when the panic in Constantinople is then described.[36] Moorehead quotes sympathetically Keyes's later assertion that the Navy could have forced the straits at any time from 4 April onwards.[37] He returns at length to Keyes to describe his strenuous efforts in London in October to gain renewed support for the operations.[38] In contrast, Moorehead does *not* mention Guy Dawnay's similar trip to London in September on the converse mission to press for evacuation.[39]

Keyes's biographer was Cecil Aspinall-Oglander.[40] Aspinall-Oglander himself read a draft of Moorehead's book – though he apparently failed to notice startling errors, such as the claim that only the Anzacs, among those who fought at Gallipoli, went on to fight the Germans elsewhere.[41] Aspinall-Oglander *was* on the look out for his allies, however. He successfully begged Moorehead to remove a potentially damaging reference to Churchill's June 1915 Dundee speech which may have forewarned Liman von Sanders of the August attacks.[42] Aspinall-Oglander's similar comment in his official history had led to searing criticism of Churchill in the *Daily Herald*. Aspinall told Moorehead:

Never did I feel so ashamed. I had an enormous admiration for Winston's part in the whole campaign, and thought he had been dead right. He had then championed my book with all his might, only to find, on the day of its publication, that I had given the Herald its chance for further vilification! Naturally, I wrote at once to the Herald, and they had the decency to publish my letter without further comment; but as Winston sadly said to me: 'That sort of mischief can never be put right – the stigma sticks, the man impressed by the article never sees your denial, and the story goes on and on.' And here it is, after another 25 years, repeated in your lovely book. So do, please omit it.[43]

In addition to renewing interest in Gallipoli, Moorehead inspired two, perhaps three, significant works related to the campaign: Sidney Nolan's Gallipoli paintings (see figure 6), Robert Rhodes James's *Gallipoli* (1965) and possibly George Johnston's *My Brother Jack* (1964).[44] Both Nolan and Johnston were living on the Greek island of Hydra during the winter of 1955–56 when, coincidentally, Moorehead was on Spetsae writing *Gallipoli*.[45] Nolan was searching for a new theme for his painting and had become interested in ancient Troy, borrowing Johnston's copies of Homer's *Iliad* and Robert Graves's *Greek Mythology*. Nolan wanted to link the struggle for life in Australia's arid inland with Trojan tragedy, and when Johnston showed him Alan Moorehead's *New Yorker* article on Gallipoli,[46] which commented on the parallels between Gallipoli and Troy, Nolan was inspired. Johnston recalls:

> From then on, when the *retzina* circled and wild winter buffeted at the shutters of the waterfront taverns, we would talk far into the small hours about this other myth of our own, so uniquely Australian and yet so close to that much more ancient myth of Homer's. Nolan's poetic imagination saw them as one, saw many things fused into a single poetic truth lying, as the true myth should, outside time.[47]

The following spring, Nolan visited Troy, Gallipoli, Mudros and Lemnos, and thereafter began to paint his long series of elegiac paintings on that theme. In 1965, 180 of them were incorporated into a short film, *Toehold in History*, produced for the fiftieth anniversary of the landings and scripted, appropriately, by George Johnston. Nolan's biographer's comments on the film suggest that Nolan had chosen a typically Australian emphasis on the *individual* experience of the campaign:

> The main impression given by this cinematic cavalcade of subtle imagery was the immediacy of someone who had been on the spot at Gallipoli, not concerned with the grand designs of military strategy or the grandeur of

6 *Gallipoli Soldiers* (1960) by Sidney Nolan

battle, but with the human face of engagement. The emphasis was on the personal and emotional aspects of men enmeshed in bloody conflict and haunted by the ever-present spectre of death.[48]

Where Nolan is less typically Australian is in the links he made between Troy and Gallipoli, links more usually found in British works on the campaign, notwithstanding the influence of Arthur H. Adams's poem *The Trojan War, 1915*, which Bean had included in *The Anzac Book*.[49]

Nolan's paintings were used on the dust jackets of George Johnston's *My Brother Jack* and of *Cooper's Creek* by Moorehead (with whom the artist had become friendly).[50] Like Moorehead, George Johnston had been a war correspondent in the Second World War; and both were expatriate Australians. The novel describes David Meredith's rise to success as a war correspondent and contrasts him with his brother Jack who embodies the heroic virtues of the Anzac. The urge to write the novel was probably inspired more by the 1958 revelation of Johnston's serious illness (he died in 1970) than by Moorehead or Nolan.[51] It is autobiographical and is concerned with the Anzacs' position, the human spirit and national identity, rather than the Gallipoli campaign.[52]

Although Moorehead had been acclaimed by Compton Mackenzie as 'the first writer to present Gallipoli in historical perspective',[53] his style was that of a journalist. The first scholarly history of the campaign was by Robert Rhodes James, himself one of the many who wrote to congratulate Moorehead on his achievement: 'Please do accept once more my most sincere congratulations from one who was at one time prepared to be a very hostile critic indeed, but who has been completely won over.'[54] After years of scholarship, however, Rhodes James was to change his mind. In 1995 he wrote: 'the Australian mythology about Gallipoli has been too often neither objective nor fair, fuelled by Alan Moorehead's deeply flawed and grievously over-praised account'.[55]

Rhodes James explained his enduring interest in the Gallipoli campaign in his Preface. He had been familiar with the content of Aspinall-Oglander's official history, and with other accounts of the campaign, since his schooldays, 'but it was not until the late Alan Moorehead's book was published in 1956 that this intense interest developed into resolution. I did not share the extravagant praise and admiration that Moorehead's book received; it was superb literature, but doubtful history.'[56] Rhodes James carried out his research between 1962 and 1965, having been allowed early access to official papers on the campaign on the understanding that his book would not be published until 1965, when the fifty-year rule would see the release of the papers on Gallipoli.[57] His aim 'was to attempt to describe the campaign in the words of those who served on the Peninsula, and not only in those of the commanders and politicians'.[58] However, he did not do this as later historians have done by quoting extensively from the private letters and diaries of the lower ranks to describe the experience of the campaign; instead, his was an essentially top–down portrayal, focusing mainly on the politics, the strategy and the tactics of the campaign. He based his account on primary evidence from those who had participated in the campaign, quoting them often but generally briefly, so that his narrative is deeply informed by the perceptions of those inside the expeditionary force. His writing is lucid and engaging, and peppered with scholarly discussion of the evidence and his own perceptive judgements.

Rhodes James gives a sophisticated summary of pre-war Anglo-Turkish relations, carefully dissecting the fuzzy decision-making process which led to the inception of the campaign, and in doing so criticises the 'total absence of strong leadership' in the War Council.[59] He shows that the genesis of the plan lay entirely with Churchill,[60] that Kitchener took the decision to land at Gallipoli,[61] and that Hamilton and De Robeck rather than the Cabinet or the War Council decided on a joint operation.[62] He declares Hamilton's plan for the landing to have been 'bold, intelligent and ambitious', but marred by the extensive detail on trivialities while being 'excessively vague on the really important points'.[63] He gives excellent and economical descriptions of those involved, coupling them with insightful comments on individuals' flaws, the interplay of personalities and the implications for the campaign.

Rhodes James also tried to pick apart those elements of the story which are legend (in the sense of untruths) and to identify their source, noting for example, some extra details added by Ellis Ashmead Bartlett.[64] He observed the differing perceptions of the campaign as romantic[65] and enthralling,[66] and the shift from the early view that Churchill was entirely responsible to the 'equally foolish' post-Second World War view that his actions were 'uniformly wise and justified by events'.[67] Rhodes James had no truck with the romantic view of the campaign. He has written elsewhere:

> The best cure for the romantic haze which hangs over the campaign is to go to Gallipoli, in August, alone; for the intense heat, the blinding glare, and the spume of dust moving slowly across the Peninsula are not sufficient to obliterate the chilling coldness of the atmosphere. It was good to have gone there; it was better to leave. The Peninsula resents intruders.[68]

Rhodes James's own verdict on Gallipoli is that 'it was a desperately close fought campaign, waged with superlative perseverance and courage by both sides, which ended in a tactical draw; regarded strategically, it was a major defeat for the Allies'.[69] His book remains the best history of the Gallipoli campaign.

Gallipoli and academia

Moorehead and Rhodes James, the authors of the first two substantial histories of Gallipoli written post-1945, came from outside academia. Prior to their histories, academic interest in the campaign had centred on the armed forces, studying its strategic and operational lessons. During the 1920s this first modern amphibious campaign was 'exhaustively studied' by the US Marine Corps.[70] A study by William Puleston[71] and a translation of Liman von Sanders's memoirs[72] emerged from the US Naval Institute, Annapolis. Gallipoli was therefore a direct precursor to the success of the island-hopping strategy in the Pacific in the Second World War, as Moorehead broadly suggested. Gallipoli continues to be studied by today's armed forces.[73]

Yet within academia Gallipoli, the First World War and military history in general were ignored until the mid-1960s. Michael McKernan has discussed the reasons for the prior neglect by academics of Australia's military history. He suggested that military history is an uncomfortable subject for the left-leaning historians who made up the majority of the profession.[74] Furthermore, the manner in which Bean's official history series had been written, that is, predominantly by journalists and public servants, also put it outside the purview of university academics.[75]

Various suggestions have been mooted as factors explaining the development of academic interest in the First World War. Alex Danchev has suggested that Moorehead's *Gallipoli* helped to inspire a general interest in the First World War, indicating perhaps not only the power of the book, but of the Gallipoli campaign as the palatable face of the war.[76] Peter Simkins has suggested that in the mid-1960s British academic interest in the First World War was stimulated also by the fiftieth anniversary of the war, not least because this led to the opening to researchers of the British official records of the conflict, one beneficiary being Robert Rhodes James.[77] The expansion of tertiary education in Britain and Australia may also have been influential. Michael McKernan notes that in 1937 there were twelve university teachers of history in Australia, but by 1971 this figure had grown exponentially to 750, with perhaps an equal number of postgraduates. He comments: 'In history there will never be a shortage of topics for research, but clearly with this explosion of industry the range of topics developed too.'[78] One of these was military history.

Bean rediscovered

The first academic historian to study the Gallipoli campaign was Ken Inglis of the Australian National University. Perhaps significantly, Inglis was not a military but a social–cultural historian, and it was from that indirect approach that he opened up the study of Gallipoli. In a series of articles written over a decade, Inglis shifted his gaze from organised religion to what he perceived to be a civic religion, and thus turned to Anzac Day and the Anzac legend. His research has been hugely influential in opening up this field. One of the most important consequences of Inglis's work is that it led to the rediscovery of Charles Bean. This is true in several senses – first, in the most literal sense in beginning to write about the man, notably his 1965 *Meanjin Quarterly* article and his 1969 Macrossan lecture *C. E. W. Bean, Australian Historian* which traced Bean's career and impressive achievements.[79]

The second sense in which Bean was rediscovered concerned the way he wrote military history, starting from the frontline and working backwards. The revolutionary nature of Bean's work can be seen if it is placed in the later context of the modern historiography of the First World War. Much of this writing has focused upon what Peter Simkins has dubbed 'everyman at war';[80] that is, it has examined the experience of the frontline, taking a 'bottom–up' view, often making use of personal diaries, letters and oral history. This bottom–up historiographical trend applies as much to Gallipoli as to the Western Front. In particular it is the approach of two of the most popular and influential works on Gallipoli: Bill Gammage's *The Broken Years* (1974) and Patsy Adam-Smith's *The Anzacs* (1978). Gammage drew upon the diaries and letters of approximately 1,000 Australians who fought in the frontline during the war,[81] while Adam-Smith read 7,820 letters and diaries.[82]

Adam-Smith's popular history of the campaign sold well, leading to eleven reprints or new editions between 1978 and 1991. It was the joint winner of *The Age* Book of the Year award in 1978. Simkins notes that Adam-Smith is 'refreshingly prepared to strip away some of the more romanticized elements of the Anzac legend',[83] citing her clear-eyed treatment of Simpson and the Donkey; she also included figures and details on venereal disease. Yet, in the commentary which accompanies the diary extracts, Adam-Smith often writes in the most elevated language possible in 1978; thus, in her Preface, while reminding us that 'war *is* hell'[84] and ignoring the generals and strategy, she venerates those Australians who participated:

So, to you old men, who have spent so much of the last of your time with me ensuring that I knew how you felt, why you went – and stayed – what you did and how you came home again, I dedicate this book. You had the greatest number of casualties per men on the field of all the Allied armies; you travelled the furthest, were away the longest. You were the only volunteers. You came from a newer land, were a younger race than any who entered that awful arena. When time has removed this age to a distance, our descendants will speak of you as we now speak of the three hundred at Thermopylae – but I have had the rare, and peerless, privilege of knowing you.[85]

Adam-Smith used a methodology similar to Bill Gammage's earlier and more scholarly work, yet made no reference to *The Broken Years* in her bibliography.[86]

In addition to Ken Inglis, Gammage was instrumental both in drawing Gallipoli and the Anzacs into the realms of academic study and in revivifying interest in those subjects among the wider population. As a student, Gammage had been disappointed by the neglect in academia of military history and the First World War. He wrote of his undergraduate experience of the Australian National University in 1962: 'my Australian History course that year stopped in 1914 and re-started in 1918, stopped in 1939 and re-started in 1945 [. . .] The same thing had happened in history at school.'[87] He was nonetheless keen to work on the First World War for his honours thesis. His choice was so unusual that he had to be allocated a supervisor from outside the ANU History Department (a man at the military college, Duntroon, who he never met). Gammage carried out his postgraduate research at the Australian War Memorial, and received one of the first awards under what was later formalised as the Memorial's Research Grants Scheme. He has noted that the significance of his work at the Memorial slowly dawned on him and others:

My presence ended an era for the Memorial: it would no longer be a vault, a store of memory, it would be a place of research [. . .]

I am part of the generation which took them [the Great War dead] from memory to history and I feel privileged about that.[88]

Gammage's research was published as *The Broken Years*, which he described as 'an emotional history of the AIF'.[89]

The Broken Years is a powerful and beautifully written account of the Australians' experiences of the Great War. It bears the imprint of Bean in its footnotes detailing the name, home town, occupation, birth date and often the date of death of each diarist and letter-writer quoted. It thus follows Bean in its focus on the individual. Where it is an enhancement of Bean is in its frank admittance of the vicious and callous side of war,[90] and of larrikin behaviour,[91] alongside the many other responses of these men to war. Such was the liberty of an academic historian writing in the 1970s. And in admitting and explaining those faults that emerged at times in some men, the far more numerous virtues of the men described with deep admiration and sensitivity are thrown into relief. Yet if Gammage's book is rounded in perspective in emotional terms, it lacks perspective in other crucial ways; this is the by-product of the book's methodology and aim. Far more so than Bean, it lacks tactical and strategic explanations of events – no doubt because the men did not discuss them.[92] This lack of an overarching view makes war seem pointless. Similarly, we are given no external estimates of the result of British fighting prowess – indeed the efforts at Cape Helles are almost entirely overlooked, and the admittedly poor showing of Kitchener's men at Suvla is given no mitigating explanation; nor are the overall difficulties of the campaign described – making the leadership seem less competent than it was.

Despite some similarities in methodology and focus, then, Gammage's longer term perspective and modern sensibilities led him to a quite different conclusion. Bean witnessed the entire war and drew some consolation from the sacrifice and death that he saw: Gammage quotes his hymn 'We only know – from good and great/ Nothing save good can flow.' By contrast, Gammage sees the war as an unrelieved tragedy. He has explained that his book 'sees the war as destroying an age and a generation to no purpose, and blighting our country by anchoring our national traditions and our national psyche in the past, rather than the future'.[93] Gammage's view of Gallipoli has probably attained a wider influence than has any other historian through his work as historical adviser on Peter Weir's 1981 film *Gallipoli*.[94]

The film's historical sources were the official histories of Charles Bean and *The Broken Years*. (Indeed, the Italian version of the film was named after Gammage's book.[95]) The personal focus of these works led to a film that *Variety* aptly described as 'virtually an intimate epic' that 'tackles a legend in human terms'.[96] Rather than showing the main episodes of the Gallipoli campaign or explaining its strategy, the film provides a distillation of the Anzac legend. Weir and Williamson decided on a simple story focused on two young men from Western Australia.[97] The film contrasts Archy Hamilton (played by Mark Lee), the naïve blond country boy, with Frank (Mel Gibson), the sceptic from the city.[98] Their friendship develops from an athletics race (which Archy wins); they join up together, and we see them training in Egypt before they are sent as reinforcements to Gallipoli, where in the final scene Archy dies during the attack on the Nek.

Archy had joined up eagerly (and illegally – he was too young) and he persuaded Frank to join him. Archy is associated with notions of empire – we see his family listening to a story by Kipling (in which Mowgli becomes a man),[99] while Frank initially asserts his Irish background as his objection to joining up. En route to enlistment, they get lost in the outback like Burke and Wills. During their training in Egypt, we are shown Frank and his mates mocking the monocled British officers and hitting back at locals who were mistakenly believed to be corrupt. Only the final thirty-two minutes (of a total 111) of the film are devoted to scenes on the Gallipoli peninsula.[100]

The film thus encapsulates and promotes many of the key elements of the Anzac legend. The two mates' loss of innocence and passage into manhood reflect the larger story of Australia's journey to nationhood through war. Archy, the hero, is the noble bushman, just as Bean would have had it. The Anzacs have a strong anti-authoritarian streak – as shown by their activities in Egypt – and, save for the nurses at the ball, there is no place for women in the story. It does not show the two men as warriors in action (effective or otherwise) – being good fighters is no longer such a central part of the Anzac legend.

Another much discussed element of the film is the anti-British sentiment that it promotes. It should be noted that Gammage denies that this was ever its purpose; it is, nonetheless, its effect.[101] The crucial scene is that of the attack at the Nek. We are incorrectly told that this was in support of the British landing further up the coast at Suvla Bay (it was in fact to assist the New Zealand advance on Chunuk Bair).[102] The inexperienced and badly led British troops landing at Suvla notoriously made little headway, but there is no evidence to support the film's allegation that they sat on the beach and drank tea.[103] This lassitude is contrasted with Archy and his comrades going to their deaths in a series of attacks. The continuation of those attacks, although clearly entailing deaths, is ordered by an officer whose English background will be inferred by many from his accent, although military buffs will recognise his Australian uniform.[104] In reality he was Colonel Antill, who came from New South Wales.

Some commentators have criticised the film for the inconsistencies at its heart. It caricatures the English but obscures the fact that the Anzacs were fighting for them. It is a patriotic film, but the featured Australians were not fighting for their own country.[105] Like much modern writing on the First World War, it honours their heroism and self-sacrifice while denying any purpose to their deaths. Gerard Henderson argued:

> Now that there is a revival in nationalist feeling, the left is attempting to win back lost ground. It was once intellectually fashionable to sneer at those (primarily conservatives) who honoured the Anzacs and glorified both their sacrifices and the causes for which they fought.
>
> Now this has changed. The current Anzac revival – of which *Gallipoli* is a central part – attempts to distinguish between the Anzacs as individuals and the cause for which they fought. The former are to be glorified but the latter is condemned since it led to the death or disfigurement of so many Australian sons.[106]

This injection of the modern view of war as futile into the Anzac legend was surely prompted by the film-makers' reliance on Gammage's *The Broken Years*. This view provides a contrast to Roger McDonald's novel *1915* (1979), which also features two young friends going to war.[107] Other modern touches, such as Frank's espousal of republican sentiments,[108] Archy's friendly relations with Aborigines and the duo's misfounded accusations of corruption against the Egyptians,[109] were helpful in making the film acceptable to a modern audience, and thereby reinforcing the Anzac legend.[110] But such window-dressing disappointed Sylvia Lawson who criticised the film's failure to question the myth. She argued that the film

> seeks to produce a consensus in the audience, an acceptance that this is still an appropriate way to recount Australia's part in WWI, and that, by implication this is still – after all, and notwithstanding – a Great Story. As with some new and idiomatic Life of Jesus, reverence is assumed, or at least a suspension of irreverence: *Gallipoli*, untainted by any grain of ambiguity, offers no other position [. . .]
>
> It seems hardly credible that in 1981 avowedly liberal commentators can disregard the position of the myth – a highly-wrought selection from historical materials – as the centre of a demi-official State religion, one which has sustained the worst of the old white Australia in its persistent looking-back, its racism and sexism, and its readiness for pro-British or pro-American militarism.[111]

The film-makers' decision to focus on two friends, celebrating their youth and heroism while largely ignoring the cause for which they fought, ridiculing their unthinking allegiances and denigrating their allies created some confusion among reviewers. Brian McFarlane suggested that it was neither a 'war film' nor an 'anti-war film', but a film about the reactions to war.[112] Sandra Hall thought it 'not a war film, but a film about friendship'.[113] By contrast, Kenneth Jackson declared it 'one of the greatest anti-war movies of all time'.[114] Most academic commentators discuss it in terms of its portrayal of a national myth,[115] and the powerful communication of that myth is the film's principal achievement.

Some more recent works on Gallipoli have, however, served to question the Anzac legend. Gammage's method has been partially followed by Nigel Steel and Peter Hart who used the testimony of ordinary men and their officers to recount the experience of the campaign. They conducted oral history interviews and used the resources of the Imperial War Museum, and so their book was the first to pay substantial attention to the experience of British soldiers at Gallipoli. This is done in the context of a careful discussion of events on the ground. Prior to their collaboration, Steel had written a guide to the peninsula in which he tried to evoke the calmn enchantment of the place for those who could not travel there in person.[116] Harking back to the tantalising idea of the campaign having been 'within an ace of success', Steel and Hart initially planned to entitle their book 'Narrowest of Margins', but they decided to use only the envisaged subtitle; as a result their book has the most uncompromising title of any book on the campaign: *Defeat at Gallipoli* (1994).[117] They conclude unequivocally:

> Many of the major protagonists of the campaign have sought to demonstrate the worthiness of the Gallipoli project by explaining how close the campaign came to a magnificent success. As Gallipoli was a comprehensive strategic failure, this has been an impossible task, and attention has therefore centred on a few 'key' moments in the campaign which have been portrayed as 'lost opportunities' where the British would have swept to a crushing success and achieved all their strategic aims but for a crucial mistake or a piece of cruel misfortune which thwarted them [. . .]
>
> A worthwhile strategic concept is not negated by tactical failure on the battlefield, but tactical failure can be made almost inevitable if the strategy is faulty: and the British strategy was fundamentally flawed.[118]

In a similar vein, Alistair Thomson's *Anzac Memories* (1994) drew on interviews with Australian working-class veterans from the ranks.[119] Thomson's book is not a history of the campaign. Rather, as its title suggests, it is as much to do with oral history, the workings of memory and the continued reinterpretation of an experience over time as it is about the Anzac legend *per se*. Thomson found that his interviewees recalled little romance or heroism in their experiences. The influence of Thomson's book on my own work will be clear – in particular, his view that 'Bean's Anzac legend-making provides a superb example of the "hegemonic" process whereby a legend was created, not by excluding the varieties and contradictions of digger experience, but by using selection, simplification and generalisation to represent that complexity'.[120] Furthermore, the veterans' memories serve to confirm Samuel Hynes's thesis of the 'whole story' being encapsulated in the soldiers' tale: 'their testimony records a war experience that was much more complex and multifaceted than the homogeneous identity of the legend, and which sometimes even contradicts the legend'.[121]

John Robertson's beautifully illustrated book, published in 1990, sought 'to tell a story through the words of Australians who fought at Gallipoli'.[122] He does so more in the style of Rhodes James, weaving short quotations into his narrative, rather than using extended passages from original sources like Steel and Hart, and Gammage. The nature and scope of his book are indicated by its title: *The Tragedy and Glory of Gallipoli: Anzac and Empire*.

Robertson sets the Australian experience of Gallipoli within its imperial context, explaining its political and strategic implications – thus avoiding some of the limitations of Gammage's *The Broken Years*. Robertson's narrative of events on the peninsula does not seek to discuss the tactics of the campaign – Bean's 'superlative account' has already done that, he says.[123] Instead he homes in on important episodes like the Nek,[124] Keith Murdoch,[125] and the botched medical arrangements (to which he devotes two extended chapters),[126] amid a more general account. He combines these with intermittent discussion of perceptions in Australia of the campaign's course (for example, the dawning realisation that it had failed),[127] thereby tracing the steady development of Australian nationalism and its 'intricate relationship' to empire loyalty.[128] Other original and useful features are his discussion of prisoners of war (who suffered from the Turks' indifference and brutality, though not to the same extent as would prisoners of the Japanese in the Second World War),[129] the Dardanelles Commission[130] and the developments leading to Anzac Day;[131] and an excellent historiographical survey is appended.[132]

Informing Robertson's book are his admiration of Bean and what may be regarded as a return to Bean's attitudes. He is thus fiercely critical of historiographical trends such as the dissection of the Anzac legend:

The notion that the 'Anzac legend' was 'created' by Charles Bean or was a figment of his imagination seems to be becoming fashionable among a younger generation of historians. The evidence in this book shows conclusively that this attitude does not accord with the facts. Eliminate Bean's writing from the story, and the same picture emerges of bravery, recklessness, a cynical or disrespectful attitude towards authority outside battle, stern discipline under fire, and so on.[133]

For Robertson such work denigrates those who fought at Gallipoli:

One wonders what qualifies people who have never experienced the rigours of campaigning or the terrifying savagery of battle to belittle the valour of those who have. Australians in 1915 were anxious to make a mark on the world and so were very receptive to the views of Ashmead-Bartlett, Masefield and others of like mind. With remarkable rapidity Australians enshrined these views in their national psyche. But it cannot be said that they exaggerated or misled each other. They simply drew inspiration from what had happened on the battlefield.[134]

Robertson also attacks another common attitude to war in general, leading him to a strong defence of Australia's role in the Great War (despite doubts as to whether the Gallipoli campaign itself was worthwhile).[135] He concludes: 'These men sacrificed much for what they rightly considered a noble cause. It is sadly ironic that a later generation has doubted the value of their cause.'[136]

In Adam Smith, Gammage, Steel and Hart, Thomson and Robertson we have six authors whose books about Gallipoli were based on the testimonies of individuals who fought there in the frontline.[137] These works are radically different both from each other and from the participants' histories of an earlier era. Those authorswho rely to a greater extent on the words of individual participants to explore the events – Gammage, Steel and Hart, Thomson – avoid the more overt assertions of the romance of the campaign. Is there a paradox here? I have argued that with Gallipoli, in contrast to the Western Front, the possibility of focusing on the individual in describing war – particularly as practised by Charles Bean – facilitated the development of a romantic portrayal. Have these revisionist texts echoed Bean's approach but warped it in a way that serves to denigrate the men of Gallipoli and weaken the Anzac legend as Robertson feared?[138] It seems not. The popularity of Gammage's book, for example, has coincided with a remarkable growth in the Australian public's interest in Gallipoli. Perhaps the incorporation of the modern sense of the futility of war into the broader romantic myth has facilitated the latter's persistence by keeping it tolerable for new generations who know nothing of war. The need for a myth to evolve in step with societal values is surely the reason why gentle, care-giving heroes such as Simpson and the donkey are now placed centre-stage in the Anzac legend, where earlier the focus might have fallen on the martial heroics of Albert Jacka, VC, who held a trench single-handedly, killing seven Turks in the process.[139]

Peter Cochrane (1992) has investigated the development of the Simpson legend.[140] E. M. Andrews's excellent *The Anzac Illusion* (1993) pointed out the parochialism, delusions and exaggerations of the legend.[141] Along with Thomson's work, research of this type, interrogating Bean and the Anzac legend, has been among the most stimulating and original recent work on Gallipoli. Not only is the Anzac legend strong enough to survive such questioning, but it is a necessary part of ensuring its survival. This process maintains the legend's relevance. Criticism provokes interest and the restatement of the original version, perhaps with slight modification. Thesis and anti-thesis lead to synthesis.

This argument is illustrated by Les Carlyon's *Gallipoli* (2001).[142] It is a narrative history of the campaign that topped the best-seller charts in Australia. The author is a journalist and former editor of Melbourne's *The Age*, and his book is a worthy successor to the work of Moorehead, the earlier journalist–historian of the campaign. Carlyon seeks to contextualise the extraordinary phenomenon of Anzac Day and the nature of the peninsula today by telling the story of the campaign from the point of view of the politicians, the generals and admirals, the Turks and the men. Above all, Carlyon's book is the story of Australians. Thus the French receive fairly cursory coverage, and the evocative individual pen-portraits are largely of Anzacs rather than British Tommies.

A typical bias therefore remains, despite Carlyon's inherent fairness – for instance, he acknowledges that the landings at Helles were far bloodier than at Anzac[143] and that Peter Weir's film unfairly implies that a British officer, and not Antill, had been responsible for the continuation of the attack at the Nek.[144] In some respects, Carlyon is updating Bean, echoing his definition of heroism, 'The epic was in the hanging on',[145] but taking the opportunity to be more critical and enquiring. For example, he uses the case of Ivor Margetts, a teacher from Hobart, who returned to the beach to look for reinforcements, as a means to introduce the controversy over straggling.[146] Carlyon is critical of New Zealand and Australian officers such as Godley and Johnston,[147] but he saves his greatest venom for Hunter Weston and Stopford.[148] The ferocity of his sarcasm in such instances sets his approach apart from the usual academic tack, as also do his occasional references to his own experiences of the peninsula[149] and his flights of imagination.[150]

Perhaps these elements in his engaging style are integral to conveying the mythic aspects of Gallipoli; certainly Carlyon argues that 'the siren-call of this beach has little to do with facts or common sense or the dessicated footnotes of academics'.[151] He further evokes the romantic aura of the campaign through references to 'history's stadium', 'Samothrace, home of Poseidon', Napoleon and Alexander, the Via Dolorosa and Golgotha, Homer and Shakespeare.[152] Hamilton is cast as Don Quixote, and more akin to Hamlet than to Henry V.[153] Indeed, Carlyon is largely sympathetic to the commander-in-chief, perhaps in part because he takes *Gallipoli Diary* at face value.[154] He thus combines the romanticism of Hamilton, the heroic individualism of Bean and the revisionism of Thomson, while producing a coherent whole. Finally, one unusual addition underlines Carlyon's post-modernity: the attack at the Narrows hampered by the minefield, he says, is nothing short of a scene from *Catch 22*.[155] The success of Carlyon's book demonstrates the continuing resonance of the heroic–romantic myth and particularly the Anzac legend, and that they may be blended together and reinvigorated with contemporary attitudes and recent research so that Gallipoli once more captures the imagination.

Notes

1 Lord Hankey, *The Supreme Command 1914–1918*, 2 vols (London, 1961). Hankey began writing this book in 1931: 'The brain of war', *Times Education Supplement*, 14 April 1961, Churchill College, Cambridge, Hankey Papers, HNKY 2/7.

2 Catalogue details of Major John North, BA, LLB (1894–1973), Liddell Hart Centre for Military Archives, King's College London.

3 Publicity release, 'Gallipoli again', North Papers, I/4a/5.

4 John North, *Gallipoli: The Fading Vision* (London, 1936), p. 17.

5 *Ibid.*, p. 19.

6 *Ibid.*, p. 20.

7 *Ibid.*, unpaginated dedication and p. 16.

8 *Ibid.*, p. 360.

9 *Ibid.*, pp. 187–8.

10 Hamilton to North, 2 November 1934, North Papers, I/3/238; Hamilton to

North, 18 December 1934, North Papers, I/3/240; North to unidentified reviewer, 20 March 1936, North Papers, I/3/360.

11 John North, 'The last of the Bayards', *The Red Poppy* (25th anniversary edition), National Library of Australia, Canberra, Moorehead Papers, MS 5654, box 13, folder 109.

12 North, *Fading Vision*, p. 244.

13 *Ibid.*, pp. 317–18. This passage is also by implication criticising the arguments put forward in Churchill's *The World Crisis 1915*.

14 *Ibid.*, p. 54.

15 *Ibid.*, p. 347.

16 *Ibid.*, p. 32.

17 Cecil Aspinall-Oglander, 'Gallipoli comes of age – the twenty first anniversary', proof article for *Observer*, CRO, Newport, Isle of Wight, Aspinall-Oglander Papers, OG 113; this review was published on 22 March 1936, North Papers, I/4a/71.

18 North to Still, 31 March 1936, North Papers, I/3/447.

19 North, *Fading Vision*, p. 354.

20 Harold Nicolson, 'Gallipoli Epic', *Daily Telegraph*, 27 March 1936, North Papers, I/4a/71.

21 Alan Moorehead, *Gallipoli* (Ware, 1997 [1956]).

22 *Ibid.*, unpaginated Introductory note.

23 *Ibid.*, p. 86.

24 John Connell, 'From Imbros over the sea', *Time and Tide*, 5 May 1956, Moorehead Papers, box 13, folder 107.

25 Norman Podhoretz, 'Books. Romance and reality', proof version, *The New Yorker*, 20 October 1956, Moorehead Papers, box 13, folder 108.

26 Tom Pocock, *Alan Moorehead* (London, 1990), p. 262.

27 Moorehead Papers, box 13, folder 107.

28 'Television: Granada Tonight', *Evening Chronicle* (Manchester), 30 July 1956, Moorehead Papers, box 13, folder 108.

29 Moorehead, *Gallipoli*, pp. 304–5. Noted by Cyril Falls, 'Gallipoli in retrospect', *Times Literary Supplement*, May 4 1956, Moorehead Papers, box 13, folder 107; and Raymond Postgate, 'Gallipoli: the end of a world', *New York Nation*, 29 September 1956, Moorhead Papers, box 13, folder 108.

30 Noted by John Connell, 'From Imbros over the sea', *Time and Tide*, 5 May 1956, Moorehead Papers, box 13, folder 107; and 'The epic of Gallipoli', *New Zealand Herald*, 21 June 1956, Moorhead Papers, box 13, folder 108.

31 References to the Second World War in Moorehead can be found on pp. 192, 196, 200, 213, and 305 of *Gallipoli*; noted variously, including '40 years after comes a superb book about . . . the Gallipoli tragedy', *RSA Review* (Wellington, New Zealand), August 1956, Moorehead Papers, box 13, folder 108.

32 Moorehead, *Gallipoli*, p. 306; noted by Leon Gellert, 'Story of Gallipoli', *Sydney Morning Herald*, 14 July 1956; and Drew Middleton's book review, 'The Dardanelles, 1915: heroic failure of a great idea', *New York Times*, 16 September 1956, Moorehead Papers, box 13, folder 108.

33 Moorehead, *Gallipoli*, p. 305. He published two books about Churchill: *Winston Churchill in Trial and Triumph* (Boston, MA, 1955) and *Churchill: A Pictorial Biography* (London, 1960).

34 Moorehead, *Gallipoli*, p. 131.

35 *Ibid.*, p. 211. This is anachronistic, although Monash had certainly become an accomplished leader by 1918, aspects of his record at Gallipoli have been questioned.

36 *Ibid.*, pp. 57–66.

37 *Ibid.*, p. 77.

38 *Ibid.*, pp. 264–76.

39 Perhaps a more egregious omission is Moorehead's failure to discuss the landings at W Beach on 25 April (p. 121).

40 C. F. Aspinall-Oglander, *Roger Keyes* (London 1951). Cyril Falls's review 'Gallipoli in retrospect' commented on the similarity of the arguments presented in Aspinall-Oglander's official history and Moorehead's book.

41 Moorehead received 'roughly 500 furious letters' correcting this error: Moorehead to Robert Rhodes James, 9 January (no year given), Churchill College, Cambridge, Robert Rhodes James Papers, RHJS 1/7.

42 Moorehead Papers, box 13, folder 104, typescript draft, p. 286; Moorehead, *Gallipoli*, p. 206.

43 Cecil Aspinall-Oglander to Moorehead, 7 November 1955, Moorehead Papers, box 13, folder 109.

44 George Johnston, *My Brother Jack* (Sydney, 1964). This is the first novel in the Meredith trilogy, published in Sydney, 1988.

45 Barry Smith, 'George Johnston's Anzac: the role of Sidney Nolan and Peter Finch', *Quadrant*, 119:21:6 (1977), pp. 66–9.

46 Alan Moorehead, 'Return to a legend', *New Yorker*, 2 April 1955, pp. 101–2.

47 George Johnstone [misspelt], 'Gallipoli paintings', *Art and Australia*, 5:2 (September 1967), p. 455.

48 Brian Adams, *Sidney Nolan: Such Is Life* (Hawthorn, Victoria, 1987), p. 178. The film was premiered in Canberra before Governor-General Lord De L'Isle in mid-March 1965. The first major exhibition of Nolan's Gallipoli paintings was in Sydney in April 1966. See also Tom Heath, 'Sydney [*sic*] Nolan: the Gallipoli paintings', *Architecture in Australia*, 55:4 (July 1966), pp. 86–7; Gavin Fry, *Nolan's Gallipoli* (Adelaide, 1983); and T. G. Rosenthal, *Sidney Nolan* (London, 2002).

49 D. A. Kent has noted that this poem was plagiarised from *The Bulletin*: D. A. Kent, '*The Anzac Book* and the Anzac legend: C. E. W. Bean as editor and image-maker', *Historical Studies*, 21:84 (April 1985), p. 380.

50 Adams, *Sidney Nolan*, p. 170.

51 Peter Sekuless, *A Handful of Hacks* (St Leonards, New South Wales, 1999), p. 98; and Garry Kinnane, *George Johnston: A Biography* (Ringwood, Victoria, 1989).

52 See also George Johnston, 'Anzac . . . a myth for all mankind', *Walkabout* (April 1965), pp. 13–16; and 'As myths fade – we need an identity', *Walkabout*, 36:2 (February 1970), pp. 5–8.

53 Compton Mackenzie, 'The Dardanelles', 29 April 1956 (unidentified newspaper), Moorehead Papers, box 13, folder 107.

54 Robert Rhodes James to Moorehead, 16 May 1956, Moorehead Papers, box 13, folder 107.

55 Robert Rhodes James, *Gallipoli: A 'British' Historian's View*, Public lecture delivered at the University of Melbourne, 24 April 1995 (Melbourne, 1995), p. 2.

56 Robert Rhodes James, *Gallipoli* (London, 1974 [1965]), p. v; in a series of footnotes throughout the book, Rhodes James points out and corrects Moorehead's factual errors (see pp. 56, 92, 104, 134, 235–6, 237–8, 267, 271, 284, 290, 297, 317, 348, 352), though he does endorse Moorehead's observation that the campaign was 'a mighty destroyer of reputations' (p. 349).

57 *Ibid.*, p. v.

58 *Ibid.*, p. v.

59 *Ibid.*, p. 25.

60 *Ibid.*, p. 31.

61 *Ibid.*, p. 54.

62 *Ibid.*, p. 69.

63 *Ibid.*, p. 89.

64 *Ibid.*, p. 104.

65 *Ibid.*, p. 200.

66 *Ibid.*, p. 353.

67 *Ibid.*, pp. 352–3.

68 Robert Rhodes James, 'A visit to Gallipoli', *Australian Army Journal*, 191 (April 1965), pp. 37–40, Churchill College, Cambridge, Robert Rhodes James Papers, RHJS 1/7.

69 Rhodes James, *Gallipoli*, p. 353.

70 Allan R. Millett, *Semper Fidelis: The History of the United States Marine Corps* (New York, 1980), p. 321; see also Ian Speller, 'In the shadow of Gallipoli? Amphibious warfare in the inter-war period' in Jenny Macleod (ed.) *Gallipoli: Making History* (forthcoming).

71 William Dilworth Puleston, *The Dardanelles Expedition: A Condensed Study* (Annapolis, 1927 [1926]); Hamilton wrote the Foreword to W. D. Puleston's *High Command in the World War* (London, 1934).

72 Liman von Sanders, *Five Years in Turkey* (Annapolis, 1927 [1920]); another German memoir of Gallipoli translated into English in the same period was Hans Kannengiesser, *The Campaign in Gallipoli* (London, 1928).

73 See, for example, Geoffrey Till and Gary Sheffield (eds) *Challenges of High Command in the Twentieth Century* (Camberley, 2000).

74 Michael McKernan, 'Writing about war' in M. McKernan and M. Browne, *Australia: Two Centuries of War and Peace* (Canberra, 1981), p. 16.

75 *Ibid.*, p. 18; the exception is volume 11, *Australia During the War*, by Ernest Scott, professor of history at the University of Melbourne, though this is not military but political and social history.

76 Alex Danchev, ' "Bunking" and debunking: the controversies of the 1960s' in Brian Bond (ed.) *The First World War and British Military History* (Oxford, 1991), p. 264. Dan Todman is studying generational explanations for this interest: D. Todman, 'Representations of the First World War in British popular culture 1918–1998' (PhD, Cambridge University, 2003).

77 Peter Simkins, 'Everyman at war: recent interpretations of the front line experience' in Bond (ed.) *The First World War and British Military History*, p. 289.

78 McKernan, 'Writing about war', p. 18.

79 K. S. Inglis, 'The Anzac tradition', *Meanjin Quarterly*, 100 (1965), pp. 25–44; *C. E. W. Bean, Australian Historian*, John Murtagh Macrossan Lecture, 1969 (St Lucia, Queensland, 1970); see Introduction for further bibliographical details. Some of the material in this section was first published in Jenny Macleod, 'The fall and rise of Anzac Day: 1965 and 1990 compared', *War & Society*, 20:1 (May 2002), pp. 149–68.

80 Simkins, 'Everyman at war', pp. 289–313.

81 Bill Gammage, *The Broken Years: Australian Soldiers in the Great War* (Canberra, 1974), p. xiii.

82 Patsy Adam-Smith, *The Anzacs* (London, 1991 [1978]), p. x.

83 Simkins, 'Everyman at war', p. 307.

84 Adam-Smith, *Anzacs*, p. viii.

85 *Ibid.*, p. xi; these claims are inaccurate: until conscription was introduced in 1916, all British soldiers were volunteers, while the South Africans and the Indians remained volunteers to the end.

86 This omission provoked criticism from Gammage, writing in *Quadrant* (April 1979); quoted by Gerard Henderson, 'The Anzac legend after *Gallipoli*', *Quadrant*, 179:26:7 (1982), p. 62.

87 Bill Gammage, 'The broken years', *Journal of the Australian War Memorial*, 24 (April 1994), p. 34.

88 *Ibid.*, pp. 34, 35.

89 *Ibid.*, p. 34.

90 For example, see the extended discussion of Australians' attitudes towards killing, in Gammage, *The Broken Years*, pp. 95–8.

91 For example, see the discussion of the Wasser riots in *ibid.*, pp. 39–40.

92 A phenomenon already observed in chapter 4's consideration of frontline soldiers' published personal narratives.

93 Gammage, 'The broken years', p. 35.

94 Bill Gammage, David Williamson and Peter Weir, *The Story of Gallipoli: The Film About the Men Who Made a Legend* (Ringwood, Victoria, 1981); Bill Gammage, 'Working on *Gallipoli*' in Anne Hutton (ed.) *The First Australian History and Film Conference Papers 1982* (North Ryde, New South Wales, 1982), pp. 67–72.

95 Patricia Lovell, *No Picnic: An Autobiography* (Sydney, 1995), p. 256.

96 'Gallipoli', *Variety*, 5 August 1981; *Variety Film Reviews 1981–1982* (New York, 1986).

97 Peter Weir, 'Gallipoli: "I felt somehow I was really touching history"', *Literature/Film Quarterly*, 9:4 (1981), p. 214. See also Brian McFarlane and Tom Ryan, 'Peter Weir: towards the centre', *Cinema Papers*, 34 (September–October 1981), pp. 323–9 and 'Peter Weir. Interview by Katherine Tulich', *Cinema Papers*, 80 (August 1990), pp. 6–11. Mel Gibson was interviewed by Margaret Smith in *Cinema Papers*, 42 (March 1983), pp. 13–17.

98 The themes and imagery of the film have been discussed by Livio Dobrez and Pat Dobrez, 'Old myths and new delusions: Peter Weir's Australia', *Kunapipi*, 4:2 (1982), pp. 61–75; Chris Flaherty and Michael Roberts, 'The reproduction of Anzac symbolism', *Journal of Australian Studies*, 24 (May 1989), pp. 52–69; Marek Haltof, 'In quest of self-identity: *Gallipoli*, mateship and the construction of Australia national identity', *Journal of Popular Film & Television*, 21:1 (1993), pp. 27–36; Josef Marek Haltof, 'When cultures collide: the cinema of Peter Weir' (PhD thesis, University of Alberta, 1995); Michael Bliss, *Dreams Within a Dream: the Films of Peter Weir* (Carbondale & Edwardsville, 2000), ch. 5.

99 Stuart Ward, ' "A war memorial in celluloid": the Gallipoli legend in Australian cinema, 1940s–1980s' in Jenny Macleod (ed.) *Gallipoli: Making History* (forthcoming).

100 Available (accessed 4 January 2001): http://arts.adelaide.edu.au/person/DHart/Films/Gallipoli.html, p. 2.

101 Williamson has made derogatory comments about Britain in an interview: Ray Willbanks, *Australian Voices: Writers and Their Work* (Austin, TX, 1991), p. 179.

102 Henderson, 'The Anzac legend', p. 63. See also Tim Travers, '*Gallipoli*: film and the traditions of Austrailian [*sic*] history', *Film & History*, 14:1 (February 1984), pp. 14–20; Robin Prior, 'The Suvla Bay tea-party: a reassessment', *Journal of the Australian War Memorial*, 7 (October 1985), pp. 25–34; Kenneth T. Jackson, 'Gallipoli' in Ted Mico, John Miller-Monzon and David Rubel (eds) *Past Imperfect: History According to the Movies* (New York, 1996), pp. 182–5.

103 Bliss writes (*Dreams*, p. 89) that Gammage is the only historian to make this claim.

104 *Ibid.*, pp. 88–90.

105 Dobrez and Dobrez, 'Old myths', pp. 66, 70.

106 Henderson, 'The Anzac legend', p. 63; see also Travers, '*Gallipoli*: film', p. 18.

107 Henderson, 'The Anzac legend', p. 62.

108 Jane Freebury, 'Screening Australia: *Gallipoli* – a study of nationalism on film', *Media Information Australia*, 43 (February 1987), p. 8.

109 Dobrez and Dobrez, 'Old myths', p. 63.

110 *Ibid.*, p. 70.

111 Sylvia Lawson, 'Gallipoli: you are being told what you are to remember', *Film News* (November–December 1981), p. 11.

112 Brian McFarlane, 'Gallipoli', *Cinema Papers*, 33 (July–August 1981), p. 285; Brian McFarlane, 'Gallipoli' in Scott Murray (ed.) *Australian Film 1978–1994: A Survey of Theatrical Features* (Melbourne, 1995), p. 74.

113 Sandra Hall, *Critical Business: The New Australian Cinema in Review* (Adelaide, 1985), p. 69.

114 Jackson, 'Gallipoli', p. 185.

115 Freebury, 'Screening Australia', p. 7.

116 Nigel Steel, *The Battlefields of Gallipoli: Then and Now* (London, 1990).

117 Nigel Steel and Peter Hart, *Defeat at Gallipoli* (London, 1994). Thanks to Nigel Steel for this information. Another book piecing together details of the campaign through individuals' private papers (though without extensive discussion) is Peter Liddle's *Men of Gallipoli: The Dardanelles and Gallipoli Experience, August 1914 to January 1916* (Trowbridge, 1998 [1976]).

118 Steel and Hart, *Defeat*, p. 419.

119 Alistair Thomson, *Anzac Memories: Living with the Legend* (Melbourne, 1994); see also Alistair Thomson, 'A past you can live with: digger memories and the Anzac legend' in Alan Seymour and Richard Nile (eds) *Anzac: Meaning, Memory and Myth* (London, 1991), pp. 21–31.

120 Thomson, *Anzac Memories*, p. 47.

121 *Ibid.*, p. 26.

122 John Robertson, *The Tragedy and Glory of Gallipoli: Anzac and Empire* (London, 1990), p. 7.

123 *Ibid.*, p. 7; despite focusing specifically on the Anzacs, he excuses himself for ignoring the New Zealanders by pointing to Chris Pugsley's *Gallipoli: The New Zealand Story* (1984).

124 Robertson, *Anzac and Empire*, pp. 126–30.

125 *Ibid.*, pp. 155–8.

126 *Ibid.*, pp. 192–212.

127 *Ibid.*, pp. 131–3.

128 *Ibid.*, p. 261.

129 *Ibid.*, pp. 213–23.

130 *Ibid.*, pp. 224–44.

131 *Ibid.*, pp. 245–58.

132 *Ibid.*, pp. 268–76.

133 *Ibid.*, p. 259.

134 *Ibid.*

135 *Ibid.*, pp. 262–3.

136 *Ibid.*, p. 267.

137 The renewed interest in publishing personal narratives of Gallipoli, such as Albert Facey's *A Fortunate Life* (Fremantle, 1981), notwithstanding its brief coverage of Gallipoli, might be attributed to this historiographical trend set in train by Gammage *et al.*

138 Thomson provides a robust response to Robertson's criticisms and reproduces two newspaper cartoons disparaging his work: Thomson, *Anzac Memories*, pp. 218–19.

139 'Jacka, Captain Albert' in Peter Dennis, Jeffrey Grey, Ewan Morris and Robin Prior (eds) *The Oxford Companion to Australian Military History* (Melbourne, 1995), p. 320.

140 Peter Cochrane, *Simpson and the Donkey: The Making of the Legend* (Carlton, Victoria, 1992).

141 E. M. Andrews, *The Anzac Illusion: Anglo-Australian Relations During World War One* (Cambridge, 1993).

142 Les Carlyon, *Gallipoli* (Sydney, 2001).

143 *Ibid.*, pp. 148, 189.

144 *Ibid.*, p. 409.

145 *Ibid.*, p. 169.

146 *Ibid.*, pp. 137–40, 169–70.

147 *Ibid.*, pp. 398, 238, 374.

148 *Ibid.*, pp. 194, 225, 279, 305, 330, 350, 387, 420.

149 *Ibid.*, pp. 1–11, 165, 411.

150 *Ibid.*, pp. 16, 113, 217.

151 *Ibid.*, p. 9.

152 *Ibid.*, pp. 4, 11, 48, 28, 9, 16.

153 *Ibid.*, p. 18, 504.

154 *Ibid.*, p. 24, 79, 213.

155 *Ibid.*, p. 34.

Conclusion

Gallipoli is still regarded as distinctive as compared to the Western Front. This has always been the case. Gallipoli's distinctiveness was an important aspect of its early romance and its continued romanticisation. It was fought on a scale – in terms both of men and of land – that is comprehensible, with comparatively low casualties in a location that was utterly different from the plains of Northern Europe. It shares this sense of exotic glamour with the campaign in Palestine – there Britain focuses on the activities of Lawrence of Arabia, Australia on those of the men of the Light Horse. Moreover, its strategic potential as a means of delivery from the attrition of the Western Front – however remote that was in reality – has been a continuous theme in its heroic–romantic myth. Indeed, part of the Eastern Command's strategy's initial attractiveness was as an alternative to the Western Front.

The continued power of this contrast stems from the popular perception of the Western Front as one of unmitigated disaster. As Peter Simkins suggests, 'British popular perceptions of the First World War are still stuck fast in the mud of Passchendaele.' He describes this British fascination with defeat as 'historical masochism'.[1] Despite the ultimate victory of 1918, which rested on improved tactics and the development of operational capability, increasingly skilled soldiers and a successful naval blockade, the popular image of the Western Front is of a grotesque and futile war fought in a quagmire at the behest of donkey-like generals.[2] This sense of the distinctiveness of Gallipoli is the source of its resonance in Britain; in Australia it is the nation-building Anzac legend that resonates, and that meaning has proved far more powerful. This is demonstrated by the commemoration of the campaign in the two countries.

In Britain, a great deal of the commemorative activity on 'Gallipoli Day' appears to have been inspired by Australian connections with the campaign. Among specific local ceremonies are those at Leighterton Church's cemetery in Gloucestershire (where Australian Flying Corps casualties are buried);[3] Harefield (St Mary's) churchyard in Middlesex (where veterans of both wars are buried, the majority of the 120 First World War graves being those of Australians who died in No. 1 Australian Auxiliary Hospital at Harefield Park); Cannock Chase War Cemetery in Staffordshire (which was begun during 1914–18 when there was a large military camp there at which the New Zealand Rifle Brigade was based); and Sutton Veny (St John's) churchyard in Wiltshire (the 29th Division was concentrated at Sutton Veny in April 1915, as was No. 1 Australian Command from the end of 1916 to October 1919, and it was also the location of a military hospital – 143 of the 168 First World War burials in the churchyard are Australian).[4] Events at the Cenotaph and West-minster Abbey on Anzac Day are organised alternately by the Australian and the New Zealand High Commissions. There are also ceremonies in Warrington, Bury and elsewhere which stem from English regiments' connections with the campaign.[5]

Another notable element in commemorative activities in Britain is the work of the Gallipoli Memorial Lecture Trust in Eltham, south-east London. The Lecture Trust grew out of an annual memorial service begun by Henry Hall, chaplain to the 29th Division who, after the war, became vicar of Holy Trinity, Eltham. The Lady Chapel at Eltham com-memorates the fallen of the campaign. When the numbers of veterans and their relatives attending the annual commemorative service began to dwindle the decision was taken to institute an annual lecture set in the context of an act of remembrance centred on the suffering on both sides. These ran from 1985 to 2000 and attracted high-profile speakers.[6] It was then decided that the series had run its course and that it should be replaced by Sunday Evensong. The lecture consistently attracted around 250 people, and it peaked at 390 for the final one. The audience was made up largely of members of the Gallipoli Association, regimental associa-tions, senior military officers, representatives from the Turkish Embassy and the Australian and New Zealand High Commissions, and those with family connections to the campaign.[7] It was thus a dedicated and well-informed audience, but not one that was broadly based.

This specialised interest in Gallipoli is apparent in comparisons with the observance of Remembrance Sunday in Britain and Anzac Day in Australia. The anniversary of the Armistice each November is marked not only by commemorative services but by the wearing of a poppy – this is perhaps a less onerous gesture to make, but one that is observed by millions rather than hundreds. Armistice Day is also widely observed in Australia, but there it is overshadowed by Anzac Day, which has become the most significant date in the national calendar. Large crowds attend commemorative events, including 15,000 on the peninsula itself.[8] In Sydney in 2001, 24,000 veterans and their descendants participated in the march while an estimated 4 million people in New South Wales watched the TV coverage of the event.[9] Such a committed response is due to the resonance of the Anzac legend and the manner in which it has come to encapsulate what it is to be Australian. It has taken on a meaning that transcends the campaign itself.

In 2000, a new memorial was unveiled on Gallipoli by the prime ministers of Australia and New Zealand,[10] but the most significant commemorative event on the peninsula in recent years occurred in 1990, the seventy-fifth anniversary of the campaign. The elaborate nature of Anzac Day 1990 has been discussed elsewhere;[11] my concern here is the differing emphases of the addresses by the prime ministers of Australia and Britain, Bob Hawke and Margaret Thatcher, since they indicate the survival of the Anzac legend and the heroic–romantic myth. Thatcher followed the usual British line regarding Gallipoli, defending Churchill and describing his strategy as 'brilliant', but accepting that organisation was terrible. She went on to claim that the lessons of the campaign had assisted the 1982 success in the Falklands.[12] Her opinion of the Gallipoli strategy was echoed by Churchill's grandson and by Kim Beazley, former Australian defence minister. Hawke, meanwhile, was refining the Anzac legend by extracting the elements most useful for modern Australia – the examples set of comradeship and of respect for the enemy, the Turks – and thus continued the process that was begun at Gallipoli of detaching Australia from Britain.

Hawke made two major speeches on Anzac Day. At Lone Pine, his speech turned on the idea of comradeship and quoted Bean on the matter.[13] His speech at the Dawn Service sought to encapsulate what Gallipoli now meant in Australia. It was about the character of a nation – the mettle of the men, as Bean put it.[14] In a conscious echo of Bean, Hawke explained that they had not achieved their military objectives (he does not say because they were defeated or that they failed); yet,

> because of the courage with which they fought, because of their devotion
> to duty and their comradeship, because of their ingenuity, their good

humour and their endurance, because these hills rang with their voices and ran with their blood; this place is in one sense a part of Australia.[15]

Hawke's comments on Turkey show how far attitudes to that country have changed: while there has always been admiration for the Turks since 19 May 1915, now that part of the legend is played up. He told his Turkish hosts:

It is remarkable to reflect that the tragedy of our first encounter has been the source of nationhood for both our countries.

It was through his brilliant defence of the Gallipoli Peninsula, as well as his exploits on other fronts in the First World War, that the great Mustapha Kemel Ataturk demonstrated the singular qualities of leadership which enabled him subsequently to create the Turkish Republic.[16]

He went on to praise the Turks for the respect shown to the memory of a departed enemy. Such comments are in sharp contrast to the less public remarks he made about Australia's *ally* at Gallipoli: en route to Turkey, prior to the Gallipoli commemorative activities, Hawke lambasted the British for 'unbelievably inept planning', singling out Churchill and Hamilton.[17]

Cultural historians of the First World War have tended to focus either on Paul Fussell's idea of the war (specifically the Western Front) as a supreme irony and a disillusioning experience or on the development of the Anzac legend.[18] This book has demonstrated that Fussell's idea does not apply to the Gallipoli campaign. On the contrary, Gallipoli has retained a powerful and durable sense of romance, a romance based on the Anzac legend *in combination with* the heroic–romantic myth. These two strands are complementary: they are the particular national emphases within the grand narrative of Gallipoli.

This romantic grand narrative of Gallipoli was established prior to 1939. Indeed it was firmly in place by the time John North wrote *The Fading Vision* in 1936; most of the pieces of the jigsaw were there following Churchill's *The World Crisis* in 1923, and they certainly were by 1932 when the second volume of Aspinall-Oglander's official history came out. The themes of romance and heroism are threaded throughout the narratives of Gallipoli. Sometimes these themes are overtly apparent, as in the lyrical propaganda of John Masefield or the juvenile and sickly Ernest Raymond. The stoical General Sir Ian Hamilton demonstrated the romance of striving, and he sought to propagate his view of the campaign both clandestinely and publicly.

Charles Bean, perhaps the most prolific and effective mythologiser of Gallipoli, and specifically of the Anzacs, told the world of the romance of combat. This was an old notion, but one shorn of the grandiloquence of high diction, and refreshed and reinvigorated in the context of a national epic poem.

Even those narratives that are less obviously romantic have contributed to the myths of Gallipoli. A. P. Herbert set out to criticise army discipline, but in describing the fall of Harry Penrose he presented Gallipoli as an innocent and romantic mirror of the young Harry. Even a critic of the campaign itself like Ashmead-Bartlett did much to promote its reputation initially through his dispatches. Thereafter his status continued to rely on that of the campaign and he therefore perpetuated the idea of its strategic merit, which is fundamental to the campaign's attractiveness. The same idea was central to Aspinall-Oglander's official history that broke from the norms of British official history to justify the planning and the conduct of the operations. Furthermore the Dardanelles Commission, in choosing not to castigate the soldiers at Gallipoli and in soothing the debate about the campaign, left open the opportunity to portray Gallipoli in a more positive light. Similarly, the soldiers' personal narratives are notable for the fact that they did not condemn the campaign outright and thereby failed to provide evidence to contradict those who said it was romantic.

Three themes have emerged in the course of this attempt to explain each author's motivation in writing about the campaign: bearing witness; commemoration; and exculpation. These categories are not necessarily exclusive of each other. Bearing witness and commemoration merge into one where the author aspires to remember and record the experience of the campaign or record participation in it. This is particularly true of Bean. In his journalistic dispatches, published piecemeal, his role was to bear witness to the Australians' part in the campaign. When that story was retold in his official history it was elevated to become a national memorial. This elevation of the campaign entails romance and is the key to both commemoration and exculpation. The latter is the key motivation of the prominent British figures associated with Gallipoli, such as Hamilton, Aspinall-Oglander and Churchill. Given this context, it is possible that the heroic–romantic myth was essentially a product of the upper echelons of British society. It certainly was not repeated in the soldiers' narratives of frontline participants. But it has been seen that not all soldiers' narratives fitted Hynes's thesis. Moreover, it is not the complexities and confusion of the soldiers' tale that have survived, but the simplified romantic narrative made from the British heroic–romantic myth and the Australian Anzac legend.

The survival of the notion of Gallipoli as a romantic, heroic, tragic, epic failure rather than as the futile, attritional, sickness-ridden defeat that it also was, is testament to its continuing fascination and to the resonance of the heroic–romantic myth of Gallipoli. That this notion has been propelled to a much more prominent place in Australia's national consciousness is testament to the even greater resonance of the Anzac legend. The combined power of the myth and the legend has ensured that a small and almost marginal campaign is remembered throughout the world, while most operations on the Western Front have been all-but forgotten. Romance, it seems, is the key to the survival of narratives of war.

Notes

1 Peter Simkins, 'Everyman at war: recent interpretations of the front line experience' in Brian Bond (ed.) *The First World War and British Military History* (Oxford, 1991), p. 311.

2 See G. D. Sheffield, ' "Oh! What a futile war": representations of the Western Front in modern British media and popular culture' in Ian Stewart and Susan L. Carruthers (eds) *War, Culture and the Media: Representations of the Military in 20th Century Britain* (Trowbridge, 1996), pp. 54–74; one of the most powerful representations of this view is the play *Oh! What a Lovely War*, which halts its satirical portrayal of the war in 1917.

3 David Goodland and Alan Vaughan, *Anzacs Over England: The Australian Flying Corps in Gloucestershire 1918–1919* (Stroud, 1992).

4 This information was provided by Peter Francis of the Commonwealth War Graves Commission.

5 Other ceremonies in April 2002 included commemorations held in, Arbroath, Brockenhurst, Cambridge, Carisbrooke, Chepstow, Chilworth, Dallachy Strike Wing, Edinburgh, Norwich, Oxford, Peterborough, Preston, Shaftesbury, St Albans, Stapleford, Walton-on-Thames and at the Gallipoli Memorial in the Crypt of St Paul's Cathedral: *The Gallipolian* (spring 2002); see the final chapter of Geoffrey Moorhouse's *Hell's Foundations: A Town, its Myths and Gallipoli* (London, 1992) for a description of the commemoration of Gallipoli in Bury.

6 Speakers included Sir Martin Gilbert, Professor Sir Michael Howard, Professor Robert O'Neill, HRH The Duke of Edinburgh, the Right Honourable Sir Edward Heath and the Right Reverend and Right Honourable Lord Runcie; the lectures have been collected in Martin Gilbert (ed.) *The Straits of War: Gallipoli Remembered* (Stroud, 2000).

7 Information provided by Wing Commander John Towey, OBE, hon. secretary of the Gallipoli Memorial Lecture Trust.

8 Paul McGeough, 'Magic touches a Gallipoli beach', *Sydney Morning Herald*, 26 April 2001, available online: www.smh.com.au

9 'Thousands pay respects', *The Age* (available online: www.theage.com.au), 26 April 2001; TV audience estimate courtesy of Dr Peter Stanley of the Australian War Memorial and his contacts at the ABC. New South Wales' total population is just over 6 million.

10 '5,000 mourn Anzac troops at Gallipoli', *Times*, 26 April 2000.

11 Jenny Macleod, 'The fall and rise of Anzac Day: 1965 and 1990 compared', *War & Society*, 20:1 (May 2002), pp. 149–68.

12 'Heroes return . . . Gallipoli lessons aided Falklands: Thatcher', *Daily Telegraph* (Sydney), 26 April 1990, AWM, Canberra, News clippings: Anzac Day 1990, folder 70; see also Admiral Sandy Woodward with Patrick Robinson, *One Hundred Days: The Memoirs of the Falklands Battle Group Commander* (London, 1992), p. 86; and Robert Rhodes James, *Gallipoli: A 'British' Historian's View*, Public Lecture Delivered at the University of Melbourne on 24 April 1995 (Melbourne, 1995), p. 5.

13 'Gallipoli Revisited. Anzac Cove 1990', ScreenSound Australia, Canberra; AWM, R. J. L. Hawke Papers, MSS 1300.

14 C. E. W. Bean, *The Story of Anzac from the Outbreak of War to the End of the First Phase of the Gallipoli Campaign, May 4, 1915*, vol. 1 of the Official History of Australia in the War of 1914–1918 (St Lucia, Queensland, 1981 [1921]), p. 607.

15 Text of prime minister's speech, Anzac Cove 25 April 1990, AWM, Canberra, News clippings: Anzac Day 1990, folder 62; this passage has echoes also of Rupert Brooke, Atatürk's speech of 1934 and Abraham Lincoln's Gettysburg Address.

16 'PM opens an old wound with Brits', *Mercury* (Hobart), 24 April 1990, AWM, Canberra, News clippings: Anzac Day 1990, folder 59.

17 *Ibid.*

18 Paul Fussell, *The Great War and Modern Memory* (London, 1975); the work of other cultural historians such as Modris Eksteins, Samuel Hynes, Jay Winter, George Mosse and Rosa Maria Bracco was discussed in the Introduction.

Select bibliography

Archival collections

Public Record Office, Kew

CAB 16/52–3; CAB 17/132; CAB 17/184; CAB 19/28; CAB 19/30; CAB 19/33; CAB 27/182; CAB 44/428; CAB 45/238; CAB 45/244; CAB 103/1–10; CAB 103/68; CAB 103/73; CAB 103/76; CAB 103/82–3; CAB 103/102

Private papers

Australian War Memorial, Canberra

Charles Bean Papers: AWM38 3DRL 606, items 10, 17, 24; AWM38 3DRL 6673, items 2, 11, 180, 234, 270, 271; AWM38 3DRL 8039, items 1, 7; AWM38 3DRL 8042, items 3, 47

William Birdwood Papers: 3DRL 3376/11/5

R. J. L. Hawke Papers: MSS 1300

Frederick Sydney Loch Papers: MSS 1367

Press cuttings file: Anzac Day, 1990; Biography, Monash

Bodleian Library, Oxford

Henry Herbert Asquith Papers: II/28, II/29, II/30

Henry Nevinson Papers: MS Eng misc c.497; MS Eng misc e.619; MS Eng misc e.620

Churchill Archives Centre, Churchill College, Cambridge

Winston Churchill Papers: CHAR 2/74; CHAR 2/106/94; CHAR 2/106/152; CHAR 2/106/174–5; CHAR 2/164/9–10; CHAR 2/177/72; CHAR 8/45

Maurice Hankey Papers: HNKY 1/1; HNKY 1/3

Robert Rhodes James Papers: RHJS 1/7

County Records Office, Newport, Isle of Wight

Cecil Aspinall-Oglander: OG 111; OG112; OG 113; OG114; OG116

Harry Ransom Centre, University of Texas at Austin, Texas
Compton Mackenzie Papers

Imperial War Museum, London
Guy Dawnay Papers: 69/21/1; 69/21/5
Orlo Williams: Diary 2

Liddell Hart Centre for Military Archives, King's College, London
James Edmonds Papers: III/16
Ian Hamilton Papers: 7/3/1; 7/3/11; 7/4/9; 7/9/15; 7/9/19–20; 7/10/3; 7/10/12;
    8/1/4; 8/1/7; 8/1/10–11; 8/1/13; 8/1/15–16; 8/1/21; 8/1/26; 8/1/31; 8/1/38;
    8/1/40; 8/1/43; 8/1/46; 8/1/57; 8/1/66; 8/2; 8/2/22; 8/2/24; 8/2/28–29; 13/24;
    13/113; 17/38; 17/43; 17/47; 17/52
Basil Liddell Hart Papers: LH 1/23
John North Papers: 1/3; 1/4a

Mitchell Library, State Library of New South Wales, Sydney
Ellis Ashmead-Bartlett Papers: ML A1583; ML A1584; ML A1585

National Library of Australia, Canberra
Ellis Ashmead-Bartlett Papers (on microfilm): mfm M2582–6
(Originals held at Institute of Commonwealth Studies, London)
Sir John Monash Papers: MS 1884/955; MS 1884/1623; MS1884/1624
Alan Moorehead Papers: MS 5654/107; MS 5654/108; MS 5654/109
Keith Murdoch Papers: MS 2823/2/1; MS 2823/2/5; MS 2823/2/13; MS 2823/5;
    MS 2823/11/9

ScreenSound Australia, Canberra
'Gallipoli revisited. Anzac Cove 1990'

Printed sources

Newspapers

The following newspapers are additional to collections of cuttings found in
various archives:
The Age
Daily Mail
Daily Telegraph
Independent
Sydney Morning Herald
The Times

Official reports and command papers

Commonwealth of Australia Gazette
First Report of the Dardanelles Commission (Parliamentary Papers 1917–18, vol.
    10, Cd 8490)

Final Report of the Dardanelles Commission (Parliamentary Papers 1919, vol. 13, Cd 371)

House of Commons Parliamentary Debates
Report of the Committee Appointed to Investigate the Attacks Delivered on and the Enemy Defences of the Dardanelles Straits (Admiralty, M.01167 1919)
Statistics of the Military Effort of the British Empire in the Great War 1914–1920 (HMSO, 1922)
Supplement to First Report of the Dardanelles Commission (Parliamentary Papers 1917–18, vol. 10, Cd 8502)

Official histories
The Official History of Australia in the War of 1914–1918 (12 vols)
Bean, C. E. W., *The Story of Anzac: From the Outbreak of War to the End of the First Phase of the Gallipoli Campaign, May 4, 1915*, vol. 1 (St Lucia, Queensland, 1981 [1921])
—— *The Story of Anzac: From 4 May, 1915 to the Evacuation of the Gallipoli Peninsula*, vol. 2 (St Lucia, Queensland, 1981 [1924])
—— *The Australian Imperial Force in France 1916*, vol. 3 (St Lucia, Queensland, 1982 [1938])
—— *The Australian Imperial Force in France During the Allied Offensive, 1918*, vol. 6 (St Lucia, Queensland, 1983 [1942])
Scott, Ernest, *Australia During the War*, vol. 11 (Sydney, 1937)

History of the Great War Based on Official Documents
Edmonds, Brigadier-General Sir James E., *Military Operations, France and Belgium, 1914*, vol. 1: *August-October: Mons, the Retreat to the Seine, the Marne and the Aisne, August–October 1914* (London, 1925 [1922])
—— *Military Operations, France and Belgium 1915*, vol. 2: *Battle of Aubers Ridge, Festubert, and Loos* (London, 1928)
Aspinall-Oglander, Brigadier-General C. F., *Military Operations, Gallipoli*, vol. 1: *Inception of the Campaign to May 1915* (London, 1992 [1929])
—— *Military Operations, Gallipoli*, vol. 2: *May 1915 to the Evacuation* (London, 1992 [1932])
Corbett, Sir Julian S., *Naval Operations*, 3 (London, 1923)

Books and articles by Gallipoli participants
Alexander, Major H. M., *On Two Fronts: Being the Adventures of an Indian Mule Corps in France and Gallipoli* (London, 1917)
Anon., 'The end of war? A correspondence between the author of *All Quiet on the Western Front* and General Sir Ian Hamilton GCB, GCMG', *Life and Letters*, 3 (July 1929 to December 1929), pp. 399–411

'Anzac', *On the Anzac Trail: Being Extracts from the Diary of a New Zealand Sapper* (London, 1916)

Ashmead-Bartlett, E., *Ashmead-Bartlett's Despatches from the Dardanelles: An Epic of Heroism* (London, 1916)

—— *Some of My Experiences in the Great War* (London, 1918)

—— *The Uncensored Dardanelles* (London, 1928)

Ashmead-Bartlett, E., C. E. W. Bean and NSW Department of Public Instruction, *Australians in Action: The Story of Gallipoli* (New South Wales, 1915)

Aspinall-Oglander, C. F., *Roger Keyes* (London, 1951)

Bean, C. E. W., *On the Wool Track* (Sydney, 1945 [1910])

—— (ed.) *The Anzac Book* (London, 1916)

—— 'Sidelights of the war on Australian character', *Royal Australian Historical Society Journal & Proceedings*, 13:4 (1927), pp. 209–23

—— 'Writing the war history', *Reveille* (1 June 1933)

—— 'The writing of the Australian Official History of the Great War – sources, methods and some conclusions', *Royal Australian Historical Society Journal & Proceedings*, 24:2 (1938), pp. 85–112

—— *The Old AIF and the New* (Sydney, 1940)

—— 'The technique of a contemporary war historian', *Historical Studies Australia and New Zealand*, 2:6 (November 1942), pp. 65–79

Beeston, J. L., *Five Months at Anzac: A Narrative of Personal Experiences of the Officer Commanding the 4th Field Ambulance, Australian Imperial Force* (Sydney, 1916)

Birdwood, Field Marshal Lord, *Khaki and Gown: An Autobiography* (London, 1941)

Brereton, Major C. B., *Tales of Three Campaigns* (London, 1926)

Campbell, Captain R. W., *The Kangaroo Marines* (London, 1915)

Cooper, Bryan, *The Tenth (Irish) Division in Gallipoli* (London, 1918)

Creighton, Reverend O., *With the Twenty-Ninth Division in Gallipoli: A Chaplain's Experiences* (London, 1916)

Cutlack, F. M. (ed.) *War Letters of General Monash* (Sydney, 1934)

De Loghe, Sydney (F. S. Loch), *The Straits Impregnable* (London, 1917)

Dinning, Hector, *By-Ways on Service: Notes from an Australian Journal* (London, 1918)

Ellison, Lieutenant-General Sir Gerald, *The Perils of Amateur Strategy as Exemplified by the Attack on the Dardanelles Fortress in 1915* (London, 1926)

Ewing, William, *From Gallipoli to Baghdad* (London, 1918)

Facey, A. B., *A Fortunate Life* (Fremantle, 1981)

Fallon, Captain David, *The Big Fight (Gallipoli to the Somme)* (London, 1918)

Fewster, K. (ed.) *Gallipoli Correspondent: The Frontline Diary of C. E. W. Bean* (Sydney, 1983)

Foster, Reverend H. C., *At Antwerp and the Dardanelles* (London, 1918)

Gallishaw, John, *Trenching at Gallipoli: A Personal Narrative of a Newfoundlander with the Ill-Fated Dardanelles Expedition* (New York, 1916)

Gillam, Major J. G., *Gallipoli Diary* (London, 1918)

Gillam, John, *Gallipoli Adventure* (London, 1939)

Gillon, Captain Stair, *The Story of the 29th Division: A Record of Gallant Deeds* (London, 1925)

Godley, General Sir Alexander, *Life of an Irish Soldier* (London, 1939)

Hamilton, General Sir Ian S. M., *Ian Hamilton's Final Despatch* (London, 1916)

—— *Ian Hamilton's Despatches from the Dardanelles* (London, 1917)

—— *Gallipoli Diary*, 2 vols (London, 1920)

—— *The Soul and Body of an Army* (London, 1991 [1921])

—— *Listening for the Drums* (London, 1944)

Hankey, Lord, *The Supreme Command 1914–1918* (London, 1961), vol. 2

Hanman, E. F., *Twelve Months with the 'Anzacs'* (Brisbane, 1918)

Hanna, Henry, *The Pals at Suvla Bay (Being the Record of 'D' Company of the 7th Royal Dublin Fusiliers)* (Dublin, 1916)

Hargrave, John, *At Suvla Bay* (London, 1916)

Hatton, S. F., *The Yarn of a Yeoman* (London, 1930)

Herbert, A. P., *The Secret Battle* (Oxford, 1982 [1919])

Herbert, Aubrey, *Mons, Anzac and Kut* (London, 1930 [1919])

Hogue, Oliver, *Trooper Bluegum at the Dardanelles: Descriptive Narratives of the More Desperate Engagements on the Gallipoli Peninsula* (London, 1916)

Hope, Stanton, *Richer Dust: A Story of Gallipoli* (London, 1930)

Hurst, Gerald B., *With Manchesters in the East* (Manchester, 1918)

Idriess, Ion L., *The Desert Column* (Sydney, 1932)

Jerrold, Douglas, *The Royal Naval Division* (London, 1923)

—— *Georgian Adventure* (London, 1937)

Juvenis, *Suvla Bay and After* (London, 1916)

Kannengiesser, Hans, *The Campaign in Gallipoli* (London, 1928)

Knyvett, Captain R. Hugh, *'Over There' with the Australians* (New York, 1918)

Liman von Sanders, Otto, *Five Years in Turkey* (Annapolis, 1927)

Lushington, R. F., *A Prisoner with the Turks 1915–1918* (London, 1923)

Mackenzie, Compton, *Gallipoli Memories* (London, 1929)

—— *My Life and Times: Octave Five 1915–1923* (London, 1966)

Marshall, Lieutenant-General Sir William, *Memories of Four Fronts* (London, 1929)

Masefield, John, *Gallipoli* (London, 1916)

McCustra, Trooper L., *Gallipoli Days and Nights* (London, 1916)

Moseley, Sydney, *The Truth About the Dardanelles* (London, 1916)

—— *The Truth About a Journalist* (London, 1935)

Nevinson, Henry W., *The Dardanelles Campaign* (London, 1918)

—— *Last Changes, Last Chances* (London, 1928)

Partridge, Eric, *Frank Honywood, Private: A Personal Record of the 1914–1918 War* (Melbourne, 1987 [1929])

Patterson, Lieutenant-Colonel J. H., *With the Zionists in Gallipoli* (London, 1916)

Pebody, E., *Experiences in the Dardanelles of the 1st/5th Beds. Regiment TF* (Olney, 1916)

Priestman, E. Y., *With a B-P Scout in Gallipoli: A Record of the Belton Bulldogs* (London, 1916)

Raymond, Ernest, *Tell England: A Study in a Generation* (London, 1922)

—— *The Story of My Days: An Autobiography 1888–1922* (London, 1968)

—— *Please You, Draw Near: Autobiography 1922–1968* (London, 1969)

Ross, Malcolm and Noel Ross, *Light and Shade in War* (London, 1916)

Schuler, P. F. E., *Australia in Arms: A Narrative of the Australasian Imperial Force and Their Achievement at Anzac* (London, 1916)

—— *The Battlefields of Anzac: On Which the Australasians Won Deathless Fame* (Melbourne, 1916)

Smith, Lieutenant The Honourable Staniforth, *Australian Campaigns in the Great War* (Melbourne, 1919)

Sparrow, Geoffrey and J. N. Macbean Ross, *On Four Fronts with the Royal Naval Division* (London, 1918)

Springthorpe, Dr J. W., *The Great Withdrawal: Story of a Daring Plan. Last Days at Anzac. How Our Soldiers Left. A Vivid Narrative* (Melbourne, March 1916)

Teichman, Captain O. *The Diary of a Yeomanry MO: Egypt, Gallipoli, Palestine and Italy* (London, 1921)

Thompson, Colonel R. R., *The Fifty-Second (Lowland) Division 1914–1918* (Glasgow, 1923)

Tilton, May, *The Grey Battalion* (Sydney, 1933)

Westerman, Percy F., *The Fight for Constantinople: A Story of the Gallipoli Peninsula* (London, 1915)

Weston, Lieutenant-Colonel C. H., *Three Years with the New Zealanders* (London, 1918)

White, Major-General Sir C. B. B., *Some Reflections Upon the Great War* (Sydney, 1921)

Williams, Orlo, 'The Gallipoli tragedy: part I', *The Nineteenth Century and After*, 106 (July–December 1929), pp. 82–94

Wright, Stanley Sherman, *Of That Fellowship: The Tragedy, Humour and Pathos of Gallipoli!* (London, 1931)

Young, Lieutenant-Colonel James, *With the 52nd (Lowland) Division in Three Continents* (Edinburgh, 1920)

Printed secondary works

Books and articles

Adam-Smith, Patsy, *The Anzacs* (London, 1978)

Adams, Brian, *Sidney Nolan: Such Is Life* (Hawthorn, Vic., 1987)

Adcock, A. St. John, *Australasia Triumphant! With the Australians and New Zealanders in the Great War on Land and Sea* (London, 1916)

'An uncensored war correspondent', *The Army Quarterly*, 16 (April–July 1928), pp. 323–7

Andrews, E. M., 'Bean and Bullecourt: weaknesses and strengths of the official history of Australia in the First World War', *Revue internationale d'histoire militaire* (August 1990), pp. 25–47

—— *The Anzac Illusion: Anglo-Australian Relations During World War One* (Cambridge, 1993)

Anon., *The Song of Roland*, introduced and trans. C. H Sisson (Manchester, 1983)

Avieson, John, 'The correspondent who stopped the war', *Australian Journalism Review*, 8 (1986), pp. 64–71

—— 'Sir Keith Murdoch: the unwilling witness', *Australian Journalism Review*, 11 (1989), pp. 43–9

Babington Smith, Constance, *John Masefield: A Life* (Oxford, 1978)

Barret, John, 'Robin Gerster, *Big Noting: The Heroic Theme in Australian War Writing*', *Journal of Australian Studies*, 23 (November 1988), pp. 106–8

Barrett, John, 'No straw man: C. E. W. Bean and some critics', *Australian Historical Studies*, 23:89 (April 1988), pp. 102–14

Bartov, Omer, *Murder in Our Midst: The Holocaust, Industrial Killing and Representation* (Oxford, 1996)

Beaumont, Joan, 'The Anzac legend' in Joan Beaumont (ed.) *Australia's War 1914–18* (St Leonard's, NSW, 1995), pp. 149–80

Beckett, Ian, 'Frocks and brasshats' in Brian Bond (ed.) *The First World War and British Military History* (Oxford, 1991), pp. 89–112

Bennett, S., *Gallipoli: The Heroic Story of the Australasians at Anzac. Complete Official and Other Accounts – Illustrated* (Sydney, 15 January, 1916)

Blake, George, *The Path of Glory* (London, 1929)

Bond, Brian, 'British "anti-war" writers and their critics' in Hugh Cecil and Peter Liddle (eds) *Facing Armageddon: The First World War Experienced* (London, 1996), pp. 817–29

Bourke, Joanna, *An Intimate History of Killing: Face to Face Killing in Twentieth Century Warfare* (London, 1999)

Bourne, John, 'British generals in the First World War' in G. D. Sheffield (ed.) *Leadership and Command: The Anglo-American Military Experience since 1861* (London, 1997), pp. 93–116.

Bowen, James, 'Education, ideology and the ruling class: Hellenism and English public schools in the nineteenth century' in G. W. Clarke (ed.) *Rediscovering Hellenism: The Hellenic and the English Imagination* (Cambridge, 1989), pp. 161–86

Bracco, Rosa Maria, *Merchants of Hope: British Middlebrow Writers and the First World War 1919–1939* (Providence, RI, and Oxford, 1993)

Buley, E. C., *Glorious Deeds of Australasians in the Great War* (London, 1915)

Burness, Peter, *The Nek* (Kenthurst, NSW, 1996)

Bushaway, Bob, 'Name upon name: the Great War and remembrance' in Roy Porter (ed.) *Myths of the English* (Cambridge, 1992), pp. 137–67

Caesar, Adrian, 'Robin Gerster, *Big Noting: The Heroic Theme in Australian War Writing*', *Journal of the Australian War Memorial*, 14 (April 1989), pp. 58–9

Callwell, Major-General Sir C. E., *Campaigns and Their Lessons: The Dardanelles* (London, 1919)

Cannadine, David, 'War and death, grief and mourning in modern Britain' in Joachim Whaley (ed.) *Mirrors of Mortality: Studies in the Social History of Death* (London, 1981), pp. 187–242

Carlyon, Les, *Gallipoli* (Sydney, 2001)

Cecil, Hugh, 'British war novelists' in Hugh Cecil and Peter Liddle (eds) *Facing Armageddon: The First World War Experienced* (London, 1996), pp. 801–16

Churchill, W. S., *The World Crisis 1915* (London, 1923)

Coates, Tim (ed.) *The Dardanelles Commission, part 1: Lord Kitchener and Winston Churchill, 1914–15* (London, 2000)

—— (ed.) *Defeat at Gallipoli – The Dardanelles Commission, part 2: 1915–16* (London, 2000)

Cochrane, Peter, *Simpson and the Donkey: The Making of the Legend* (Carlton, Victoria, 1992)

Cohen, Eliot A. and John Gooch, *Military Misfortunes: The Anatomy of Failure in War* (New York, 1990)

Craven, Digger and W. J. Blackledge, *Peninsula of Death – as Told to W. J. Blackledge by Digger Craven* (London, 1937)

Danchev, Alex, ' "Bunking" and debunking: the controversies of the 1960s' in Brian Bond (ed.) *The First World War and British Military History* (Oxford, 1991), pp. 263–88

Davis, Paul, *Ends and Means: The British Mesopotamia Campaign and Commission* (Cranbury, NJ, 1994)

Delage, Edmond, *The Tragedy of the Dardanelles* (London, 1932)

Dobrez, Livio and Pat Dobrez, 'Old myths and new delusions: Peter Weir's Australia', *Kunapipi*, 4:2 (1982), pp. 61–75

Dungan, Myles, *Irish Voices from the Great War* (Blackrock, Co. Dublin, 1995)

Dyer, Geoff, *The Missing of the Somme* (London, 1994)

Eksteins, Modris, *Rites of Spring: The Great War and the Birth of the Modern Age* (London, 1989)

Ely, Richard, 'The first Anzac Day: invented or discovered?' *Journal of Australian Studies*, 17 (November 1985), pp. 41–58

Falls, Cyril, 'Edmonds, Sir James Edward (1861–1956)'in E. T. Williams and H. M. Palmer (eds) *Dictionary of National Biography 1951–60* (Oxford, 1971), pp. 327–9

—— *War Books* (London, 1989 [1930])

Fewster, Kevin, 'Ellis Ashmead-Bartlett and the making of the Anzac legend', *Journal of Australian Studies*, 10 (June 1982), pp. 17–30

Flaherty, Chris and Michael Roberts, 'The reproduction of Anzac symbolism', *Journal of Australian Studies*, 24 (May 1989), pp. 52–69

French, David, ' "Official but not history?" Sir James Edmonds and the official history of the Great War', *RUSI: Journal of the Royal United Services Institute for Defence Studies*, 131:1 (March 1986), pp. 58–63

—— 'The Dardanelles, Mecca and Kut: prestige as a factor in British Eastern strategy, 1914–1916', *War and Society*, 5:1 (May 1987), pp. 45–61

—— 'Sir James Edmonds and the official history: France and Belgium' in Brian Bond (ed.) *The First World War and British Military History* (Oxford, 1991), pp. 69–86

Fussell, Paul, *The Great War and Modern Memory* (London, 1975)

Gammage, Bill, *The Broken Years: Australian Soldiers in the Great War* (Canberra, 1974)

—— 'Working on *Gallipoli*' in Anne Hutton (ed.) *The First Australian History and Film Conference Papers 1982* (North Ryde, NSW, 1982), pp. 67–72

—— 'Anzac' in John Carroll (ed.) *Intruders in the Bush: The Australian Quest for Identity* (Melbourne, 1992), pp. 54–66

—— 'The broken years', *Journal of the Australian War Memorial*, 24 (April 1994), pp. 34–5

Gammage, Bill, David Williamson and Peter Weir, *The Story of Gallipoli: The Film About the Men who Made a Legend* (Ringwood, Victoria, 1981)

Gerster, Robin, *Big Noting: The Heroic Theme in Australian War Writing* (Melbourne, 1987)

Gibbs, Philip, *Realities of War* (London, 1929 [1920])

—— *The War Dispatches* (London, 1964)

Gilbert, Martin, *Winston S. Churchill*, vol. 3: *1914–16* (London, 1971)

—— *Winston S. Churchill*, vol. 3: *Companion Part I: July 1914–April 1915* and *Companion Part 2, May 1915–December 1916* (London, 1972)

—— *Winston S. Churchill*, vol. 4: *1916–22* (London, 1975)

—— *Winston S. Churchill*, vol. 4: *Companion Part 2, July 1919–March 1921* (London, 1977)

—— *In Search of Churchill* (London, 1994)

—— (comp. and ed.) *The Straits of War: Gallipoli Remembered* (Stroud, 2000)

Girouard, Mark, *The Return to Camelot: Chivalry and the English Gentleman* (New Haven, CT, 1981)

Gregory, Adrian, *The Silence of Memory: Armistice Day 1919–1946* (Oxford 1994)

Grey, Jeffrey, 'Denis Winter's *Haig's Command: A Reassessment*', *Journal of the Society for Army Historical Research*, 71:285 (spring 1993), pp. 60–3

—— *A Commonwealth of Histories: The Official Histories of the Second World War in the United States, Britain and the Commonwealth*, Trevor Reese Memorial Lecture, 1998, Sir Robert Menzies Centre for Australian Studies, Institute of Commonwealth Studies, University of London (London, 1998)

Grieves, Keith, 'Early historical responses to the Great War: Fortescue, Conan Doyle and Buchan' in Brian Bond (ed.) *The First World War and British Military History* (Oxford, 1991), pp. 15–39

—— 'Making sense of the Great War: regimental histories, 1918–23', *Journal of the Society for Army Historical Research*, 69:277 (spring 1991), pp. 6–15

—— 'C. E. Montague, Manchester and the remembrance of war, 1918–25', *Bulletin of the John Rylands University Library of Manchester*, 77:2 (summer 1995), pp. 85–104

—— 'Remembering an ill-fated venture; personal and collective histories of Gallipoli in a southern English community 1919–1939' in Jenny Macleod (ed.) *Gallipoli: Making History* (forthcoming)

Haltof, Marek, 'In quest of self-identity: *Gallipoli*, mateship and the construction of Australian national identity', *Journal of Popular Film and Television*, 21:1 (1993), pp. 27–36

Hamilton, Ian B. M., *Happy Warrior: A Life of General Sir Ian Hamilton, GCB, GCMG, DSO by his Nephew* (London, 1966)

Hartesveldt, Fred R. Van, *The Dardanelles Campaign, 1915: Historiography and Annotated Bibliography* (New Haven, CT, 1997)

Harvey, A. D., *A Muse of Fire: Literature, Art and War* (London, 1998)

Heath, Tom, 'Sydney Nolan: the Gallipoli paintings', *Architecture in Australia*, 55:4 (July 1966), pp. 86–7

Henderson, Gerard, 'The Anzac legend after *Gallipoli*', *Quadrant*, 179:26:7 (July 1982), pp. 62–4

Henderson, K. T., *Khaki and Cassock* (Melbourne, 1919)

Herbert, Sir Alan, *A. P. H. His Life and Times* (London, 1970)

Hickey, Michael, *Gallipoli* (London, 1995)

Hoffenberg, Peter, 'Landscape, memory and the Australian war experience, 1915–18', *Journal of Contemporary History*, 36:1 (2001), pp. 111–31

Hynes, Samuel, *A War Imagined: The First World War and English Culture* (London, 1990)

—— 'Personal narratives and commemoration' in J. M. Winter and E. Sivan (eds) *War and Remembrance in the Twentieth Century* (Cambridge, 1999), pp. 205–20

—— *The Soldiers' Tale: Bearing Witness to Modern War* (New York, 1997)

Inglis, K. S., 'The Anzac tradition', *Meanjin Quarterly*, 100 (1965), pp. 25–44

—— *C. E. W. Bean, Australian Historian*, John Murtagh Macrossan Lecture 1969 (St Lucia, Queensland, 1970)

—— 'The Australians at Gallipoli – I', *Historical Studies*, 14:54 (April 1970), pp. 219–30

—— 'The Australians at Gallipoli – II', *Historical Studies*, 14:55 (October 1970), pp. 361–75

—— 'A sacred place: the making of the Australian War Memorial', *War and Society*, 3:2 (September 1985), pp. 99–126

—— 'Anzac revisited: the Anzac tradition in Australia and New Zealand' in Alan Seymour and Richard Nile (eds) *Anzac: Meaning, Memory and Myth* (1991), pp. 13–20

—— 'War memorials: ten questions for historians', *Guerres mondiales et conflits contemporains*, 167 (July 1992), pp. 5–21

—— *Sacred Places: War Memorials in the Australian Landscape* (Melbourne, 1998)

—— *Anzac Remembered: Selected Writings of K. S. Inglis*, ed. John Lack (Melbourne, 1998)

Inglis, K. S. and Jock Phillips, 'War memorials in Australia and New Zealand: a comparative survey' in John Rickard and Peter Spearritt (eds) *Packaging the Past? Public Histories* (Melbourne, 1991), pp. 179–91

Jenkyns, Richard, *The Victorians and Ancient Greece* (Oxford, 1980)

Jerrold, Douglas, *The Lie About the War* (London, 1930)

Johnston, George, *My Brother Jack* (Sydney, 1964)

—— 'Anzac . . . a myth for all mankind', *Walkabout* (April 1965), pp. 13–16

Johnstone, George, 'Gallipoli paintings', *Art and Australia*, 5:2 (September 1967), pp. 466–9

Jones, Max, ' "Our king upon his knees": the public commemoration of Captain Scott's last Antarctic expedition' in G. Cubitt and A. Warren (eds) *Heroic Reputations and Exemplary Lives* (Manchester, 2000)

Keegan, John, *The Face of Battle* (London, 1976)

Kent, D. A., '*The Anzac Book* and the Anzac legend: C. E. W. Bean as editor and image-maker', *Historical Studies*, 21:84 (April 1985), pp. 376–90

—— '*The Anzac Book*: a reply to Denis Winter', *Journal of the Australian War Memorial*, 17 (October 1990), pp. 54–5

Kinnane, Garry, *George Johnston: A Biography* (Ringwood, Victoria, 1989)

Kipling, Rudyard, *The Irish Guards in the Great War* (London, 1923)

Kitley, Philip, 'Anzac Day ritual', *Journal of Australian Studies*, 4 (June 1979), pp. 58–69

Knightley, Phillip, *The First Casualty: The War Correspondent as Hero, Propagandist, and Myth Maker from the Crimea to Vietnam* (London, 1975)

Lee, John, 'Sir Ian Hamilton and the Dardanelles, 1915' in Brian Bond (ed.) *Fallen Stars* (London, 1991), pp. 32–50

—— 'Sir Ian Hamilton after the war: a liberal General reflects' in Hugh Cecil and Peter Liddle (eds) *Facing Armageddon: The First World War Experienced* (London, 1996), pp. 879–87

—— *A Soldier's Life: General Sir Ian Hamilton 1853–1947* (London, 2000)

Liddell Hart, B. H., *The Real War 1914–1918* (London, 1930)

—— *The British Way in Warfare* (London, 1932)

—— 'Responsibility and judgment in historical writing', *Military Affairs* (spring 1959), pp. 35–6

Liddle, P. H., 'The distinctive nature of the Gallipoli expedition', *RUSI: Journal of the Royal United Services Institute for Defence Studies*, 122:2 (June 1977), pp. 51–6

—— *Men of Gallipoli: The Dardanelles and Gallipoli Experience, August 1914 to January 1916* (Trowbridge, 1988 [1976])

Lloyd, D. W., *Battlefield Tourism, Pilgrimage and the Commemoration of the Great War in Britain, Australia and Canada, 1919–1939* (Oxford, 1993)

Londey, Peter, 'A Greek inscription at the Australian War Memorial', *Journal of the Australian War Memorial*, 23 (October 1993), pp. 50–1

Luvaas, Jay 'The first British official historians' in Robin Higham (ed.) *Official*

Histories: Essays and Bibliographies from Around the World (Kansas, 1970), pp. 488–502

Macleod, Jenny, 'General Sir Ian Hamilton and the Dardanelles Commission', *War in History*, 8:4 (2001), pp. 418–41

—— 'The fall and rise of Anzac Day: 1965 and 1990 compared', *War and Society* 20:1 (May 2002), pp. 149–68

Mandle, W. F., *Going it Alone: Australia's National Identity in the Twentieth Century* (Ringwood, Victoria, 1977)

Mansfield, Wendy M., 'The importance of Gallipoli: the growth of an Australian folklore', *Queensland Historical Review*, 6:2 (1977), pp. 41–53

McCarthy, Dudley, *Gallipoli to the Somme: The Story of C. E. W. Bean* (London, 1983)

McCartney, H. B., 'Interpreting unit histories: Gallipoli and after' in Jenny Macleod (ed.) *Gallipoli: Making History* (forthcoming)

McKernan, Michael, 'Writing about war' in M. McKernan and M. Browne, *Australia: Two Centuries of War and Peace* (Canberra, 1987), pp. 11–24

Millett, Allan R., *Semper Fidelis: The History of the United States Marine Corps* (New York, 1980)

Moorehead, Alan, *Gallipoli* (Ware, 1997 [1956])

Moorhouse, Geoffrey, *Hell's Foundations: A Town, its Myths and Gallipoli* (London, 1992)

Moriarty, Catherine, 'Christian iconography and First World War memorials', *Imperial War Museum Review*, 6 (1992), pp. 63–75

Moses, John A., 'The struggle for Anzac Day 1916–1930 and the role of the Brisbane Anzac Day Commemoration Committee', *Journal of the Royal Australian Historical Society*, 88:1 (June 2002), pp. 54–74

Mosse, G., 'The two world wars and the myth of the war experience', *Journal of Contemporary History*, 21:4 (October 1986), pp. 491–513

Moynihan, Michael (ed.) *God on Our Side* (London, 1983)

North, John, *Gallipoli: The Fading Vision* (London, 1936)

O'Neill, Robert, 'Alliances and intervention: from Gallipoli to the 21st century', *RUSI Journal*, 146:5 (October 2001), pp. 56–61

Paris, Michael, *Warrior Nation: Images of War in British Popular Culture, 1850–2000* (London, 2000)

Parker, Peter, *The Old Lie: The Great War and the Public School Ethos* (London, 1987)

Pedersen, P. A., *Monash as Military Commander* (Melbourne, 1985)

Penn, Geoffrey, *Fisher, Churchill and the Dardanelles* (London, 1999)

Phillips, Jock, Nicholas Boyack and E. P. Malone (eds) *The Great Adventure: New Zealand Soldiers Describe the First World War* (Wellington, 1988)

Pocock, Tom, *Alan Moorehead* (London, 1990)

Pound, Reginald, *A. P. Herbert: A Biography* (London, 1976)

Prior, Robin, *Churchill's 'World Crisis' as History* (London, 1983)

—— 'The Suvla Bay tea-party: a reassessment', *Journal of the Australian War Memorial*, 7 (October 1985), pp. 25–34

Prior, Robin and Trevor Wilson, 'Paul Fussell at war', *War in History*, 1:1 (March 1994), pp. 63–71

Pugsley, Christopher, *Gallipoli: The New Zealand Story* (Auckland, 1984)

Puleston, William Dilworth, *The Dardanelles Expedition: A Condensed Study* (Annapolis, 1927 [1926])

Remarque, Erich Maria, *All Quiet on the Western Front* (London, 1929)

Repington, C. à Court, *The First World War* (London, 1920)

Rhodes James, Robert, 'A visit to Gallipoli', *Australian Army Journal*, 191 (April 1965), pp. 37–40

—— *Gallipoli* (London, 1965)

—— 'General Sir Ian Hamilton' in Field Marshal Sir Michael Carver (ed.) *The War Lords: Military Commanders of the Twentieth Century* (London, 1976), pp. 84–92

—— *Gallipoli: A 'British' Historian's View*, Public lecture delivered at the University of Melbourne on 24 April 1995 (Melbourne, 1995)

Robertson, John, *The Tragedy and Glory of Gallipoli: Anzac and Empire* (London, 1990)

Robson, L. L., 'The origin and character of the First AIF, 1914–1918: some statistical evidence', *Historical Studies* 15 (1973), pp. 737–49

—— 'C. E. W. Bean: a review article', *Journal of the Australian War Memorial*, 4 (1984), pp. 54–7

Roskill, Stephen, *Hankey: Man of Secrets*, vol. 1: *1877–1918* (London, 1970)

Ross, Jane, *The Myth of the Digger: The Australian Soldier in Two World Wars* (Sydney, 1985)

—— 'Review: *Frontline Gallipoli*, etc.', *Australian Historical Studies*, 24:97 (October, 1991), pp. 478–9

Royle, Trevor, *War Report: The War Correspondent's View of Battle from the Crimea to the Falklands* (London, 1989)

Sekuless, Peter, *A Handful of Hacks* (St Leonard's, NSW, 1999)

Sellers, Leonard, *For God's Sake Shoot Straight* (London, 1995)

—— *The Hood Battalion, Royal Naval Division: Antwerp, Gallipoli, France 1914–1918* (London, 1995)

Shadbolt, Maurice, *Voices of Gallipoli* (Auckland, 1989)

Sheffield, G. D., ' "Oh! What a futile war": representations of the Western Front in modern British media and popular culture' in Ian Stewart and Susan L. Carruthers (eds) *War, Culture and the Media: Representations of the Military in 20th Century Britain* (Trowbridge, 1996), pp. 54–74

Sillars, Stuart, *Art and Survival in First World War Britain* (London, 1987)

Simkins, Peter, 'Everyman at war: recent interpretations of the front line experience' in Brian Bond (ed.) *The First World War and British Military History* (Oxford, 1991), pp. 289–313

Simpson, Keith, 'The reputation of Sir Douglas Haig' in Brian Bond (ed.) *The First World War and British Military History* (Oxford, 1991), pp. 141–62

Sixsmith, E. K. G., *British Generalship in the Twentieth Century* (London, 1970)

Speller, Ian, 'In the shadow of Gallipoli? Amphibious warfare in the inter-war period' in Jenny Macleod (ed.) *Gallipoli: Making History* (forthcoming)

Spiers, Edward, 'Gallipoli' in Brian Bond (ed.) *The First World War and British Military History* (Oxford, 1991), pp. 165–88

Stanley, Peter, 'Reflections on Bean's last paragraph', *Sabretache*, 24:3 (July–September 1983), pp. 4–11

—— 'Gallipoli and Pozières: a legend and a memorial', *Australian Foreign Affairs Record*, 56:4 (April 1985), pp. 281–289

Steel, Nigel, *The Battlefields of Gallipoli: Then and Now* (London, 1990)

Steel, Nigel and Peter Hart, *Defeat at Gallipoli* (London, 1994)

Sydenham of Combe, Colonel The Lord *et al.*, The World Crisis *by Winston Churchill: A Criticism* (London, 1928)

Thomson, Alistair, ' "Steadfast until death"? C. E. W. Bean and the representation of Australian military manhood', *Australian Historical Studies*, 23:93 (October 1989), pp. 462–77

—— 'A past you can live with: digger memories and the Anzac legend' in Alan Seymour and Richard Nile (eds) *Anzac: Meaning, Memory and Myth* (London, 1991), pp. 21–31

—— ' "The vilest libel of the war"? Imperial politics and the official histories of Gallipoli', *Australian Historical Studies*, 25:101 (October 1993), pp. 628–36

—— *Anzac Memories: Living with the Legend* (Melbourne, 1994)

Travers, Tim, *The Killing Ground: The British Army, the Western Front and the Emergence of Modern Warfare 1900–1918* (London, 1987)

—— 'Command and leadership styles in the British Army: the 1915 Gallipoli model', *Journal of Contemporary History*, 29 (1994), pp. 403–42

—— *Gallipoli 1915* (Stroud, 2001)

Turner, E. R., 'Some books about the war', *Sewanee Review*, 25 (1917), p. 497

Turner, John, *British Politics and the Great War: Coalition and Conflict 1915–1918* (London, 1992)

Umbreit, Hans, 'The development of official military historiography in the German Army from the Crimean War to 1945' in Robin Higham (ed.) *Official Histories: Essays and Bibliographies from Around the World* (Kansas, 1970), pp. 160–8

Ward, Stuart, ' "A war memorial in celluloid": the Gallipoli legend in Australian cinema, 1940s–1980s' in Jenny Macleod (ed.) *Gallipoli: Making History* (forthcoming)

Welborn, Suzanne, *Lords of Death: A People, a Place, a Legend* (Fremantle, 1982)

White, Richard, *Inventing Australia: Images and Identity 1688–1980* (Sydney, 1981)

—— 'Robin Gerster, *Big Noting: The Heroic Theme in Australian War Writing*', *Australian Historical Studies*, 23:92 (April 1989), pp. 323–4

Wilcox, Craig (ed.) *Observing Australia 1959 to 1999: K.S. Inglis* (Melbourne, 1999)

Williams, John, *Anzacs, the Media and the Great War* (Sydney, 1999)

Wilson, S. S., *The Cabinet Office to 1945* (London, 1975)

Wilson, Trevor, *The Downfall of the Liberal Party 1914–1935* (London, 1966)

—— *The Myriad Faces of War* (Cambridge, 1986)

Winter, Denis, 'The Anzac Book: a re-appraisal', *Journal of the Australian War Memorial*, 16 (April 1990), pp. 58–61

—— *Haig's Command: A Reassessment* (London, 1991)

—— (ed.) *Making the Legend: The War Writings of C. E. W. Bean* (St Lucia, Queensland, 1992)

—— *25 April 1915: The Inevitable Tragedy* (St Lucia, Queensland, 1994)

Winter, J. M., 'Catastrophe and culture: recent trends in the historiography of the First World War', *Journal of Modern History*, 64 (September 1992), pp. 525–32

—— *Sites of Memory, Sites of Mourning: The Great War in European Cultural History* (Cambridge, 1995)

Zwar, Desmond, *In Search of Keith Murdoch* (Melbourne, 1980)

Unpublished papers and dissertations

Ball, Martin, 'Rereading Bean's last paragraph', unpublished paper presented to the conference 'Australia in War and Peace', 1–4 October 2002, Çanakkale, Turkey

Curran, Bernard, 'The Australian warrior–hero and the classical component', unpublished paper presented at the Australian War Memorial Conference, 12–15 November 1991

Fewster, Kevin J., 'Expression and suppression: aspects of military censorship in Australia during the Great War', unpublished PhD thesis, University of New South Wales (1980)

Hiley, N. P., 'Making war: the British news media and government control, 1914–1916', unpublished PhD thesis, Open University (1985)

Mackie, Chris, 'Troy and Gallipoli: patterns in comparative myth making', unpublished paper presented at the conference 'Australia in War and Peace', 1–4 October 2002, Çanakkale, Turkey

Macleod, Jennifer, 'General Sir Ian Hamilton and the re-writing of the history of the Gallipoli campaign 1915–30', unpublished MPhil. dissertation, Cambridge University (1996)

—— 'The Gallipoli campaign as assessed by some British and Australian participants, 1915–1939', unpublished PhD thesis, Cambridge University (2000)

Stryker, Laurinda S., 'Languages of sacrifice and suffering in England in the First World War', unpublished PhD thesis, Cambridge University (1992)

Index

Note: literary works can be found under authors' names.

Adam-Smith, Patsy, *The Anzacs* (1978) 221–2
Andrews, E. M. 70–5 *passim*
    The Anzac Illusion (1993) 229
Anzac Day 4, 221, 227, 229, 238–41
    compared to Armistice Day 4, 239–40
Anzac legend 221
    classical allusions 8–9, 162, 217
    defined 5–6
Ashmead-Bartlett, Ellis 14, 17, 103–37, 191,
        219, 228, 242
    censorship 120–31, 133
    character and career 105–10
    contrast with Bean 105, 110–15
    contrast with Mackenzie 119–20
    criticisms of Hamilton 108, 124
    finances 106–7
    incident with Murdoch 39, 40, 41, 44
    The Uncensored Dardanelles (1928) 107–9,
        134
    unreliability 108–10, 115–17
    written style 111–15, 115–20
Aspinall-Oglander, Brigadier-General Cecil
        Faber 9, 14, 47, 115, 163, 212, 215–16
    British official history (*Military
        Operations, Gallipoli* (1929 and
        1932))15, 17, 57, 82–93, 218, 241,
        242
        compared to Australian official history
            82, 90–2, 92–3
        influence of his experience as staff
            officer 81–2, 85, 91–2
        struggle to discuss general context of
            war 83–4, 92, 200
        written style 87–90
        see also Daniel; Edmonds; Hankey;
            official history
    career/background 81, 131–2
Asquith, Herbert 2, 25–7, 28, 34, 46, 127–8,
        132, 134, 135, 201
Australian War Memorial 222

Bean, Charles Edwin Woodrow
    The Anzac Book (1916) 6, 217
    attitudes 73–5

admiration for Australian soldiers 74,
        188
    definition of heroism 75, 77, 149, 229
    romance of war 75, 77–80, 90
Australian official history (*The Story of
        Anzac* (1921 and1924)) 17, 148
    compared to British official history 82,
        90–2, 92–3
    compared to personal narratives 148,
        168
    criticisms of 70–1, 72, 75, 77, 78, 79
    frontline perspective 72, 76, 78, 90
    portrayal of Turks 78
    purpose 67–8, 72–3
    working methods and sources 69–72
    written style 76; footnote style 72, 79,
        222; minimises negative aspects
        78–80, 223
    career/background 65–7, 104
    influence 4–5, 221, 227, 228, 230, 240,
        242
    war correspondent 103–37
        censorship 106, 125–6
        compared to Ashmead-Bartlett 105,
            110–15, 115–17
        criticisms of Ashmead-Bartlett 110,
            115–17, 135
        criticisms of his work 115, 117
        working habits 115
        written style 111–13
Birdwood, Lieutenant-General Sir William 2,
        34, 36, 47, 85
Braithwaite, Major-General Walter 30, 31,
        35, 36, 38, 164, 195
Brooke, Rupert 10, 11–12, 162, 184–5

Campbell, Alec 1
Carlyon, Les, *Gallipoli* (2001) 229–30
casualties 13, 82, 187
chaplains 155, 159, 161
children's fiction 161
Churchill, Winston
    attitude to war correspondents 121
    British official history 64, 84, 200, 216

Dardanelles Commission 29–32, 45, 46, 200
historian 4, 9, 15, 17, 85, 242
   The World Crisis 1915 (1923) 199–202, 215, 241
politician 134, 215
relationship with Fisher 29, 202
relationship with Hamilton 29–32, 182–3, 193, 198, 202
strategist 2, 14, 77, 156, 211, 219
Cochrane, Peter 229
Creighton, Reverend Oswin 155–6

Daniel, Colonel E. Y. 57–60
Dardanelles Commission 17, 25–56, 57, 82, 92, 227, 242
  compared to Mesopotamia Commission 46
  compared to Mitchell committee 48
  conclusions 44–9
  membership 27
    Cromer, Lord Evelyn 35
    Grimwood Mears, Edward 44
    Mackenzie, Sir Thomas 37, 38, 46, 47
    Nicholson, Field-Marshal Lord William 37–9, 43
    Pickford, Sir William 38, 43
    see also Fisher, Andrew
  potential effect in Australia 33, 34
  reasons for its establishment 25–7
Dawnay, Major Guy 131–3, 134, 215
De Lisle, General Beauvoir 199
De Loghe, Sydney (F. S. Loch)
  The Straits Impregnable (1917) 148–55
  'Turn'd, but Not Torn' (MS 1934) 154–5, 159
De Robeck, Admiral John 30, 114, 183, 212
Doughty-Wylie, Lieutenant Colonel Charles, VC 201

Edmonds, Brigadier-General Sir James 17, 61–5, 71, 79–80, 89, 91, 92
Ellison, Major-General Sir Gerald 80–1

Fisher, Andrew 27, 34, 37, 39, 40, 42, 43
Fisher, John, Admiral of the Fleet Lord ('Jackie') 28, 29, 45, 183, 202
Fussell, Paul 8, 12, 13–14, 73, 115, 241

Gallipoli campaign
  causes of failure 3–4
  compared to Mesopotamia 25–7
  compared to Palestine 238
  compared to Western Front 9, 12, 13, 82, 89, 185, 213, 228, 238, 243
  lessons for later campaigns 220, 240
  living conditions 7, 40, 45, 89, 151, 152, 185–6
  outline 2–4

significant events
  armistice 79, 163
  Chunuk Bair 3, 116, 118, 224
  evacuation 3
  Krithia (2nd battle of) 122–4
  landings at Anzac 3, 111–15, 194
  landings at Helles 3, 194
  Lone Pine 3, 157–8
  Majestic sinks 109, 119–20, 127
  Nek 3, 78, 224, 227
  River Clyde 157
  Suvla 85, 88, 157, 190–1, 224
  Turkish attack (18 May) 187
  strategy defended 9, 82, 197–8, 200, 214
Gallishaw, John 153
Gammage, Bill, *The Broken Years* (1974) 221–8
Gibson, Mel 223
Gillam, Major John Graham 155–8

Hall, Reverend Henry 199, 239
Hamilton, General Sir Ian 2, 14, 15, 17, 30, 85, 164–5, 241
  career 3, 32, 176–7
  character 4, 81, 85, 176–7, 190–5, 197
  Dardanelles Commission
    concern for effect in Australia 32–4
    his response to its report 45, 48, 177–8, 180, 195
    his strategy in dealing with 35–7, 195
  Gallipoli Diary (1920) 17, 82, 176–208, 230
    defends strategy 190–8
    memoirs presented as diary 180–3
    portrayal of heroism 187–90
    portrayal of romance of war 183–7
    portrayal of Turks 189
    purpose 177–80
    reviews 198–9
  influence on other authors 88, 167–8, 178, 202, 211, 230
  official dispatches 47, 113–14, 123, 124–5, 178, 181, 202
  other publications
    The Commander (1957) 197
    The Soul and Body of an Army (1921) 184
    A Staff Officer's Scrap Book (1907) 198
  relationship with Braithwaite 31, 35, 36, 38, 42, 195
  relationship with Churchill 29–32, 182–3, 193, 198, 202
  relationship with Kitchener 38, 85, 124, 191, 193–4
    Hamilton's need to blame 29–31, 179, 195–8
  war correspondents 103, 104, 119, 121
    Ashmead Bartlett 107, 109, 120, 121, 126–31, 191
    Murdoch 40–4, 198
  written style 88, 183

Hankey, Lieutenant-Colonel Maurice
  Dardanelles Commission 26–7, 28–9, 33,
    48–9
  official history 58–61, 84
  The Supreme Command (1961) 209
Hanna, Henry 165
Hawke, Bob 240–1
Herbert, A. P., *The Secret Battle* (1919)
    161–2, 163, 242
heroic–romantic myth of Gallipoli 5, 6–15
  celebration of failure 10, 12–13
  classical allusions 7, 8, 11, 77, 87–8, 89,
    118, 156, 157, 160, 162, 167, 179, 185,
    210, 213–14, 216–17, 230
Hogue, Major Oliver ('Trooper Bluegum')
    104, 157–8
Hunter Weston, Major-General Aylmer 85,
    194, 230
Hynes, Samuel 2, 14, 17, 77, 93, 181, 227,
    242
  The Soldiers' Tale (1997) 16, 147–75

Idriess, Ion 153
Inglis, Ken 4, 73, 77, 79, 221

Jacka, Captain Albert 229
Johnston, George 5–6, 216, 218
journalists
  censorship arrangements 120–1, 125, 129
  quasi-independent role 103, 120, 134–7
  war correspondents at Gallipoli 103–5
  see also Ashmead-Bartlett; Bean; Moseley;
    Murdoch; Nevinson; Ross; Schuler

Kemal, Mustapha 78, 85, 86, 241
Keyes, Commodore Roger 30, 81, 85, 121,
    215
Kirke report 92
Kitchener, Field-Marshal Lord H. H. 2, 3, 26,
    27, 123, 180, 200
  see also Hamilton
Knyvett, Captain R. Hugh 158

Lawson, Harry 128–31 *passim*
Leeper, Janet (Ian Hamilton's niece) 180
Liddell Hart, Basil 9, 83, 84, 89
Liman von Sanders, General 135, 213, 215,
    220

McDonald, Roger 225
Mackenzie, Compton 8, 15, 128, 136, 166,
    190
  Gallipoli Memories (1929) 162–5, 218
  war correspondent 104, 109, 119–20
Masefield, John 155, 167, 180, 202, 228, 241
  Gallipoli (1916) 6–7, 15
Monash, General Sir John 17, 215
  War Letters of General Monash (1934) 182

Monro, General Sir Charles 3, 133
Moorehead, Alan 180, 229
  Gallipoli (1956) 212–16
Moorhouse, Geoffrey, *Hell's Foundations*
    (1992) 5
Moseley, Sydney 104, 109, 121, 129, 136
Murdoch, Keith 34, 39–44, 79, 130–1, 132,
    136–7, 198, 227

Nevinson, Henry 15, 47, 106, 135, 177, 178,
    180, 202
  The Dardanelles Campaign (1918) 165–8
  war correspondent 44, 104, 121, 127,
    129
Nolan, Sidney 216–18
North, John 15, 77
  Gallipoli: The Fading Vision (1926)
    209–12, 241

official history
  principle discussed 57–61
  selection of authors 62, 66–7, 80–1
  see also Aspinall-Oglander; Bean; Edmonds

Prior, Robin 85, 201–2
Puleston, William 220

Raymond, Ernest, *Tell England* (1922)
    158–61, 163, 241
Remarque, Erich Maria, *All Quiet on the
    Western Front* (1929) 154, 184
Rhodes James, Robert 77, 132, 192
  Gallipoli (1965) 4, 216, 218–19, 220
Robertson, John 199
  Anzac and Empire (1990) 227–9
Ross, Malcolm 104, 116, 129

Schuler, Phillip 41, 105
  Australia at War (1916) 165–8
Shield, Mary 180
Simpson and the Donkey 221, 229
Steel, Nigel and Peter Hart, *Defeat at
    Gallipoli* (1994) 15, 226
Stopford, General Sir Frederick 45, 85, 133,
    193, 194, 230

Thatcher, Margaret 240
Thomson, Alistair 74, 79, 90, 230
  Anzac Memories (1994) 226–7
Turkish perspective 4
  impact on Turkish army 9
  portrayal of Turks 74, 78, 189
  see also Kemal

Weir, Peter, *Gallipoli* (1981) 223–6, 229
Williams, Orlo 88, 132, 164, 192
Winter, Denis 70, 95–6n.38
Wright, Stanley 26

DATE DUE

GAYLORD		PRINTED IN U.S.A.